American Government

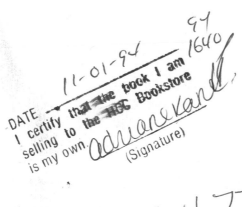

American Government

SIXTH EDITION

Walter E. Volkomer
Hunter College of the City University of New York

with the editorial assistance of Carolyn D. Smith

 PRENTICE HALL, *Englewood Cliffs, New Jersey*   07632

Library of Congress Cataloging-in-Publication Data
Volkomer, Walter E.
    American government / Walter E. Volkomer; with the editorial
assistance of Carolyn D. Smith.— 6th ed.
        p.   cm.
    Includes bibliographical references and index.
    ISBN 0-13-028861-6
    1. United States— Politics and government.   I. Smith, Carolyn D.
II. Title.
JK274.V65   1992
320.973— dc20   91-19749
                                                                    CIP

Acquisitions editor: Karen Horton
Editorial/production supervision: Serena Hoffman
Interior design and page layout: Andy Zutis
Prepress buyer: Debra Kesar
Manufacturing buyer: Mary Ann Gloriande
Copy editor: Ann Hofstra Grogg
Photo editor: Lorinda Morris-Nantz
Photo researcher: Joelle Burrows
Supplements editor: Sharon Chambliss
Editorial assistant: Dolores Mars
Cover designer: Bruce Kenselaar
Cover photo: Superstock

 © 1992, 1989, 1986, 1983, 1979, 1975 by Prentice-Hall, Inc.
A Simon & Schuster Company
Englewood Cliffs, New Jersey 07632

Printed in the United States of America
10   9   8   7   6   5   4   3   2

ISBN 0-13-028861-6

Prentice-Hall International (UK) Limited, *London*
Prentice-Hall of Australia Pty. Limited, *Sydney*
Prentice-Hall Canada Inc., *Toronto*
Prentice-Hall Hispanoamericana, S.A., *Mexico*
Prentice-Hall of India Private Limited, *New Delhi*
Prentice-Hall of Japan, Inc., *Tokyo*
Simon & Schuster Asia Pte. Ltd., *Singapore*
Editora Prentice-Hall do Brasil, Ltda., *Rio de Janeiro*

Brief Contents

Contents

9 The Federal Bureaucracy

10 The Judiciary

PART IV   THE RIGHTS OF THE INDIVIDUAL

11 Civil Liberties   293

Appendixes

Preface

In the almost three years since the fifth edition of this textbook was published, there have been many important developments in both domestic and international politics. At home, Republican George Bush was elected as this nation's forty-first President in a one-sided contest with his Democratic opponent, Michael Dukakis.

During the 1988 campaign, many observers viewed George Bush as indecisive and lacking the necessary qualities of a leader. He began his service as President with many doubts about his executive abilities. The Bush administration soon began to have problems with its domestic policies. The President reneged on his election promise not to raise taxes ("Read my lips"), and in the fall of 1990 the Democratic-controlled Congress raised taxes and enacted a budget law that they had largely shaped. In other domestic areas, the Bush administration made promises but made no serious attempt to implement them. Indeed, it seemed to many that the President had little real interest in domestic matters, and that it was international affairs that most concerned him.

Events on the world scene favored George Bush. In his first year as President, the eastern European empire of the Soviet Union collapsed. After more than four decades of Soviet domination, Poland, Bulgaria, Czechoslovakia, Hungary, and Romania all regained their political independence and struggled to create new, more democratic forms of government. Further, the division between East and West Germany was ended, and a new, united nation was created. The cold war tensions that had existed between the Soviet Union and the United States since the end of World War II declined, even if they did not entirely disappear. And a degree of democracy emerged in the Soviet Union after seventy years of rigid communist control.

In China, a student revolution against the communist government took place in 1989. The students erected a replica of the American Statue of Liberty in the main square of their nation's capital to symbolize their hopes for democracy. But the government brought in the army to crush the rebellion, and China quickly returned to totalitarian rule.

Movement toward greater freedom and democracy occurred in other parts of the world as well during the early years of President Bush's administration. Even South Africa, long under the repressive rule of a white minority, began to dismantle its system of apartheid and took its first steps towards granting equal rights to its African majority.

The defeat of communism and the yearning for freedom and democracy among people in many parts of the world seemed to many Americans to represent the triumph of this nation's values. President Bush basked in the reflected glory of the dramatic changes in the world, and his popularity at home soared.

But his leadership on the international scene was yet to be tested. The President met that test in the 1991 war with Iraq. Following Iraq's conquest of neighboring Kuwait, the President assembled a worldwide coalition of nations to oppose that conquest. He helped win the backing of the United Nations for an international embargo against trade with Iraq and its consent to wage war against Iraq if it did not leave Kuwait by January 15, 1991. The Congress of the United States, somewhat reluctantly, gave him its support for military intervention by United States forces against Iraq. When that country did not withdraw by the deadline, the President led an international armed force and won a quick and decisive victory over Iraq that restored the legitimate government of Kuwait.

Despite the hunger for democracy in many parts of the world and the preeminent position of the United States as a symbol of freedom and democracy, many Americans are indifferent and uninformed about their own governmental system. The election turnout of eligible voters in the United States is one of the lowest of all democratic nations. Various public opinion polls in recent years show that Americans know appallingly little about their governmental system and basic rights; 59 percent of adult Americans interviewed in one poll did not know what the Bill of Rights is, and only 46 percent could identify it as the first ten amendments to the United States Constitution!

My minimum hope in writing this book is that its readers will be able to give correct answers to such basic questions. Of course, I would be delighted if they learned a good deal more about this nation's governmental system. My maximum hope is that many would develop a lifelong interest in government and politics, and come to appreciate the importance of these subjects to their lives.

Finally, I want to restate something I have said in the preface to earlier editions of this book. In writing this text, I have always tried to keep the reader in the forefront of my thoughts. Too many authors of college textbooks have forgotten what it is like to be a first- or second-year student being introduced to new and often confusing areas of human knowledge. This loss of perspective too often results in textbooks that are research oriented, filled with technical jargon, and needlessly long and overwritten.

I have attempted to write a book that students will find both interesting and readable. The book does not avoid difficult topics, but rather seeks to handle them in a manner that is understandable to the average student. I have drawn on scholarly research in political science without employing its all-too-frequent abuse of the English language.

Again, a word of thanks to the members of the Hunter College Library staff who have helped me track down and obtain information and sources. My work has also been helped by the criticisms and suggestions of a number of reviewers, especially: Professor Lindsey Back, Morehead State University; Professor Timothy A. Cantrell, Lexington Community College; Professor Gerard S. Gryski, Auburn University; Dr. Larry Elowitz, Georgia College; Professor Donald F. Kerle, Pittsburg State University; Dr. Joseph S. Trachtenberg, Clayton State College; Professor John Sistarenik, Jefferson Community College. Any errors in the book are, of course, entirely my responsibility.

Walter E. Volkomer

ABC News/PH Video Library for American Government

Video is the most dynamic of all the supplements you can use to enhance your class. But the quality of the video material and how well it relates to your course can still make all the difference. For these reasons, **Prentice Hall** and **ABC News** have decided to work together to bring you the best and most comprehensive video ancillaries available in the college market.

Through its wide variety of award-winning programs—*Nightline, This Week with David Brinkley, and World News Tonight*—ABC offers a resource for feature and documentary-style videos related to text concepts and applications. The programs have extremely high production quality, present substantial content, and are hosted by well-versed, well-known anchors. Prentice Hall, its authors, and its editors provide the benefit of having selected videos on topics that will work well with this course and text and give the instructor teaching notes on how to use them in the classroom.

The **ABC News/PH Video Library for American Government** will offer video material on the 1992 election. Part I, available for classes in the fall of 1992, will cover the campaign trail and the primaries. Part II, available for classes in the spring of 1993, will cover the conventions, election results, and analysis. A video guide will carefully integrate the videos into your lecture.

The New York Times

The New York Times and **Prentice Hall** are sponsoring *A Contemporary View:* a program designed to enhance student access to current information of relevance in the classroom.

Through this program, the core subject matter provided in the text is supplemented by a collection of time-sensitive articles from one of the world's most distinguished newspapers, *The New York Times*. These articles demonstrate the vital, ongoing connection between what is learned in the classroom and what is happening in the world around us.

To enjoy the wealth of information of *The New York Times* daily, a reduced subscription rate is available. For information, call toll-free: 1-800-631-1222.

Prentice Hall and **The New York Times** are proud to co-sponsor *A Contemporary View.* We hope it will make the reading of both textbooks and newspapers a more dynamic, involving process.

American Government

1

Questions for Thought

What is political power?

What is the view of elitists about political power?

What is the view of pluralists about political power?

What is the difference between direct and representative democracy?

What are the main political ideas of John Locke, and how did they influence the framers of the United States Constitution?

Why are the principles of majority rule and minority rights both important in a democracy?

Politics, Democracy, and the American People

DURING a debate in the United States Senate in the 1940s, Senator Tom Connally of Texas said to Senator Styles Bridges of New Hampshire, "If the Senator from New Hampshire would approach these matters with an open mind instead of an open mouth, he could understand these matters."[1] Connally's remark points up a common feature of political debate: Political opinions often are not backed up by adequate information.

The main purpose of this book is to provide information to back up opinions. Answers to today's political questions will not be found here; instead, we will convey basic facts about the structure and functioning of American government. Armed with this information and an open mind, you will be better able to understand—and perhaps participate in—American politics.

1

■ The Nature of Politics

Politics has been defined as the art of governing humanity by deceiving it. It has also been seen as the conduct of public affairs for private advantage. Such definitions reflect a view of politics as synonymous with deception and dishonesty. Many Americans see politicians as self-seeking, not very competent, even ruthless.[2] These ideas may arise from a tendency to confuse politics as a whole with the activities of certain politicians. Examples of scandal and corruption in government increase the prevalence of this cynicism toward politics. To people who hold this view, all political activities are suspect, and politics serves as a convenient whipping boy for the evils of society.

Not everyone is cynical about politics, however. Many people have a different and more positive view of the subject. Most political leaders and private citizens show genuine interest in bringing about needed changes and improving the welfare of all members of society. By demonstrating that the actions of concerned citizens can affect the social and political environment, they have encouraged others to develop a favorable opinion of politics and to participate in political activity at the local, state, or national level.

Politics and Power

More than fifty years ago, the political scientist Harold Lasswell spoke of **politics** as the study of "who gets what, when, how."[3] A generation later, another political scientist refined this definition when he described politics as a process by which values are authoritatively allocated for a society—in other words, a method of deciding who gets what.[4] These definitions go to the heart of what politics is about and point to the concerns of political scientists as they study this area of human activity.

Closely related to the concept of politics is that of **political power**—the ability to influence the political behavior of others. Political power is sought for the sake of the rewards and benefits that can be gained from it. A political candidate tries to influence voters in order to win an election; an interest group tries to influence key members of Congress in the hope that they will support or oppose a particular bill. Politics, then, is concerned with the use of power to achieve specific benefits and with the way in which those benefits are distributed among individuals and groups in society.

We all deal with "politics" in our daily lives—office politics, school politics, family politics. These are the areas in which ordinary people compete for personal advantage. The power at stake in such contests is usually limited, and the size of the group affected is relatively small. The politics that are of interest to political scientists, on the other hand, affect large numbers of people and involve significant amounts of power. These activities can even affect the entire society.

Any person or group can seek to exercise political power. For example, church groups normally engage in nonpolitical activities of a spiritual and social nature. But some churches have become active in opposing or supporting legalized abortion, which is a political issue as well as a moral and ethical one.

Political Power in America: Two Views

In theory, no group in society is entirely lacking in political influence, but in practice political power is never distributed evenly. Some political theorists stress the dispersal of power in a democracy and are known as **pluralists.** Others, referred to as **elitists,** believe that power is concentrated in the hands of a few individuals.

The pluralist view holds that political power is not limited to those who possess wealth. Other resources exist besides money—organizational skills and popular support in elections, for example. Those resources tend to be distributed unequally, with some individuals having access to certain kinds of resources but not to others. Large corporations may have access to great amounts of wealth but lack political backing by the majority of Americans. Conversely, other groups may have popular support but have little money. And some people or organizations may be better able to use the resources available to them than others with similar means. An experienced politician, for example, can usually use political, economic, and organizational resources more effectively than someone who is running for office for the first time. Moreover, pluralists contend, people who possess power do not always use it for political ends. Many wealthy people do not participate in political activity and may choose instead to contribute to philanthropic or cultural causes.[5]

In contrast, the elitist view holds that the nation is literally ruled by a relatively small elite of wealthy, powerful individuals, usually men, who are able to maintain their positions over time. Their power comes from the important positions they hold in industry and finance, as well as in government and the military. The result, according to one writer, is that "government often represents the privileged few rather than the needy many, and . . . participating in elections and the activities of political parties and exercising the right to vote are insufficient measures against the influences of corporate wealth."[6]

It is unlikely that the debate between the pluralist and elitist views of American political life will ever be resolved. The two sides examine different materials, use different methods of analysis, and have fundamentally different perceptions of politics and society. For these and other reasons, it is impossible to obtain a definitive answer to the question: Who really rules?

A corporate boardroom. Elitists contend that business dominates American society, a view pluralists strongly reject.

3

The Bases of Political Power

In discussing political power, we are not referring to power that is based solely on force or coercion. Instead, we are referring to *legitimate* power. A political official can exercise legitimate power only if most people accept that power and believe that the rules and decisions stemming from it are right and proper. According to the German sociologist Max Weber, **legitimacy** in politics is derived from three sources: tradition, charisma, and legality.[7]

Weber believed that positions of power become legitimate over time; that is, they become *traditional.* American political parties provide an example of this kind of legitimacy. The Constitution contains no mention of a two-party system or even of political parties, yet a two-party system has existed almost from the beginning of the nation's history. So-called third parties have rarely won elections and have had a very limited effect on election results.

Weber also stressed the importance of personality in creating political legitimacy. The great popularity of some leaders is due in part to their personal magnetism, or *charisma.* Such twentieth-century political leaders as Dwight Eisenhower, Winston Churchill, and Charles de Gaulle have won acceptance for their ideas through sheer force of personality. Some—like Rev. Martin Luther King, Jr.—held no formal political position but because of their charisma were able to win the loyalty of large numbers of people not only to themselves but also to their ideas.

Finally, Weber pointed to the importance of *law* in creating legitimacy. Some political activities are considered legitimate simply because they are legal, that is, based on an accepted body of laws. In the United States, the

The Reverend Martin Luther King, Jr. (1929-1968). Minister, civil rights leader, and recipient of the 1964 Nobel Peace Prize.

POLITICS, DEMOCRACY, AND THE AMERICAN PEOPLE

written constitutions of the national and state governments and the laws passed by Congress and state and local legislatures provide the foundation on which legitimate authority is exercised by government over the people.

Politics and Government

It is important to understand that *government* is not the same as *politics.* The term **government** refers to the institutions and processes by which rules are made and enforced for all members of a society. Congress, the Supreme Court, and the President are all parts of the government of the United States. They have the power to make decisions or rules for all the members of society, and they have the power to enforce those decisions. For the government to exercise this power over citizens, the citizens must accept it as legitimate. Without such acceptance, a government cannot function well. In contrast, the governing units of labor unions, schools, churches, and social clubs are far more limited both in their jurisdictions and in their power to enforce their regulations.

A key phrase in the definition of government is *all members of a society.* If a few people break the rules of a union or club, at worst they may be thrown out of the organization; after that, its rules no longer apply to them. Nonmembers do not view the organization as having legitimate power over them. But if the same people break the rules of government, they can be punished whether they agree with those rules or not.

Individuals and groups may be deeply involved in politics but not be part of government. A labor union, a corporation, or a group concerned with protecting civil liberties and civil rights can influence government decisions that will affect society as a whole. These organizations, therefore, have political power but cannot make and enforce rules for all members of society.

■ Democracy as a Political System

Politics and government are sometimes viewed as elements of a political system. A *system* is any group of related elements that serves a specific function. The human digestive system is an example; so are a basketball team and a computer. A **political system** serves the function of making decisions that affect an entire society. According to one definition, a political system is a "system of behavior through which society is able to make decisions that most people accept as authoritative or binding most of the time."[8] The product of a political system is **public policy,** which includes all the rules that are made and enforced at the various levels of the political system—laws, judicial and administrative decisions, treaties with other nations, executive orders, and so forth.

There are numerous political systems in the United States: the national government in Washington, D.C., the fifty state governments, and many thousands of local governments—towns, townships, counties, cities, and

*A town meeting in Sand-
wich, New Hampshire.*

school districts, for example. Each operates within its assigned legal sphere of authority and provides services to the people who live within its jurisdiction.

Defining Democracy

Most Americans would agree that their nation is a democracy, but few have a clear understanding of what that means. **Democracy** is a form of government in which the policy decisions of the government are based on the freely given consent of the people, and the people are guaranteed certain basic rights. Democracy in the United States is **representative democracy** as opposed to **direct democracy.** In a direct democracy, each voter is able to participate directly and personally in the decision-making process. This assumes that all the participants can gather in one place for a general debate and discussion of policy. It must therefore be confined to political units with relatively small populations that cover a small geographic area.

In a representative democracy, on the other hand, citizens transfer their decision-making power to people whom they elect to represent them. These elected representatives are held responsible for their official acts through the election system. Representative democracy thus requires that there be regularly scheduled elections that cannot be postponed or suspended by the government. It also requires the freedom to discuss political ideas and the freedom to form political parties and contest elections. The political economist Joseph A. Schumpeter once defined modern democracy as an "institutional arrangement for arriving at political decisions in which individuals acquire the power to decide by means of a competitive struggle for the people's vote."[9]

Representative democracy (sometimes called *republican government*) is found in political units that are much larger in terms of both area and population than those that practice direct democracy. Today, however, it is also used in small units of government in which it might be theoretically possible to practice direct democracy. This is so because direct democracy is too difficult to apply in today's complex and mobile society. In the United

States, therefore, direct democracy is found only in some rural New England communities, which still hold town meetings. A twentieth-century variation of direct democracy, the *referendum* (in which citizens vote on specific issues) is allowed under the constitutions of many states and the charters of many local governments.

The Bases of Democracy

Self-Government. A basic principle of American democracy is the belief that people are capable of governing themselves. This idea was set forth by the British philosopher John Locke (1632–1704) in his *Two Treatises on Government*, which had a strong influence on the political leaders of eighteenth-century America. Locke believed that people are rational enough to perceive and understand the higher law—the so-called *natural law*—that provides a standard of human conduct. This leads to the recognition of certain *natural rights*, such as the rights to life, liberty, and property. These rights exist separately from society and government and, as such, should not be abridged by any political state; the state, in fact, exists solely to protect them. Locke's views on law were in sharp contrast to those of many other political and legal theorists, who viewed law as a creation of people and government, not as a system derived from nature.

Locke not only stressed the natural rights of all people but also believed that the individual is qualified to participate in a government established to protect those rights. He understood that some restraints must be placed on people's conduct. But he rejected the idea that people are not capable of governing themselves and that strong government is necessary to control their activities and maintain order.

The men who drafted the United States Constitution in 1787 believed that people were rational enough to govern themselves and did not need a king or tyrant to regulate their conduct. Despite this belief, however, they were not overly optimistic about human nature, tending to agree with the

John Locke (1632–1704). British philosopher and author of Two Treatises on Government *(1689), which strongly influenced the thought of late eighteenth-century America and the writing of the United States Constitution.*

7

political ideas of two other British writers: Thomas Hobbes (1588–1679) and David Hume (1711–1776). To varying degrees, both Hobbes and Hume were skeptical of human reason and stressed the role of passion and self-interest in human behavior. Thus James Madison, the most important figure in the writing of the United States Constitution, stated his views on human nature and government as follows:

> But what is government itself, but the greatest of all reflections on human nature? If men were angels, no government would be necessary. If angels were to govern men, neither external nor internal controls on government would be necessary. In framing a government which is to be administered by men over men, the great difficulty lies in this: you must first enable the government to control the governed; and in the next place oblige it to control itself.[10]

The Social Contract. Locke's belief that people are capable of governing themselves became a basic principle of American democracy. But why should there be a government at all? Why not simply let each person govern himself or herself?

Locke's political philosophy was based on the idea that early in human existence people lived in a "state of nature," without organized society or government. That state was unsatisfactory precisely because it was unorganized. There were no laws, judges, or penalties to prevent some people or groups from oppressing others. Eventually this chaotic situation led to the formation of civil society, in which there is a method for "making laws with penalties . . . for the regulating and preserving of property, and of employing the force of the community, in the execution of such laws . . . all this only for the public good."[11] This was done by means of a **social contract,** an agreement among the members of the society in which they accepted existing laws and penalties as binding. A second contract created government. It went into effect when a majority of the people agreed on the form of government that was to be created by the contract.

Government, in Locke's view, can possess only limited powers. It is established to protect people's natural rights to life, liberty, and property. If the government should fail to do this, the people have the right to replace it. They can then create a new government that will perform its proper function of protecting individuals and not oppressing them. This right was eloquently expressed by Thomas Jefferson in the American Declaration of Independence:

> We hold these truths to be self-evident, that all men are created equal, that they are endowed by their Creator with certain unalienable Rights, that among these are Life, Liberty and the pursuit of Happiness. That to secure these rights, Governments are instituted among Men, deriving their just powers from the consent of the governed. That *whenever any Form of Government becomes destructive of these ends, it is the Right of the People to alter or to abolish it,* and to institute new Government, laying its foundation on such principles and organizing its powers in such Form, as to them shall seem most likely to effect their Safety and Happiness. (Italics added.)

Majority Rule. According to Locke's social contract theory, a person who lives in a civil society no longer has to fear the arbitrary use of power

Thomas Jefferson (1743–1826). Author of the Declaration of Independence, diplomat, philosopher, Vice-President (1797), and the third President of the United States (1801–1809).

by other people, as was the case in the state of nature. But Locke did not believe that people are totally free in a civil society. They are now governed by the will of the majority. Locke believed that the decisions of government should be based on this principle. The doctrine of **majority rule** is an extension of his idea that people are able to make rational decisions and that they understand what policies would best serve their interests.

The concept of majority rule has been criticized, however. Perhaps the best-known challenge came from the French nobleman and social historian Alexis de Tocqueville, who was concerned about the possibility of a "tyranny of the majority." In the course of his extensive travels in the United States in the early 1830s, Tocqueville observed American democracy in operation. In his brilliant analysis of the American political system, *Democracy in America* (1835), he warned that

> if ever the free institutions of America are destroyed, that event may be attributed to the omnipotence of the majority, which may at some future time urge the minorities to desperation and oblige them to have recourse to physical force.[12]

For Tocqueville, absolute power was a danger in any form of government:

> When I see that the right and the means of absolute command are conferred on any power whatever, be it called a people or a king, an aristocracy or a democracy, a monarchy or a republic, I say there is the germ of tyranny, and I seek to live elsewhere, under other laws.[13]

It has been argued that one wise and benevolent leader, or a group of such leaders, would be better qualified to decide public policy than a majority. This argument is based on the idea that people do not have the ability to make rational decisions about public affairs. It cannot be denied that a large number of Americans vote on the basis of a candidate's

Alexis de Tocqueville (1805–1859). French liberal politician, historian, and author of Democracy in America *(1835).*

appearance or religious and ethnic background rather than on the basis of informed judgment. Supporters of majority rule argue, however, that error and injustice are much less likely under a system of majority rule. Although the public may often be uninformed or misinformed about political issues, it can quickly become involved and even outraged if it believes an injustice or wrong has taken place.

Majority rule as a governing principle may sometimes result in unwise decisions, but it does permit the correction of abuses of power and the removal of offending individuals from office. Moreover, it can be argued that a correct policy is more likely to emerge from the opinions of a majority than from the judgment of a few leaders.

Minority Rights. Although majority rule prevents tyranny by the few, the majority can violate the rights of individuals and groups in society. In a democracy, majority rule is legitimate only if it respects and protects the rights of the minority. The preservation of **minority rights** does not, of course, mean that the policies of the minority must be accepted by the majority. Rather, it means that the minority must be granted certain basic freedoms. These basic freedoms are what people usually mean when they link democracy and liberty. Liberty means freedom to express one's opinions even if they differ from those of the majority; freedom to worship—or not worship—as one chooses; freedom to join social, economic, or political organizations of almost any description; and many other such freedoms. Even the freedom to travel from one place to another, both within the United States and outside it, is a right of Americans that is not possessed by citizens of some nations.

The United States Constitution is an attempt to put into practice the ideas of limited government and minority rights. Many of its sections define and limit the power of government; others stress the need to protect the

10

rights of individuals and minorities. Nowhere is this more evident than in the Bill of Rights—the first ten amendments to the Constitution. Adopted in 1791, two years after the Constitution was ratified, the Bill of Rights sought to protect the individual against abuses of the power of government, even if the government had the support of the majority. The First Amendment, for example, guarantees freedom of speech, freedom of the press, the right to assemble, and the right to petition the government. The Fourth, Fifth, and Sixth Amendments grant important rights to people who are accused of having committed crimes, such as the right to a trial by jury and the right to have an attorney. These rights, usually referred to as **civil liberties,** will be discussed in detail in Chapter 11.

Limited Government. The idea of limited government is closely related to the belief in minority rights. Both Locke and the political leaders of late-eighteenth-century America stressed the need to place limits on the power of government, even when that government is a democracy in which the majority rules. The idea of limited government has a long history in this country. It was very popular in colonial America and during the decades after the end of the Revolution. Today Americans who distrust "big government" are expressing the same belief in the value of limited government.

The idea of limited government is associated with the principle of *constitutionalism*, which holds that the powers of government should be defined and limited in a written document that serves as the basic law of the land. The written constitution outlines the institutions of the government, their relationship to one another, and their specific powers. It puts limits on the authority of the government, and it may also guarantee certain rights to the individual. The basic structure and power of government created by the constitution can be altered only through a formal amendment process that is also stated in the document. A written constitution thus attempts to achieve the goal of limited government by stating the limits and making them legally binding on all officials of the government. The form of government that exists in the United States is often referred to as a **constitutional democracy,** meaning one that places written legal limits on the power of the majority to act.

Democratic Institutions. To be useful, democratic principles have to be translated into actual institutions. In the United States this has been done by means of a written constitution. The Constitution set up a government with three branches—executive, legislative, and judicial—run by officials with specific terms of office who were to be chosen in specific ways. It established the relationships among the three branches, as well as their powers and limitations, and created a system of elections. In addition, it divided power between a central government and the state governments.

Not all democratic governments take this form. Often power is centralized in a single national government. Nor do all democracies separate the powers of the government into three branches. In Great Britain, for example, the legislature (Parliament) is supreme and the executive and judicial functions are legally subordinate to it.

The complex system of government created by the United States Constitution is largely due to the influence of the eighteenth-century French philosopher Montesquieu (1689–1755). The basic functions of

Baron de Montesquieu (1689–1755). French political philosopher and author of The Spirit of the Laws *(1748), which strongly influenced the writing of the United States Constitution.*

government (i.e., legislative, executive, and judicial) had been recognized by political theorists before the eighteenth century. But it was Montesquieu who argued that if any two of these functions were held by the same person or group, political liberties would be destroyed. He therefore advocated that the three functions of government be separated. The authors of the United States Constitution adopted this theory, but they went even further: They created a system of checks and balances designed to prevent one branch from dominating the others, and they set up a federal system of government that divided power between a central government and the state governments. These topics will be discussed more fully in Chapters 2 and 3.

Free Elections. Free elections are essential in a government based on the will of the people. In the United States, elections are regularly scheduled and open to all citizens over the age of 18 who meet certain brief residency requirements. In addition, all states conduct primary elections in which citizens nominate the candidates who will run in the general election.

In the course of the nation's history, the right to vote has been granted to increasing numbers of people. At first it was restricted to white male property owners; later it was granted to white males who did not own property, then to blacks, to women, and most recently to 18-year-olds.

Another important aspect of the American electoral system is the secret ballot. Voters may be pressured to vote for a particular candidate, but they cannot be forced to do so. The frequency of elections is also significant. Presidential elections are held every fourth year; U.S. senators are elected every six years and members of the House of Representatives every two years. This means that elected officials must repeatedly win the approval of their constituents and respond to the challenges of opposing candidates.

Free elections fulfill several functions. They give citizens a chance to select policy-making officials and to express their preferences on public policy, and they encourage elected officials to be responsive to the desires of their constituents. Clearly, these functions are basic to a representative democracy. An additional effect of the electoral process is that it solves the difficult problem of determining how the power of government will pass from one group of rulers to another. If the election system is operating properly, its results will be accepted by the officials who have been removed from power and by the citizens who supported the losing candidates. Nations that rely on elections avoid violence as a means of replacing rulers.

An Organized Opposition. One feature that distinguishes a democracy from other forms of government is the presence of an organized opposition that is free to criticize people in positions of power. In the United States this is done primarily by the **political parties**—organized groups that support candidates for public office. When the Republicans control Congress or the presidency, for example, the Democrats serve as the organized opposition; they examine the policies of those in power and attempt to persuade the public that their program would be superior.

Some critics of the American two-party system claim that the parties do not offer real policy choices and thus do not truly oppose each other. Whether or not the parties differ significantly, one can hardly deny that each performs the valuable service of criticizing the other, especially at election time. The party in power is highly sensitive to accusations by the opposition, and such charges are answered—not silenced, as they are in nations that do not possess a democratic form of government.

Free Expression of Ideas. The First Amendment to the Constitution guarantees freedom of speech, press, and assembly and the right to petition government. It is, as Justice Benjamin Cardozo wrote, "the matrix, the indispensable condition, of nearly every other form of freedom."[14] The freedom to express opinions on issues and to hear the opinions of others is what makes democratic dialogue possible. Such exchanges of opinion can range from presidential press conferences to informal discussions among friends. In the United States the primary channel for the discussion and debate of politics is the mass media—newspapers, magazines, television, and radio.

Although political discussion may not bring all the facts on an issue into the open, it gives people a basis for making decisions, forces them to think about public problems in new ways, challenges them to defend their points of view, and encourages them to develop more rational opinions. Moreover, the free expression of ideas forces public officials to defend their policies to the public. The result may be not only responsive government but a more responsible public as well.

Equality. Like the concept of liberty, that of *equality* is often mentioned in connection with democracy. The concept of equality is one of the noblest and perhaps least understood aspects of democratic theory. In a democracy equality should apply in many areas of human life: equality before the law, equality of political rights, equality of economic and social opportunity, and equality of economic condition. Democratic theory has always stressed legal and political equality and the right of each person to have an equal chance to advance economically and socially. The idea that economic equality is necessary for the existence of a democratic society—that every person should have an adequate income and there should not be major differences in wealth among members of a society—is fairly recent. It has become an important idea only in the twentieth century.[15]

Contemporary critics who focus on the need for greater economic equality are alarmed by studies that show the extent of poverty in the United States. In 1989, for example, the U.S. Census Bureau reported that more than 31.7 million people, or 13 percent of Americans, lived below the official "poverty line" (defined as $12,675 for a family of four).

This form of inequality was not a matter of concern to the nation's founders. When Thomas Jefferson, the author of the Declaration of Independence, wrote that "all men are created equal," he was not expressing the belief that all people are equal in intellectual ability or that they should be equal in income and possessions. The equality Jefferson spoke of was a moral equality, one that would give each individual equality of opportunity. This kind of equality would not result in equality of wealth or position. It seemed obvious to Jefferson that people are born with different talents and they respond differently to the opportunities life offers them. But he believed strongly that people should not be kept from realizing their full potential by arbitrary laws or by distinctions based on factors like religion or family background.

Jefferson's view of equality included equality under the law. Jefferson also believed in broad political rights, such as the right to vote and the right to express political ideas. It should be noted, however, that like other late-eighteenth-century thinkers he did not apply the concept of equality to all human beings. In particular, black slaves and women did not share in the legal and political equality posessed by American citizens.

Some observers have expressed the fear that an excessive devotion to equality in a democratic society can lead to the loss of liberty. Tocqueville, for example, believed that democracy is more strongly linked to equality than to liberty and that people might tend to choose equality at the expense of liberty. "Equality every day confers a number of small enjoyments on every man," and as a result "the passion for equality penetrates . . . into men's hearts, expands there, and fills them entirely." Any challenge to equality will arouse their fury and distract them so that they will not notice "freedom escaping from their grasp."[16]

Universal Education. Thomas Jefferson claimed that a nation cannot be both ignorant and free. An early advocate of public education, he defended the cost of a system on the grounds that it would prepare citizens to make wise political choices and would instill in them the values of democracy. A few nations have succeeded in maintaining a democratic political system despite widespread illiteracy and poverty; India is a good example. But such conditions only make the task of establishing and maintaining democratic institutions more difficult.

The importance of education to democratic government is evident. Democracy requires that citizens have some understanding of public issues and the ability to make electoral choices on the basis of that knowledge. It also requires tolerance, respect for the rights of others, and the ability to compromise on public issues. These are attitudes that are developed through education. For poor people in America, therefore, the quality of education is a matter of particular concern. Inadequate education acts as a major obstacle to their understanding of political issues and their ability to participate in the nation's political system.

Democracy and Diversity

Democracy is said to have arisen in Athens in the fifth century B.C. There, for the first time in history, every citizen had an equal voice in government. But there is little similarity between democracy as it was practiced in ancient Athens and democracy as it exists in the United States today. For one thing, in Athens the privileges of democracy were granted only to free males, not to women or slaves. For another, Athens was a small, self-contained city-state, whereas the United States is an immense nation with a population whose diversity is almost beyond description.

Think of it! From a few small, rural, largely Protestant colonies with a fairly homogeneous population, the nation has expanded to cover an entire continent. And its people have become incredibly diverse. According to the Census Bureau, in 1988 the Nations almost 250 million inhabitants included 30.2 million blacks, 19.8 people of Hispanic origin, about 1.7 million Native Americans, and millions of people whose family background

The annual Cinco de Mayo Mexican festival, Denver, Colorado. People of hispanic background make up a rapidly growing part of the population of the United States.

is Scottish, English, Asian, German, Polish, Russian, Italian, Scandinavian, Irish, or one of over thirty other nationalities from which Americans claim descent.

Throughout most of American history, most immigrants came from Europe—first from the nations of Western Europe and later from those of Eastern Europe. That pattern changed sharply during the 1980s. During that decade the large majority of legal immigrants to the United States came from Asia—China, Korea, and the Philippines—and from the Americas—Mexico, the Dominican Republic, and Cuba, for example. This trend is likely to continue through the 1990s and will add to the great mix of peoples who make up the population of the United States.

This diversity of background is matched by diversity of religious affiliation, educational attainment, household composition, and many other characteristics.

Such immense diversity creates special problems for a democracy. Diversity leads to wide differences of opinion, making it difficult to obtain agreement on proposed solutions to political problems. The size of the population compounds this problem. For example, each member of the House of Representatives must vote according to the desires of more than 580,000 people, and within a group of that size there is bound to be a great deal of disagreement. In short, the task of running a democracy as large and diverse as the United States is enormously challenging.

■ Summary

In this chapter we have described the American political system in theoretical terms. We have seen that in setting up a representative democracy based on a written constitution, the nation's founders did not merely establish a new political system. They believed that they were creating a better form of government because, for the first time, the rights of the citizen would be protected. By means of a written constitution that embodied such devices as the separation of powers, federalism, and a bill of rights, the nation's founders hoped to guarantee to each person freedom from the arbitrary exercise of governmental power.

We have also examined the roots of what the political scientist Samuel P. Huntington has called the American creed: "liberty, equality, individualism, democracy, and the rule of law under a constitution."[17] Although this creed has been modified somewhat since it was first stated in the Declaration of Independence and the Constitution, its basic elements have not changed much in 200 years.

How has American democracy worked out in practice? Did the founders achieve their goal? Is the American political system open to influence by many individuals and groups, as pluralist theorists maintain? Or is it an essentially closed system that is dominated by the privileged few, as the proponents of an elitist view of American politics contend? In evaluating American democracy, we must keep in mind not only the intent of the founders but also the problems the nation has faced at various times in its history. When we encounter instances in which democratic institutions have failed to protect the rights of the citizen, we must ask whether such failures are due to faults in the institutions of democracy, faults in human nature, or simply the difficulty of running a democracy in a nation as large as ours.

■ Key Terms

politics

political power

pluralists

elitists

legitimacy

government

political system

public policy

democracy

representative democracy

direct democracy

social contract

majority rule

minority rights

civil liberties

constitutional democracy

political parties

■ Suggested Reading

CRICK, BERNARD. *In Defense of Politics*, 2nd ed. Chicago: University of Chicago Press, 1973.

DAHL, ROBERT A. *Democracy, Liberty, Equality.* New York: Oxford University Press, 1987.

FLATHMAN, RICHARD E. *The Philosophy and Politics of Freedom.* Chicago: University of Chicago Press, 1987.

GRAHAM, GEORGE J., JR., and SCARLETT G. GEORGE, EDS. *Founding Principles of American Government.* Chatham, N.J.: Chatham House, 1984.

HARTZ, LOUIS. *The Liberal Tradition in America.* New York: Harcourt Brace Jovanovich, 1955.

LIPSET, SEYMOUR MARTIN. *The First New Nation.* New York: Basic Books, 1963.

LOWI, THEODORE J. *The End of Liberalism*, 2nd ed. New York: Norton, 1979.

MCCLOSKY, HERBERT, and JOHN ZALLER. *The American Ethos: Public Attitudes toward Capitalism and Democracy.* Cambridge, Mass.: Harvard University Press, 1985.

MERELMAN, RICHARD. *Making Something of Ourselves: On Culture and Politics in the United States.* Berkeley: University of California Press, 1984.

SCHATTSCHNEIDER, E. E. *The Semi-Sovereign People: A Realist's View of Democracy in America.* New York: Holt, Rinehart & Winston, 1961.

■ Notes

1. Quoted in Leon A. Harris, *The Fine Art of Political Wit* (New York: Dutton, 1966), p. 222.

2. Roper poll, cited in *Wall Street Journal*, April 27, 1984, p. 1.

3. Harold D. Lasswell, *Politics: Who Gets What, When, How* (New York: McGraw-Hill, 1936).

4. David Easton, *The Political System* (New York: Knopf, 1953), pp. 129–134.

5. Robert A. Dahl, *Who Governs?* (New Haven, Conn.: Yale University Press, 1961), p. 129.

6. Michael Parenti, *Democracy for the Few*, 5th ed. (New York: St. Martin's Press, 1988), p. 2. See also Thomas R. Dye and L. Harmon Ziegler, *The Irony of Democracy*, 7th ed. (Monterey, Calif.: Duxbury Press, 1987), pp. 2–7.

7. Max Weber, *The Theory of Social and Economic Organization*, trans. A. M. Henderson and Talcott Parsons (New York: Oxford University Press, 1947), p. 328.

8. David Easton and Jack Dennis, *Children in the Political System* (New York: McGraw-Hill, 1969), p. 4.

9. Joseph A. Schumpeter, *Capitalism, Socialism, and Democracy*, 3rd ed. (New York: Harper & Row, 1950), p. 269.

10. *The Federalist Papers*, no. 51.

11. Quoted in George H. Savine, *A History of Political Theory*, rev. ed. (Fort Worth, Tex.: Holt, Rinehart & Winston, 1955), pp. 531–532.

12. Alexis de Tocqueville, *Democracy in America*, ed. Phillips Bradley (New York: Vintage, 1954), vol. I, p. 279.

13. Ibid., p. 270.

14. *Palko* v. *Connecticut*, 302 U.S. 319, 327 (1937).

15. See, e.g., John Rawls, *A Theory of Justice* (Cambridge, Mass.: Harvard University Press, 1971).

16. de Tocqueville, *Democracy*, vol. II, pp. 101–102.

17. Samuel P. Huntington, *American Politics: The Promise of Disharmony* (Cambridge, Mass.: Belknap Press of Harvard University Press, 1981), p. 14.

2

Chapter Outline

The Road to Independence
Early Attempts at Cooperation
The First Continental Congress
The Revolution
The Declaration of Independence

The Articles of Confederation
Government under the Articles
Shays' Rebellion

The Constitutional Convention
The Delegates
The Issues
Ratification

The United States Constitution
Federalism
Separation of Powers
Checks and Balances: Shared Powers
Judicial Review
Popular Sovereignty
National Supremacy

Constitutional Change and Development
Amending the Constitution
Other Means of Constitutional
  Development

Questions for Thought

*What were the main features of the
Articles of Confederation?*

*What were the major weaknesses of the
Articles of Confederation?*

*What issues most divided the delegates to
the Philadelphia Convention?*

*What arguments against ratification of the
Constitution were made by the
antifederalists?*

*What are the main principles of the
United States Constitution?*

*What procedures must be followed in
order to amend the Constitution?*

From Colonialism to Constitutionalism

LEXIS DE TOCQUEVILLE was among the first Europeans to examine the American political system closely. After his visit to the United States, he wrote:

> I confess that in America I saw more than America; I sought there the image of a democracy itself, with its inclinations, its character, its prejudices, and its passions, in order to learn what we have to fear or to hope from its progress.[1]

The United States' experience with democracy from the colonial period to the late twentieth century is unique in world history, and the political system that has evolved as a result is also unique.

As we saw in Chapter 1, the American political experience had its roots in the traditions brought by the colonists from England in the seventeenth and eighteenth centuries. In fact, the colonists thought of themselves as English, and their ideas about politics, religion, law, and individual rights were rooted in their English background. The American legal system, for example, is derived from English ideas and practices. It is based on the English common law, a system of law built on judicial decisions and precedents that developed over many centuries.

Perhaps most important, the American political and legal system owes a major debt to the English tradition of individual rights. According to the **Magna Charta** of 1215, the king was bound by the law and must respect the rights of his subjects. The **English Bill of Rights** of 1689 established basic guarantees, such as the right to trial by jury and the right to petition the government. Thus, when the American colonists finally rebelled against British rule and demanded their rights, they were demanding the rights possessed by English citizens.

■ The Road to Independence

Throughout the period before the American Revolutionary War, the colonists thought of themselves as English citizens. The idea of a separate nation independent of English rule was not widely accepted until just before the Revolution, which began in 1775. There were, however, numerous instances in which the colonists cooperated in attempts to solve shared problems. These efforts were the first step along the road to independence.

Early Attempts at Cooperation

The first of the early efforts to cooperate occurred between 1643 and 1684, when four New England colonies formed the New England Confederation to deal with the danger of Indian attacks. Another attempt was made in 1754, when delegates from the Iroquois nation and from several northern colonies met in Albany to discuss Indian relations. On his way to this meeting, Benjamin Franklin devised a proposal for colonial government known as the Albany Plan. The proposal called for the creation of a general government with the power to make treaties with the Native American tribes, to settle and purchase western lands, and to make war and peace and regulate trade with the Indians. But the British rulers of the colonies rejected Franklin's plan.

After 1760 the cooperative efforts of the colonies were spurred by British policies, some of which were intended to raise revenue for England at the expense of the colonists. The first of these was the American Revenue Act, better known as the Sugar Act, which was adopted by Parliament in 1764. Among other things, this law placed import duties on coffee, certain wines, and other goods imported by the colonists. Shortly after the passage of this act, "taxation without representation" (i.e., without the consent of the colonists) was denounced at a Boston town meeting. One of the fundamental rights of English citizens was the guarantee that taxes could be imposed on them only by their elected representatives. The colonists agreed that Parliament could make some laws for them, but as they had no representatives in that body, they claimed it did not have the power to tax them without their consent.

In 1765 the resentment aroused by the Sugar Act was intensified by the passage of the Quartering Act. This act required some of the colonies to provide supplies for the British troops that were stationed there and to house them in inns and unoccupied buildings. Even more exasperating to the colonists was the Stamp Act, also passed in 1765. This act, which imposed a tax on items like newspapers, legal documents, and playing cards, met with strong opposition throughout the colonies.

In 1770 the growing tension between the citizens of Boston and the British soldiers quartered there came to a head. A fistfight between a colonist and a soldier developed into a riot that ended in the so-called Boston Massacre, in which five colonists were killed.

The grievances of the colonists led to the formation of "committees of correspondence" in several of the colonies. The purpose of the committees was to communicate with one another regarding actions of Parliament that were viewed as threatening to the colonies. One such action was the passage of the Tea Act of 1773, which gave the East India Company a monopoly on the American tea trade. This placed a hardship on American merchants, whose protests eventually led to the famous Boston Tea Party in which a group of Bostonians disguised as Mohawk Indians boarded a ship loaded with tea and dumped much of its cargo into Boston Harbor.

After the Boston Tea Party there was little pretense of harmony between the colonists and the British government. In 1774 Parliament passed a series of measures that came to be known as the Coercive Acts, including a bill that prohibited the loading or unloading of ships in any part of Boston Harbor. At about the same time, the Quartering Act was renewed and its provisions were extended to all of the colonies. Americans began to feel that the colonies were being occupied rather than governed. The protest against British rule gathered momentum.

The First Continental Congress

The growing outcry against British control led to numerous calls for the creation of a congress at which the colonies might agree on a joint response to the actions of the British. In September 1774 delegates from all the colonies except Georgia met in Philadelphia for the First Continental Congress. The announced purpose of the congress was "to deliberate and determine on wise and proper measures . . . for the restoration of union and harmony between Great Britain and America." But, led by radical delegates like Samuel Adams of Boston, it ended up adopting a "declaration of rights" that listed a number of violations of colonial rights and stated that Parliament had no authority over the colonies.

The British government was not impressed by the colonists' protests. The Continental Congress had little real power and did not appear to pose a serious threat to British rule. However, Britain's leaders failed to consider the colonists' growing sense of national identity, as expressed in Patrick Henry's statement that "the distinctions between Virginians, Pennsylvanians, New Yorkers, and New Englanders are no more. I am not a Virginian, but an American."

The Revolution

The colonists' frustration at the British government's attitude led to violent action. On the morning of April 19, 1775, six companies of British soldiers traveled west from Boston to Concord to search for hidden arms and arrest rebel leaders. The colonists had been warned the night before by Paul Revere, and when the British soldiers reached Lexington, they found the road blocked by about sixty Massachusetts minutemen armed with muskets. Historians cannot determine which side fired the first shot, but shots were fired and eight minutemen were killed. The war for independence had begun.

The **Second Continental Congress** met in Philadelphia in May 1775. It had no more authority than the first congress, but the reality of war had caused most of the colonists to see the need for at least a temporary central government: Troops had to be raised, money printed, and ambassadors sent

The Battle of Lexington, Massachusetts, April, 1775, was one of the first engagements of the American Revolutionary War.

"The Liberty Bell," Independence Hall, Philadelphia. Its ringing announced the signing of the Declaration of Independence on July 4, 1776.

to foreign powers. Congress became responsible for guiding the efforts of the colonists in their fight against the British.

The Declaration of Independence

Even with the Revolution under way, some colonists continued to hope that peaceful relations with England could be restored. Thomas Paine's pamphlet *Common Sense*, which called the king a "royal brute" and claimed that "of more worth is one honest man . . . than all the crowned ruffians that ever lived," is credited with turning the tide of public opinion in favor of a formal break with England. By the summer of 1776 the idea of independence had become popular throughout the colonies.

On June 7, 1776, Richard Henry Lee of Virginia submitted two proposals to the Continental Congress, one recommending that the colonies form a permanent confederation and the other calling for a positive declaration that "these United Colonies are, and of right ought to be, Free and Independent States." The latter proposal was debated for nearly a month and was finally adopted on July 2. Thomas Jefferson had been asked to prepare a statement to be read to the public, and this document, the Declaration of Independence, was adopted on July 4.[2]

■ The Articles of Confederation

Although the Declaration of Independence announced America's independence to the world, the "United Colonies" were recognized only by France and the Netherlands. To the rest of the world, the American states were still British colonies rebelling against British rule. In fact, from 1776 until 1781 the United Colonies had no real common government but consisted of thirteen separate states. But at the same time that the Continental Congress put forth the Declaration of Independence, it began work on the **Articles of Confederation**—a plan of government that would establish an association of the states to deal with common problems. The Congress finished its work in November 1777, and the document was sent to the states for their approval. The Articles of Confederation required the consent of all thirteen states, and this was not obtained until March 1781, when the Maryland legislature approved the Articles.

The Articles of Confederation created a Congress in which each state had one vote. The new government had very little power, however. It did not have a separate executive branch or a national court system. Congress did not have the authority to regulate interstate commerce, and it could neither tax citizens nor draft them into the military during times of war. It could request money and soldiers from the states, but it had no authority to enforce its requests. Moreover, amendments to the Articles of Confederation required the unanimous consent of the states—a condition that was virtually impossible to meet.[3]

Government under the Articles

The Revolution ended two years after the adoption of the Articles of Confederation. The new nation managed to survive the war, but with little help from its central government. The long years of fighting and the collapse of the British colonial system led to economic depression and a weakening of the national spirit. Most of the states failed to give the central government financial support, and the new nation had almost no standing among foreign powers. But the main problems facing the central government under the Articles arose from the fact that it lacked the power to tax individuals and the power to regulate commerce. Thus, of the $10 million that Congress had requested from the states, it had collected only $1.5 million by the end of 1783. Unable to regulate commerce, it left the job to the states, and they handled it badly. To protect their own economies, they imposed tariffs on products imported from other states. A series of trade wars developed in which states used tariffs to keep out goods and produce of other states.

The situation within the states was no better. The economic problems of the time led the debtor class, mainly the poorer farmers, to demand action by the state legislatures. Some legislatures responded by passing laws that extended the period for making payments on mortgage debts. A majority also issued paper money, which increased the amount of money in circulation, making it easier to repay debts. But these actions angered creditors and failed to solve the economic problems of the states.

Shays' Rebellion

In Massachusetts the picture was especially bleak. Massachusetts had taxed its citizens so heavily that by 1786 its economy was crippled. Mortgage foreclosures were at an all-time high, and the prisons were full of debtors; whole towns were demanding tax reductions. Under the leadership of a former Revolutionary War captain named Daniel Shays, the Massachusetts debtors took action. They marched on the courthouse in Northampton and denied entrance to judges who were preparing to foreclose mortgages on local farms. **Shays' Rebellion** lasted for nearly a year and was finally ended by the state militia.

Shays' Rebellion was one of several factors that led to the calling of a constitutional convention. But other forces were also at work. In 1785 Virginia and Maryland reached an agreement resolving the problem of the

Shays' Rebellion (1786–1787) was an armed insurrection against the government by farmers in western Massachusetts. This painting portrays followers of Shays taking possession of a local courthouse.

commercial use of the Potomac River. The Virginia legislature then advanced the idea of a convention to deal with the common interstate commercial problems of all the American states. Only five states sent delegates to the convention, which met at Annapolis, Maryland, in September 1786. But the representatives of these states—New York, New Jersey, Pennsylvania, Delaware, and Virginia—went beyond simply dealing with commercial issues. They also recommended that a convention be held for the purpose of devising remedies for the nation's ills. This idea was approved by Congress, which called for a convention to be held in Philadelphia beginning May 14, 1787, "for the sole and express purpose of revising the Articles of Confederation."

The movement to alter the Articles of Confederation had broad support, but it also had opponents. Some groups favored the existing system, either because they benefited from it economically or because they were fearful of a more centralized form of government. As a result of these opposing views, drafting an acceptable constitution and obtaining public approval for the new document would prove to be a difficult process. Yet the outcome of these efforts has endured. Today, more than two centuries after it was written and ratified, the United States Constitution is the oldest written constitution still in use in the world today.

■ The Constitutional Convention

Bad roads and heavy rains delayed the opening of the **Constitutional Convention** until May 29, 1787, when delegates from nine states were present and the first official session was held. The sessions were closed to the public, but several delegates, notably James Madison, kept records of the proceedings, and these have been of great value to historians and political scientists in putting together an account of what actually happened at the Convention.[4]

The Delegates

The delegates who attended the Philadelphia Convention were not elected by the people but appointed by their respective state legislatures. James Madison called them "the most respectable characters in the United States . . . the best contribution of talents the state could make for the occasion." Jefferson went further, calling them "an assembly of demigods." Indeed, they were an exceptional group. Among them were George Washington, commander-in-chief of the Revolutionary War army and one of the richest men in the nation; Madison, who had served in the Virginia Assembly and had studied the governments of many nations; Benjamin Franklin, the noted statesman, scientist, inventor, and writer; Roger Sherman, a longtime judge on the Connecticut Supreme Court and the only person to sign the Declaration of Independence, the Articles of Confederation, and the Constitution; James Wilson of Pennsylvania, a lawyer,

Portrait of George Washington by the American painter Joseph Wright (1756–1793).

legislator, and signer of the Declaration of Independence; Gouverneur Morris, also of Pennsylvania, who, because of his brilliant command of language, was called upon to draft the final version of the Constitution; and George Mason, author of the Virginia Declaration of Rights.

As a group, the delegates to the Convention represented the nation's economic and social elite. Many had served in Congress or as state governors; more than half had attended American colleges or received a university education in England; and most were wealthy. The middle class, on the other hand—the shopkeepers, artisans, and successful farmers—was not represented at the Convention, nor was the lower class—hunters and trappers, less successful farmers, and laborers. No women participated in the Philadelphia Convention, nor were there any blacks or Native Americans among the delegates.

The Issues

At the first official session of the Convention, Governor Edmund Randolph of Virginia presented the so-called **Virginia Plan,** which included a proposal that "a national government ought to be established consisting of a supreme legislative, executive, and judiciary." This proposal clearly went beyond revising the Articles of Confederation, yet it was approved with little debate as a basis for starting the proceedings of the Convention. The decision to scrap the Articles and write a totally new constitution was probably the single most important decision made at the Convention.

A National Government versus States' Rights. The decision to write a new constitution was closely related to another basic problem faced by the Convention: Should it create a truly national government, or should it continue the system established by the Articles of Confederation, in which the states possessed most of the legal authority of government? Nationalist feelings were strong among the delegates. A large majority wanted to create a national government, one in which each citizen would have both national and state citizenship and would have a legal relationship to both governments. The Virginia Plan envisioned a strong central government composed of legislative, executive, and judicial branches with the power to veto state laws. In addition, the legislative power of Congress would be expanded, and it would gain the authority to make laws that directly affected the people and not just the state governments. It would, for example, have the power to tax citizens rather than requesting funds from the states, as had been the case under the Articles of Confederation. This last feature clearly showed the national character of the government proposed by the Virginia Plan and its fundamental departure from the confederate system.

Not all of the delegates favored a national form of government, however. Supporters of the Articles of Confederation made an attempt to prevent the adoption of the Virginia Plan. One of them, William Paterson, presented the **New Jersey Plan,** which would have preserved the basic elements of the confederate system. Under the New Jersey Plan, Congress would consist of one house in which all the states would be represented equally. It would have to obtain the approval of the states to impose duties on foreign goods, regulate foreign and interstate commerce, impose postal fees, and the like. In presenting his proposal, Paterson said, "If the confederacy was radically wrong, let us return to our States, and obtain larger powers, not assume them of ourselves."

In reality, the decision to draft a new constitution and the decision to set up a national government could not be separated. The New Jersey Plan would not solve the problems that had brought the delegates to the Convention. The two plans were debated for several days and then put to a vote. The New Jersey Plan was voted down, and the Convention undertook to establish a national system of government that would have the power to act directly on the people.[5]

Large States versus Small States. Another issue that divided the delegates was the nature of the proposed legislature. The Virginia Plan, which was generally supported by the larger states, called for a *bicameral*, or two-house, national legislature, with the number of representatives in both houses to be determined by population or taxes paid; the members of the lower house would be elected by the people and those of the upper house would be appointed by the lower house. This arrangement favored large states, such as Virginia, New York, Massachusetts, and Pennsylvania, which had larger populations and paid more taxes than smaller states like New Jersey, Delaware, and Maryland. Under the Virginia Plan, the larger states would dominate the legislature and, thus, the government.

The small states generally objected to the adoption of such a legislative system. They favored the creation of a *unicameral*, or single-house, legislature, with each state having equal representation. When this idea was defeated, the small states insisted on equal representation in at least one house of the bicameral legislature.

The division over the issue of representation should not be viewed as solely a conflict between large and small states. The conflict had a strong regional aspect as well. Most of the small states were in the Mid-Atlantic and

FROM COLONIALISM TO CONSTITUTIONALISM

James Madison (1751–1836), fourth President of the United States (1809–1817). Madison represented Virginia in the Continental Congress, the Congress of the Articles of Confederation, and was a member of the House of Representatives from 1789 to 1797. He served as President Jefferson's Secretary of State between 1801 and 1809. Madison wrote a majority of the Federalist Papers *and was the principle drafter of the United States Constitution and the Bill of Rights. Portrait by Gilbert Stuart.*

the North; they included New Jersey, Connecticut, New Hampshire, Maryland, and Delaware. New York, a state with a large population and territory, generally voted with the northern states on questions of representation. On the other hand, the large states, which included Pennsylvania and Massachusetts, received the backing of the four southern states: populous Virginia as well as thinly settled North Carolina, South Carolina, and Georgia.

The Convention almost collapsed because of the deep division on the subject of representation. To resolve the conflict, the Convention formed a committee to work out a compromise. The committee's proposal, known as the **Connecticut Compromise,** called for a bicameral legislature in which the number of representatives in the lower house (the House of Representatives) would be determined by population, while each state would have equal representation in the upper house (the Senate). This arrangement satisfied both sides and ended the conflict.

North versus South. Other differences between the northern and southern states also created problems at the Convention. The economies of the northern states were based on commerce, shipping, and industry, whereas those of the southern states were based on agriculture, slave labor, and the export of farm products. The southern states were afraid that the northern states, which outnumbered them, would interfere with their export trade. They therefore argued for a clause in the Constitution stating that "no tax or duty shall be paid on articles exported from any state." They also insisted that all treaties with foreign governments be approved by a two-thirds vote in the Senate. This would give the South the power to block any treaty that would harm the economic interests of that region. Both of these proposals were accepted by the Convention and included in the final draft of the Constitution.

Slavery was also a major concern of the southern states. They would not accept any constitution that would interfere with its continued existence. It is likely that a majority of the delegates opposed the slave trade and that some were morally opposed to slavery. Luther Martin of Maryland declared that slavery was "dishonorable to the American character." But North and South Carolina and Georgia would not yield. John Rutledge of South Carolina pointed to the political reality that confronted the Convention: "The true question . . . is whether the Southern states shall or shall not be parties to the Union."

Although the framers of the Constitution never used the word *slavery*, the document sanctioned its existence. One section of the original document required all states to return escaped slaves to their masters. In addition, the Constitution gave Congress the authority to outlaw the importation of slaves into the United States after 1808. But this deadline provided the South with a period of twenty years in which to continue the slave trade and build up the size of the slave population. (In 1808 Congress acted to outlaw the importation of slaves from outside the United States, but it did not legislate against the slave trade within the nation.)

The Convention also dealt with the question of how slaves were to be counted in determining a state's population and in levying direct taxes. The southern delegates failed in their attempt to have slaves included in the total population so that their states would obtain more seats in the House of Representatives. The delegates ultimately agreed to adopt a three-fifths rule, by which each slave would be counted as three-fifths of a person in determining the number of representatives each state would send to the House and for purposes of imposing direct taxes.

These provisions remained in the Constitution until after the Civil War, when slavery was abolished by the Thirteenth Amendment and the three-fifths rule was ended by the Fourteenth Amendment. In effect, the delegates to the Constitutional Convention accepted slavery as part of the nation's legal and economic system. As one scholar has written,

> [The delegates] nourished a generous vision of American citizenship. That vision did not include the Negro slave. Indeed, according to [pre–Civil War] abolitionists, the delegates bought union and liberty for the white man at the expense of slavery for the black. . . . Many seemed to suppose that slavery was dying in the face of economic and humanitarian sentiment. Perhaps a few truly wanted a slave empire. However these matters may be, the fact remains that the Constitution paved the way to an entrenchment of [slavery].[6]

Electing Government Officials. The delegates agreed on the need for a government based on the consent of the people, but they had difficulty agreeing on how that consent should be obtained. There was a division between those who favored a more democratic system of government, which would give greater authority to the people, and those who had a more aristocratic view and were afraid of giving too much power to the people.

In the debate over how members of the House of Representatives were to be elected, there was overwhelming backing for the idea of direct election by the people. But the question of who would be eligible to vote for those members was bypassed. The Convention was unable to agree on a national standard for voting. Instead, it was decided that the standards used by each state in choosing members for the lower house of its legislature would be used in determining who could vote for members of the House of Representatives. Under state law at the close of the eighteenth century only adult white males were qualified to vote, and some states also imposed property and religious requirements for voting.

The Convention resolved the question of how senators were to be chosen in a very different manner. The proposal that senators be chosen by the people was soundly defeated. The idea of having them selected by the state legislatures emerged during the debate on this subject and was ultimately adopted.[7] Supporters of this method of electing senators favored it because it would directly represent the state governments in Congress and would also serve as a check on the popularly elected House.[8]

The Convention had made the important decision to create an executive branch of government headed by a president. But it had great difficulty deciding how the nation's chief executive would be chosen. There was conflict between delegates who favored direct popular election and those who believed that the President should be selected by Congress. Most delegates did not believe that the people were wise enough to make such an important choice. In addition, delegates from the small states feared that direct election would give too much influence to the larger states. Moreover, it would have been impossible to hold a single national election, given the great difficulty of travel and the limited means of communication that existed at the close of the eighteenth century. Support for the idea of legislative election of the President was strong, but many delegates to the Philadelphia Convention were unwilling to accept this system. They were afraid it would make the President a captive of the legislative branch.

This problem was not resolved until the closing days of the Convention and was one of the last major decisions made by the delegates. A specially appointed committee proposed an indirect system for selecting the President: an **electoral college.** After some changes, this plan was accepted by the Convention. In accepting this proposal, the Convention rejected a parliamentary form of government, such as existed in Great Britain, and gave its support to a presidential model of government.

Under the electoral college system, each state would choose a number of electors equal to its total number of senators and representatives in Congress. The state legislatures were free to decide how the electors were to be chosen. The electors would meet in each state and cast votes for two people, at least one of whom was not a resident of that state. The votes of each state would be sealed, sent to the U.S. Senate, and then opened and counted before a joint meeting of both houses of Congress. The person who obtained the largest number of votes would become President as long as he received a majority of the total number of electoral votes. If there was a tie in the electoral votes cast or if the candidate with the most votes did not receive a majority of the votes, the House of Representatives was given the power to select the President from among the candidates with the five highest vote totals. In voting for the President, the House would vote by

The inauguration of George Washington as the first President of the United States at Federal Hall, New York City, on April 30, 1789.

state, with each state having a single vote. The candidate with the second-highest number of electoral votes would become Vice President, but if two or more people had equal numbers of votes, the Senate was to make the choice.[9]

Ratification

The Constitution was signed by thirty-nine delegates on September 17, 1787. It was then submitted to the Congress of the Confederation and to the states for **ratification.** The Convention had made an important decision in requiring that ratification of the proposed Constitution be achieved when only nine of the thirteen states gave their approval. Moreover, the decision to ratify was to be made not by the state legislatures, in which opposition to the new system of government was likely to be strong, but by specially created conventions.

The supporters of the Constitution were called **Federalists** and its opponents **Antifederalists.** The latter were at a disadvantage because they could only voice opposition to the proposed Constitution; they did not have an alternative plan. Still, the contest was a very close one.

Supporters of the new Constitution tended to live in the states with small populations. With the exception of New Hampshire and Rhode Island, the small states—Delaware, New Jersey, Georgia, and Connecticut—were the first to ratify. These states were satisfied with the compromise that gave

FROM COl ONIALISM TO CONSTITUTIONALISM

each state equal representation in the Senate, and they felt that a stronger central government would make them more secure. (Georgia, for example, was concerned about the presence of hostile foreign powers—Spain and France—on its borders.)

Opposition to the new Constitution was greatest in the most populous states. Most of the people in those states lived in rural areas, not in cities like New York and Philadelphia. While city dwellers tended to favor the Constitution, farmers often opposed it because they were suspicious of the economic and social elite who had drafted it. As a result, by June 1788, when New Hampshire became the ninth state to ratify, Virginia and New York had not yet given their consent. Without the approval of these major states, the Constitution was doomed even though it had been ratified by the required number of states.

Age also influenced people's attitudes toward the Constitution. The leading Federalists were an average of ten to twelve years younger than the most prominent Antifederalists. As the historian Samuel Eliot Morison has noted, "The warmest advocates were eager young men."[10]

The Federalists and Antifederalists differed in other respects. For one thing, their careers were quite different. The Federalists had begun their public lives during the Revolutionary War and had developed a "continental" outlook as a result of serving in national institutions such as the Continental Army and the Continental Congress. The Antifederalists did not

The Bill of Rights, as it was submitted to the states for ratification by Congress on September 24, 1789. Note that the first and second amendments were rejected by the states. The remaining proposals became the first ten amendments to the United States Constitution—the Bill of Rights.

share this outlook. Their careers had begun in the years before the Revolution and had consisted largely of service in the state governments.[11]

The Antifederalists were critical of the Constitution for a number of reasons, but perhaps their most effective point was the failure of its authors to include a list of individual rights—a **bill of rights**—that would protect individuals against the power of the new central government. The document did include certain basic protections, such as the right to a jury trial in criminal cases, a narrow definition of treason against the government, and restrictions on the power of the national government to pass *ex post facto laws* or *bills of attainder* and to suspend the *writ of habeas corpus*. (See Chapters 3 and 11.) Yet the Antifederalists argued that unless the basic rights of the people were listed in the Constitution, the national government could ignore those rights and oppress the citizens. The absence of a bill of rights was the single issue that united Antifederalists throughout the country.

A leading spokesman for the Antifederalists was George Mason of Virginia. In his speeches to the Constitutional Convention, Mason pointed out that the Constitution did not adequately protect the people against the power of the central government, since it lacked a bill of rights. Such a statement of individual freedoms was essential to prevent the new government from becoming either a monarchy or a tyrannical aristocracy, he argued.

The fear of a highly centralized government exercising its power over a large geographic area was another basis for Antifederalist opposition to the proposed Constitution. Numerous essays on this subject were published, with the authors sometimes borrowing the names of leading figures of the ancient Roman republic. One of the best of those essays was signed "Brutus"; it attacked the idea of a centralized government extending over a large geographic area. "Brutus" claimed that such a government would inevitably become arbitrary and impersonal and would ultimately eliminate the states altogether. To "Brutus" and other Antifederalists, a republic could not survive unless it was geographically small—like the Greek and Roman republics—and its citizens close to those who governed them.[12]

The most important arguments of the Federalists in favor of ratification were published in a series of eighty-five essays that appeared in New York newspapers and are collectively known as *The Federalist Papers*. Written under the pseudonym "Publius" by James Madison, Alexander Hamilton, and John Jay, *The Federalist Papers* remain a valuable and influential expression of the ideas and political philosophy of the writers of the Constitution.[13]

The authors of *The Federalist* criticized the Articles of Confederation and argued that small republics tend to quarrel among themselves and to be easily dominated by more powerful nations. They favored a geographically large republic with a strong government, which they believed would be most likely to provide both security and liberty for its citizens. These goals could be achieved through the devices of federalism, separation of powers, checks and balances, popular sovereignty, national supremacy, and judicial review, all of which are embodied in the United States Constitution. (These devices are discussed in the next section of the chapter.)

Eventually the Federalists admitted the need to guarantee the rights of individual citizens. They promised that as soon as the Constitution went into effect, it would be amended to include a bill of rights. This compromise helped turn the tide toward ratification in both Virginia and New York. In the early summer of 1788 both states voted by narrow margins to ratify the Constitution.

The United States Constitution

The delegates to the Philadelphia Convention were practical men who were willing to compromise on some issues in order to achieve their overall objective of writing a new constitution that would create a strong central government. But the delegates were also motivated by certain fundamental ideas, and those ideas shaped the character of the final document. While they wanted to create a central government with adequate powers, they also wanted to restrain those powers. They sought to achieve this goal through the use of several constitutional devices: federalism, separation of powers, and checks and balances. The power of the courts to exercise judicial review, though not expressly stated in the Constitution, was also intended to act as a restraint on the power of government.

The delegates were fundamentally opposed to both monarchy and autocratic government. They desired to establish a republican form of government based on the concept of *popular sovereignty*. The idea that the people were sovereign was a novel one at the end of the eighteenth century, but it was an idea that was to have great influence from that time on.

Finally, the authors of the Constitution wanted to guarantee that the newly created central government would be supreme within the area of its legal authority. To accomplish this purpose, they made the principle of *national supremacy* part of the new Constitution.[14]

Federalism

Federalism is a system for organizing government that is based on a geographic division of power. In a federal system, a national government has authority over the entire territory, while regional governments have authority only within their own area. Under the United States Constitution, the national government has specific powers, such as the right to regulate interstate commerce. States have the general power to legislate in areas that have not been delegated to the national government or denied them by the Constitution.

In a federal system, power can be divided in different ways. The constitutions of some countries, unlike that of the United States, delegate specific powers to the states or provinces and reserve all other authority to the central government. Regardless of how power is distributed, federalism always serves the basic purpose of limiting the power of government by dividing it along geographic lines.

Separation of Powers

Having divided the powers of government between the states and the national government, the writers of the Constitution went on to separate the operations of the national government into three distinct branches: legislative, executive, and judicial. This was accomplished in the first three articles of the Constitution. Article I states that "all legislative Powers herein granted shall be vested in a Congress of the United States"; Article II, that "the executive Power shall be vested in a President of the United States of America"; and Article III, that "the judicial Power of the United States, shall be vested in one supreme Court, and in such inferior Courts as the Congress may from time to time ordain and establish."

The nation's founders believed that this system of **separation of powers** would limit the powers of the government by preventing any one of the three branches from dominating the other two. They were especially fearful of legislative power, since it was believed that in a popular form of government, power tends to flow to the legislature, which is most directly responsive to the wishes of the people.

Checks and Balances: Shared Powers

The authors of the Constitution did not believe in absolute separation of governmental powers. Once they had formally separated the three branches of government, they introduced a system of **checks and balances** in which the power of government is shared by the legislative, executive, and judicial branches. The main purpose of checks and balances is to limit the power of government by making each branch dependent on the others; Congress can pass laws, for example, but the President can veto them. The President has the power to negotiate treaties with foreign nations, but such agreements must be approved by a two-thirds vote of the Senate. The federal courts can interpret the meaning of laws and of the Constitution, but they are limited by the broad authority of Congress to shape the structure of the federal judicial system and to define the types of cases courts can hear.

The checks-and-balances system is also illustrated by the methods found in the Constitution for removing public officials. The President, the Vice President, federal judges, and other officials can be removed from office only by **impeachment** and conviction, the first the responsibility of the House of Representatives and the second of the Senate. The House is given the sole power to impeach—that is, to formally accuse a public official of wrongdoing. But the Senate alone has the authority to convict and remove the accused person from office, and this action requires a two-thirds vote of the senators present. Thus in the removal process, the power of the House of Representatives is checked by that of the Senate.

The system for choosing federal officials embodies an even more complex system of checks and balances. The Constitution requires that members of the various branches of the national government be elected by different groups or constituencies: Senators represent the people of an entire state; members of the House of Representatives represent the voters of smaller districts within a state; and the President represents all the citizens of the nation (though he is actually elected by the electoral college, which is organized by states). Moreover, the Constitution assigns different terms of office to senators (six years, with one-third of the senators elected every two years); representatives (two years); the President (four years); and federal judges (life). The staggered terms for the President and members of Congress were designed to prevent the government from being "captured" or totally controlled by the officials chosen in any one election year.

The nation's founders believed that this complex election system would limit government by introducing different points of view into debates on public issues. Local viewpoints would conflict with state and national viewpoints. Senators elected in one year would represent different interests than would senators elected two years later, but both would serve together in the upper house of the legislature. The life tenure of federal judges would make them independent of public opinion, and this would provide stability and continuity.

Judicial Review

The term **judicial review** refers to the power of courts to declare legislative and executive actions unconstitutional. Although judicial review is not mentioned in the Constitution, there is evidence that its authors intended the federal courts to have this authority. Judicial review had been used on a number of occasions by courts in colonial America and by state courts in the years following the Revolutionary War. The first time this power was exercised by the Supreme Court to nullify an act of Congress came in 1803 in the famous case of *Marbury v. Madison.*[15] Chief Justice John

John Marshall (1755–1835). Diplomat, Virginia Congressman, and fourth Chief Justice of the United States. His opinion in Marbury v. Madison *(1803) provided the precedent for the power of judicial review. Later opinions strengthened the authority of the central government in relation to the states.*

Marshall's opinion in that case established the precedent that judicial review could be used by the federal courts to limit the legislative power of Congress.

The Supreme Court's power of judicial review extends not only to actions of the United States Congress and the President but also to acts of the state governments. As early as 1796, the Supreme Court invalidated a Virginia law that violated a provision of the peace treaty made by the United States with Great Britain after the Revolutionary War.[16] The federal courts have exercised the power of judicial review over state governments on many hundreds of occasions over the course of the nation's history.

Popular Sovereignty

The word *sovereignty*—ultimate legal authority—is not mentioned in the Constitution, but it is clear that the delegates had definite ideas on this subject. And those ideas were decidedly different from those that had been expressed by commentators on government up to that time. In Europe, sovereignty had been viewed as indivisible and residing in a single source—usually the monarch.

But this conception of sovereignty was at odds with the new republican theory of government that took hold in the United States after the Revolutionary War. This new theory was based on the idea of **popular sovereignty**—the belief that the people are the source of all legal authority.

The writers of the Constitution accepted the idea of popular sovereignty and rejected the notion that either the state or the federal government was the final source of legal authority. Critics argued that two systems of government could not function in the same geographic area, since this denied all traditional ideas of sovereignty. But, as several constitutional scholars have pointed out, dual government "was precisely what American federalism provided for, and the doctrine of popular sovereignty made it possible. Created by the people, state and federal government could legislate and govern concurrently over the same population in the same territory."[17]

National Supremacy

Article VI of the Constitution declares that

> This Constitution, and the Laws of the United States which shall be made in Pursuance thereof; and all Treaties made, or which shall be made, under the Authority of the United States, shall be the supreme Law of the Land; and the Judges in every State shall be bound thereby, any Thing in the Constitution or Laws of any State to the Contrary notwithstanding.

This important provision of the Constitution—originally proposed as part of the New Jersey Plan—established two major principles. First, the United States Constitution and all federal laws and treaties are superior to conflicting provisions of state constitutions and laws; this is the principle of **national supremacy.** Second, the supremacy clause makes clear that the Constitution is enforceable as law by judges and is not merely a statement of political or moral rules.

Constitutional Change and Development

Amending the Constitution

If it is not to become obsolete, a constitution must include a procedure for changing or revising the original document—an **amendment** process. The nation's founders understood this need, but they also realized that there was a danger in making the amendment process too easy: The fundamental rules created by the Constitution could then be readily changed, and the document would take on the character of a lengthy legislative code. The delegates therefore made it difficult to amend the Constitution.

Article V establishes a two-step amendment procedure: *proposal* and *ratification.* Amendments can be proposed using either of two methods: by a two-thirds vote of both houses of Congress or by a national convention called by Congress at the request of the legislatures of two-thirds of the states. Only the first method has been used to date. Similarly, there are two procedures for ratifying an amendment: It must be approved by the legislatures of three-fourths of the states or by specially elected ratifying conventions in three-fourths of the states. (See Table 2.1.) The latter method has been used for only one of the amendments ratified thus far—the Twenty-first, which repealed the Eighteenth (Prohibition) Amendment.

TABLE 2.1 *Amendments to the Constitution: Time between Congressional Approval and Ratification*

	Amendment	*Year ratified*	*Ratification time*
1–10	Bill of Rights	1791	1 year, 2½ months
11	Suits against states	1798	3 years, 10 months
12	Election of the President	1804	8½ months
13	Slavery	1865	10½ months
14	Civil rights	1868	2 years, 1½ months
15	Voting right for blacks	1870	1 year, 1 month
16	Income tax	1913	3 years, 7½ months
17	Direct election of senators	1913	1 year, ½ month
18	Prohibition	1919	1 year, 1½ months
19	Voting rights for women	1920	1 year, 2½ months
20	Terms of office	1933	11 months
21	Repeal of Prohibition	1933	9½ months
22	Two-term limit for Presidents	1951	3 years, 11½ months
23	Voting in presidential elections for Washington, D.C.	1961	9 months
24	Abolition of the poll tax	1964	1 year, 5½ months
25	Presidential succession	1967	1 year, 6½ months
26	Voting right for 18-year-olds	1971	4 months

Approximately 6,000 proposed constitutional amendments have been introduced in the Congress since 1789, but only 26 have been ratified. The time between congressional approval and ratification of an amendment has never been longer than 4 years. Eight amendments were proposed by Congress but never ratified by the necessary number of states.

Congress can determine which of the two ratifying procedures must be used, and it can set a time limit for ratification by the states.

The Constitution has been amended only twenty-six times in all and only sixteen times since 1791. The first ten amendments, the Bill of Rights, were proposed by the First Congress to meet the popular demand for a written statement of rights that would protect individuals against oppression by the national government. Many of the remaining amendments were designed to make the political system more responsive to the people. The post–Civil War amendments—the Thirteenth (1865), Fourteenth (1868), and Fifteenth (1870)—abolished slavery and were intended primarily to guarantee and protect the rights of black people. The Seventeenth Amendment (1913) provided for direct popular election of U.S. senators; the Nineteenth (1920) outlawed discrimination on the basis of sex in determining who shall have the right to vote; the Twenty-third (1961) gave the District of Columbia votes in the electoral college; the Twenty-fourth (1964) barred the state and national governments from denying a person the right to vote in primary and national elections because of failure to pay a poll tax; and the Twenty-sixth (1971) denied the state and national governments the right to discriminate against people 18 years of age or over in granting the right to vote (age 21 had been the generally accepted standard).

Other amendments have dealt with a variety of matters. The Eighteenth (1919) prohibited the manufacture, sale, and transportation of alcoholic beverages. This "noble experiment"—Prohibition—ended with the adoption of the Twenty-first Amendment (1933), which repealed it. The Eleventh (1798), Twelfth (1804), Twentieth (1933), and Twenty-fifth (1967) Amendments dealt with various technical and procedural problems. The Twenty-second Amendment (1951) prevents any person from being elected President more than twice. (It also provided that a Vice President who becomes President as a result of the impeachment, death, or resignation of his predecessor can be elected to two full terms only if he has served less than two years of the former President's term of office.)

In every session of Congress, many constitutional amendments are introduced. A few of the proposed amendments have been subjects of serious national debate. Among these are proposals to allow prayer in public schools and to return to the states the full right to legislate on the subject of abortion, thus reversing the 1973 decision of the Supreme Court in *Roe* v. *Wade*. In 1990 Congress debated several constitutional proposals that would have required a balanced federal budget. None of these ideas received the necessary two-thirds vote of the legislature.

Many less serious proposals are introduced in Congress each year and receive little or no attention. For example, there have been suggestions to end congressional immunity from traffic citations received en route to and from the Capitol, to reduce the terms of federal judges to eight or ten years, and to allow voters in national elections to enact or repeal federal laws.[18]

Since the Civil War almost all amendments proposed by Congress have been ratified by the states. Two of the three exceptions occurred recently. The Equal Rights Amendment, which would have barred all discrimination on the basis of gender, was proposed by Congress in 1972 but fell three states short of the number needed for ratification. And in 1978 Congress proposed a constitutional amendment that would have given the citizens of the District of Columbia full voting representation in Congress. But by the time this proposal expired in 1985, only sixteen states had ratified it.

The second method of proposing a constitutional amendment—in which two-thirds of the states ask Congress to call a constitutional convention—has never been used. However, on one occasion it indirectly led to the adoption of an amendment. In the early years of the twentieth century, growing public support for the direct election of United States senators was resisted by Congress. A movement to call a constitutional convention received the support of all but one of the necessary two-thirds of the states. Congress finally acted, thereby avoiding the need for a convention. In 1912 it proposed the Seventeenth Amendment, which provided for the popular election of senators; the states quickly ratified the amendment.

At present some thirty-two states—two short of the necessary thirty-four—have requested that Congress call a constitutional convention largely for the purpose of proposing an amendment to require a balanced federal budget. But no new states have added their support for a number of years. By mid-1990 fifteen states had called for a constitutional convention to modify a 1985 Supreme Court decision—*Garcia* v. *San Antonio Metropolitan Transit Authority*[19]—that narrowly interpreted the powers of the states under the Tenth Amendment to the Constitution. (This case is discussed more fully in Chapter 3.)

Other Means of Constitutional Development

The Constitution provides a written outline for the American political system. Some aspects of this system, however, are not found in the words of that document but are derived from experience and accepted practice. For example, there is no mention in the Constitution of political parties or the Cabinet.

The political parties had their origins in the debate over ratification of the Constitution. They were a natural outgrowth of the fact that people rarely agree in their political views, let alone their economic and personal interests. The Antifederalists opposed the Federalists on the issue of ratification of the Constitution, and during Washington's presidency the Jeffersonians (Republicans) opposed the Hamiltonians (Federalists) on issues related to domestic and foreign policy issues. These groups evolved into the two major parties that are familiar to us today.

The Cabinet likewise is not mentioned in the Constitution and has no formal legal status. It serves as a means by which the heads of government departments can meet with the President to discuss policies. The Cabinet was founded by George Washington both as a way of saving time (he could meet with all the department heads at once instead of one at a time) and as a way of testing the opinions of his advisers.[20] Since Washington's time, some Presidents have continued to use the Cabinet in these ways, but it has rarely functioned as a policy-making body, and most modern Presidents have not used it extensively.

The United States Supreme Court plays the most significant role in developing the meaning of the Constitution. Through its many decisions over two centuries, the Court has given life and force to the general rules set forth in the Constitution. Without judicial interpretation, such important but broad principles as national supremacy, due process of law, equal protection of the laws, and freedom of speech would exist as mere words on paper, without specific meaning. The United States Constitution is a living instrument of government largely because of the role played by the Supreme Court as its final interpreter.

In sum, the Constitution should be viewed as a living document that includes not just the written text but the whole set of customs, traditions, practices, and understandings that have developed in the more than two hundred years since it went into effect in 1789.[21]

■ Summary

For over two centuries the Constitution has served as the basic instrument of government for the United States. It has done so despite the nation's transformation from a largely rural country confined to the Atlantic seaboard to a heavily urbanized industrial society spread across a continent. The Constitution has survived these great changes because the nation's founders understood that it had to be made flexible enough to adapt to changing needs. At the same time, the basic principles embodied in the Constitution remain intact: popular sovereignty, federalism, separation of powers, checks and balances, national supremacy, and judicial review.

In two centuries the Constitution has survived a civil war, several international wars, economic depressions, and major scandals in government. In the future the nation will undoubtedly face new challenges both at home and abroad, and the Constitution will be tested again. During those crises some critics will say that the United States Constitution is outdated and inadequate. But if American history is any guide, the critics will be proved wrong, and the document written during the hot Philadelphia summer of 1787 will be equal to the challenge.

■ Key Terms

Magna Charta
English Bill of Rights
First Continental Congress
Second Continental Congress
Articles of Confederation
Shays' Rebellion
Constitutional Convention
Virginia Plan

New Jersey Plan
Connecticut Compromise
electoral college
ratification
Federalists
Antifederalists
Bill of Rights
federalism

separation of powers
checks and balances
impeachment
judicial review
popular sovereignty
national supremacy
amendment

FROM COLONIALISM TO CONSTITUTIONALISM

Suggested Reading

BERNSTEIN, RICHARD B. *Are We To Be a Nation? The Making of the Constitution.* Cambridge, Mass.: Harvard University Press, 1987.

CAREY, GEORGE W. *The Federalist: Design for a Constitutional Republic.* Champaign, Ill.: University of Illinois Press, 1989.

KAMMEN, MICHAEL. *A Machine That Would Go of Itself: The Constitution in American Culture.* New York: Random House, 1986.

KERBER, LINDA. *Women of the Republic: Intellect and Ideology in Revolutionary America.* New York: Norton, 1986.

LEVINSON, SANFORD. *Constitutional Faith.* Princeton, N.J.: Princeton University Press, 1988.

LEVY, LEONARD W., ED. *Essays on the Making of the Constitution,* 2nd ed. New York: Oxford University Press, 1987.

MACDONALD, FORREST F. *Novus Ordo Seclorum: The Intellectual Origins of the Constitution.* Lawrence, Kans.: University of Kansas Press, 1985.

MCCOY, DREW R. *The Last of the Fathers: James Madison and the Republican Legacy.* New York: Columbia University Press, 1989.

MEAD, WALTER B. *The United States Constitution: Personalities, Principles, and Issues.* Columbia, S.C.: University of South Carolina Press, 1987.

PANGLE, THOMAS L. *The Spirit of Modern Republicanism: The Moral Vision of the American Founders and the Philosophy of Locke.* Chicago: University of Chicago Press, 1988.

ROSSITER, CLINTON. *1787: The Great Convention.* New York: Macmillan, 1965.

STORING, HERBERT J. *What the Anti-Federalists Were For.* Chicago: University of Chicago Press, 1981.

Notes

1. Alexis de Tocqueville, *Democracy in America*, ed. Phillips Bradley (New York: Vintage, 1954), vol. I, p. 15.

2. The complete text of the Declaration of Independence appears in Appendix A at the end of this book.

3. The complete text of the Articles of Confederation appears in Appendix B.

4. The best brief study of the Convention may be found in Max Farrand, *The Framing of the Constitution of the United States* (New Haven, Conn.: Yale University Press, 1913). This book has been issued in a number of modern editions. Much of the discussion that follows is based on Farrand's study.

5. C. Herman Pritchett, *Constitutional Law of the Federal System* (Englewood Cliffs, N.J.: Prentice-Hall, 1984), p. 12.

6. David G. Smith, *The Constitution and the Convention: The Political Ideas of the Founding Fathers* (New York: St. Martin's Press, 1965), p. 52.

7. The Seventeenth Amendment to the Constitution, adopted in 1913, provided for direct election of U.S. senators by the people.

8. See, e.g., *The Federalist Papers*, no. 62, by James Madison.

9. Some features of this method of selecting the President and Vice President were changed by the Twelfth Amendment to the Constitution, ratified in 1804. See Chapter 6 for a more complete discussion of the present workings of the electoral college.

10. Samuel Eliot Morison and Henry Steele Commager, *The Growth of the American Republic*, 5th ed. (New York: Oxford University Press, 1962), vol. I, p. 194.

11. Stanley M. Elkins and Eric McKitrick, "Youth and the Continental Vision," in Leonard W. Levy, ed., *Essays on the Making of the Constitution*, 2nd ed. (New York: Oxford University Press, 1987), pp. 241–245.

12. Excerpts from George Mason's writings and the essay by "Brutus" appear in Appendix C.

13. The complete text of two of the most influential essays, no. 10 and no. 51, appears in Appendix D.

14. The complete text of the Constitution appears in Appendix E.

15. 1 Cranch 137 (1803).

16. *Ware* v. *Hylton*, 3 Dallas 199 (1796).

17. Alfred H. Kelly, Winfred A. Harbison, and Herman Belz, *The American Constitution*, 6th ed. (New York: Norton, 1983), pp. 105–106.

18. Francis J. Flaherty, "The Amend Corner," *National Law Journal*, March 26, 1984, p. 3.

19. 469 U.S. 528 (1985).

20. Louis W. Koenig, *The Chief Executive*, 4th ed. (Orlando, Fla.: Harcourt Brace Jovanovich, 1981), p. 33.

21. Kelly, Harbison, and Belz, *American Constitution*, p. xv.

3

Chapter Outline

Federalism in the Constitution
Powers of the National Government
Concurrent Powers
Limitations on the National Government
Powers of the States
Limitations on the States
Interstate Relations

Mutual Obligations
Obligations of the National Government to
the States
Obligations of the States to the Union
National Supremacy

Federalism in Theory and Practice
Competitive Federalism
Cooperative Federalism
Centralized Federalism
Growth of the Grant System
The New Federalism

Questions for Thought

What are the main features of a federal form of government?

How does a federal form of government differ from a confederacy? From a unitary government?

What types of powers are given to the national government by the Constitution?

What types of powers are given to the states by the Constitution?

What are federal grants-in-aid?

Why do grants-in-aid play such an important part in the present operation of our federal system?

The Federal System

AS Morton Grodzins and Daniel Elazar have written, "government in the United States is chaotic."[1] We do not have a single, central government with power over every aspect of life. Nor can it be said that we have fifty-one governments—a national government and fifty state governments—with political and legal power divided among them, although this is what the Constitution says we have. In reality there are thousands of governments in the United States—cities, townships, counties, and a large number of special-purpose governments, such as local school districts, in addition to the national and state governments. Most citizens are under the jurisdiction of—and pay taxes to—at least three local governments.

How is this complex system of governments within governments possible? The answer is that in a federal system different levels of government are assigned different powers and duties. Such a system is somewhere between a unitary, or centralized, government and a confederation. In a **unitary government** like that of France, the United Kingdom, or Israel, the central government has ultimate legal authority over citizens. It grants specific powers to local governments, but in theory it can reclaim those powers at any time. In a **confederation,** by contrast, the powers of the central government are granted to it by the state governments. The central government can make laws for the nation as a whole, but it cannot regulate the actions of citizens. For example, it can request financial support from the states, but it cannot impose a tax on individuals. Authority over the individuals in any given area is in the hands of the state government. Such a system existed in the United States under the Articles of Confederation during the 1780s and in the confederacy created by the southern states during the Civil War; the present government of Switzerland is also a confederacy.

Under **federalism,** neither the central government nor the state governments have absolute power. Political and legal power is divided between them, usually in a written constitution. Today the word *federal* is used to refer to an activity or institution of the national (i.e., central) government, whereas *federalism* refers to a system in which decisions and functions are divided between two levels of government.

In American federalism the states are not merely administrative units that manage programs adopted in Washington. Although they may administer some national programs, they are separate political units, acting

U.S. Marine F/A-18 Hornets fly over Kuwait on their way to bomb Iraqi military positions during the 1991 Persian Gulf War. Military and foreign policy are areas the Constitution assigns exclusively to the national government.

independently within their legal sphere of activity. The power to conduct foreign affairs, however, rests exclusively with the central government; the states have no legal authority in this area. Federalism, therefore, applies only to the nation's internal, or "domestic," affairs.

Under federalism, different units of government theoretically have authority over different areas of life: the federal government makes decisions concerning broad national issues, such as interstate commerce; the state governments control local matters like education and road construction. In practice, however, the distribution of power in a federal system is less clear-cut, and the powers of various units overlap.

■ Federalism in the Constitution

The colonists who came to America before the Revolution were fleeing from arbitrary, often oppressive, governments. When they found that political conditions in the colonies were not much better, they rebelled. Having won their independence after a long struggle, the colonists did not want to create a strong central government. Under the Articles of Confederation, therefore, power was distributed among a set of largely independent states. But the confederation was unable to deal with many of the problems facing the new nation. A major goal of the Constitutional Convention of 1787 was to create a stronger central government. The result, after many compromises, was a federal form of government.

The Constitution that went into effect in 1789 established the basic pattern of American federalism, though later amendments and judicial decisions have made some changes in this system. The nation's founders created a form of government that delegated specific powers to the national government and reserved most of the remaining powers for the states. In the words of James Madison, the framers of the Constitution created "neither a national nor a federal Constitution, but a composition of both."[2]

In addition to establishing a system of shared powers, the Constitution sets forth the limitations on the national government and its obligations to the states. It denies specific powers to the states, and it defines the obligations of one state to another as well as to the national government. It also provides for a Supreme Court. One of the main functions of the Court is to settle conflicts that rise from the distribution of powers among the various governments that make up the federal system. It therefore plays a key role in defining and shaping the American federal form of government.

In this chapter we will discuss the powers and limitations of the national and state governments and look at how they are applied in practice.

Powers of the National Government

The Constitution gives two basic types of powers to the national government: **delegated powers** (also called expressed or enumerated powers) and *implied powers.* Delegated powers are named in the Constitution; implied powers are derived from the "necessary and proper" clause of Article I, Section 8.

Delegated Powers. Article I, Section 8, of the Constitution lists many of the delegated powers of Congress. In domestic matters the most important of these are the authority to impose taxes and the power to regulate interstate commerce. The expansion of the national government has been based largely on these powers. The taxing authority is used by Congress not only to obtain revenue but also to regulate certain types of behavior. The federal tax on gasoline, tobacco products, and alcoholic beverages, for example, is designed both to raise money and (because the tax increases the price) to discourage use of these products.

The power to regulate interstate commerce also has far-reaching effects. By the late 1930s the Supreme Court had interpreted this power in such a way as to support broad governmental regulation of business, labor, and agriculture. For example, it upheld the Fair Labor Standards Act of 1938, which set wage and hour standards for workers engaged in interstate commerce.[3] In the Civil Rights Act of 1964 Congress used the commerce clause to outlaw racial discrimination in hotels, motels, and many restaurants. Because their customers and the food they serve move from one state to another, discrimination restricts the flow of these forms of commerce. The Supreme Court ruled that these provisions of the act are constitutional.[4]

Article I, Section 8, also grants Congress important powers in foreign and military affairs. It gives it the authority to raise an army and navy and to declare war. But in Article II the President is given the primary power to act in foreign affairs. The President is designated as commander-in-chief of the armed forces; granted the right to receive ambassadors from foreign nations and (with Senate approval) appoint American ambassadors; and empowered to negotiate treaties with foreign nations (with the advice and consent of two-thirds of the Senate). Article II also delegates to the President important domestic powers, such as ensuring that the laws are faithfully executed.

Implied Powers. Article I, Section 8, of the Constitution gives Congress the right "to make all laws which shall be necessary and proper for carrying into Execution the foregoing Powers, and all the Powers vested by this Constitution in the Government of the United States, or in any Department or Officer thereof." This **necessary and proper clause** can be cited to justify the use of an unstated, or implied, power as a means of carrying out an expressed power. For example, although the Constitution gives Congress the expressed power to raise an army and navy, it does not say how this is to be done. A variety of methods have been adopted by Congress during the twentieth century—including lotteries, selective service, and, currently, a volunteer system—all constitutionally justified by the necessary and proper clause.

The precedent for a broad interpretation of the implied powers of Congress was set in the famous case of *McCulloch* v. *Maryland* (1819).[5] Congress had created a system of national banks that was extremely unpopular in some parts of the nation. Maryland had imposed a tax on the operation of the system's Baltimore branch, which the bank refused to pay.

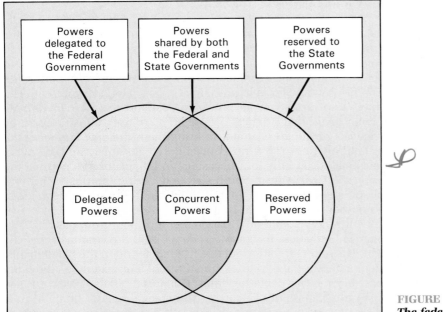

FIGURE 3.1
The federal system.

One of the central issues raised in the case was whether Congress had the power to create a national banking system. The Constitution does not expressly grant such a power, but the government argued that Congress had the implied power to do so in order to carry out its delegated authority to borrow and coin money. The state maintained that the federal banking system was unconstitutional; it sought to persuade the Supreme Court to accept a very narrow reading of the necessary and proper clause. Chief Justice John Marshall rejected Maryland's arguments and upheld the constitutionality of the banking system. He took a broad view of the implied powers clause, a view that has been accepted ever since. "Let the end be legitimate," he wrote, "let it be within the scope of the Constitution, and all means which are appropriate, which are plainly adapted to that end, which are not prohibited, but consistent with the letter and spirit of the Constitution, are constitutional." (See Figure 3.1.)

Concurrent Powers

Concurrent powers are those that can be exercised by both the states and the federal government. The major example is the power to tax and spend. The states may impose taxes on people and businesses within their jurisdictions. Without this power, they would be unable to function and would be entirely dependent on the national government. Other concurrent powers include the power to borrow money, to take property for public purposes after compensating the owner (this is known as the power of *eminent domain*), to establish courts, and to enforce the laws.

Limitations on the National Government

In Article I, Section 9, the Constitution denies Congress specific powers. Among these is the power to pass **bills of attainder** (legislative acts that single out certain people for punishment without trial) and **ex post facto laws** (laws that make an act criminal that was legal when it was performed or increase the penalty for a crime after it has been committed). The government is also limited in its power to suspend the **writ of habeas corpus,** a court order that protects people from arbitrary imprisonment by requiring officials of the government to bring them to court and state the reasons for holding them. (This most ancient of Anglo-American legal rights has been suspended on only four occasions in U.S. history: in parts of the nation during the Civil War; in South Carolina during the post–Civil War Reconstruction period; in 1905 in the Philippines during the American occupation of that nation; and in Hawaii during World War II.)

The Constitution also bars the national government from passing laws or engaging in activities that would deny rights guaranteed by the Constitution. The main limitations of this type are found in the Bill of Rights, the first ten amendments to the Constitution. For example, the First Amendment begins by declaring that Congress "shall make no law respecting an establishment of religion." Congress therefore may not pass legislation that favors one religion over another, nor may it grant federal funds to religious groups to advance their religious purposes.

Powers of the States

The Constitution does not assign specific powers to the states, but the Tenth Amendment makes it clear that all powers that are not delegated to the national government or denied to the states are reserved for the states or the people. The powers of the states under the United States Constitution are referred to as **reserved powers.** The states have the authority to pass laws that promote the health, welfare, safety, and morals of their citizens. Education and fire and police protection are among the principal functions exercised by state and local governments.

The states may enact legislation under their reserved powers without expressed authority from the national constitution. They may not, however, invade areas that are assigned to the national government (e.g., foreign affairs). Nor may the states violate any specific limitations on their power based on provisions of either the United States Constitution or their own state constitutions.

Limitations on the States

Certain powers are denied to the states by the Constitution. Article I, Section 10, contains a number of limitations. For example, the states may not pass bills of attainder or ex post facto laws, nor may they "enter into any Treaty, Alliance, or Confederation" with a foreign nation. (For example,

Public education is one of the main powers reserved to the state governments in this nation's federal system.

Texas could not enter into a treaty with Mexico to settle problems related to their common border.) States cannot levy any tax on imports or exports without the approval of Congress. Several amendments to the Constitution, including the Thirteenth, Fourteenth, Fifteenth, Nineteenth, Twenty-fourth, and Twenty-sixth, impose a variety of limitations on the states.

The **due process clause** and **equal protection clause** of the Fourteenth Amendment have become especially important sources of restrictions on the states during the past half-century. The due process clause ("nor shall any State deprive any person of life, liberty, or property, without due process of law") imposes a variety of restraints on the ability of the states to act. Most important, the Supreme Court has interpreted the word "liberty" in the clause to include most of the provisions of the Bill of Rights, thereby guaranteeing those freedoms against infringement by both the state and federal governments.

The equal protection clause ("No State shall . . . deny to any person within its jurisdiction the equal protection of the laws.") has been applied by the Supreme Court to outlaw racial discrimination and many forms of sex discrimination by state governments.

Interstate Relations

The Constitution also sets forth a number of important rules governing relations among the states:

1. The **full faith and credit clause** of Article IV, Section 1, requires the states to honor the final civil rulings of other states—including marriages, divorce decrees, and final court judgments. (It does not apply to criminal cases.) This clause was intended to protect the rights of citizens both in their home state and in other states. Thus a marriage or divorce that is validly granted under the laws of one state must be recognized in all other states.

2. According to Article IV, Section 2, "The Citizens of each State shall be entitled to all Privileges and Immunities of Citizens in the several States." Although this **privileges and immunities clause** has never been clearly defined, various Supreme Court decisions have created some general rules. The Court has held that the clause does not guarantee complete legal equality between citizens and noncitizens of a state. It protects only the "fundamental rights" that are "basic to the maintenance and well-being of the nation."[6] Thus, for example, a state may not discriminate against a noncitizen with respect to providing police protection and medical care. But a doctor or lawyer who is licensed to practice in one state does not have a constitutional right to practice in another state without first meeting that state's licensing requirements.

3. The **interstate rendition clause** of Article IV, Section 2, states that "a person charged in any State with Treason, Felony or other Crime, who shall flee from Justice, and be found in another State, shall on Demand of the executive Authority of the State from which he fled, be delivered up to be removed to the State having jurisdiction of the Crime." In the vast majority of situations, interstate rendition, or *extradition*, presents few problems. Fugitives usually agree to be returned to the state where they are wanted. When prisoners do not agree to be returned, state governors routinely comply with the extradition requests of other states. However, the Supreme Court has held that the federal courts have no power to force a governor to extradite a wanted fugitive.[7]

4. Article I, Section 10, of the Constitution provides that "no State shall, without the Consent of Congress, . . . enter into any Agreement or Compact with another State." In this indirect way the Constitution permits the states to settle mutual problems through the use of **interstate compacts,** or agreements between two or more states. An interstate compact is normally negotiated by the states' governors and approved by their legislatures. If its provisions would affect the federal system, it must also receive the approval of the United States Congress.

Throughout the nineteenth century interstate compacts were used almost exclusively to settle boundary disputes between states. In the twentieth century they have been used to resolve more complex problems. Some compacts still deal with relatively minor issues, but a growing number are concerned with difficult transportation problems, environmental issues, crime control, and a variety of commercial problems.

Perhaps the best-known interstate compact is the one that created the Port Authority of New York–New Jersey in 1921. The Port Authority operates many aspects of transportation in the New York–New Jersey area, including interstate bridges and tunnels, port facilities for ships, bus terminals, and a small railroad system. It also owns two 110-story

The George Washington Bridge, which spans the Hudson River between New York and New Jersey, is one of many transportation facilities operated by the New York-New Jersey Port Authority.

office buildings (the World Trade Center) and several airports serving both interstate and international travelers.

A more recent example of an important interstate compact is an agreement reached by California, Arizona, North Dakota, and South Dakota in 1987. Under the terms of the compact, California will accept all low-level nuclear waste generated in the four states for thirty years. After that, the state that generates the next-highest volume of radioactive waste will accept all such waste from the member states. The compact was created in response to a federal law requiring all states to come up with plans for the safe disposal of mildly radioactive waste. It is not limited to the four states included in the original agreement; other states may apply for membership.[8]

5. In the case of a dispute between two or more states (e.g., when one state sues another over a disputed boundary line), Article III gives the Supreme Court **original jurisdiction;** that is, the Supreme Court sits as a trial court to settle the problem. The Court has, however, heard relatively few such cases in the course of the nation's history.

■ Mutual Obligations

Obligations of the National Government to the States

Article IV, Section 4, of the Constitution declares that the United States shall guarantee to the states a "Republican Form of Government." There is no definition of the term *republican* and nothing to indicate which branch of the federal government has the duty of applying this provision. The

Supreme Court has always refused to become involved in issues arising under this **guarantee clause.** It has claimed that all such questions are "political," not "judicial," and therefore must be decided by either Congress or the President. Thus the Court would not decide whether the provisions of the Oregon State Constitution, which permitted direct legislation by the people through the procedures known as initiative and referendum, denied the state a republican form of government.[9]

Article IV, Section 4, also requires the national government to protect the states against foreign invasion or internal violence. On the rare occasions in the nation's early history when a state was invaded by a foreign power (during the War of 1812 the British attacked Washington, D.C., Baltimore, and New Orleans), the national government used its military forces to oppose the invasion.

Finally, Article IV, Section 4, provides that upon the application of the state legislature (or the governor if the legislature cannot be convened), the United States shall protect the states against internal or domestic violence. The states have requested federal aid in suppressing domestic violence on about sixteen occasions since the nation's founding.

The federal government has the right to intervene within a state "in cases of domestic violence" even in the absence of a request by the state. Congress has delegated to the President the power to put down domestic violence by using federal troops or calling the state militia into federal service. The President can also act on the basis of his own constitutional authority. He has the legal right to act in order to protect federal property and to prevent interference with the federal mails and the movement of interstate commerce.[10] In addition, the President can act to uphold federal court orders. For example, in 1957, acting against the wishes of state officials, President Dwight Eisenhower used federal troops to subdue violence and enforce a federal court order requiring desegregation of public schools in Little Rock, Arkansas. In 1962 federal troops were used to maintain order at the University of Mississippi, which had been ordered by the federal courts to admit its first black student. And in 1965 President Lyndon Johnson sent federal troops to Selma, Alabama, to protect the participants in a voting rights march led by Rev. Martin Luther King, Jr.

Obligations of the States to the Union

The Constitution also imposes certain legal obligations on the states. They are required to maintain a republican form of government, preserve peace within their borders, hold elections for members of Congress, fill vacancies in their delegations to Congress, choose presidential electors, and consider proposed constitutional amendments submitted by Congress or by a national convention under the provisions of Article V.

National Supremacy

In a federal system of government there is bound to be some conflict between the central and state governments over the exercise of various powers. In Article VI, the framers of the Constitution made a clear and unambiguous decision in favor of national supremacy when such a conflict exists: "This Constitution, and the Laws of the United States which shall be made in Pursuance thereof; and all Treaties made, or which shall be made, under the Authority of the United States, shall be the supreme Law of the Land."

Article VI does not make the states completely subordinate to the national government. Rather, it prevents the states from exercising power in areas that the Constitution has assigned to the national government. States may not, therefore, pass laws or establish policies that conflict with the Constitution, constitutional acts of Congress, or valid national treaties. When such a conflict arises, Article VI requires that the state policy give way to that of the national government.

The United States Supreme Court is the main vehicle for resolving conflicts within the federal system. The Court is, in fact, the umpire of American federalism. This role was firmly established early in the nineteenth century. In *McCulloch* v. *Maryland*, for example, Chief Justice Marshall, after upholding Congress' right to establish a national bank, declared unconstitutional a state law that taxed the bank on the ground that it violated the national supremacy clause of Article VI. Early in the nineteenth century the Supreme Court also upheld the right of Congress to create an appeals system in which decisions of state courts involving questions of federal law could be reviewed by the Supreme Court.[11] This method of appeal, which has been used throughout American history, permits the Supreme Court to serve as the final interpreter of federal law. This procedure guarantees that federal, not state, judges will have the final say on issues arising under the Constitution, federal law, and national treaties.

A modern example of the Supreme Court's serving as umpire of the federal system is the case of *Philadelphia* v. *New Jersey*.[12] A New Jersey law prohibited bringing into the state "any solid or liquid waste which originated or was collected outside [the] state." The Supreme Court declared the law to be "impermissible under the Commerce Clause of the Constitution," which bars one state from setting up discriminatory laws designed "to isolate itself in the stream of commerce from a problem shared by all."

On a few occasions in the nation's history federal troops have been used to uphold national supremacy when groups of people or local governments have used force or legal obstructions to prevent implementation of federal law. As noted earlier, the civil rights struggles of the 1950s and 1960s created several such situations.

■ Federalism in Theory and Practice

The framers of the Constitution created only an outline of a federal system; they did not present a precise theory of this system of government. It has therefore been possible for several very different theories of federalism to be developed in the course of American history. During that time the practice as well as the theory of federalism has changed dramatically.

Competitive Federalism

The competitive theories of federalism, in which the basic question is which level of government should have the most power, include nation-centered federalism, state-centered federalism, and dual federalism. *Nation-centered federalism*, the oldest of these theories, was advocated by Alexander Hamilton, Secretary of the Treasury under President Washington, and Chief Justice Marshall. This theory emphasized national supremacy. It held that the Constitution expresses the will of the American people and that the national government, which the people created, has the bulk of the political power in the United States and is responsible for satisfying the needs of the people.

State-centered federalism developed in response to nation-centered federalism. Among the supporters of this theory were Thomas Jefferson and John C. Calhoun. They argued that the Constitution was written as a result of state action; the states sent delegates to the Constitutional Convention, and state ratifying conventions made the Constitution legal. State-centered federalism was based on the belief that the federal government is entitled only to the powers listed in the Constitution, interpreted as narrowly as possible, and that if government expands beyond these limits, it is encroaching on the rightful power of the states.

The concept of *dual federalism,* in which governmental functions are divided between the national and state governments, grew in importance in the period before the Civil War and remained influential in the early decades of the twentieth century. Supporters of this theory believed that the federal and state governments are separate centers of power. Each has jurisdiction in a specific area and is barred from interfering with the other's activities. As Madison explained it, the states would "form distinct and independent portions of the supremacy, no more subject within their respective spheres to the general authority than the general authority is subject to them within its own sphere."[13] The Supreme Court gave support to this view of federalism in many of its decisions between the 1890s and the 1930s.

Cooperative Federalism

Since the 1930s federalism has been modified to deal more effectively with the problems of the heavily urbanized, industrial society of twentieth-century America. In particular, it has been reshaped to handle the financial problems confronting state and local governments throughout the United States. These governments have been unable to pay the costs of the many public services that Americans have come to expect in such fields as education, health, transportation, and social welfare.

To understand the financial difficulties faced by the states and their subdivisions, it is necessary to understand the nature of the tax system. The federal government benefits from the most productive and flexible tax, the personal income tax. As national wealth increases, federal tax revenues also rise. State tax money is collected from a variety of other taxes, which are not as responsive to increases in wealth. These include small personal and business income taxes, sales taxes, and excise taxes on products like liquor and tobacco. Local governments are forced to rely on an even less desirable tax—the tax on real property. This tax, unlike the personal income tax, is relatively inflexible. As the land values of a community increase, tax revenues from the property tax do not rise in the same proportion.

It is also important to recognize that there are great differences in wealth among various states and regions of the United States. Mississippi and Arkansas, for example, are much less prosperous than Delaware or California. Moreover, within a state some cities or counties may be relatively affluent and others relatively poor.

The dilemma that has confronted American federalism for much of this century is that demands for more, and increasingly expensive, public services have been placed on local and state governments, which lack the taxing ability to pay for those programs. The federal government, on the other hand, has greater access to taxable wealth but relatively little responsibility for actually providing basic domestic services.

Efforts to resolve this dilemma resulted in what is known as *cooperative federalism,* "a new style and new philosophy of federalism distinguished by *joint undertakings* between the federal and state governments and the expansion of the use of *federal grants-in-aid.*"[14] A **grant-in-aid** is a sum of money given by a higher level of government to a lower level to be used to pay for a specific program in an area such as education, health, welfare, or transportation. (See Table 3.1.) Such grants are of fundamental importance to the operation of the nation's federal system.

In this approach to federalism, the emphasis is on cooperation between the state or local government and the national government in achieving

Federal grants-in-aid helped pay the costs of building much of America's highway system, such as this San Diego freeway interchange.

TABLE 3.1 *Federal Grant-in-Aid Outlays by Function (In Billions of Dollars)*

Function	Actual 1988	ESTIMATE					
		1989	1990	1991	1992	1993	1994
National defense	0.2	0.2	0.2	0.2	0.2	0.2	0.2
Energy	0.5	0.4	0.4	0.3	0.3	0.3	0.3
Natural resources and environment	3.7	3.7	3.6	3.4	3.0	2.6	2.3
Agriculture	2.1	1.7	1.5	1.3	1.2	1.0	1.0
Commerce and housing credit	*	....	....	....	....	....	....
Transportation	18.1	18.2	17.9	17.2	16.7	16.5	16.1
Community and regional development	4.3	4.3	4.3	4.2	3.7	3.3	3.2
Education, training, employment, and social services	19.9	22.4	22.3	22.7	22.6	22.5	22.7
Health	32.6	36.6	38.4	41.8	45.5	49.3	52.8
Income security	31.6	33.4	32.8	32.7	34.2	35.9	37.1
Veterans benefits and services	0.1	0.1	0.1	0.2	0.2	0.2	0.2
Administration of justice	0.3	0.4	0.4	0.3	0.2	0.2	0.2
General government	1.9	2.1	1.9	1.9	1.9	1.9	2.0
Total outlays	115.3	123.6	123.6	126.1	129.7	134.0	138.1

*$50 million or less.

Source: Executive Office of the President, Office of Management and Budget, *Special Analyses Budget of the United States Government: Fiscal Year 1990* (Washington, D.C.: Government Printing Office, 1989), p. H19.

goals determined by the national government. Although Congress does not have direct power to regulate public health, safety, or welfare, it can employ its power to tax and spend for the general welfare to establish a system that will reward the states for performing these functions.[15]

Cooperative federalism was the dominant theory during the New Deal administration of President Franklin D. Roosevelt. Several programs that required both financial and administrative cooperation between federal and state or local officials were undertaken. Most of these programs were financed by grants-in-aid, and all of the grants were *categorical*—to be used for a specific, narrowly defined purpose. They also tended to be *matching grants*—the state or local government receiving the grant was required to pay some of the costs of the project. In addition, they were *competitive*—state and local governments submitted applications to federal agencies, which decided how grants-in-aid would be distributed.

Centralized Federalism

During the Great Society administration of President Lyndon Johnson in the mid-1960s, a new approach to federalism developed. Sometimes referred to as *centralized federalism*, this approach entailed more forceful control of grants by the federal government. The goal was to persuade state and local governments to undertake programs that they might have preferred to avoid. This approach was applied most fully in the area of civil rights, job training, welfare, and housing for the poor. It abandoned any pretense of a state and local government role in making policy for the nation; the federal government assumed the power to define national problems and set national goals. In effect, centralized federalism was centralized government.[16]

The United States Supreme Court has given its approval to this highly centralized view of the federal system. In *Garcia* v. *San Antonio Metropolitan Transit Authority* (1985)[17] the Court upheld the power of Congress to impose minimum wage and overtime provisions on employees of state governments who perform governmental functions. It rejected the claim that this 1974 legislation interfered with the sovereignty of the states and hence violated the Tenth Amendment to the Constitution. According to the Court, the rights of the states are protected through their representation in Congress and by their role in the election of the President, not by the Tenth Amendment or the Supreme Court.

Many state and local officials have strongly opposed the *Garcia* decision. Indeed, their opposition has been so intense that some state legislatures have adopted resolutions requesting Congress initiate an amendment to the Constitution to modify the ruling. By mid-1990 fifteen states had taken this action, which would change the Tenth Amendment so as to require that the courts decide issues involving the allocation of powers within the federal system rather than compelling the states to turn to Congress for relief from oppressive national legislation.

Growth of the Grant System

The grant-in-aid system is the primary means by which governmental power has gradually become centered in Washington. Although grants have been employed throughout American history—beginning with land grants for such purposes as the establishment of public schools—in the twentieth century the use of grants has increased dramatically. In 1902 the national government operated five grant programs that distributed a total of $3 million, or less than 1 percent of state and local government revenues. By the 1989 fiscal year the total amount distributed under federal grant programs had risen to 123.6 billion, accounting for 18.7 percent of state and local government revenues. (See Table 3.2.) Most of the growth occurred in the 1960s and 1970s. The number of grant programs, for example, increased from 51 to 530 between 1964 and 1971.

The primary reason for the growth of the grant system was dissatisfaction with state and local government actions. As one political scientist has put it:

> People who wanted problems addressed and who were unsatisfied with state and local responses went to Washington. Responding to their problems through grants enabled officials at different levels of government to share the credit for fighting crime, combating poverty, or improving educational opportunities.[18]

TABLE 3.2 *Historical Trend of Federal Grant-in-Aid Outlays (Fiscal Years; Dollar Amounts in Billions)*

| | | FEDERAL GRANTS AS A PERCENT OF | | | |
| | | FEDERAL OUTLAYS[1] | | State and local expenditures[3] | Gross National Product |
	Total grants-in-aid	Total	Domestic programs[2]		
Five-year intervals:					
1950	$ 2.3	5.3%	11.6%	10.4%	0.8%
1955	3.2	4.7	17.2	10.1	0.8
1960	7.0	7.6	20.6	14.6	1.4
1965	10.9	9.2	20.3	15.2	1.6
1970	24.1	12.3	25.3	19.2	2.4
1975	49.8	15.0	23.1	22.7	3.3
Annually:					
1980	91.5	15.5	23.3	25.8	3.4
1981	94.8	14.0	21.6	24.6	3.2
1982	88.2	11.8	19.0	21.6	2.8
1983	92.5	11.4	18.6	21.3	2.8
1984	97.6	11.5	19.6	20.9	2.6
1985	105.9	11.2	19.3	20.9	2.7
1986	112.4	11.3	19.8	20.5	2.7
1987	108.4	10.8	19.0	18.3	2.4
1988	115.3	10.8	18.9	18.2	2.4
1989 estimate	123.6	10.9	18.7	NA	2.4
1990 estimate	123.6	10.7	18.7	NA	2.3
1991 estimate	126.1	10.4	17.8	NA	2.2
1992 estimate	129.7	10.4	17.4	NA	2.1
1993 estimate	134.0	10.5	17.2	NA	2.0
1994 estimate	138.1	10.5	17.1	NA	2.0

[1]Includes off-budget outlays; all grants are on-budget.
[2]Excludes outlays for national defense, international affairs, and net interest.
[3]As defined in the national income and product accounts.
NA = Not available.

Source: Executive Office of the President, Office of Management and Budget, *Special Analyses Budget of the United States Government: Fiscal Year 1990* (Washington, D.C.: Government Printing Office, 1989), p. H22.

The New Federalism

In the late 1960s state and local officials became increasingly critical of the federal grant system. They claimed that it had become excessively complex and fragmented. Moreover, they felt that the system forced them to operate programs favored by the federal government at the expense of programs that their own citizens would have preferred. Federal officials were too far away to understand the unique problems of each locality, and voters felt that they were losing control over policies that affected their lives.

When he became President in 1969, Richard Nixon announced a "new federalism" designed to restore the balance of power between the federal government and the states. The centerpiece of Nixon's program was general **revenue sharing,** a system of financial aid in which a certain portion of federal tax money was returned to the states and cities with no strings attached. The funds were allocated according to a formula based on numerous factors such as population, income, and urbanization. Nixon's New Federalism also made greater use of the **block grant,** a sum of money given by the national government to a state to be used for a broad, general purpose. Such a grant may be used for purposes related to law enforcement, for example, in contrast to categorical grants for the purchase of police cars or the improvement of prison facilities.

Although revenue sharing and block grants became important components of federal aid to states and localities, the goals of Nixon's New Federalism were not achieved. Revenue sharing never accounted for more than 12 percent of the federal grant system, and block grants did not succeed in replacing categorical grants.

When he took office in 1981, President Ronald Reagan announced a revised version of the New Federalism whose goal was to increase the flexibility of the federal grant system and reduce federal involvement in the states' domestic affairs. This was to be achieved in two ways: by combining existing categorical grant programs into larger, more loosely defined block grants and by dividing up major responsibilities between the federal government and the states. For example, the federal government would be responsible for providing food and medical care for the poor, while the states would provide cash assistance to poor families with children. An underlying objective of Reagan's program—which amounted to a form of dual federalism—was to reduce domestic spending by the federal government.

At first state and local government officials welcomed Reagan's New Federalism, but they soon realized that they were being asked to take on more responsibility while receiving less federal aid (see Figure 3.2). Congress also rejected some of the President's proposals, such as the plan to eliminate national grants for Aid to Families with Dependent Children.

The Reagan administration was successful in achieving some of its goals. Revenue sharing was ended in 1986 after fourteen years of existence. The end came as no great surprise. Although the program had distributed $83 billion to state and local governments, it had declined in importance since 1980. And because the federal government's budget deficit was growing rapidly during this period, revenue sharing had few supporters in Congress.[19]

President Reagan also increased the use of block grants and reduced the total number of federal grant programs from 539 in 1981 to approximately 340 in 1986. But he was able only to slow the rate at which the costs of federal grants increased. The amount was reduced during his first year in office but grew during subsequent years. The federal government spent $88.2 billion on state and local grants in fiscal year 1982; by fiscal year 1989—the last budget year for President Reagan—the amount had reached $123.6 billion.[20]

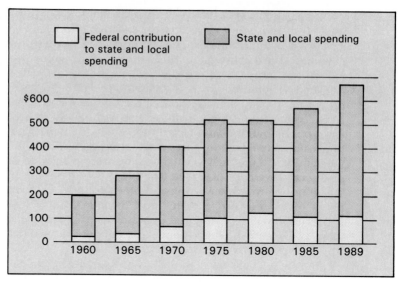

FIGURE 3.2 *A heavier burden for the states (Figures in billions of 1988 dollars).*

Source: Advisory Commission on Intergovernmental Relations, *The New York Times*, December 30, 1990, p. 1. Copyright © 1990 by the New York Times Company. Reprinted by permission.

Reagan's New Federalism differed from Nixon's in some significant ways. Whereas Nixon's was an activist program designed to decentralize governmental functions in a rational manner, Reagan's program was focused on restraint, on reduction of government spending, and withdrawal of federal influence from state and local programs. In the words of one political scientist: "The Reagan administration waged a comprehensive assault on the intergovernmental dimensions of public sector activism."[21]

Unlike Presidents Nixon and Reagan, George Bush came to office without stating a theory of federalism. But he did declare that the federal government should take greater responsibility for education, drug prevention, AIDS research, and environmental protection. However, huge federal budget deficits effectively prevented any significant increases in federal spending for these domestic programs.

By the early 1990s many states were experiencing severe financial problems. Tax revenues and federal grants were not adequate to pay for the expenses of government. This occurred at a time when the cost of state programs for education, health, nursing home care, and law enforcement were growing rapidly.

The financial difficulties of the states were compounded by the fact that all states, with the exception of Vermont, are legally required to have a balanced budget. The choices left to the states were, therefore, limited to either raising taxes or cutting services. Since new taxes have been strongly opposed by the public, the response of many states was to dismiss workers, impose hiring freezes, cut back on services, and raise college tuitions and various fees and fines. State officials also pleaded for more federal contributions toward state and local programs mandated by Washington.

The fiscal crisis of American federalism during the early 1990s was starkly real. One long-time observer of our federal system commented darkly, "I think you would have to go back to the Great Depression [of the 1930s] to find similar anguish, in terms of the number of states that are facing an unprecedented cutback in service or significant increases in taxes."[22]

■ Summary

A federal form of government has both advantages and drawbacks. On the positive side, federalism results in flexible government, helps prevent abuses of power, encourages experimentation in policy making, stimulates competition among governments (thereby promoting efficiency and responsiveness), augments citizen participation in government, and, by establishing free trade within a nation, helps bring about economic growth. On the negative side, federalism has been criticized for being unable to coordinate the policies of different levels of government, for being unresponsive to public needs, for promoting local rather than national interests, for perpetuating inequality in public services and in the protection of individual rights, for failing to hold public officials fully accountable for their actions, and for favoring affluent members of society over the poor.[23]

To the average American, these theoretical issues are probably less important than the more practical questions related to the way the federal system works. Throughout the first 150 years of the nation's history Americans looked to the states and localities to provide the services they expected from government. During the past fifty years they have increasingly turned to Washington for solutions to their problems. The central government has grown in both size and power, often at the expense of the state and local governments.

The Reagan administration was partially successful in its efforts to reverse this trend and return power to the states and localities. The increased use of block grants gave these governments greater freedom in deciding how to spend federal money. The end of revenue sharing and the slowdown in the growth of total federal grants compelled state and local governments to rely more fully on their own financial resources.

Faced with these new realities, many states took on new responsibilities. Indeed, the 1980s were an expansionary era for state and local policy. Using more broad-based tax systems and public-private partnerships, state and local governments became increasingly active in education, children's programs, and economic development. State spending grew as federal contributions levelled off. But as each state and city was left to fend for itself, the affluent areas fared well while the poor ones suffered. And as the 1990s began, a series of economic problems appeared on the horizon. A growing recession struck many parts of the nation. This factor, coupled with spiraling costs in such areas as medical care and prison maintenance, caused many states and localities to consider raising taxes and cutting back services.[24]

■ Key Terms

unitary government	due process clause
confederation	equal protection clause
federalism	full faith and credit clause
delegated powers	privileges and immunities clause
implied powers	interstate rendition clause
necessary and proper clause	interstate compact
concurrent powers	original jurisdiction
bill of attainder	guarantee clause
ex post facto law	grant-in-aid
writ of habeas corpus	revenue sharing
reserved powers	block grant

■ Suggested Reading

ANTON, THOMAS J. *American Federalism and Public Policy.* Philadelphia: Temple University Press, 1989.

BERGER, RAOUL. *Federalism: The Founders' Design.* Norman, Okla.: University of Oklahoma Press, 1987.

BOWMAN, ANN O'M., and RICHARD C. KEARNEY. *The Resurgence of the States.* Englewood Cliffs, N.J.: Prentice-Hall, 1986.

ELAZAR, DANIEL. *American Federalism: A View from the States,* 3rd ed. New York: Harper & Row, 1984.

———. *Exploring Federalism.* Tuscaloosa, Ala.: University of Alabama Press, 1987.

KETTL, DONALD F. *The Regulation of American Federalism.* Baltimore: Johns Hopkins University Press, 1987.

NATHAN, RICHARD P., and FRED C. DOOLITTLE, *Reagan and the States.* Princeton, N.J.: Princeton University Press, 1987.

O'TOOLE, LAURENCE J., JR., ED. *American Intergovernmental Relations.* Washington, D.C.: Congressional Quarterly Press, 1985.

PETERSON, PAUL E., BARRY G. RABE, AND KENNETH K. WONG. *When Federalism Works.* Washington, D.C.: Brookings Institution, 1986.

VAN HORN, CARL E. *The State of the States.* Washington, D.C.: Congressional Quarterly Press, 1989.

■ Notes

1. Morton Grodzins and Daniel Elazar, "Centralization and Decentralization in the American Federal System," in Robert A. Goldwin, ed., *A Nation of States: Essays on the American Federal System,* 2nd ed. (Chicago: Rand McNally, 1974), p. 1.

2. *The Federalist Papers,* no. 39.

3. *United States* v. *Darby,* 312 U.S. 100 (1941).

4. *Heart of Atlanta Motel* v. *United States,* 379 U.S. 241 (1964).

5. 4 Wheat. 316 (1819).

6. *Baldwin* v. *Montana Fish and Game Commission,* 436 U.S. 371 (1978).

7. *Kentucky* v. *Dennison,* 24 How. 66 (1861).

8. Eugene Carlson, "Quick, Name a State Willing to Accept Radioactive Waste," *Wall Street Journal,* June 30, 1987, p. 33. For a discussion of the use of interstate compacts, see David C. Nice, "State Participation in Interstate Compacts," *Publius,* 17 (Spring 1987), 69–83.

9. *Pacific States Telephone and Telegraph Co.* v. *Oregon,* 223 U.S. 118 (1912). See also *Luther* v. *Borden,* 7 How. 1 (1849).

10. *In re Debs,* 158 U.S. 564 (1895).

11. *Martin* v. *Hunter's Lessee,* 1 Wheat. 304 (1816); *Cohens* v. *Virginia,* 6 Wheat. 264 (1821).

12. 437 U.S. 617 (1978).

13. *The Federalist Papers*, no. 39.

14. Jeffrey R. Henig, *Public Policy and Federalism: Issues in State and Local Politics* (New York: St. Martin's Press, 1985), p. 15. Italics in original.

15. Thomas R. Dye, *American Federalism: Competition among Governments* (Lexington, Mass.: Lexington Books, 1990), p. 7.

16. Ibid., pp. 7–8.

17. 469 U.S. 528 (1985).

18. David C. Nice, *Federalism: The Politics of Intergovernmental Relations* (New York: St. Martin's Press, 1987), p. 55.

19. Steve Blakely, "Revenue Sharing: Ups and Downs," *Congressional Quarterly*, September 17, 1986, p. 7.

20. U.S. Bureau of the Census, *Statistical Abstract of the United States, 1990*, 110th ed. (Washington, D.C.: Government Printing Office, 1990), Table 459.

21. Timothy Conlan, *New Federalism: Intergovernmental Reform from Nixon to Reagan* (Washington, D.C.: Brookings Institution, 1988), pp. 221–224.

22. Henry Aaron, as quoted in Michael de Courcy Hinds with Erik Eckholm, "80's Leave States and Cities in Need," *New York Times*, December 30, 1990, pp. 1, 16–17.

23. Nice, *Federalism*, pp. 13–20.

24. Neal R. Pierce, "Reagan's Surprise Legacy to States and Cities," *National Journal*, January 21, 1989, p. 145; Pierce, "State Budgets: Calm Now, Stormy Seas Ahead," *National Journal*, March 4, 1989, p. 541.

4

Chapter Outline

The American Political Culture

Political Socialization

The Nature of Public Opinion

Measuring Public Opinion
Scientific Polling
How Polls Are Conducted
Criticisms of Public Opinion Polling

The Role of the Media
The Paid Media
The Free Media
Proposals for Reform

How Americans Participate

The Changing American Voter
Who May Vote?
Who Votes?
How Do Americans Vote?

Questions for Thought

How are scientific polls conducted?

What are exit polls?

What is meant by the free media? The paid media?

Who are the nonvoters in American politics?

What groups in American society tend to support the Democratic Party?

What groups in American society tend to support the Republican Party?

Public Opinion, Mass Media, and Voting

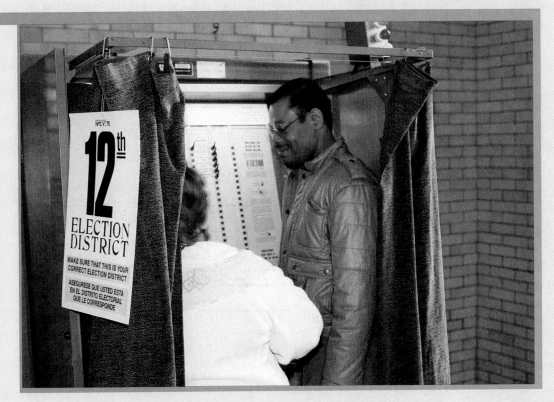

O
N AUGUST 11, 1988, an ABC News Poll showed George Bush ahead of Michael Dukakis in the race for the presidency by 49 percent to 46 percent. A series of polls a few days earlier had placed Dukakis ahead by between 7 and 14 percentage points. On August 14, ABC found that Dukakis was leading by 55 percent to 40 percent. Other polls showed the two candidates running almost even. Both the poll takers and the public were confused.

In the end the polls were quite accurate in forecasting the results of the 1988 presidential election. None predicted victory for Dukakis, and most were within two percentage points of Bush's actual margin of victory. This was a far more accurate performance than that of the 1980 presidential election polls, most of which failed to predict Ronald Reagan's landslide victory and some of which even predicted victory for Jimmy Carter.

Why were the polls conducted during the early months of the 1988 campaign so undependable? This is an important question to political analysts, since polls can have an immense impact on the way politicians organize their campaigns and on the way voters perceive the candidates, as well as on how the campaigns are covered by the press and television.

In this chapter we will examine the role of polls and the media in the political process and their impact on the voting behavior of Americans. We will begin, however, by discussing the processes through which people form political opinions and the ways in which they express those opinions—when they choose to do so.

■ The American Political Culture

Public opinion in the United States must be viewed within the context of the nation's **political culture**—the fundamental, widely supported values that hold American society together and give legitimacy to its political institutions. The American political culture is, obviously, democratic. The democratic goals of equality, individual freedom, and due process of law are among the most basic values of the American people. These goals can be achieved through democratic procedures such as *majority rule* and protection of *minority rights.*

While almost all Americans support the basic goals of democracy, there is less agreement when it comes to the application of democratic procedures. For example, one study showed that while 95 percent of Americans support the right of a group of their neighbors to circulate a petition, this figure drops to 52 percent for a group that wants to legalize marijuana use. But most studies show that the American public has become more tolerant of unpopular political ideas in the past few decades; this is especially true of citizens with more education. Note, however, that these attitudes may have little meaning for the public and may not influence actual behavior or even represent the public's attitudes during times when democratic principles are under attack.[1]

It should also be understood that the nation's political leaders support democratic goals and procedures more strongly than the general public does.[2] The fact that public officials are especially likely to support democratic procedures is important. It means that they will generally make decisions that maintain those procedures even if those procedures lack widespread public support. It is not at all certain that democratic political systems require public commitment to basic democratic principles:

> Hostility to democratic procedures is fatal, whether among the leaders or the public, but support of these procedures may prove essential only among leaders. Perhaps the public need not agree on basic principles so long as it does not demand disruptive policies and procedures.[3]

■ Political Socialization

The process by which a society's political culture is transmitted from one generation to the next is known as **political socialization.** The process begins in early childhood, when children acquire a general orientation toward political issues from their parents, and it continues throughout life.[4] People's political ideas are influenced by all the groups of which they are members: immediate, personal groups like family and friends as well as larger, less personal groups such as political parties or labor unions. They are also affected by social categories—race, religion, place of residence, income level, education, and the like. Of course, historical events and political issues may also affect a person's attitudes.

THE FAMILY. The earliest and perhaps most powerful influence on a person is the family. Young children have very little contact with people outside the family. Many children learn about their parents' political party during the preschool years, and often this party identification persists in later life. The family also has a strong effect on a person's later interest in politics. Children of people who show interest in political matters generally express such an interest as adults.

The pledge of allegiance in schools is an example of the socialization process.

THE SCHOOL. Many social scientists believe that the school's impact on the socialization process is almost as great as the family's. This is not surprising, since after their preschool years children spend much of their time in the classroom. Here they are taught discipline, patriotism, and respect for the law. In addition, teachers serve as models for many schoolchildren and influence their attitudes and behavior.[5]

THE PEER GROUP. Children's friends, classmates, teammates, and other associates also influence their attitudes. As an adult, a person may belong to peer groups within his or her religious community, political party, and ethnic association, as well as other more or less formal groups (e.g., bridge clubs, bowling leagues, PTAs, etc.). Relations among the members of peer groups are often highly personal, and certain groups can have a lasting effect on a person's political opinions.

SOCIAL CLASS: INCOME, OCCUPATION, AND EDUCATION. Although the United States is often thought to be a classless society, there are several fairly distinct social classes—upper middle, lower middle, working—based on income, occupation, education, and related factors. Americans can and often do move from one social class to another.

It is sometimes difficult to obtain information about the political opinions of members of various social classes. Some people, for example, do not consider themselves to be members of the class in which a political scientist might place them. Despite this difficulty, however, enough information has been gathered to permit some conclusions about the relationships between social class and political opinions. Generally, people with higher incomes, more education, and higher job status are more conservative in their political opinions and tend to support the Republican party. Unskilled workers, by contrast, are generally more liberal in their political views and support the Democratic party.

RACE AND RELIGION. Certain patterns of political opinion can be traced to race or religion. On such issues as civil rights, abortion laws, and aid to Israel, members of racial and religious groups have strong opinions, are very active, and in some cases have a significant influence. Blacks, for example, have been very active on civil rights issues; Catholics generally oppose abortion; and Jews support Israel.

PLACE OF RESIDENCE. The area in which people live can also influence their political opinions. Since World War II the suburbs of America's large cities have been strongly Republican, while most of the nation's largest cities have been Democratic throughout most of this century. Certain sections of the country—the Rocky Mountain states, for example—have been Republican strongholds. By contrast, the Democratic party's almost complete dominance of the South for a century after the Civil War caused political analysts to refer to it as the "solid South."

HISTORY AND POLITICAL EVENTS. Attitudes are also influenced by the important events that occur in a person's lifetime. Military service in Vietnam during the 1960s and 1970s has probably had a long-term effect on the opinions of many Americans regarding issues of war and peace and American foreign policy in general. But the involvement with history need not be a direct, personal one. The opinions of most members of a society are influenced by the events of their time. This is especially true of major developments like wars and economic depressions.

■ The Nature of Public Opinion

As people grow older, they gather a variety of impressions of the political system in which they live. Very early in life they begin to develop their own attitudes toward political activities—attitudes that are influenced by the many different kinds of people with whom they come into contact, by factors in their society, and by historical events. These attitudes shape their political opinions.

Political opinion is a form of **public opinion,** the range of opinions expressed by citizens on any subject. The subject may be anything from their favorite television programs to the team that is going to win the World Series. There is no single public opinion on any given issue; rather, there are as many public opinions as there are possible views on an issue. **Political opinion** is the set of opinions expressed by the members of a community on political issues (i.e., issues that involve some aspect of public policy). Issues like taxation, welfare, social security, and foreign policy can—and usually do—generate political opinions, and those opinions are just as varied as opinions on nonpolitical issues. In this chapter, when we refer to *public opinion* we will be concerned mainly with opinions on political subjects.

Although views on political subjects can vary greatly, even within the same family, it is possible to identify some general features of political opinions. These have been labeled *intensity, concentration, stability, distribution,* and *salience* (importance or relevance). Political opinions can also be either transitory or lasting.

Intensity refers to how strongly an opinion is held. It varies according to the individual—some people feel more strongly about certain issues than others do. Intensity also varies according to how important an issue seems to a person. Topics like civil rights and taxation tend to evoke stronger opinions among many Americans than do such matters as farm subsidies and antitrust law.

An opinion is said to be *concentrated* if it is held by a small portion of society. For example, corn and wheat farmers in the Midwest benefit from federal farm subsidies. Accordingly, public opinion in favor of farm subsidies tends to be concentrated in the midwestern states.

When the intensity and concentration of a given political opinion are fairly constant over a long period, the opinion is said to be *stable.* The opinion that democracy is a good form of government is clearly a stable one; if it were not, radical attempts to change the American political system would have succeeded long ago. It should be noted, however, that opinions are never absolutely stable; change is always possible.

The *distribution* of opinion refers to the number of people who support various positions on a given issue. In the case of abortion, for instance, opinion is distributed between two major camps—those who are opposed and those who believe it is a matter for individual decision. In other cases, however, opinion may be distributed fairly evenly along a continuum. An example would be the opinions Americans hold on a subject such as the future of the American economy, that is, whether the nation will prosper or decline in coming years.

The term _salience_ refers to the importance or relevance of an issue to a person or group. To most Americans, such issues as the state of the economy or whether the United States should engage in military conflicts are salient, whereas U.S. policy toward small businesses is not.

Some political opinions are short-lived or transitory, while others are lasting. Many political issues at the national, state, and local levels change fairly rapidly; political opinions on these issues will be formed and will last only as long as the issue is important. Some political opinions remain constant and are long-lived. People's core attitudes—whether they are liberal or conservative, for example—may remain basically the same throughout their lives.

■ Measuring Public Opinion

In a democracy, politicians and public officials always want to know what the public is thinking about issues and candidates. Historically, they found out by talking to citizens directly and by reading the letters that came to their offices. They also kept track of public opinion as it was expressed in the media, especially the press.

During the nineteenth century various journals began presenting public opinion in a new form known as the _straw poll_. These polls simply asked the same question of a large number of people, and the results were counted and made public. Straw polls were thought to give the press more trustworthy information than could be obtained by interviewing party leaders. Newspapers favored the polls as a means of demonstrating independence and professionalism: They could support a particular candidate even though news stories showed that the candidate was trailing in the race. By the turn of the century straw polls had become a routine practice.[6]

In the 1940s a new method of measuring public opinion was developed: prediction of election results on the basis of past voting information. This information is collected in a variety of ways. One is through interviewing people in neighborhoods that have almost always supported the candidates of one of the major parties and finding out how many plan to vote for that party's candidate in the coming election. In this way it is possible to learn what issues are important to people in, say, Catholic or black neighborhoods and how they are likely to vote. Another approach is to study the historical record and project trends on that basis. If, for example, the number of people voting for Democratic candidates has risen by 5 percent in each of the past five elections, this method predicts that it will increase to a similar extent in the next one.[7]

drawbacks → Both of these techniques have drawbacks. For example, they are based on the incorrect assumption that the ratio of Democrats to Republicans in an area will stay the same. It was to correct such problems that the computer was first used as a tool for predicting election results. Since

President Harry Truman holds aloft a copy of the Chicago Tribune *that confidently announced the election of Governor Thomas Dewey as President in the November 1948 election. The* Tribune's *analysis of early voting returns was in error in predicting the actual outcome; Truman won and became President for the next four years.*

computers can digest much larger amounts of information than an individual researcher can, they made it possible to refine greatly the methods used to discover and analyze public opinion. Thus in the early 1960s campaign organizations and television networks began using computers to analyze voting patterns. Information from so-called bellwether districts—areas whose voting patterns are viewed as good predictors of national patterns—was fed into the computer, and the results were announced early in the evening on election day.

Even computers have their faults, however—as is often noted, they are only as good as the information that is fed into them. For example, in 1960 CBS's computer was fed election results in the order in which they came into the network's studio. The vote from heavily Republican Kansas came in first, and the computer compared it with the vote that had come in first in 1956, which happened to be from the less Republican state of Connecticut. The result was an erroneous prediction of a Nixon victory.[8]

Scientific Polling

Today the most important method used to find out about public opinion is **scientific polling,** the use of scientific methodology and mathematical probability to analyze public attitudes toward issues and candidates in electoral campaigns. Scientific polling was first used in advertising and market research. Since World War II it has also become widely used in academic research and in politics, journalism, and the media. Political polling is less common than commercial polling (product surveys, etc.), but it is still a big business.

One of the earliest polling organizations was the American Institute of Public Opinion, better known as the Gallup Poll. The first organization to attempt a nationwide poll (in 1944) was the University of Chicago's National Opinion Research Center (NORC). Since then a large number of polling organizations have been established. Some of them, such as the Gallup and Harris polls, sell their results to clients. Others are academic research organizations like NORC and the Center for Political Studies at the University of Michigan. The main goal of the polls conducted by both kinds of organizations is to discover the public's views on political issues and candidates during election campaigns, especially presidential nomination and election campaigns.

Many of the clients of polling organizations are politicians and candidates for office who want to know what people believe the main issues to be and how they feel about those issues. Candidates also want to know how popular they are compared with other candidates. The results of surveys conducted for candidates often are not made public unless the candidate thinks publication of the findings would benefit his or her campaign.

Polling organizations also sell their results to newspapers and magazines. Those results, of course, are "news" and are published by the media. Modern media polls are conducted mainly by the three major television networks, some national news magazines, and many newspapers. Media polling has grown rapidly since the 1970s and is now more important than the polls conducted by the older polling organizations.

How Polls Are Conducted

Polling organizations employ a common methodology which provides the scientific basis for their activities.[9]

Sampling. The basic tools of modern scientific polling are the sample and the survey. **Sampling** is the process of choosing a relatively small number of cases to be studied for information about the larger population from which they have been selected. (A *population* is any group of people, organizations, objects, or events about which the researcher wants to draw conclusions; a *sample* is any subgroup of a population that is identified for analysis.)

To be of value to the researcher, a sample must be *representative;* that is, every major attribute of the population from which the sample has been drawn must be present in the sample in roughly the same proportion or

A representative of a polling organization conducts an interview in Miami, Florida. Public opinion polling is relied upon in both politics and commerce.

frequency as it is in the larger population. For example, a representative sample of the U.S. population must, among other things, contain the same proportions of blacks, whites, Native Americans, people of Spanish origin, and other groups as the population as a whole.

The method used to choose a representative sample is known as *random sampling*. Although it may involve sophisticated statistical analysis, random sampling is essentially a lottery system: The sample is chosen in such a way that each and every case (or individual) in the entire population has an equal opportunity to be selected for analysis, just as in a properly run lottery every number has an equal chance of being the winning number.

Survey Research. Once a random sample has been selected, the researcher can carry out the actual study. If the purpose of the study is to find out what people think or how they act, the best (and sometimes the only) way is to ask them. The method used is known as **survey research.** It may be defined as a method of data collection in which information is obtained directly from individuals who have been selected so as to provide a basis for making inferences about some larger population. The techniques used in survey research include direct questioning through face-to-face or telephone interviews and mailed or self-administered questionnaires.

Survey research can be broken down into a series of steps, beginning with specifying the purpose of the research and ending with reporting the findings. Some key steps in the research process are *instrumentation* (drafting the questions and other items that will appear on the questionnaire or interview guide), *pretesting* (administering the survey instrument to a small sample to ensure that the instructions can be interpreted correctly), *surveying* (administering the survey instrument to the entire sample), *coding* (reducing the data collected to numerical terms), and *analyzing* the data.

Telephone Polls. As noted earlier, polls conducted by the media have become the most important form of political polling: Media polls use two basic methods: the **telephone poll** and the exit poll. The findings of polls like the CBS News/*New York Times* and ABC/*Washington Post* polls are generally based on telephone surveys, in which telephone numbers are selected through random-digit dialing; up to four callbacks are made in order to reach the selected respondent. Such a poll usually takes about 15 or 20 minutes to administer. Some telephone polls are conducted on a quarterly or monthly basis and measure public opinion on such subjects as support for presidential policies or pending legislation. Some are shorter surveys intended to monitor opinion on a particular governmental action or event.

Telephone surveys always include standard demographic questions on such matters as household income, education, and marital status and may include questions about party identification, participation in past elections, interest in the current campaign, and the like. The data gathered can be weighted to match nationwide population distributions by region, race, sex, age, and education; the resulting figures provide reasonable estimates of public opinion for all adult Americans.

A variant of the telephone survey that has been used by the media since 1984 is the *tracking poll.* Such a poll may include up to 1,000 interviews in a single day and will indicate changes in voter preferences from day to day during the week or so preceding an election.[10]

Exit Polls. Another frequently used polling method is the **exit poll,** in which voters are interviewed at the polls on election day. This method was developed in the 1960s but did not become common until the next decade. At first such polls were used to determine voter preferences in a few selected precincts; soon, however, journalists discovered that they could use them to predict the outcome of an election while it is still in progress.

The questionnaires used in exit polls may contain thirty or forty items, but they can be completed in a few minutes. This speed is important, since the television networks need to obtain the results of the polls within an hour or less after the last interview to use them on the evening news programs.

In an exit poll, the interviewer attempts to sample voters leaving the polling place in a systematic way throughout the day. The interviewer may, for example, approach every nth voter, with the "n" varying according to the size of the precinct. (The precincts in which the poll is to be conducted are randomly selected.) The voter is asked to fill in the questionnaire and place it in a receptacle; the results are collected three times during the day and are tallied and entered into a computer.

A typical national exit poll collects information from as many as 10,000 voters. This total is large enough to contain subgroups (e.g., Jews, Hispanics, professional women) whose voting preferences may be compared and analyzed. An even more important feature of exit polls is their immediacy: Voters are interviewed right after they have voted and before the results are known. This immediacy has made the exit poll an increasingly popular method for learning about voting patterns as well as predicting election results. By 1988 there was at least one network exit poll in every state, and all three major networks conducted national exit polls.[11]

Polling organizations allow themselves a margin of error of 3 to 4 percent; that is, if the actual outcome is within 3 or 4 percent of the stated outcome, they consider their analysis to be accurate. As a result, in a close election their prediction of voter intentions can be accurate, given the margin of error they allow themselves, but they may name the wrong candidate as the winner. (The pollsters themselves would not say that they are predicting anything, just that they are determining public opinion at the time of the poll.)

Criticisms of Public Opinion Polling

Over the years, public opinion polls have provided much valuable information about public thinking on major issues. They have been subjected to criticisms, however. The most fundamental criticism has to do with faulty procedures. Pollsters may use too small a sample, or they may interview registered voters without finding out whether they are planning to vote. The way in which questions are phrased can affect how people respond to them. It can also be argued that a poll cannot determine with reasonable accuracy how voters will actually behave when they enter the voting booth on election day. But there are other, more fundamental difficulties associated with opinion polling.

A major problem of preelection telephone polling is finding out who is likely to vote. In most elections only about one-third of eligible voters actually vote; a poll that samples the two-thirds who do not vote will obtain misleading information. Most telephone polls do not include procedures for identifying likely voters because of the effort and expense involved.[12] Exit polls, of course, gather information from people who have already voted, but they suffer from a related problem in that the conclusions derived from the data are based on assumptions about the likely voter turnout in each precinct, which in turn are based on past voting patterns. If those patterns change, the assumptions become misleading.

Another problem is that poll takers fail to take account of the strength of voters' commitment to a particular candidate. If one candidate has the support of very loyal voters and the other candidate's support is weak, there may be a last-minute shift of votes from the second candidate to the first, a shift that would not be anticipated in the results of a poll. A further difficulty is that respondents to telephone polls may answer in ways that are socially acceptable or that they believe the questioner wants to hear. A white respondent, for example, may say that he or she will vote for a black candidate but may not actually do so on election day.

Until recently, polling organizations stopped calling on the Friday before election day. This practice resulted in some highly inaccurate predictions, because many voters change their minds in the final days of a campaign. Since 1980 pollsters have attempted to continue polling as late as possible.[13]

Polling in primary elections (i.e., nominating elections—see Chapter 5) poses special problems. Primaries often do not receive as much media coverage as general elections, and voters may not yet have made up their minds at the time that the polls are conducted. But what makes primary polling especially difficult is the fact that voter turnouts for those elections are often very small. A surge of support for one candidate among a relatively few voters could change the outcome and cause the poll results to be inaccurate.

Exit polls also encounter some special problems. Since voters fill out questionnaires and place them in a box, there is no reason for them to lie on an exit poll. However, the problem mentioned earlier—flawed assumptions about precinct turnouts—can skew the results. In addition, many voters do not wish to be polled; in some communities, as many as 40 percent have declined to fill out the questionnaires. If poll takers fail to keep track of the sex, race, and apparent age of those who do not participate and weight the responses accordingly, the results of the poll may be misleading.

Another problem of exit polls is the need to stop polling an hour before the polls close to prepare results to be broadcast at closing time. If voters who support one candidate are likely to turn out earlier than voters who support the other candidate, again the results will be inaccurate.[14]

Finally, critics of exit polls have argued that these polls could discourage some people from voting in the belief that "it's already over." The failure of those voters to turn out could affect the results of some close elections. Indeed, there is some evidence that in presidential elections exit polls have contributed to reduced voter turnout in the western states, which are in later time zones and so the polls are the last to close. Such polls may also have affected the outcomes of a number of close congressional and state elections.

During the 1990s the normal problems of polling have been complicated by some additional difficulties. The widespread public antagonism and cynicism toward politics and politicians causes many people to refuse to talk to poll takers. These attitudes also make voters more volatile, more likely to change their minds at the last minute in ways that are not anticipated in the polls.

Despite all the criticisms, polls have become a central feature of American politics. The number of polls has proliferated; not only the major television networks but at least 40 percent of American newspapers conduct polls. The quality of those polls varies, partly because the demand for polling has grown beyond the supply of trained poll takers. Accurate or not, these polls have an immense impact on the conduct of American politics. They influence the behavior of politicians and journalists, and probably that of the American public as well.[15]

■ The Role of the Media

In earlier periods of American history, candidates for public office campaigned primarily by giving speeches—called *stump speeches*—at as many locations as possible. With the rise of the railroads in the nineteenth century, candidates for national office traveled throughout the country by train, making frequent appearances before local audiences. This method was made obsolete by the arrival of the airplane; since the 1950s candidates have traveled around the nation by plane, giving speeches and appearing on platforms and in motorcades.

In the twentieth century, changes in communications technology have had a major impact on the way candidates conduct campaigns. Since the 1920s, radio speeches and news have played an important part in supplying Americans with information about candidates and politics. Newspaper advertising and news coverage continue to play a role in campaigns, but television now dominates political campaigning at the national and state levels. Indeed, today television is the source of much of the information the public receives about politics.

In considering the role of the media in politics, it is important to distinguish between the paid media and the free media. *Paid media* are advertisements whose content is controlled by a particular campaign organization; these messages are sent through several channels, including radio, television, newspapers, and direct mail. They can convey anything the candidate wishes, limited only by libel laws, good taste, and available funds. *Free media* are not controlled by campaign organizations; they include news stories and analyses, editorials, interviews, and debates. Naturally, candidates and their staffs try to influence the content of these media to the extent possible.[16]

The Paid Media

Today it is impossible to run a national political campaign without heavy reliance on television, and it is virtually impossible for a candidate to run for office at the state level without extensive use of television commercials. In fact, television advertising accounts for about two-thirds of the budget of a typical statewide campaign. The costs of television advertising vary according to the size of the population to be reached, the number of markets in which the candidate must advertise, and the number of exposures desired. (It is generally assumed that between three and five exposures are required for a message to "sink in."[17]) Differences in the size of state populations and the cost of television advertising in different states play a significant role in a campaign organization's choices about the use of television advertising.

Television is less important in congressional campaigns than in national and statewide campaigns. The use of television in congressional primary contests varies in different regions of the country, depending on cost and the degree of correspondence between the television market and the congressional district. In the Southwest, where television advertising is relatively inexpensive, three-quarters of House candidates buy television advertising. On the West Coast the proportion falls to one-quarter; in the Middle Atlantic region fewer than one-fifth of congressional candidates use television. In the general election, fewer than half of all House candidates use television advertising. Various studies have shown that the cost efficiency and market potential of television ads are greater in the midwestern and southern states than in New England and the western states. Television also is generally more effective in rural districts than in urban areas.[18]

Candidates for local offices are unlikely to use broadcast advertising. Instead, they rely on direct voter contact, both in person and by mail and telephone. These methods are preferred because they can be more readily targeted at district audiences. Mail is used extensively in urban congressional districts, where it can reinforce intensive personal voter contact.[19]

In recent campaigns there has been a dramatic increase in the frequency of *negative advertising*—ads that attack the opponent. In the 1988 presidential race, for example, one commentator claimed that the candidates used advertising "at least as much to bash the other side as to promote themselves."[20] A prime example is the Bush campaign's advertisement in which Michael Dukakis was attacked for allowing a convicted murderer named Willie Horton to be released from prison; after his release, Horton committed another serious crime. These ads, which are often referred to as "attack ads," were a striking feature of the 1988 campaign.

The 1990 congressional and gubernatorial elections also emphasized negative advertising. The California gubernatorial race was notable for its reliance on attack ads: Republican Pete Wilson accused Democrat Dianne Feinstein of supporting quotas for appointments in state government; Feinstein counterattacked by accusing Wilson of being influenced by the savings and loan industry; such exchanges continued throughout the long fall campaign. Although there were some indications of a backlash against negative advertising, many candidates continued to make extensive use of such ads.

Political consultants say that there is a simple explanation for the trend toward negative advertising: It works. Their research has shown that although people often express a dislike for such advertising, they also tend to remember the ads. Positive advertising must be repeated numerous times to have the same impact. Another cause of the increase in negative advertising is the growing cost of paid media. Since negative ads are more likely to be remembered, they are more cost effective than positive ads. Nor can negative ads be ignored; if the candidate who is attacked by such an ad does not quickly answer the charges, he or she is likely to lose ground in the polls. Failure to respond was a major factor in Michael Dukakis' loss to George Bush in the 1988 presidential contest.

The Free Media

The free media include the print media, especially newspapers, and the electronic media—television and radio. Although they try to influence the free media, candidates cannot exercise any direct control over the political content of what is published or broadcast.

In their search for news, journalists look for something that actually happens. As a result, they tend to focus on politics as a sort of horse race rather than on the issues and policies being discussed in a campaign. Moreover, most reporters do not analyze or evaluate the policy proposals of candidates. Instead they report on such matters as the candidates' standings in the polls, the amount of money they raise, and the endorsements they attract.

Journalists also have a tendency to focus on incumbents rather than on challengers and to pay more attention to better-known candidates than to those who are less well known. It is easier to cover incumbents; many of

President George Bush answering questions at a White House press conference. Presidential press conferences, covered extensively by television networks and the press, are examples of the free media.

their official activities would be reported anyway, and they have already established a relationship with the media. In addition, an incumbent has a much better chance of winning the election. (The advantageous position of incumbents is discussed in Chapter 6.)

There are some significant differences between the print and electronic media in their coverage of political campaigns. For one thing, the electronic media present much less news than the print media. A political story on the network news, for example, receives between thirty seconds and two minutes of coverage. Television reporters rarely give in-depth coverage to candidates and campaigns. In addition, a television news story must have an interesting background if it is to hold viewers' attention. If a campaign event does not take place in interesting surroundings, it is likely to be ignored.

The 1988 presidential election campaign appeared to many observers to be managed almost solely for the benefit of the television news. Every campaign stop and public appearance was carefully planned and scripted with the evening news programs in mind. The candidates' images were crafted to appeal to viewers, and each day had a theme—the message to be delivered to the voters that evening. Little attention was given to substantive issues, and there was almost no contact with actual voters. As two analysts concluded, "Political operatives are seeking to isolate not just the candidate but the entire campaign from anything resembling spontaneous reality."[21]

A key feature of television coverage of campaigns—both in the paid and free media—is the *sound bite*. This technique developed out of the advertising industry's recognition that people are likely to remember short, punchy messages. Coupled with the tendency of politics to become increasingly image conscious, this recognition has resulted in campaign coverage that is dominated by brief, narrowly focused vignettes in which the candidate may speak for only a few seconds. Perhaps reflecting an increasingly fast-paced society, the average length of a sound bite decreased from 42.3 seconds in 1968 to only 9.8 seconds in 1988.[22]

Radio news programs give much more coverage than television to political events. They often have available time that needs to be filled. Thus radio stations may even use political press releases in the form in which they were written by a candidate's campaign staff; sometimes they feature comments that have been taped by candidates and offered to radio stations. The latter are especially desirable, since they sound like news and can easily be included in news programs. Candidates who have difficulty getting attention from television and newspaper reporters may compensate by taking advantage of the availability of radio air time.

The free media devote much more attention to presidential campaigns than to other campaigns. Coverage of a presidential campaign may begin as long as two years before the election, and by the beginning of the election year it is the subject of daily reports. In contrast, coverage of gubernatorial races does not begin until Labor Day, and coverage of senatorial races often does not start until a month before the election. Congressional candidates and candidates for state office also receive much less scrutiny than presidential candidates.

The free media rarely devote much space to local campaigns. Free media coverage sometimes helps challengers gain recognition, but only if the candidate has also raised enough money to gain visibility through paid advertising.[23]

Proposals for Reform

The increasing dependence of political campaigns on the media, especially television, has become a matter of concern to many analysts of

American politics. Critics believe that negative advertising has given a nasty tone to many campaigns, while excessive use of sound bites has tended to trivialize important public issues. These observers see much news coverage of political campaigns as superficial, focusing on images rather than issues and providing little of substance for viewers to evaluate in deciding how to vote.

Some newspapers now keep watch on televised political advertising and publish reports on the accuracy of the content and the methods used to create the ads. Some California newspapers, for example, reprint the text of new political advertisements, accompanied by an analysis that may challenge, clarify, contradict, or present a context for claims made in the commercial. These *truth boxes* have had some effect on campaign advertising; media consultants have become somewhat more careful about documenting their claims. However, the truth boxes themselves have sometimes been used as ammunition by candidates, thereby adding to the amount of negative advertising rather than providing a solution to the problem.

The newspaper truth boxes have other drawbacks as well. For one thing, they are only published once, whereas a commercial may be repeated dozens or even hundreds of times. For another, they focus on literal statements rather than on the visual and aural content of ads. Yet viewers recall video images more effectively than written or spoken statements. "People tend to believe what they see more than what they hear," comments one expert. "You can try to counteract it by explaining what a candidate is trying to do. But people still succumb to the beautiful visuals."[24]

In an attempt to counteract the trend toward dependence on paid commercials and brief news spots, public television is planning to provide air time for candidates during the 1992 elections. Each candidate will be allowed to speak uninterrupted for up to fifteen minutes at regular intervals: once a week during September and most of October and each day during the final week before election day.

There have also been proposals to address the problem through legislation. One proposal would attempt to curb negative advertising by requiring candidates to appear in person in their commercials, thereby forcing the candidate to take personal responsibility for the content of the ad. Some experts question the constitutionality of this proposal, since it could be viewed as interfering with the First Amendment guarantee of freedom of speech. An alternative plan is to provide public financing in the form of vouchers that could be used to purchase television time in blocks of one to five minutes. The purpose of this proposal is to reduce candidates' dependence on brief television sound bites and equalize the opportunity for candidates to purchase TV time.

Many media experts do not believe that longer advertisements and news spots will solve the problem of negative advertising. Some scholars and public officials favor an approach in which free television time would be granted to parties rather than to candidates. This approach, which is widely used in other democracies, has won the approval of a Senate task force on campaign reform. However, most of the countries that currently use this approach are parliamentary democracies with multiparty systems that are quite different from the candidate-centered, two-party system of the United

States. Also, most of these countries are smaller and have fewer television stations than the United States, so those who watch television will be likely to see the programs the political parties present. In the United States the multiplicity of television stations and cable services fragments the television audience, with the result that any given message is unlikely to reach a majority of viewers.

Even reforms like those just described may not be enough to counteract the superficiality of American political campaigns. Such an action may require more fundamental changes in American culture. As one political scientist has pointed out, "You cannot improve discourse. Lack of education, lack of demands by the public that a certain level of discourse be reached are the problem. That will not change with free time. That is corrected with more and better civic education, starting from kindergarten."[25]

■ How Americans Participate

For public opinion to influence government policy, it must be translated into actions; in other words, to have an effect on the political system, people must participate in that system. Political scientists have studied how

TABLE 4.1 *Percentage of Public Engaging in Twelve Different Acts of Political Participation*

Type of political participation	Percentage
1. Report regularly voting in presidential elections	72
2. Report always voting in local elections	47
3. Active in at least one organization involved in community problems	32
4. Have worked with others in trying to solve some community problems	30
5. Have attempted to persuade others to vote as they were	28
6. Have ever actively worked for a party or candidates during an election	26
7. Have ever contacted a local government official about some issue or problem	20
8. Have attended at least one political meeting or rally in last three years	19
9. Have ever contacted a state or national government official about some issue or problem	18
10. Have ever formed a group or organization to attempt to solve some local community problem	14
11. Have ever given money to a party or candidate during an election campaign	13
12. Presently a member of a political club or organization	8

Source: Sidney Verba and Norman H. Nie, *Participation in America* (New York: Harper and Row, 1972), Table 2–1. Copyright © 1972 by Sidney Verba and Norman H. Nie. Reprinted by permission of Harper and Row, Publishers, Inc.

Americans participate in the political system. They have found that participation can take many forms: voting in presidential or local elections, joining with others in trying to solve community problems, actively working for a party or candidate during an election, attending a political meeting or rally, contacting a government official about a political issue, giving money to a party or candidate during an election, and joining a political club or organization.[26] (See Table 4.1.)

When participation is examined in terms of social status, a significant pattern emerges. Of those who participate least, a greater percentage are members of lower socioeconomic classes; those who participate most tend to be higher in social and economic status. Political participation is likely to result in more favorable action by government officials. Therefore, those who participate most obtain the most benefits from the government—benefits like tax reductions, favorable decisions on the routing of highways and the location of power plants, and the passage of laws supporting their views on energy or the economy. But those who participate less may need such benefits more: A person living in an inner-city slum, struggling to support a family on a small income, is probably too busy trying to scrape together a living even to think about politics, yet such people need the benefits of participation more than those who become involved. It is for this reason that activists who want to obtain more benefits for certain groups spend a great deal of energy trying to get members of those groups to vote and to participate more in political activities.[27]

The Changing American Voter

The way Americans participate most is by voting. Voting is, in fact, the only form of political activity that is engaged in by a majority of adult Americans. This final section of the chapter will be devoted to a discussion of who may vote, who actually votes, and how they vote.

Who May Vote?

When the United States Constitution was adopted, only adult white males who owned property or paid taxes could vote (state laws varied as to the amounts required), and some states imposed religious qualifications on the right to vote. The vote therefore was limited to a small percentage of the population.

Over the course of American history, restrictions on voting have gradually been lowered or eliminated. Amendments to state constitutions and changes in laws adopted by the state legislatures brought about many of these changes. Judicial decisions and amendments to the United States Constitution also contributed to the expansion of voting rights. Today the goal of **universal suffrage**—the right of all adult men and women to vote—has largely been achieved. Only a small percentage of the adult population is ineligible to vote: noncitizens, people who have been convicted of serious crimes, and the mentally incompetent. Some people are temporarily unable to vote because they recently changed their place of residence. But Supreme Court decisions have outlawed excessively long residency laws, and federal law places a thirty-day limit on the states in setting residency requirements for national elections.

Many Americans believe that the right to vote is granted by the Constitution, but this is not actually the case. Article I, Section 2, of the Constitution provides that the standards set by each state for elections to the lower house of the state legislature are to be used for national elections as well. Moreover, the states have broad authority to control most aspects of voting procedure, such as the times and places for holding elections and the methods for nominating candidates for public office (Article I, Section 4).

But a series of constitutional amendments—the Fifteenth, Nineteenth, Twenty-fourth, and Twenty-sixth—have barred the states from using standards of race, sex, or age (above 18) or the paying of a poll tax as voting requirements. The Twenty-third amendment granted the residents of the District of Columbia the right to vote in presidential elections. Although these amendments have had the effect of extending the vote to a large portion of the American public, they do not actually grant the right to vote. The amendments prevent certain forms of discrimination by the states in determining who may vote.

The movement toward universal suffrage in the United States can be seen as consisting of four stages. First, the right to vote was extended to all adult white men, regardless of their religion or whether they owned property or paid taxes. The next step was the granting of the vote to women. This step was followed by a prolonged struggle to include blacks, who had the right to vote but not the freedom to exercise it. Finally the vote was extended to all people over the age of 18.

White Male Suffrage. The states that were admitted to the Union at the close of the eighteenth century and in the first decades of the nineteenth were the first to eliminate religious and economic requirements for voting. The original thirteen states followed suit, and by the 1850s all states had abolished the property requirement.

Women's Suffrage. In the late 1800s and early 1900s, several western states gave women the right to vote. In the nation as a whole, however, women were denied the suffrage. A movement that became widespread at the beginning of the twentieth century demanded the right to vote, with women picketing the White House and making speeches throughout the country. In 1919 Congress finally proposed the Nineteenth Amendment, which states that "the right of citizens of the United States to vote shall not be denied or abridged by the United States or by any state on account of sex"; the amendment became part of the Constitution in 1920.

Black Suffrage. The third step along the road to universal suffrage was by far the most difficult. In the early nineteenth century free blacks could vote in many New England states, in New York and Pennsylvania, and even in Tennessee and North Carolina. This right, however, was based on loopholes in the state laws, and by 1840 most of them had been closed. (For example, in 1837 Pennsylvania amended its constitution to bar blacks from voting.)

Women march in Washington, D.C., in 1919 demanding the right to vote. The Nineteenth Amendment to the Constitution was ratified a year later in response to demonstrations of this type.

In the period following the Civil War, three new amendments were added to the Constitution. The Thirteenth, ratified in 1865, outlawed slavery. The Fourteenth (1868) granted blacks national and state citizenship and other legal protections, and the Fifteenth (1870) stated that "the right of citizens of the United States to vote shall not be denied or abridged by the United States or by any State on account of race, color, or previous condition of servitude." Despite these amendments, however, following Reconstruction the southern states were able to prevent blacks from voting for almost one hundred years. The Democratic party in the South held **white primaries,** in which only whites could vote. Blacks in southern states were also denied the vote by **grandfather clauses,** under which a person who had voted before 1867 or was descended from someone who had voted before that year was not required to meet various other requirements for voting. Anyone else—meaning blacks—had to pass discriminatory literacy, or "good character" tests. **Literacy tests** were examinations given by white state election officials which required prospective voters to interpret and explain provisions of the United States or state constitutions. The officials

Black citizens registering to vote with a federally appointed voting registrar in Canton, Mississippi, in August 1965. The Voting Rights Act, passed earlier that year, produced a dramatic increase in the number of blacks registered to vote in the southern states.

administered these laws in an arbitrary manner, passing whites and systematically failing blacks.

The Voting Rights Act of 1965 was an important step toward ending discrimination in this area. It suspended literacy tests in counties where less than half the voting-age population was registered to vote, and it permitted the use of federal examiners to register voters and monitor elections. This law was highly successful in increasing the number of registered black voters in the South, and it helped motivate blacks to register in greater numbers in all parts of the nation. (The struggle of black Americans to secure the right to vote is discussed more fully in Chapter 12.)

Lowering the Voting Age. Although the Constitution made no mention of a voting age, the Fourteenth Amendment refers to "male citizens twenty-one years of age." Traditionally, 21 had been considered the minimum age at which citizens are qualified to vote. During the 1960s and early 1970s, however, many young Americans argued that if they were old enough to fight for their country in Vietnam they were old enough to vote. They demanded that the voting age be lowered to 18.

In response to these demands, Congress passed the Voting Rights Act of 1970, which lowered the voting age to 18 in all national, state, and local elections. But in *Oregon* v. *Mitchell* (1970) the Supreme Court ruled that

Congress could regulate only national elections.[28] This ruling created major difficulties for almost all the states. They either had to amend their constitutions to lower the voting age for their local elections or to provide separate registration books, ballots, and voting booths for younger voters in national elections. The solution to this dilemma was an amendment to the Constitution. Proposed in 1971 and quickly ratified, the Twenty-sixth Amendment prohibits the states and the national government from discriminating against citizens 18 years of age or older in voting.

Who Votes?

"The act of voting," explain scholars who have studied the American voter, "requires the citizen to make not a single choice but two: He must choose between rival parties or candidates. He must decide also whether to vote at all."[29] Apparently, many Americans make only one choice—not to vote.

Voter turnout—the percentage of eligible voters who actually vote—in presidential elections has varied during different periods of American history. It was high—over 70 percent—in the nineteenth century, but between the 1860s and the 1920s it declined considerably, reaching a low of about 45 percent in 1924. After that the turnout rate rose again until 1940, when it was about 63 percent. But then it dropped sharply, rose briefly to an estimated 60 percent in 1960, and again began a decline, to slightly more than 50 percent in the most recent presidential elections. In the 1988 presidential election 91.6 million Americans, or 50.1 percent of the eligible voters, cast ballots, a decline from 53.1 percent in 1984. The 1988 figure was the lowest turnout of voters in a presidential election since 1924. (See Figure 4.1.)

Participation in midterm (or "off-year") congressional elections has traditionally been lower than in presidential elections. In 1990 only about 36 percent of the approximately 186 million eligible American voters cast

FIGURE 4.1 *Participation in presidential elections has been dropping steadily.*

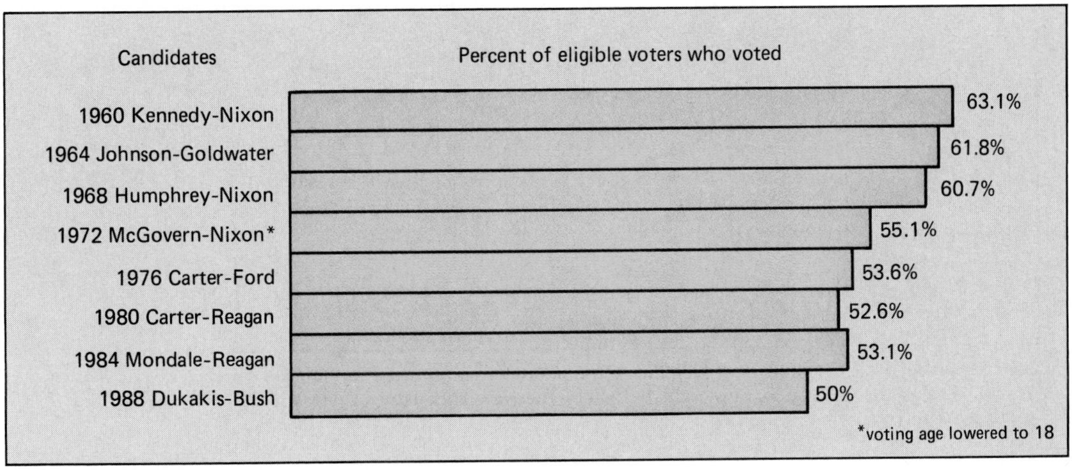

Candidates	Percent of eligible voters who voted
1960 Kennedy-Nixon	63.1%
1964 Johnson-Goldwater	61.8%
1968 Humphrey-Nixon	60.7%
1972 McGovern-Nixon*	55.1%
1976 Carter-Ford	53.6%
1980 Carter-Reagan	52.6%
1984 Mondale-Reagan	53.1%
1988 Dukakis-Bush	50%

*voting age lowered to 18

ballots. This figure was about the same as in 1986, the year in which the smallest turnout occurred in an off-year election since the end of World War II.

Voter turnout in the United States is often compared unfavorably with turnout rates in European democracies, which are considerably higher. These comparisons are somewhat misleading, however. For one thing, turnout rates in foreign countries are usually based on the number of registered voters (i.e., those whose names are on government voting lists), not on the total number of eligible voters (i.e., all citizens over 18 years of age). In addition, turnout rates for the United States do not take into account state restrictions, such as registration requirements, that have prevented some people from voting who otherwise might have done so.[30] Unlike the situation in most European nations, where the government maintains a list of the names of all residents, Americans must register to vote by a certain date before the election in order to qualify to vote. **Registration** requires a

FIGURE 4.2 *Percentage of voting-age population registered to vote (1988).*

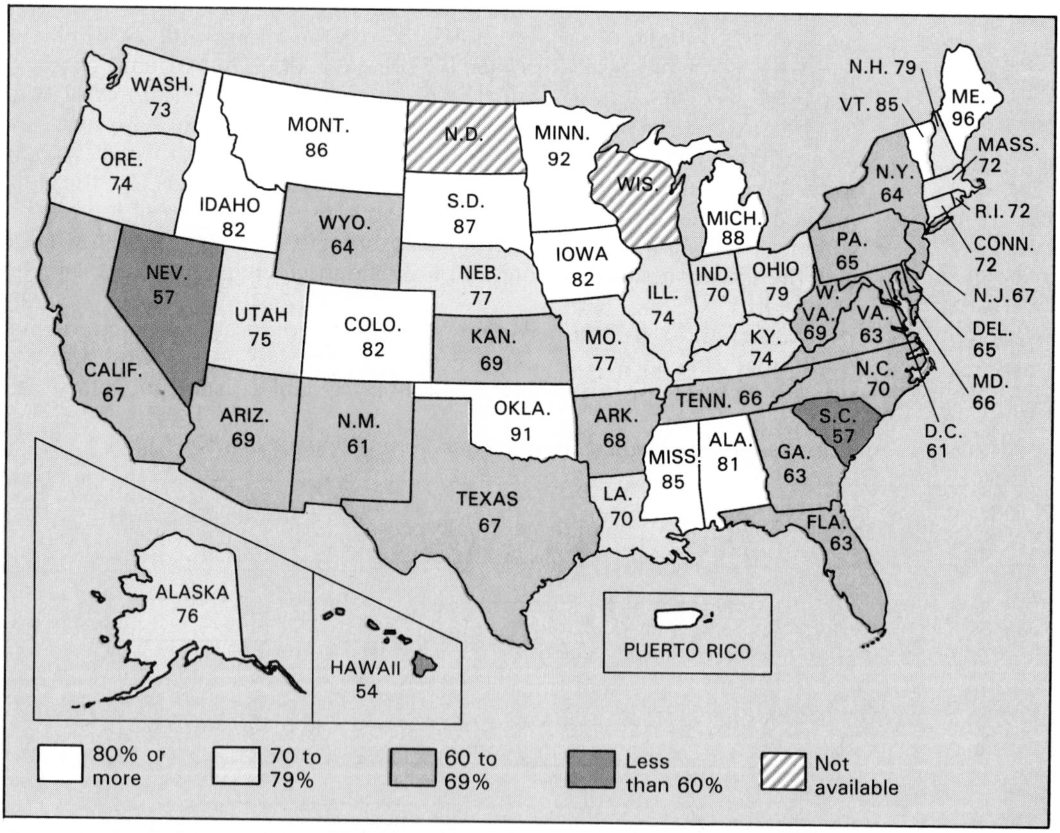

Source: National Clearinghouse on Election Administration, as reported in *The New York Times*, October 21, 1990, p. 34. Copyright © 1990 by the New York Times Company. Reprinted by permission.

PUBLIC OPINION, MASS MEDIA, AND VOTING

certain amount of effort, and millions of eligible voters do not make this effort.[31] (See Figure 4.2.)

Regardless of how voter turnout is calculated, it is still true that many Americans do not vote. Leaving aside the need to register and other legal restrictions such as residency, the main explanation for low turnout is lack of interest, information, and political involvement on the part of citizens. People who are interested in the outcome of an election and are informed about the candidates and issues are more likely to vote than those who are not. (See Table 4.2.)

TABLE 4.2 *Voters and Nonvoters Compared*

	Percent of voting public who . . .	*Percent of nonvoting public who . . .*
Demographic characteristics		
Were under 30 years of age	16%	39%
Have not attended college	59	68
Reported annual household income under $30,000	44	53
Are men	42	51
Are women	58	49
Are white	87	82
Are black	11	12
Have moved in the last two years	7	19
Civic attitudes		
Say they have been paying "a lot" of attention to election campaigns in their state this year	37	16
Say people like themselves do not have much say about what government does	54	62
Say things go on as before no matter who is elected	37	47
Trust government to do what is right only some of the time or never.	75	72
Partisanship		
Strongly identify with a party	35	21
Describe themselves as independent or decline to identify with a party	30	41
Prefer Republican candidate for Congress	39	35
Prefer Democratic candidate for Congress	44	42
Approve of the way George Bush is handling his job as President	51	52

Based on telephone interviews with 1,445 adults nationwide Oct. 28–31. The "voting public" and "nonvoting public" are identified by using the "Probable Electorate," which estimates individual respondents' likelihood of voting or not voting on election day from their answers to questions about registration, past voting history, and intention to vote in 1990.

Source: The New York Times/CBS News Poll, reported in *The New York Times*, November 7, 1990, p. B6. Copyright © 1990 by The New York Times Company. Reprinted by permission.

A recent study of the 1988 presidential election reached pessimistic conclusions about the attitudes and knowledge of many Americans regarding elections. It found a public both indifferent and poorly informed. For example, two months before the November election half of the voting-age public did not know the name of either party's vice presidential candidate or which political party controlled Congress. The researchers also found that citizens were so poorly informed about politics that they could not protect themselves against false or misleading political advertising.[32]

Many studies have attempted to determine which groups in American society do not vote. Their conclusions have generally identified young people, members of minority groups, and people with less education. An analysis of the 1988 presidential election conducted by the U.S. Census Bureau found that only 36 percent of people between the ages of 18 and 24 voted, while 68 percent of those between the ages of 45 and 64 did so. It also found that 52 percent of African Americans and 46 percent of Hispanic Americans voted in 1988, compared to 59 percent of whites. Finally, only 37 percent of persons with an eighth-grade education voted, whereas 78 percent of college graduates cast ballots.[33] (For a state-by-state analysis of voting in the 1988 national election, see Figure 4.3).

Political scientists have long known that the young and the less educated are less likely to vote. Nonvoting by the young—even after the adoption of the Twenty-sixth Amendment in 1971—can be explained partly by lack of interest. It may also be explained by the fact that young people often change their place of residence and hence fail to meet residency requirements for voting.[34]

But patterns of nonvoting are not static, and significant changes have taken place in the behavior of some groups. Thus, while whites still vote in greater proportions than African Americans, the difference has narrowed in recent presidential and congressional elections. The elimination of discriminatory barriers to voting during the 1960s and 1970s, the growth of a better-educated, more prosperous black middle class, and the increase in the number of black candidates for high public office help explain the growing number of blacks who register and vote.

Similarly, women voted less than men from 1920, when the Nineteenth Amendment was passed, until recently. The women's movement, increased education, and greater prosperity have greatly changed the political behavior of women. The gender difference in voter turnout decreased steadily during the 1970s and early 1980s. In 1984 the Census Bureau reported that for the first time the percentage of women voters surpassed that of men. This occurred again in 1988, when 58 percent of women voted, compared to 56 percent of men.[35]

Most people who are registered will vote at election time. Therefore, those who are concerned about low voter turnout have concentrated on reforms that will make it easier for citizens to register to vote. A few states allow individuals to appear at the polling place on election day and qualify at that time. Turnout has increased in those states, but because of the possibility of fraud this system has failed to gain widespread acceptance. Other reformers have argued that registration of voters should take place in

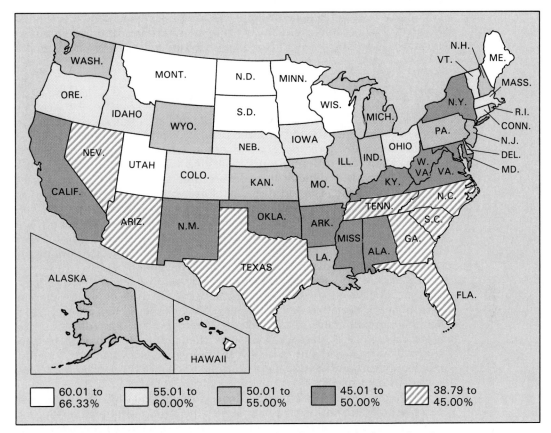

FIGURE 4.3 *Percentage of voting-age population that voted in the national election (1988).*

Source: Election Data Services, as reported in *The New York Times*, April 22, 1990, Section 4, p. 4. Copyright © 1990 by The New York Times Company. Reprinted by permission.

more public places, such as shopping malls, and should be conducted throughout the year; in most states registration now takes place in schools and other public buildings, usually for limited periods.

In 1990 the House of Representatives passed the National Voter Registration Act. That law included provisions that would have required the states to register people who have applied for driver's licenses and renewals and to permit voter registration by mail. A number of states already have adopted systems that combine voter registration with motor vehicle registration; they have reported sharp increases in numbers of registered voters. Although the Senate failed to pass the proposed legislation, it is likely that this reform will again be brought before Congress for consideration.

Not all observers are convinced that the registration system is the main reason for low voter turnout in the United States. One study has put forth the theory that the nation has entered a "postelectoral" political era. Increasing numbers of voters believe that elections are no longer important.

The traditional significance of elections has been replaced by a system in which major decisions are made by congressional investigating committees and the courts, and through revelations in the media.[36]

How Do Americans Vote?

Social scientists have devoted considerable attention to analyzing the types of Americans who support the two major political parties. Of course, not all Americans are supporters of either the Democratic or Republican parties. Many are **independents**—persons who do not identify with a political party. It is difficult to make accurate statements on this subject, given the immense size and diversity of the voting-age population and its increasing independence. But studies of American voting behavior have identified a number of important factors that influence party support; it is therefore possible to make reasonably accurate generalizations on this subject. The factors that have been identified as most important are education, income, place of residence, race, religion, and sex.

Education and income are closely related. Education usually determines a person's occupation and income and, hence, his or her social class. And there is a direct correlation between higher social class and voting for Republican candidates. Conversely, individuals with less education and lower incomes are more likely to vote Democratic. In the 1988 election approximately 65 percent of people in the highest social groups voted for the Republican presidential candidate; 62 percent of those from the lowest social groups voted for the Democratic candidate.

Place of residence also has an effect on voting behavior. The Republican party was organized in the 1850s, shortly before the outbreak of the Civil War. It has traditionally been the party of the North, especially farmers and residents of small towns especially in the Midwest. Since the end of World War II it has also gained strong support in the suburbs of large cities and in the rapidly growing western states.

From the end of the Civil War until recent decades, the Democratic party could count on the support of the so-called solid South. For almost one hundred years the Republican party hardly existed in the states of the old Confederacy. Since the 1950s, however, the Republicans have gained greater support among white voters in that area. In 1960, for example, 57 percent of southern whites voted Democratic and 40 percent voted Republican. In 1988, 67 percent voted Republican and only 32 percent Democratic.[37]

Much of the success of Republican presidential candidates in recent decades has been a result of the change in allegiance among southern white voters. In the past several presidential elections, most southern states have cast their electoral votes for Republican presidential candidates. And although the Democrats still dominate at the local level and control most state legislatures in the South, a growing number of Republican candidates have been elected to the House of Representatives, the Senate, and state governorships.

Place of residence influences voting patterns in other ways as well. Since the election of Franklin D. Roosevelt to the presidency in 1932, during the Great Depression, the Democratic party has received strong backing from voters in large cities in the North. Cities like Boston, New York, Philadelphia, and Chicago have long given overwhelming support to Democratic candidates.

Race is another factor that affects voting behavior. From the Civil War until the 1930s, blacks who were able to vote supported the Republicans, the party of Abraham Lincoln. But during the 1930s the New Deal benefited many poor blacks, and they switched their allegiance to the Democratic party. Indeed, blacks today are more strongly associated with the Democratic party than any other group in American society. In all recent presidential elections, blacks have strongly supported Democratic candidates. It is estimated that 86 percent of black voters cast their ballots for the Democratic candidate, Michael Dukakis, in the 1988 presidential election.

Religion is also a factor that influences voting. Catholics and Jews have a long tradition of support for the Democratic party. Between 1880 and 1920 many Catholics and Jews came to the United States as poor immigrants and settled in the large cities. It was usually the Democratic party that provided them with jobs and various social services and gained their political loyalty. President Roosevelt's New Deal served to reinforce their ties to the Democratic party. In the past several decades, however, the Republican party has made inroads on the Catholic vote, especially in presidential elections and among more affluent and better-educated Catholics. Ronald Reagan was especially successful in gaining the support of Catholic voters during his 1980 and 1984 presidential campaigns.

The influence of religion on voting can also be seen in the support many Protestants have given to the Republican party. Since the mid-nineteenth century, Protestants outside of the South have tended to vote Republican. And as we have already seen, in recent presidential elections the Republican party has sharply increased its support among the largely Protestant white voters in the South.

In recent years there has been considerable discussion of the so-called *gender gap*—the alleged tendency of women to see political issues differently than men do. There is growing evidence to support this claim. On some issues, public opinion polls have revealed significant differences between the views of women and men. Women, for example, are much less likely than men to back the use of military force against another nation. With regard to voting, more women than men are registered as Democrats and vote for Democratic candidates. In the 1988 election women, regardless of age or education, were more likely to vote for Democrat Michael Dukakis than were men of the same age or educational level.

In sum, the Democratic and Republican parties can best be understood as loose *coalitions*, or alliances, of voters from a variety of backgrounds. (See Table 4.3.) Republicans tend to be white, Protestant, and better educated, have higher incomes and live on farms, in small towns, or in the suburbs of large cities and in the western part of the United States or (especially with respect to presidential elections) in the South. The Democratic coalition includes blacks, many Catholics, Jews, southerners (at least in state and local elections), members of labor unions, the less well educated, the poor, people who live in the cities of the Northeast and the upper Midwest and many intellectuals—writers and college professors, for example.

TABLE 4.3 *Portrait of the Electorate, 1988*

	Voted for Bush	Voted for Dukakis
Total	53%	45%
Gender		
Men	57	41
Women	50	49
Race/Ethnic Background		
Whites	59	40
Blacks	12	88
Hispanics	30	69
Age		
18–29 years	52	47
30–44 years	54	45
45–59 years	57	42
60 and over	50	49
Religion		
White Protestant	66	33
Catholic	52	47
Jewish	35	49
Region		
East	50	49
Midwest	52	47
South	58	41
West	52	46
Education		
Not a high school graduate	43	56
High school graduate	50	49
Some college education	57	42
College graduate	56	43
Postgraduate education	50	48
Occupation		
Unemployed	37	62
Blue-collar worker	49	50
Teacher	47	51
Full-time student	44	54
White-collar worker	57	42
Professional or manager	59	40
Income		
Family income under $12,000	37	62
$12,000–$24,999	49	50
$25,000–$34,999	56	44
$35,000–$49,999	56	42
$50,000–$100,000	61	38
Over $100,000	65	32

Source: The New York Times/CBS News Poll, as reported in *The New York Times*, Nov. 10, 1988, p. B6. Data based on questionaires completed by 11,645 voters leaving polling places around the nation on Election Day. Copyright 1988 by The New York Times Company. Reprinted by permission.

PUBLIC OPINION, MASS MEDIA, AND VOTING

■ Summary

Despite the growing influence of television and the media on public opinion, the voter remains the ultimate source of authority in the American political system. The decisions of voters determine the outcome of elections and, hence the shape of American politics.

Using the abundance of information derived from public opinion research—information that was not available until recent decades—scholars have developed two contrasting theories about the typical American voter. These theories see the voter as either *dependent* or *responsive.*

In the dependent-voter portrait, the voter chooses a candidate on the basis of factors other than political events or issues. In this view, voters are influenced by social forces or party loyalty; often they make up their minds before the campaign begins and they are not overly concerned about the outcome of the election. Their choices are basically those of a group rather than those of individuals, and the group is usually the political party. This portrait presents the voter as unable to make rational decisions and likely to be influenced by a party label or a political slogan.

In the responsive-voter portrait, the voter is aware of public issues and bases voting decisions on the candidates' statements about these subjects. In this view, many factors influence voters' decisions, and different voters respond to different factors. Although voters may identify with a particular political party, they do so in the belief that their interests will be best served by that party's candidates.

Which of these theories comes closer to the truth? Probably the responsive-voter portrait. People know somewhat more about politics and political issues today than in the past, partly because of the widespread impact of television and partly because of the higher average level of education of the American people. Voters have increasingly shown greater independence in making voting decisions. And although the average voter may not have much detailed information about candidates or issues, most voters are well aware of their own interests and the basic differences between candidates. These factors, and not simply party or personality, shape the way most Americans vote today.

■ Key Terms

political culture
political socialization
public opinion
political opinion
scientific polling
sampling

survey research
telephone poll
exit poll
universal suffrage
white primary

grandfather clause
literacy test
voter turnout
registration
independent

■ Suggested Reading

ASHER, HERBERT B. *Polling and the Public.* Washington, D.C.: Congressional Quarterly Press, 1987.

BAXTER, SANDRA, and MARJORIE LANSING. *Women and Politics: The Invisible Majority.* Ann Arbor: University of Michigan Press, 1983.

Cantril, Albert H. *The Opinion Connection: Polling, Politics, and the Press.* Washington, D.C.: Congressional Quarterly Press, 1990.

Conway, M. Margaret. *Political Participation in the United States,* 2nd ed. Washington, D.C.: Congressional Quartery Press, 1990.

Cornell, Stephen. *The Return of the Native: American Indian Political Resurgence.* Berkeley: University of California Press, 1988.

Graber, Doris A. *Mass Media and American Politics,* 3rd ed. Washington, D.C.: Congressional Quarterly Press, 1988.

————, ed. *Media Power in Politics,* 2nd ed. Washington, D.C.: Congressional Quarterly Press, 1990.

Hallin, Daniel C. *The "Uncensored War": The Media and Vietnam.* Berkeley: University of California Press, 1989.

Iyengar, Shanton, and Donald R. Kinder. *News That Matters: Television and American Opinion.* Chicago: University of Chicago Press, 1987.

Jennings, M. Kent, and Richard G. Niemi. *Generations and Politics: A Panel Study of Young Adults and Their Parents.* Princeton, N.J.: Princeton University Press, 1981.

Nagel, Jack H. *Participation.* Englewood Cliffs, N.J.: Prentice-Hall, 1987.

Wolfinger, Raymond and Steven J. Rosenstone. *Who Votes?* New Haven, Conn.: Yale University Press, 1980.

■ Notes

1. William H. Flanigan and Nancy H. Zingale, *Political Behavior of the American Electorate,* 6th ed. (Boston: Allyn & Bacon, 1987), pp. 172–173.

2. Herbert McClosky, "Consensus and Ideology in American Politics," *American Political Science Review,* 58 (1964), 365.

3. Flanigan and Zingale, *Political Behavior,* p. 175.

4. David Easton and Jack Dennis, *Children and the Political System: Origins of Political Legitimacy* (New York: McGraw-Hill, 1969), pp. 73–91.

5. Robert D. Hess and Judith U. Torney, *The Development of Political Attitudes in Children* (Garden City, N.Y.: Doubleday/Anchor, 1968), pp. 105–108, 111.

6. Kathleen A. Frankovic, "Media Polls: Monitoring Changes in Public Opinion," *ICPSR Bulletin* (Interuniversity Consortium for Political and Social Research), February 1990, p. 1.

7. Nelson W. Polsby and Aaron Wildavsky, *Presidential Elections: Strategies of American Electoral Politics,* 6th ed. (New York: Scribner's, 1984), pp. 199–201.

8. Ibid., pp. 201–202.

9. The discussion of sampling and survey research is based on Jarol B. Manheim and Richard C. Rich, *Empirical Political Analysis: Research Methods in Political Science* (White Plains, N.Y.: Longman, 1986), pp. 86–91, 105–107.

10. Frankovic, "Media Polls," pp. 1–2.

11. Ibid.

12. Michael Oreskes, "In Year of Volatile Vote, Polls Can Be Dynamite,"*The New York Times,* November 2, 1990, p. A19.

13. Andres Rosenthal, "Surveys' Accuracy Fails To Curb the Criticism," *New York Times,* November 10, 1988, p. B5.

14. Adam Clymer, "Election Day Shows What the Opinion Polls Can't Do," *New York Times,* November 12, 1989, p. 4E.

15. Oreskes, "Polls Can Be Dynamite," p. A19.

16. Barbara G. Salmore and Stephen A. Salmore, *Candidates, Parties, and Campaigns,* 2nd ed. (Washington, D.C.: Congressional Quarterly Press, 1989), p. 139.

17. Jerry Hagstrom and Robert Guskind, "Shopping for Airtime," *National Journal,* February 20, 1988, pp. 462–467.

18. Edie N. Goldenberg and Michael W. Traugott, *Campaigning for Congress* (Washington, D.C.: Congressional Quarterly Press, 1984), pp. 116–119; John R. Alford and Keith Henry, "TV Markets and Congressional Elections," *Legislative Studies Quarterly* 9 (November 1984): 665–675.

19. Salmore and Salmore, *Candidates, Parties, and Campaigns,* pp. 143–144.

20. Michael Oreskes, "TV's Role in '88: The Medium Is the Election," *The New York Times,* October 30, 1988, p. 1.

21. Gerald F. Seib and Michel McQueen, "A Campaign Becomes a 'Made for TV' Race: A Picture a Day Obviates Thousands of Words," *Wall Street Journal,* September 16, 1988, p. 48.

22. Randall Rothenberg, "Politics on TV: Too Fast, Too Loose?" *The New York Times,* July 15, 1990, sec. 4, pp. 1, 4.

23. Salmore and Salmore, *Candidates, Parties, and Campaigns,* pp. 149–154.

24. Doris A. Graber, quoted in Randall Rothenberg, "Newspapers Watch What People Watch in the TV Campaign," *The New York Times,* November 4, 1990, sec. 4, p. 5.

25. Larry J. Sabato, quoted in Rothenberg, "Politics on TV," p. 4.

26. Sidney Verba and Norman H. Nie, *Participation in America* (New York: Harper and Row, 1972), p. 31.

27. Ibid., pp. 118–119.

28. 400 U.S. 112 (1970).

29. Angus Campbell, Philip E. Converse, Warren E. Miller, and Donald E. Stokes, *The American Voter* (New York: John Wiley, 1960), p. 49.

30. Flanigan and Zingale, *Political Behavior*, pp. 8–9; Ronald C. Moe, "Myth of the Non-Voting American," *Wall Street Journal*, November 4, 1980, p. 28.

31. Stanley Kelley, Jr., Richard E. Ayres, and William G. Brown, "Registration and Voting: Putting First Things First," *American Political Science Review*, 61 (June 1967), 359–380. In a few democratic countries, such as Australia and Belgium, citizens are fined for not voting. Turnout in those nations is consequently very high.

32. Markel Commission on the Media and the Electorate, cited in *The New York Times*, May 6, 1990, p. 32.

33. Richard L. Berke, "Voter Decline Is Found Among Most Groups," *The New York Times*, March 12, 1989, p. 25.

34. Flanigan and Zingale, *Political Behavior*, p. 19.

35. Ibid.

36. Benjamin Ginsberg and Martin Shefter, *Politics by Other Means* (New York: Basic Books, 1990).

37. Michael Oreskes, "Civil Rights Act Leaves Deep Mark on the American Political Landscape," *The New York Times*, July 2, 1989, p. 16.

5

Chapter Outline

Political Parties

The American Two-Party System
One-Party Areas
The Nature of American Parties
Minor Parties

The Structure of Political Parties
The Decentralization of Party Power
The Decline of Party Identification
Reform or Status Quo?

Interest Groups
The Growth of Interest Groups
The Structure of Interest Groups
Types of Interest Groups
New Types of Interest Groups
The Activities of Interest Groups
The Funding of Interest Groups
The Power of Interest Groups

Questions for Thought

Why does the United States have a two-party system?

Why is it correct to describe American political parties as decentralized?

What are interest groups? How do they differ from political parties?

How do interest groups seek to influence the decisions of government?

What are political action committees?

What criticisms have been made of the role of political action committees?

Political Parties
and Interest Groups

I N CHAPTER 4 we mentioned the various ways in which people participate in the political system, and we discussed in some detail the most common form of participation, voting. In this chapter we turn our attention to organized political activity, that is, to how *groups* participate in politics.

There are two basic types of groups that use political power to influence public policy: political parties and interest (or "pressure") groups. **Political parties** try to influence policy primarily by getting their members elected or appointed to government offices. Interest groups, by contrast, do not put forward their own candidates for public office. Instead they seek to influence government indirectly by shaping public opinion, supporting or opposing candidates, and influencing the decisions of government officials. Although the activities of political parties and interest groups overlap, it is possible to separate them for the purpose of analyzing and studying their roles in the political system.

■ Political Parties

Political parties are not mentioned in the Constitution, but there have been parties of various kinds—Federalists, Democratic-Republicans, Whigs, Democrats, Republicans—throughout the nation's history. It seems that, as one political scientist has explained, "Parties and democracy arose together; they have lived and prospered in a closely symbiotic relationship; and if one of them should ever weaken and die, the other would die with it."[1]

Parties perform a variety of functions. Along with interest groups and the mass media, parties play a role in keeping the public informed about current political issues and helping people form opinions on those issues. The minority political party—the one that does not control Congress or the presidency—serves as a check on the majority party. It examines and criticizes the proposals of the majority party and may suggest alternatives. But the main functions of political parties are the recruitment and selection of leaders, the representation and integration of group interests, and the control and direction of government.

Party activities center on the processes of recruiting, electing, and appointing political leaders to office, including administrative and judicial offices. Although parties do not control their candidates, they provide the conditions under which hundreds of thousands of elective offices can be filled in an organized manner. By proposing and campaigning for specific lists of candidates, the parties bring order and predictability to the political process.

The goal of party activities is the power and other advantages associated with public office. But in pursuing this goal the parties also provide various services to the public: They help educate voters on current issues and simplify the choices that voters face on election day. According to one political scientist, "The parties do what voters cannot do by themselves: from the totality of interests and issues in politics, they choose those that will become 'the agenda of formal public discourse.' "[2]

Another important function of parties is the representation and integration of group interests. The parties' elected officials act as "brokers" among interest groups. They consider the claims of each group, accepting some and modifying or rejecting others in a process of continual bargaining and compromise. The capacity of parties to represent diverse interests and to integrate the claims of competing groups is an important element of a democratic political system.[3]

Finally, parties recruit candidates and organize campaigns in order to gain public office, that is, to control the government. However, it is rare for one party to control all parts of the government. In recent history the party that has controlled the presidency has rarely been able to win control of both houses of Congress. Thus, while the parties can be said to organize the government, they do not fully control governmental decision making. And as we will see later in the chapter, interest groups compete with political parties in seeking to obtain public policies that are favorable to their interests; sometimes such groups are more powerful than parties.[4]

The American Two-Party System

In 1789 and 1793 George Washington was the electoral college's unanimous choice for President. But during Washington's second term in office two distinct parties—the Federalists and the Democratic-Republicans—became important political forces. By the time John Adams was elected President in 1796, both parties were operating on a national scale. Since then parties have played a major role in every election.

From its inception, the American party system—at least at the national level—has had several major traits. First, it has been a **two-party system;** almost every election in the nation has been primarily a contest between two political parties. More than two parties nominate candidates for public office in many elections, but only the candidates of the two major parties have a real chance of winning. (See Figure 5.1.) In the twentieth century, the only time a third party had a chance of winning a national election was in 1912, when ex-President Theodore Roosevelt deserted the Republican party to run on the Progressive party ticket. But Roosevelt finished behind the Democratic candidate, Woodrow Wilson.

Second, at the national level the party system has been marked by long stretches of single-party dominance. One or the other of the two major parties has controlled the presidency for long periods. From 1800 through 1860 the Democrats won eleven out of fifteen elections, and from 1860 to 1932 the Republicans were defeated only four times. The Democrats returned to power in 1932 with the election of Franklin D. Roosevelt and, except for Dwight D. Eisenhower's victories in 1952 and 1956, won every national election until 1968. Since 1968, however, the Republican party has won five of the six national elections: Richard Nixon won in 1968 and 1972, Ronald Reagan in 1980 and 1984, and George Bush in 1988. The Democrats were successful only in 1976, when their nominee, Jimmy Carter, was elected President.

Two-party systems are not found in all democracies; many democratic nations have **multiparty systems,** in which a number of parties compete successfully for elective office. Why, then, does the United States have a two-party system?

Several theories attempt to account for the existence of two dominant parties in the United States. The most widely accepted of these is the *institutional theory*, which holds that the nation's election system, especially the use of single-member districts in choosing members of Congress and of state and local legislatures, creates a two-party system. The single-member system permits only one candidate to win—the one who receives a *plurality* (the largest number) of the votes cast. All other candidates, regardless of the size of their vote, receive nothing for their efforts. Thus the opposition's best chance of winning lies in uniting to

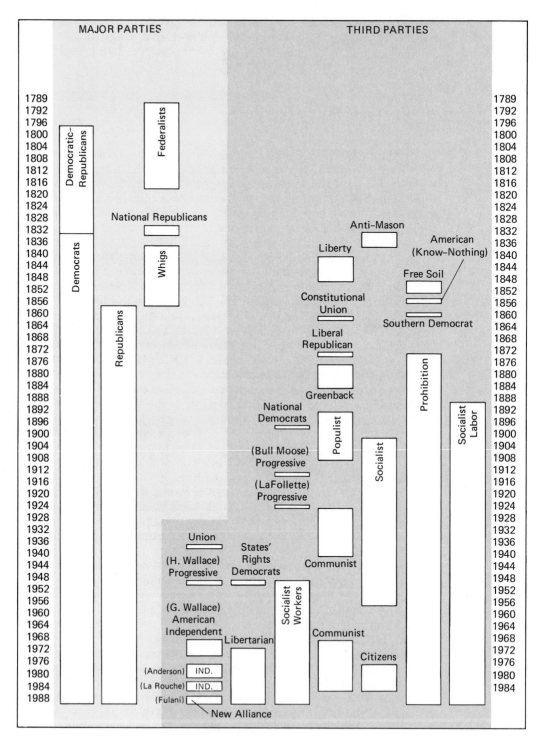

MAJOR PARTIES

THIRD PARTIES

1789		1789
1792		1792
1796		1796
1800		1800
1804		1804
1808		1808
1812		1812
1816		1816
1820		1820
1824		1824
1828		1828
1832		1832
1836		1836
1840		1840
1844		1844
1848		1848
1852		1852
1856		1856
1860		1860
1864		1864
1868		1868
1872		1872
1876		1876
1880		1880
1884		1884
1888		1888
1892		1892
1896		1896
1900		1900
1904		1904
1908		1908
1912		1912
1916		1916
1920		1920
1924		1924
1928		1928
1932		1932
1936		1936
1940		1940
1944		1944
1948		1948
1952		1952
1956		1956
1960		1960
1964		1964
1968		1968
1972		1972
1976		1976
1980		1980
1984		1984
1988		

Democratic-Republicans

Federalists

Democrats

National Republicans

Whigs

Republicans

Anti-Mason

Liberty

American (Know-Nothing)

Free Soil

Constitutional Union

Southern Democrat

Liberal Republican

Greenback

Prohibition

Socialist Labor

National Democrats

Populist

(Bull Moose) Progressive

Socialist

(LaFollette) Progressive

Union

States' Rights Democrats

(H. Wallace) Progressive

Communist

(G. Wallace) American Independent

Socialist Workers

Libertarian

Communist

(Anderson) IND.

Citizens

(La Rouche) IND.

(Fulani)

New Alliance

Source: Center for Political Studies, University of Michigan.

POLITICAL PARTIES AND INTEREST GROUPS

defeat the majority party. The formation of third parties serves only to divide the minority and strengthen the majority party's hold on the elective office. The election of Woodrow Wilson in 1912 in a three-way contest for President is a good example of this process.

The effect that an election system can have on political parties is best shown by comparing the *single-member-district method* with the system of *proportional representation* used in many democracies. Under proportional representation, legislators are elected from large districts and the parties are rewarded with seats in the legislature in proportion to the percentage of votes they obtain. Countries that use this system, such as Italy and Israel, have multiparty systems rather than only two major parties.

Other theories about the development of two-party systems may be described as *cultural*. Such theories attribute two-party systems to a willingness to compromise, which may be part of the American political culture. (See Chapter 4 for a discussion of American political culture.) In the United States, it is argued, citizens are willing to make certain compromises so that a number of diverse interests can be represented by a single major party while an opposing set of interests falls under the umbrella of the other party.

Finally, there is the *social consensus* theory. In this view, a two-party system will develop in a society in which most people agree that the nation's basic social, economic, and political institutions are legitimate. In the United States, for example, the majority of the population agrees that democracy is a good thing. As a result, parties of the antidemocratic left and right have had no success here.

It is possible, of course, that all of these explanations played a role in the development of the American two-party system. There *is* a "social consensus" concerning the American political and economic system that has existed since the Revolution. The "cultural" explanation is valid, since the major parties are clearly coalitions of diverse groups. And the electoral system used in the United States lends strong support to the "institutional" explanation.[5]

One-Party Areas

Despite the development of a two-party system and the obvious strength of that system, historically there have been some parts of the country—congressional districts, cities, states, and sometimes whole regions—where one party had such widespread support that the area was, for all practical purposes, operating under a one-party system. The South was for a long time the strongest of these one-party areas. The Democratic party almost totally controlled the politics of that region from the close of the Civil War until the past few decades; recently the region has become more competitive, especially in national elections. A number of major cities like New York and Chicago remain strongholds of the Democratic party. Kansas, Utah, and Wyoming, in contrast, are traditional Republican strongholds.

Why do one-party systems exist within a two-party system? Several reasons for this situation have been suggested. One is that there may be a local basis for party loyalty that overrides any other factor. In the South, Democratic dominance in state and local elections was based on the belief that the Republicans were responsible for the Civil War and Reconstruction. Another explanation of one-party dominance is that the people who live in a given area may be so similar that most of them support the same party. Homogeneity might, for example, explain the Republican leanings of residents of wealthy suburban areas. There are a number of other explanations, however. Among them are local tradition, the influence of powerful local officeholders, and specific local conflicts (e.g., between a major local industry and its unionized employees).[6]

Another way of looking at one-party dominance is in terms of party competition itself. One party may be the minority in a given area and unable to change the situation. Suppose, for example, that voters in a certain area have always identified with the Republican party. The Democrats are unable to win elections in that state and become known as the losing party. As such, they are unable to attract financial contributions and campaign workers, both of which are needed to win elections. As a result, they continue to lose, and the state continues to be dominated by the Republican party.

It is clear, however, that many parts of the nation that were once dominated by a single party have become more competitive in statewide elections, especially since World War II. A recent analysis has concluded that, "with a few exceptions in the South, most states have reached a substantial level of two-party competition."[7] Yet there are still many noncompetitive congressional districts, cities, and counties in which one of the two major political parties always wins on election day. This is also true of state legislatures, many of which have been controlled by one party— usually the Democrats—for generations.

Party competition thus is quite variable; in fact, it is possible to rank states and localities on a scale from noncompetitive to highly competitive. At the bottom of the scale are the one-party states and districts. Farther up the scale are areas where one party almost always elects the public officials but the minority party has enough support to pose a threat to the dominant party. Above them are areas that lean slightly toward one party or the other, and at the top are areas in which the parties are in active and continual competition.[8]

The Nature of American Parties

The most salient characteristic of the American party system is the fact that it is essentially a two-party system. However, there are other important characteristics as well. One of those characteristics is that the parties are highly decentralized. The national parties have historically been weak; the state parties are independent of national control; and within the states the county and local parties have great influence. State and local parties, for example, are free to nominate candidates and shape party positions on public issues without interference by the national party. The decentralization of power within the major parties will be discussed in more detail later in the chapter.

Another significant characteristic of the parties is that they are coalitions. Different segments of the population have traditionally supported one or the other major party. For example, during the past sixty years members of the urban working classes, union families, African Americans, Catholics, Jews, people with relatively little education, the poor, and many intellectuals have tended to support the Democratic party. The Republicans, on the other hand, have attracted the loyalty of successful businesspeople and industrialists, farmers, small-town and rural dwellers, whites, Protestants, people with higher incomes and more education, nonunion families, and "old stock" Americans.[9] This feature of parties is closely related to the voting behavior of various groups in American society, discussed in Chapter 4.

Related to this characteristic is another important aspect of American parties: ideological diversity. In order to win elections and gain power, the parties need to be adaptable—to be able to shape their programs in such a way as to attract individuals and groups with a wide range of views on issues of public policy. As a result, party ideology is not clearly defined; rather, party positions on various issues are usually set forth in such general terms that they can be interpreted differently by members of different groups.[10]

Ideological diversity tends to produce moderation. Since the parties have to appeal to many diverse groups with different political interests, they tend to avoid taking positions that are too extreme or dogmatic. Although there are important differences between the two major parties, each tries to take stands that will alienate as few voters as possible. Another reason that the parties avoid extreme positions is that most Americans hold moderate views on most public issues. Party leaders realize that they must appeal to a broad segment of the American people whose political views are generally moderate. Indeed, national elections are won by the party that successfully appeals to this moderate majority.

A natural outcome of these characteristics is that the major parties tend to nominate moderate candidates and reject those who wander too far from the middle of the political road. Nominating a candidate from the party's far right (conservative) or left (liberal) wing can be dangerous. In 1964, for example, the Republicans selected Barry Goldwater as their candidate for President. Goldwater, a conservative, lacked the support of most moderate and liberal Republicans and failed to win the votes of many Democrats and independents. (Because there are fewer Republicans than Democrats, the Republican candidate must attract Democratic and independent voters to win the election.) A similar case was the defeat of liberal Democrat George McGovern in 1972, when many independents and moderate and conservative Democrats voted for the Republican candidate, Richard Nixon.

In sum, the American two-party system is decentralized, and the parties are broad-based coalitions of ideologically different groups and interests.

But this does not mean that there is no room for other kinds of parties. Although the nation has operated under a two-party system throughout its history, there has been no shortage of minor political parties that have actively contested elections at all levels of government.

Minor Parties

Greenbackers, Free-Soilers, Bull Moosers, Populists, Socialists, Progressives, Libertarians—all have nominated candidates for national, state, and local public offices at one time or another, but rarely have those candidates won elections. Such **minor** or **third parties** exist primarily to oppose the policies and programs of the two major parties and to advance their own ideas. They do not have the power or resources to get their candidates elected.

Some minor parties are organized around a particular political ideology, such as socialism. Or they may form around a specific issue—the Prohibitionist party opposes alcoholic beverages, and the Liberty and Free-Soil parties of the nineteenth century fought against slavery. Still other minor parties fall somewhere between issue and ideology—the Progressives of 1948, for instance, combined a social-reform program with a policy of friendship with the Soviet Union.

Minor parties also differ in their origins. The Communist and Socialist Workers parties had their origins in the European politics of the early twentieth century. The Populist party arose out of a protest against the economic hardships suffered by farmers and laborers in the late nineteenth century. Other minor parties are "splinter" parties that have broken with one of the major parties. An example is the American Independent party, founded in 1968 by Alabama Governor George Wallace, which opposed the liberal policies of the Democratic party. In 1980 former Illinois Representative John B. Anderson ran for President as an independent candidate. His campaign sought to present alternatives to the domestic and foreign policies of the two major parties. But in 1990, a socialist, Bernard Sanders, won a seat in the House of Representatives from Vermont—the first socialist to serve in Congress in more than forty years.

Most minor parties disappear soon after losing one or two national elections. But a few—including the Prohibition and Socialist Labor parties—have nominated candidates for national elections for a century or more.

A minor party is sometimes given credit for taking positions that are later adopted by the major parties. The American Socialist party, for example, was an early advocate of a national social security system. But there is no way of determining the extent of this influence. It is likely that a social security system would have been adopted during the depression of the 1930s regardless of its inclusion in a third-party platform.

There have been numerous minor political parties over the course of American history, and textbooks often devote considerable space to their activities. But what have minor parties actually achieved? According to one study, minor parties "have not assumed the importance that all the attention lavished on them suggests."[11] Nevertheless, a small percentage of

Americans continue to vote for the candidates of minor political parties despite the widespread belief that a vote for a third party is a wasted vote.

■ The Structure of Political Parties

Political parties are not mentioned in the Constitution, but rules for their structure and operation are set forth in state law and in the regulations of the parties themselves. Like the government, the major political parties are organized at three levels: national, state, and local. The state and local units are, however, almost entirely independent of the national party, and most of the real authority within the parties is located at the lower levels rather than at the top. Similarly, although the structure of a state party resembles a pyramid, it should be understood that political power does not usually flow from the top down to the lower levels. Instead power is dispersed, with each unit often having a significant degree of independence.

In theory, the **national convention** is the political party's top national authority. In practice, however, it has few real powers. It meets every four years to nominate presidential and vice presidential candidates, and it adopts party rules and a party platform. But it has no voice in the selection of candidates for congressional, state, or local office; nor can it force candidates to support its platform.

Also in theory, the **national committee** of each party is the executive organ of the party during the time between meetings of the national convention. The members serve four-year terms and are elected by the convention. But this election is a mere formality. In reality, the convention simply appoints the nominees of the state parties, who have been chosen by a direct primary, state convention, or state party committee or by the delegates to the national convention.

Traditionally, the national committees of the two political parties represented states, not people or party strength. The Republican National Committee is still organized on this basis, with each state and territory receiving three seats on the committee. However, in 1974 the Democratic party adopted a charter that, among other things, provided that each state party would be allotted members on the basis of the state's population and Democratic presidential voting record. Two hundred members were added to the committee for this purpose.

Both the Democratic and Republican national committees are over-shadowed by the party's presidential candidate during campaigns, and an elected President will be the major force in his party. The national committee of a political party attains some importance in formulating policy only between presidential campaigns in which the party has not elected the President.

Like the national convention, the national committee does not have much authority. It decides where and when to hold the next convention, and it raises some campaign funds. The **national chair,** formally elected by the national committee but usually chosen by the party's presidential nominee, dominates the national committee with the help of the committee's permanent staff. But it is rare for a national chair to emerge as a strong leader of the party, especially when the party holds the presidency, for then the President is the dominant figure.

The national party committees are concerned primarily with the presidential election, although in recent elections the National Republican Committee has become more active in giving financial aid to Republican candidates for other federal and state offices. The election campaigns of representatives and senators are also assisted by their parties' Congressional and Senatorial Campaign Committees. These committees provide money, research, campaign material, and speakers to party candidates. They are active in each election year, but they are more important in nonpresidential election years, since at those times the national party committees are less active.

The state party committees differ greatly from one state to another. In some states they are made up of county party chairs, while in others they are chosen in primaries or by local party conventions. They may include anywhere from fewer than one hundred to several hundred members. The power of the state committees also varies greatly. In some states they have genuine power and are responsible for drafting the party platform, recruiting candidates for statewide office, and raising campaign funds. In other states they have little noticeable effect on state politics.

The most important local party organization in most states is the county committee, which usually consists of all the precinct officials within the county. A **precinct** is the basic unit of party organization in many states and corresponds to the small local area in which elections are administered. The committee is headed by the county chair, who is generally elected by the committee's members. The county chair is active in campaign planning and fund raising and also participates in the recruitment of candidates for public office and for membership on the precinct committees. In some states there are congressional district party organiza-

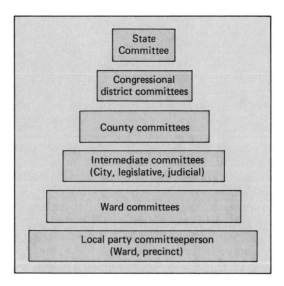

FIGURE 5.2 *Typical pyramid of party organization in a state.*

tions, which attempt to ensure that the district's representative will be relected and assist in providing services to his or her constituents.

Below the county committee are city and ward committees, which vary considerably in size and importance. (A **ward** is a local unit of party organization used in many cities and larger towns.) Like other party committees, they focus their efforts on campaigns and elections. The most basic party unit, however, is the *precinct committee*, which functions within a specific election or voting district. The strength of a precinct committee is directly related to its size: In urban areas a precinct may include as many as 2,000 voters, whereas in very rural areas there may be only a dozen voters in a precinct. Members of precinct committees engage in campaign activities, party organizational work such as recruitment of candidates and campaign workers, and dissemination of political information to voters.[12] (See Figure 5.2.)

The Decentralization of Party Power

While the government has become more and more centralized, the power of the political parties has remained in the hands of state and local units. The national parties, after all, nominate only two candidates for public office—the President and Vice President—at the party conventions held every four years. All other candidates for public office, including seats in Congress, are chosen by the state and local parties.

Even at the local level, however, the parties do not have the power they once had. The party "machines" of the late nineteenth century and the first half of the twentieth have declined in numbers and influence, though they are not yet entirely extinct. The classic *political machine* provided a host of services to the millions of immigrants from Eastern Europe who came to the United States and settled in the nation's largest cities. It helped with housing, food, legal services, employment—including government jobs— and other services. The party organization asked for only two things in return: loyalty to the machine and votes at election time.[13]

Although political machines did not develop in every large city, they were a major feature of the urban political scene for many decades. The extension of the civil service system in the twentieth century, the growth of government welfare programs as part of the New Deal in the 1930s, and the spread of economic prosperity after World War II all contributed to the decline of the big-city political machine.[14]

In contrast to the urban machine of the past, in many areas today party structure is loose and sometimes almost nonexistent. One study of political parties describes this condition as follows:

> In such cases, most of the committee positions in the party's county unit are unfilled or held by completely inactive incumbents. A chairman and a handful of loyal party officials may meet occasionally to carry out the most essential affairs of the party. Their main activity occurs shortly before the primary elections as they plead with members of the party to become candidates or offer themselves as candidates in order to "fill the party ticket." They are largely without influence or following, for often their party is a chronic minority party.

Mayor Richard Daley of Chicago at the 1976 Democratic Party National Convention in New York City. Until his death later in that year, Mayor Daley had long been a powerful figure in city, state, and national Democratic party politics. He was one of the last of the big city "bosses."

They meet infrequently, raise little money for election campaigns, and create little or no public attention.[15]

Most party organizations operate somewhere between the extremes of machine politics and disorganization, but it is fair to say that they are somewhat closer to the second than to the first. A typical county or city organization consists of a chair and an executive committee that meet frequently and are most active at election time. These officials are aided by a handful of volunteer activists who generally receive no salary and may not even have an office. The situation is even worse at the precinct level. Many precinct organizations do not have a chair or other official and do not even possess a list of local voters.[16]

The Decline of Party Identification

During long periods of U.S. history, many Americans identified strongly with one of the two major political parties. In describing the intense loyalty to the Republican party that was characteristic of the late nineteenth century, one author wrote:

> Many men were Republicans as they were church elders or lodge brothers. It was as if one belonged to an order. Their loyalties, their faith and pride in party, were often deeper, more vital to their self-respect and sense of worth than they could express. Delegates to Republican national conventions . . . sometimes had their official badges cast in gold and passed them along in their wills as precious relics.[17]

The same intensity could be seen in the devotion of many Americans to the Democratic party throughout much of the twentieth century, especially after the New Deal policies of the Roosevelt administration helped rescue the nation from the economic crisis of the 1930s. Political scientists use the term **party identification** to refer to the loyalty of voters to a particular party.

From the 1930s until the 1980s, public opinion surveys consistently showed the Democratic party with a wide lead over the Republicans in the number of people who identified with a political party. Only once in this long period (in 1946) did the Republicans reach parity with the Democrats. As recently as 1980, 41 percent of Americans said they were Democrats, while only 28 percent indicated that they were Republicans. But during the 1980s, support for the Republicans grew, and by the end of the decade, the Democrats held only a narrow lead.[18]

Another significant change in public opinion in the past fifty years has been the increase in the number of people who refer to themselves as independents. In 1940 only one out of five Americans were **independents**— people who do not identify with any political party. Today the proportion is closer to one out of three.

The decline in party identification can be seen in Americans of all ages, but it is especially striking among younger voters. Many young people who formerly identified with a party have become independents; in addition, new voters are increasingly likely to enter the electorate with no party ties. Together, these two groups account for about 75 percent of the decline in partisanship in the American electorate.[19]

Independent voters split their ticket when voting more often than those who identify with one of the major political parties. They show a moderate degree of interest in government and wait longer in the campaign before deciding on their candidate. But they are also less active politically, less knowledgeable, and less likely to vote than people who identify with a political party.[20]

Scholars have suggested several possible reasons for the general decline in party identification and the increase in the number of independent voters. One theory views the parties as going through a period of *realignment,* while a second major theory holds that they are in a period of *disintegration* or *dealignment.*

According to the realignment theory, voters are in the process of changing their party loyalties, and the result will be a system of new party allegiances.[21] Voting trends in recent national elections give some support to this theory. The Republican party's strength among white voters in the

South has sharply reduced one traditional base of Democratic party support. The Republicans have also significantly increased their share of the Catholic vote in the North, another group that once tended to vote for Democratic candidates. The Democrats have, however, continued to receive backing for these groups in local, state, and congressional elections.

According to the dealignment theory, the political parties are losing much of their importance. As the political scientist Walter Dean Burnham has written:

> The evidence lends some credence to the view that American electoral politics is undergoing a long-term transition into routines designed only to fill offices and symbolically affirm "the American way." There also seem to be tendencies for our political parties gradually to evaporate as broad and active intermediaries between the people and their rulers. . . . It is certain that the significance of party as link between government and the governed has now once again come into serious question.[22]

The effects of the decline of party identification can be seen in the coverage of elections by television and other media. References to the parties are far less frequent than they once were; at the same time, emphasis on individual candidates has increased dramatically. Indeed, Burnham has concluded, "Voting the candidate rather than the party" appears to have become part of the American political culture.[23]

As voters become less likely to use party identification as a basis for choosing among candidates, their choices become less rational. Faced with an array of candidates about whom they know very little, voters tend to rely on superficial criteria like the sound of a candidate's name or even his or her position on the ballot.[24]

The idea of a political system without parties, or with very weak parties, is a source of concern to many students of American politics. They believe that political parties are the only effective means by which citizens can hold public officials accountable for their actions or inaction. Without parties, responsibility for conduct cannot be placed on a team of officials from a single party who can be replaced at the next election. If the voters cannot blame the party for policy failures, where can responsibility be placed? Many observers see lack of accountability as a very serious problem; they believe that strong political parties are essential to the preservation of democratic government.

Reform or Status Quo?

The American two-party system has been criticized for not offering the voter a clear choice. The major party candidates, usually both middle-of-the-roaders, are more similar than they are different. It is also argued that the party has no control over its candidates once they have been elected—that it is impossible to force a candidate to keep campaign promises. In addition, the parties have been accused of being run by small groups of leaders while rank-and-file members have little say in party affairs.

Several proposals for reform of the party system have been made, including calls for a more centralized and democratic structure, more issue-oriented programs, and greater effort by officeholders to carry out their party's programs. Although there have been some revisions in party organization, the parties have ignored calls for drastic changes that would make them highly centralized, disciplined, and issue oriented.

Discussions about reform of the American political party system may be irrelevant if the parties continue to decline in importance. One observer has warned that parties are "an endangered species" and has called for "a renewed appreciation of what useful things parties—as institutions and not just as labels—are to have around." In this view, "restoring the organized parties to vigorous health . . . should be the [nation's] No. 1 reform objective."[25]

■ Interest Groups

The United States is a large nation with a large and diverse population. Interest groups reflect that diversity. Business, labor, agriculture, and consumers are represented by interest groups. So are social, religious, ethnic, and patriotic groups and people who are concerned about specific issues like the environment or abortion. Moreover, the goals of different groups in society often clash. For example, the goals of conservationists attempting to prevent the construction of nuclear power plants may conflict with those of workers in the area where a plant is to be built.

Many interests groups are formed at the local level to deal with city or neighborhood issues. Here a group meets in Austin, Texas, to discuss the need for affordable housing.

An **interest** or **pressure group** may be defined as a group of people who share common attitudes and interests and try to influence the political system by shaping public opinion, opposing or supporting candidates for public office, and influencing the decisions of government officials. Some interest groups are large and have a national membership; examples include the AFL-CIO and the American Legion. Others, such as a tenant group, may involve only a small number of people trying to solve a specific local problem. Some groups are formal, with a definite structure and a set of regulations; others are very informal and tend to dissolve when their goals have been achieved.

Almost all Americans either belong to one or more interest groups or are represented by such groups even though they are not members. In this way interest groups are similar to political parties; they represent the opinions and demands of citizens and use their strength to win benefits from the government. In fact, interest groups are a significant force in the formulation of public policy in the United States.

The Growth of Interest Groups

Interest groups of various kinds have existed throughout American history. But during the twentieth century their number has increased greatly, and since the 1970s there has been an explosion in the number of politically active groups. Of the approximately 3,000 such organizations with offices in Washington, D.C., 25 percent were founded after 1970.[26]

There are several reasons for the increase in the number of interest groups. One is the basic structure of American government; federalism and the separation of powers encourage group activity. If an interest group is unable to achieve its goals at the state level, for example, it may have more success in Washington. Or if a group cannot influence the legislative branch of the government, it can seek to gain the support of the executive branch or start a lawsuit in the courts to achieve its objectives.

The specialization of American society has also increased the number of interest groups that are active. The space program, for instance, has created new industries that are devoted to continuing and expanding that activity. These industries have similar concerns and have formed groups to represent them. The increase in the number of interest groups is also due partly to the success of many older groups, such as the American Medical Association and the National Rifle Association. Their example has convinced many Americans that the formation of an interest group is the best way to influence government.

The Structure of Interest Groups

Some interest groups have constitutions or charters, hold periodic elections, and charge membership dues. Many of the largest groups are organized like the government, with power divided between national and local levels.

The degree to which members take part in interest group activities varies widely. Some group members do not attend meetings or work for the group's goals; they are members in name only. Other members are active. They may be regular members who identify strongly with the group's goals or, in the case of the larger interest groups, professionals hired by the group to lobby on its behalf. (Lobbying will be discussed later in the chapter.)

Like political parties, interest groups depend heavily on their leaders. The leaders of a group control its professional staff and the information available to its members and to the public. The leaders also represent the group. Union leaders, for example, speak for the union as a whole. The more effective its leadership, therefore, the more powerful the group is likely to be.

Types of Interest Groups

Some interest groups are formed around a single issue and serve no purpose other than to work toward a favorable resolution of that issue. Most, however, are formed to serve their members' interests on a large number of subjects and on a continuing basis. As those interests change, so does the group's program. A number of groups have been formed to serve what they consider to be the *public interest* rather than the interests of any particular group. It is, of course, difficult or impossible to obtain agreement on what is meant by the "public interest"; some critics argue that there is no such thing as "a" public interest.

Farmers are an important interest group in the United States. Here farmers in Libertyville, Illinois, conduct a tractorcade protesting land acquisition by local open space districts.

117

In the past most interest groups have had an economic basis—agriculture, business, labor, and so forth. But there are also a variety of noneconomic interest groups based, for example, on racial or religious interests or on issues like gun control or drunk driving.

Economic Interest Groups. Most interest groups are formed to represent their members' economic interests. Agricultural groups, for instance, try to protect their members against the hardships caused by wildly fluctuating farm prices. The specialized nature of modern farming has led to a variety of groups, among them the American Livestock Association, the National Wool Growers Federation, and the National Apple Institute. There are also a number of larger groups that claim to represent farmers in general. These include the National Grange, the American Farm Bureau Federation, and the National Farmers' Union.

Business groups are similar to farmers' groups in that there are a variety of groups, called **trade associations,** that represent a single industry, as well as a few that claim to represent business as a whole. Among the former are the American Bankers Association and the Automobile Manufacturers Association. The major general business groups include the National Association of Manufacturers and the Chamber of Commerce of the United States.

Labor as a whole is represented by the AFL-CIO, a federation of more than one hundred unions. The AFL-CIO was created in 1955 by the merger of the American Federation of Labor, which is composed of skilled workers like carpenters, and the Congress of Industrial Organizations, which consists largely of unskilled workers in mass production industries like

Although their numbers have been in decline in recent years, union workers still are an important interest group in this country. Here union workers protest working conditions in local factories.

steel. Most of the nation's organized workers are affiliated with the AFL-CIO, which is very active and well financed. Membership in the AFL-CIO has declined in the past decade, largely as a result of the decline in American manufacturing. There are now about 17 million union members in the United States, or about 16.4 percent of the nation's work force, down from 24 percent in 1979.

Public employees—people who are employed by federal, state, or local governments—are the fastest-growing part of the American labor movement. Historically, governments have opposed the right of their workers to form unions. But since the 1960s this right has increasingly been recognized at all levels of government (though it is generally illegal for the unions to strike). Today unionized government workers account for 36.7 percent of the public work force.

The major unions of public employees are the American Federation of Teachers (AFT), the American Federation of State, County and Municipal Employees (AFSCME), both of which are connected with the AFL-CIO, and the National Education Association (NEA), an independent union. Not only have these groups pressed hard for increased benefits for their members, but they have also become major interest groups, spending large sums on political campaigns and lobbying on a wide variety of issues.

Professionals such as doctors and lawyers have their own interest groups. Although their membership is not large, these groups are respected because of the wealth and status of their members. **Professional associations** are concerned with licensing requirements in their states—that is, with the standards a person must meet in order to practice in the state—but they can also be very active on some issues related to government. The American Bar Association, for example, has long been concerned with the quality of appointees to the federal courts and since 1945 has been active in screening judicial nominees.

Noneconomic Interest Groups. Some noneconomic interest groups have a religious or moral basis (e.g., the National Conference of Catholic Charities, the National Council of Churches, and the American Jewish Congress); others are formed around specific issues like abortion. The interests of women are represented by several groups, of which perhaps the best known is the National Organization for Women (NOW), which has been active in eliminating gender-based discrimination. The Sierra Club is one of a number of organizations that are concerned with conservation and environmental problems. The interests of blacks are the concern of groups like the National Association for the Advancement of Colored People (NAACP), the Urban League, and the Southern Christian Leadership Conference, organized by Rev. Martin Luther King, Jr. Of the groups that claim to speak for the public interest, the largest is Common Cause, which was established in 1970 to "uphold the public interest against all comers, particularly the special interests that dominate our lives today."[27]

New Types of Interest Groups

As the strength of the political parties has declined, new kinds of groups have arisen to claim the loyalty of people who once identified with a major party. Foremost among these are the single-issue interest groups and political action committees.

Single-Issue Groups. An important trend in recent years has been the rise of **single-issue interest groups,** which focus entirely on a single issue, such as abortion or nuclear power. Groups like the National Abortion Rights Action League and the National Right to Life Committee, for example, put large amounts of money and effort into seeing that their stand on the abortion issue becomes a policy of government at all levels. They judge candidates and public officials by their views on one issue. In some primary and general elections the outcome can depend on how much pressure such groups place both on the candidates and on the voters. The result, according to some experts, is the "fragmentation" of American politics and failure to consider the overall public good.[28]

Another example of a single-issue group, one that has been far more effective than its small size would suggest, is Mothers Against Drunk Driving (MADD). Formed by mothers who have lost children in accidents caused by drunken drivers, MADD's intense lobbying efforts have been highly successful. In 1984, for example, Congress enacted a law providing that states failing to prohibit the sale of alcoholic beverages to people under 21 years of age will be ineligible to receive federal highway funds.

Political Action Committees (PACs). Labor unions and corporations are barred by federal law from making direct contributions to political campaigns, and trade unions cannot use members' dues to make contributions to candidates. To escape these prohibitions, many unions and corporations have created independent **political action committees** (PACs). The PACs have been successful in raising and spending large sums of money obtained from voluntary contributions by union members and corporate officers, and they take positions on a variety of national issues. The 1974 amendments to the Federal Election Campaign Act expressly sanctioned the creation of political action committees, and the number of such organizations has multiplied since then.

In addition to trade unions and corporations, many other types of interest groups have created PACs. The National Association of Realtors, the American Medical Association, and the National Rifle Association have three of the best-financed PACs. There are a number of ideological PACs, of which the majority are conservative. An example of the latter is the National Conservative Political Action Committee. Some PACs take an active interest in issues that affect other nations. For example, a number of pro-Israel PACs are very active in Washington.

Once an organization has established a political action committee, it can raise money from its members or employees. Under federal law the PAC can spend up to $5,000 for each candidate it supports in a particular election, with no limit on the total amount it can spend. Some PACs also engage in other kinds of political activity: assisting in voter registration, operating telephone banks, distributing campaign literature, and canvassing potential voters. The money spent on these activities does not count toward the $5,000 limit as long as the PAC's activities are kept separate from those of the candidate's personal campaign organization.

There were about 350 PACs in 1975 and 2,100 in 1980. By the late 1980s the number of trade association, corporate, labor, and private PACs had risen to 4,828.[29] The number of PACs is expected to continue to rise, though at a slower pace, unless Congress adopts new legislation to curb their influence.

In recent years the issue of ethics, both in Congress and the executive branch, has taken on greater importance in the minds of many Americans. In 1989 several prominent members of Congress, including the Speaker of the House, were forced to resign because of unethical behavior. More recent controversies over ethics have centered on the rise of PACs that spend large amounts on the campaigns of candidates for public office.[30] (See Figure 5.3.)

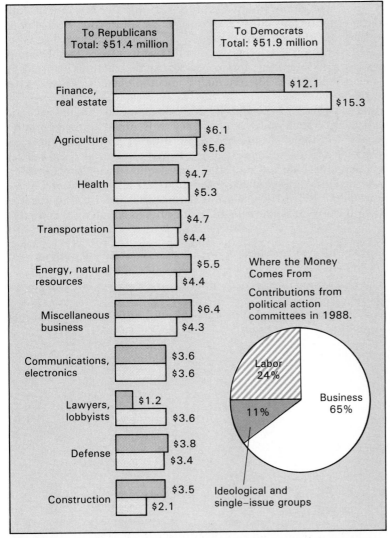

FIGURE 5.3 *Contributions by business political action committees during the 1988 Congressional races (in millions of dollars).*

Source: Center for Responsive Politics, as reported in *The New York Times*, September 16, 1990, p. 26. Copyright © 1990 by The New York Times Company. Reprinted by permission.

Since much of this money goes to incumbent legislators who are seeking reelection, the public increasingly sees government (especially Congress) as being "bought" or used by special interests. The problem of campaign spending and proposals for reform will be discussed more fully in the next chapter.

The Activities of Interest Groups

The chief method used by interest groups to influence public policy is **lobbying,** trying to persuade legislators to vote for or against a particular bill or to convince members of the executive branch that a particular program is or is not desirable. Some interest groups also attempt to achieve their policy goals by bringing lawsuits in the courts or by supporting legal actions begun by other individuals or organizations. Grassroots activity designed to influence public opinion is another frequently used strategy. Finally, many interest groups give financial and other forms of electoral support to candidates for public office. Different tactics are employed in lobbying these different audiences.

Lobbying Congress. Lobbying in Congress may be directed at individual legislators and their staffs, but much effort is aimed at the committee that deals with the issue of concern to the interest group. Lobbyists for interest groups often testify before congressional committees and submit prepared statements that present the organization's views on specific issues. These personal appearances and documents enable interest groups to present detailed information about a particular subject to members of Congress—knowledge members might not be able to obtain from any other source.

The actress Morgan Fairchild testifies before a budget committee of Congress in support of increased governmental financing of AIDS research.

POLITICAL PARTIES AND INTEREST GROUPS

Lobbyists in the corridors of Congress. They are an important feature of government in Washington, D.C., and in the state capitals of this nation.

Interest groups pay their lobbyists to keep up to date on developments within the government that could affect the group's members. Accordingly, lobbyists become experts not only in the subject their interest group is concerned with but also on the House and Senate committees and subcommittees that deal with that topic. They keep an eye on the activities of those committees and try to establish close ties with the committee members, especially the chairs.

The people who are employed by interest groups come from varied backgrounds. Some are former members of Congress who are familiar with legislative and administrative processes. Others are lawyers, public relations experts, and former administrators who have served in the federal bureaucracy. But most interest groups employ "in-house" lobbyists—staff members who work on either a full- or part-time basis as representatives of the group.[31]

Lobbying the Executive Branch. In some cases, agencies of the executive branch are more important targets of lobbying efforts than individual members and committees of Congress. Not only does the executive branch administer policies that have been enacted by Congress, but it often takes the initiative in proposing new policies. The President and his staff have an especially important role in policy making.

Although the President is less accessible than other government officials, there are numerous ways in which interest groups can influence decision making in the White House. That influence may be direct—for example, when the President asks representatives of an interest group for information and advice in drawing up a legislative proposal. More often, however, the influence is indirect, occurring through contacts with members of the President's staff. Lobbyists also seek to influence policy in the executive branch by influencing the decisions of policy-making officials in the departments and agencies of the government. The key to success in the executive branch is knowing precisely which individuals on the White House staff or in the bureaucracy have the greatest influence on policy making in a particular area.

Acting Through the Courts. The courts are protected by law from all direct lobbying activities. But there are several ways in which interest groups can indirectly influence the judiciary. One of those ways is to bring lawsuits in the courts. The best-known example of such action is the series of cases brought by groups like the National Association for the Advancement of Colored People to enforce the civil rights of African Americans. The Supreme Court case of *Brown* v. *Board of Education of Topeka* (1954),[32] which made school segregation unconstitutional, was begun by the NAACP. Similarly, the American Civil Liberties Union (ACLU) has represented many individuals in cases involving the Bill of Rights. It has been active in litigating many issues involving freedom of speech and religion and the rights of the criminally accused.

Interest groups can also file **amicus curiae** ("friend of the court") **briefs.** In such cases the group, while not a party to the actual conflict, can present its views on the issues in question and try to convince the court of the merits of its arguments. The NAACP and the ACLU frequently file amicus curiae briefs in civil liberties and civil rights cases. Groups representing labor, consumers, women, and the professions also file such briefs.

Grassroots Activities. Interest groups also engage in activities designed to influence public opinion. The goal may be to gain support for basic values (democracy, the family, the American way of life, etc.) or to shape public opinion on a specific issue. The tactics used take many forms, including obtaining exposure in the news media, buying advertisements and engaging in other forms of public relations, and publicizing the voting records of legislators.[33]

All of these campaigns seek to shape public opinion in the hope that the public will, in turn, put pressure on Congress or the executive branch to adopt the policies favored by the interest group. Lobbyists have long understood that grassroots activities are an important part of interest group politics and that their efforts in Washington "are aided by a strong show of support from those back home."[34]

Support from those back home may be expressed in the form of letters, telegrams, and telephone calls to senators and representatives. In addition, delegations from the home district or state of a member of Congress may make a personal visit to express their opinions on an issue, implying that an unfavorable response will result in loss of voter support at election time.

Pressure at the grassroots level can be quite effective. On numerous occasions in recent decades, for example, the National Rifle Association generated a flood of letters opposing proposals for tighter gun controls. On the other hand, members of Congress can often tell when an inflow of mail has been artificially created. When many letters arrive at about the same time, are printed or mimeographed, and have similar wording, the member may quickly conclude that their content represents interest group activity and not a grassroots groundswell of opinion.

Interest groups also advertise in newspapers or on television to get their "message" across to the public. They hope that the public will support their views and will put pressure on the government to adopt the policies they favor. Or they may simply hope that the public will develop a favorable attitude toward the interest group. Many large corporations, for example, help finance public television programs and radio broadcasts of cultural events.

Finally, grassroots activities may take the form of public demonstrations. When they are carried out on a large scale, these events are usually planned and organized by coalitions of groups with shared policy goals. During the 1960s and 1970s, for example, civil rights groups and groups opposed to the war in Vietnam organized many demonstrations designed to win public support for their views.

In the past several decades many other groups have held demonstra-

IN 1988, HANDGUNS KILLED
7 PEOPLE IN GREAT BRITAIN
19 IN SWEDEN
53 IN SWITZERLAND
25 IN ISRAEL
13 IN AUSTRALIA
8 IN CANADA
AND 8,915 IN THE UNITED STATES.

GOD BLESS AMERICA.

Help stop handgun violence.
Call 1-900-226-4455.
A letter will be sent in your name to your
Member of Congress urging support of stronger gun laws.
(The $2.75 cost of the call will appear on your phone bill.)
Handgun Control, Inc., 1225 Eye Street, N.W.
Washington, D.C. 20005

STOP HANDGUNS BEFORE THEY STOP YOU.

An advertisement published by a Washington, D.C., organization favoring the control of handguns. The ad seeks to obtain grassroots support for this type of legislation.

tions at both the local and national levels. At times demonstrations have been so common that their organizers have been unable to obtain media coverage for them. Yet coverage on the evening news shows is of central importance in getting the public to pay attention to the demonstration and its organizers' policy objectives.

There is always a danger that demonstrations will alienate the public. People may see them as "unruly exercises or as reflecting a narrow, selfish view." Demonstrations may also defeat their purpose if their organizers resort to excesses. This occurred, for example, when farmers drove tractors through the streets of the nation's capital to protest their economic condition. Finally, demonstrations, regardless of their form, cannot be successful unless they are combined "with other tactics in a sustained lobbying drive."[35]

Electoral Support. Many interest groups contribute money to political campaigns. The major role of political action committees in financing congressional campaigns has already been mentioned. Besides contributing funds to the candidates they favor, interest groups may also offer other forms of electoral support, such as providing political consultants, sponsoring public opinion polls, organizing campaigns to register voters, and providing workers to staff local campaign organizations.

Many ethical questions have been raised by critics of the present system of financing congressional campaigns; the role of political action committees is especially controversial. This topic will be considered in greater detail in Chapter 6.

The Funding of Interest Groups

Interest groups obtain the money to finance their activities in a variety of ways. Corporations, of course, can simply budget a particular amount for lobbying activities. Noncorporate interest groups generally raise money from several kinds of sources. Most rely on dues paid by members, but the proportion of revenues obtained in this way differs greatly from one group to another. Many groups also obtain gifts and donations from individuals and corporations and grants from foundations.

Another source of organizational income is staff-generated revenues of various kinds. These revenues come from magazines, pamphlets, informational booklets, and the like that are sold to members and the public, as well as from conferences, seminars, training sessions, and other services. A few groups also obtain income from financial investments and endowments; an example is the American Medical Association, which earns several million dollars a year in investment income.[36]

The Power of Interest Groups

Power is not evenly distributed among interest groups. Some groups are large and influential, others small and relatively unimportant. The larger groups tend to have more power because they benefit from the support of thousands and sometimes millions of members. Loyalty can also be an important factor. If a group is unified and its members are able to agree on specific goals and work together to achieve those goals, the group will be more powerful. In addition, some groups are more powerful because they are better organized and have more financial resources than others.

The uneven distribution of power in the "pressure group system" has been a subject of much criticism. Some groups, it is claimed, are simply too big, too powerful, and too effective. Some are not opposed by other groups, or if they are, the opposition is weak.

Another criticism of interest groups is that they represent only a small percentage of the population—a minority with very specific, narrow interests—and that the widely held view that interest groups represent the majority of the population is a myth. One political scientist, writing in 1960, stated that "pressure politics is essentially the politics of small groups. The system is skewed, loaded, and unbalanced in favor of a fraction of a minority"—those in the highest social, economic, and educational categories.[37] The great increase in the number of interest groups based on fairly broad citizen participation makes it unlikely that this criticism remains valid today.

Efforts to limit the power of interest groups have centered on controlling the activities of lobbyists. In 1946 Congress passed the Federal Regulation of Lobbying Act, which required lobbyists to register with the government, list their employer and salary, and file quarterly financial reports with the Senate and the House of Representatives. This legislation has been ineffective because loopholes in the law make it possible for many lobbyists to avoid registering. Only a small percentage of Washington lobbyists comply with the 1946 law.

On several occasions Congress has considered legislation that would tighten the registration and disclosure requirements governing Washington lobbyists. But it has never adopted those proposals, and it seems unlikely that it will adopt any reform legislation of this type in the foreseeable future.

■ Summary

The second half of the twentieth century has brought major changes to the American political system. The political parties have declined in importance and influence, and it seems doubtful that they will regain their former strength and power. There are many reasons for the decline of political parties. Civil service has replaced party patronage as the method by which government jobs are obtained. Most social services, which used to be provided by the parties, are now funded and administered by government.

Candidates for public office no longer depend on the political parties for the money and services needed to run campaigns; increasingly they rely on contributions from political action groups. Finally, as we will see in the next chapter, presidential campaigns are now financed by government funds. This money is given directly to candidates, not to their parties, thereby adding to the independence of presidential candidates from their party organizations.

While political parties have been in

decline, the number and importance of interest groups have grown. A wide variety of interest groups have become active in attempting to shape government policy. Of course some of these groups are not new—some date back to the nineteenth century. But many were created in the past twenty years, including most of the single-issue interest groups and political action committees.

Perhaps the most important, and in some ways the most disturbing, development of recent years is the tendency for "issue politics" to replace "party politics." A group may form around a particular issue, push for the enactment of a specific law, and keep an eye on the way that law is carried out. Many people find such activity much more satisfying than traditional party politics. For one thing, it produces visible results: Citizens working together may succeed in blocking the development of a wildlife habitat or preventing the building of a nuclear power plant. For another, issue politics permits people to choose the problem that concerns them most deeply and concentrate on it. Party politics, by contrast, deals with many public matters, and a citizen may agree with some of the party's policies but not with others.

Many observers contend that interest group activity has resulted in greater participation in the political process; more people are members of politically active organizations and more are going to meetings, writing to members of the legislature, lobbying Congress, collecting signatures on petitions, and the like. Moreover, individuals working in interest groups gain a greater sense of purpose than can be obtained from working for a party, and they can be involved year round, not just at election time.

There are drawbacks to issue politics, however. Interest groups often lack the ability to compromise the way the parties can, and they make it harder for government officials to reach workable solutions to problems. Moreover, unlike the parties, interest groups are not responsible for the success or failure of government programs. Thus, even though the proliferation of interest groups has resulted in increased representation, it has also resulted in decreased accountability and responsibility.[38]

■ Key Terms

political party
two-party system
multiparty system
minor party
national convention
national committee

national chair
precinct
ward
party identification
independent
interest group

trade association
professional association
single-issue interest group
political action committee
lobbying
amicus curiae brief

■ Suggested Reading

ALLSWANG, JOHN. *Bosses, Machines, and Urban Voters.* Baltimore: Johns Hopkins University Press, 1986.

CIGLER, ALLAN J., and BURDETTE A. LOOMIS, eds. *Interest Group Politics*, 3rd ed. Washington, D.C.: Congressional Quarterly Press, 1990.

COHEN, BENJAMIN J. *In Whose Interest?* New Haven, Conn.: Yale University Press, 1986.

POLITICAL PARTIES AND INTEREST GROUPS

Epstein, Leon D. *Political Parties in the American Mold.* Madison, Wis.: University of Wisconsin Press, 1986.

Frantzich, Stephen E. *Political Parties in the Technological Age.* New York: Longman, 1989.

Hertzke, Allan D. *Representing God in Washington: The Role of Religious Lobbies in the American Polity.* Knoxville, Tenn.: University of Tennessee Press, 1988.

Lamis, Alexander P. *The Two-Party South.* New York: Oxford University Press, 1988.

Lowi, Theodore J. *The End of Liberalism.* New York: Norton, 1969.

Rosenstone, Steven J., Roy L. Behr, and Edward H. Lazarus. *Third Parties in America: Citizen Response to Major Party Failure.* Princeton, N.J.: Princeton University Press, 1984.

Sabato, Larry J. *PAC Power: Inside the World of Political Action Committees.* New York: Norton, 1984.

————. *The Party's Just Begun: Shaping Political Parties for America's Future.* New York: Harper Collins, 1988.

Wattenberg, Martin P. *The Decline of American Parties, 1952–1984.* Cambridge, Mass.: Harvard University Press, 1986.

■ Notes

1. Clinton Rossiter, *Parties and Politics in America* (Ithaca, N.Y.: Cornell University Press, 1960), p. 67.

2. William J. Keefe, *Parties, Politics, and Public Policy in America*, 5th ed. (Washington, D.C.: Congressional Quarterly Press, 1988), p. 29.

3. Ibid., pp. 30–31.

4. Ibid., pp. 31–33.

5. Frank J. Sorauf and Paul Allen Beck, *Party Politics in America*, 6th ed. (Glenview, Ill.: Scott, Foresman, 1988), pp. 43–47.

6. Ibid., pp. 47–49.

7. Malcolm E. Jewell and David M. Olsen, *Political Parties and Elections in American States*, 3rd ed. (Chicago: Dorsey Press, 1988), p. 44.

8. Fred I. Greenstein and Frank B. Feigert, *The American Party System and the American People*, 3rd ed. (Englewood Cliffs, N.J.: Prentice-Hall, 1985), p. 84.

9. Keefe, *Parties, Politics, and Public Policy*, p. 60.

10. Ibid., p. 65.

11. Sorauf and Beck, *Party Politics*, pp. 50–56.

12. Keefe, *Parties, Politics, and Public Policy*, pp. 21–23.

13. Ruth K. Scott and Ronald J. Hrebenar, *Parties in Crisis*, 2nd ed. (New York: John Wiley, 1984), p. 119.

14. Ibid., pp. 120–123.

15. Sorauf and Beck, *Party Politics*, p. 91.

16. Ibid., pp. 91–92.

17. David McCullogh, *Mornings on Horseback* (New York: Simon & Schuster, 1981), p. 297.

18. Michael Oreskes, "Republicans Show Gains in Loyalty," *The New York Times*, January 21, 1990, p. 22.

19. Keefe, *Parties, Politics, and Public Policy*, pp. 171–173.

20. Sorauf and Beck, *Party Politics*, pp. 202–203.

21. James L. Sundquist, *Dynamics of the Party System* (Washington, D.C.: Brookings Institution, 1973), pp. 1–2.

22. Walter Dean Burnham, "The End of American Party Politics," *Transaction*, 7 (1969), 20.

23. Walter Dean Burnham, "Foreword," in Martin P. Wattenberg, *The Decline of American Political Parties, 1952–1984* (Cambridge, Mass.: Harvard University Press, 1986), p. xii.

24. Greenstein and Feigert, *American Party System*, p. 159.

25. Everett C. Ladd, Jr., *Where Have All the Voters Gone?* 2nd ed. (New York: Norton, 1982), pp. 72–73.

26. Kay Lehman Schlozman and John T. Tierney, *Organized Interests and American Democracy* (New York: Harper and Row, 1986), p. 75.

27. Quoted in Richard Halloran, "New Lobby Fights Special Interests," *New York Times*, February 3, 1971, p. 39.

28. William J. Crotty, *American Parties in Decline*, 2nd ed. (Boston: Little, Brown, 1984), pp. 142–143.

29. Report of the Federal Election Commission, quoted in Richard L. Berke, "Political Action Committees Giving More to Incumbent Democrats," *The New York Times*, April 9, 1989, p. 22.

30. David B. Magleby, "Prospects for Reform," in Margaret Latus Nugent and John R. Johannes, eds., *Money, Elections, and Democracy: Reforming Congressional Campaign Finance* (Boulder, Colo.: Westview Press, 1990), p. 246.

31. Ronald J. Hrebenar and Ruth K. Scott, *Interest Group Politics in America* (Englewood Cliffs, N.J.: Prentice-Hall, 1982), pp. 62–71.

32. 347 U.S. 483 (1954).

33. Jeffrey M. Berry, *The Interest Group Society*, 2nd ed. (Glenview, Ill.: Scott, Foresman, 1989), pp. 105–109.

34. Ibid., p. 116.

35. Berry, *Interest Group Society*, pp. 110–112.

36. Schlozman and Tierney, *Organized Interests and American Democracy*, pp. 90–92.

37. E. E. Schattschneider, *The Semisovereign People* (Fort Worth, Tex.: Holt, Rinehart and Winston, 1960), p. 35.

38. Hrebenar and Scott, *Interest Group Politics*, p. 259.

6

Chapter Outline

Nomination Procedures

Nominating a Presidential Candidate
Choosing the Delegates
The Preconvention Campaign
The National Convention

The Campaign
Campaign Financing
Reforming Campaign Financing
Congressional Campaigns
Campaign Strategy
Television Debates

The Election
Registration
Balloting
The Electoral College
Congressional Elections

Questions for Thought

What is a presidential primary? A caucus?

Should the parties continue to hold national party conventions every four years? Why?

How are presidential campaigns financed?

What is the electoral college, and how does it function?

Should the electoral college be abolished? What should take its place?

Why is there such a high reelection rate for incumbent members of the House of Representatives?

Nominations and Elections

I N this chapter we will discuss nomination and election procedures, campaign strategy, legislation affecting campaign financing, and the electoral college. Part of the chapter will focus on the complex methods by which presidential candidates are nominated. We will begin, however, with a general history and discussion of the various methods of nominating public officials at the national, state, and local levels.

■ Nomination Procedures

In most democratic nations candidates for public office are chosen by the political parties. The United States, however, has not followed this practice.

131

Since the beginning of the nineteenth century, reformers have successfully argued for the adoption of nomination systems that would be more democratic—that is, would weaken the political parties and give the people the right to choose candidates.

The earliest means of choosing candidates for public office was the *legislative caucus.* In Congress and in each state legislature, party caucuses composed of the elected legislators of each political party met privately to select their party's candidates. The legislative caucus as it originally operated had an obvious defect; districts that had elected legislators from one party were not represented in the caucus of the other party. To remedy this defect, the so-called *mixed caucus* was developed. Delegates from districts that were not represented were permitted to join the caucus to make nomination decisions.

But this reform proved to be short-lived, and it was not long before the caucus system was largely abandoned. Andrew Jackson, the popular war hero from the West, and his supporters succeeded in overturning what they called "King Caucus." In the 1824 election the party caucus failed to pick Jackson, the most popular candidate. Jackson's backers realized that the congressional caucus would never nominate him for President. They therefore sought to discredit the system by arguing that it was undemocratic.

In place of the caucus the Jacksonians favored the **convention** system, contending that it would democratize American politics. In the convention system, decisions are made by delegates, who are generally loyal party members. By the time of the 1832 election, the convention was used by both major political parties to nominate candidates for President and Vice President. It was gradually adopted by the states to nominate candidates for other national, state, and local public offices and to elect party officials and delegates. Although the convention still permitted party leaders to exercise great control over nominations, its adoption was a significant step toward making the nomination system more democratic.

Early in the twentieth century a reform movement known as progressivism pressed for the abolition of the convention system. The progressives contended that this method of nominating candidates was not sufficiently democratic. In its place they favored the use of the primary system. A **primary** is an election in which voters select a political party's candidates for local, state, and national office, and in some states select party officials such as members of party committees and convention delegates.

The primary system has been adopted by most of the states and has become the most common method of nominating people for public office. It is also used in most states to elect party officials, such as state and local committee members, and delegates to conventions, especially the national conventions. A person can get his or her name placed on a primary ballot by means of a petition signed by a required number of registered voters. Thus, there can be a number of candidates in a primary election, though frequently there is only one (i.e., there is no contest for the nomination).

Some states require the use of a **runoff primary** when none of the candidates receives a majority of the votes in a primary election. This is likely to occur in one-party areas. Many candidates may run in the dominant party's primary but be unable to garner 50 percent of the vote.

The runoff primary is a contest between the two candidates who receive the highest number of votes. Such primaries are used in most southern states and in a few strongly Democratic northern cities such as New York.

The primary system has largly replaced the convention, although conventions are still used by a small minority of the states to nominate at least some public officials, and in a few they are still used to nominate candidates for statewide offices (e.g., Michigan uses a convention to nominate its gubernatorial candidates). In several states losing candidates can demand that a primary be held if their vote in the convention was above a certain percentage.

There are two basic types of primaries: closed and open. Thirty-eight states use the **closed primary,** in which only voters who have registered with a particular party may vote. Nine states use an **open primary,** in which the voter does not have to register as a party member before taking part. On primary day the voter can select the ballot of the party in whose primary he or she wants to participate. Two states, Alaska and Washington, go even further and use a so-called **blanket primary,** in which voters do not have to choose a party and are also free to vote in more than one primary—for example, voting Republican for one office and Democratic for another.

The major political parties generally favor the closed primary. Since any person who is registered can participate in an open primary, it is harder for the party organization to control nominations. Open primaries also encourage "raiding," in which voters who normally support one political party invade the other's primary and cast their ballot for a weak or unpopular candidate. If that person wins the primary, the other party's nominee has a better chance of winning the general election.

Nominating a Presidential Candidate

The procedures for nominating a presidential candidate differ from those used to nominate other public officials. The national convention system, created by the Jacksonians in the early nineteenth century, has been retained for this purpose. The national conventions of both major parties formally choose their presidential and vice presidential candidates. But the system is complicated by the use of state primaries, caucuses, and conventions to select the delegates who will attend the national conventions.

Choosing the Delegates

Presidential Primaries. First used in Wisconsin in 1905, the **presidential primary** has now been adopted by a majority of the states. In 1956 nineteen states had primaries. By 1976 the total had reached twenty-nine, and in 1988 thirty-eight states held primaries for either or both major political parties.

States rushed to adopt the presidential primary as it became more and

Supporters of various presidential candidates near a polling place in Nashua, New Hampshire, during that state's presidential primary in February 1988.

more evident that the nominations of the major parties were being decided in the preconvention primary campaigns. Since the early 1960s a large majority of the candidates have been chosen in this way. Rather than deny voters the right to influence the selection of presidential candidates, state legislatures have adopted state presidential primary laws. The primary takes the formal selection of delegates out of the control of state party leaders and places it in the hands of the voters. Moreover, primaries not only elect delegates but also make it possible for a candidate to demonstrate the ability to attract voters. Candidates who cannot demonstrate popular support are soon eliminated from the race.

Changes in party rules have also encouraged states to adopt the primary system. The Democratic party's requirement that delegates be chosen in a nondiscriminatory manner and that they be representative of the state's population has helped make the primary the preferred method of delegate selection.[1]

The exact form of the primary varies, depending on state law. Most states have some form of presidential preference ballot in which voters are able to express their preference for a particular candidate. An increasing number of states combine the preference vote with the selection of delegates. Some states require a separate vote for the candidate and the delegates, while a few hold a presidential preference vote but select delegates through a convention system. Delegates may be chosen in primaries held at the local level *(district delegates)* or on a statewide basis *(at large delegates)*. (See Figure 6.1 for an example of a presidential primary ballot.)

Each party determines the total number of delegates who will attend its national convention. In 1988 there were 4,161 delegates to the Democratic Convention and 2,277 to the Republican Convention. These figures result from the parties' use of different formulas to assign delegates to each state and territory represented at the convention.

The formulas used by the parties to assign a number of delegates to each state are too complex to be discussed here. The consequences of

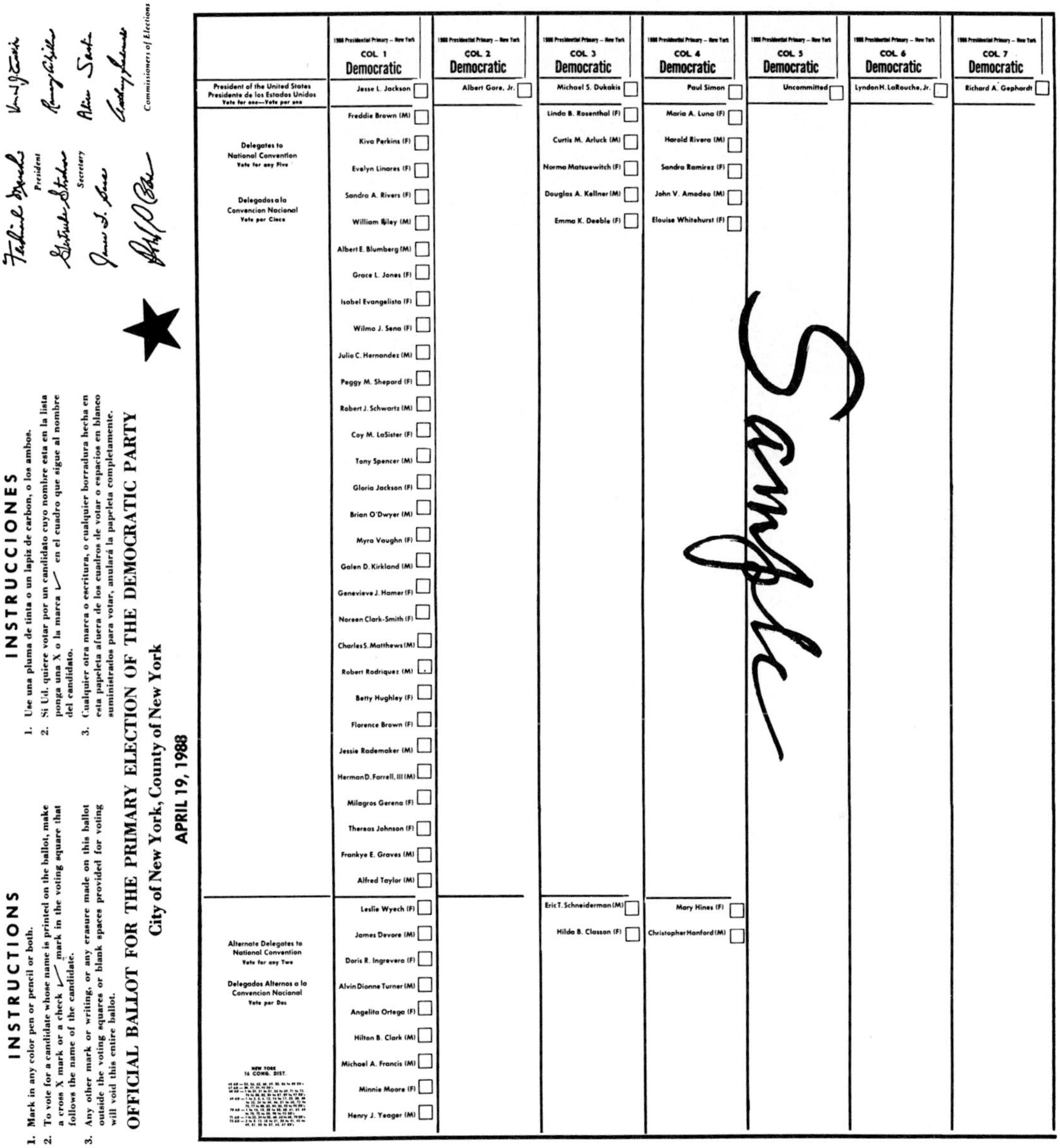
INSTRUCTIONS

1. Mark in any color pen or pencil or both.
2. To vote for a candidate whose name is printed on the ballot, make a cross X mark or a check ✓ mark in the voting square that follows the name of the candidate.
3. Any other mark or writing, or any erasure made on this ballot outside the voting squares or blank spaces provided for voting will void this entire ballot.

INSTRUCCIONES

1. Use una pluma de tinta o un lapiz de carbon, o los ambos.
2. Si Ud. quiere votar por un candidato cuyo nombre esta en la lista ponga una X o la marca ✓ en el cuadro que sigue al nombre del candidato.
3. Cualquier otra marca o escritura, o cualquier borradura hecha en esta papeleta afuera de los cuadros de votar o espacios en blanco suministrados para votar, anulará la papeleta completamente.

OFFICIAL BALLOT FOR THE PRIMARY ELECTION OF THE DEMOCRATIC PARTY
City of New York, County of New York
APRIL 19, 1988

President — Secretary — Commissioners of Elections

	1988 Presidential Primary — New York COL 1 Democratic	1988 Presidential Primary — New York COL 2 Democratic	1988 Presidential Primary — New York COL 3 Democratic	1988 Presidential Primary — New York COL 4 Democratic	1988 Presidential Primary — New York COL 5 Democratic	1988 Presidential Primary — New York COL 6 Democratic	1988 Presidential Primary — New York COL 7 Democratic
President of the United States / Presidente de los Estados Unidos / Vote for one—Vote por uno	Jesse L. Jackson	Albert Gore, Jr.	Michael S. Dukakis	Paul Simon	Uncommitted	Lyndon H. LaRouche, Jr.	Richard A. Gephardt
Delegates to National Convention / Vote for any Five / Delegados a la Convencion Nacional / Vote por Cinco	Freddie Brown (M)		Linda B. Rosenthal (F)	Maria A. Luna (F)			
	Kiva Perkins (F)		Curtis M. Arluck (M)	Harold Rivera (M)			
	Evelyn Linares (F)		Norma Matsuewitch (F)	Sandra Ramirez (F)			
	Sandra A. Rivers (F)		Douglas A. Kellner (M)	John V. Amodeo (M)			
	William Riley (M)		Emma K. Deeble (F)	Elouise Whitehurst (F)			
	Albert E. Blumberg (M)						
	Grace L. Jones (F)						
	Isabel Evangelista (F)						
	Wilma J. Sena (F)						
	Julio C. Hernandez (M)						
	Peggy M. Shepard (F)						
	Robert J. Schwartz (M)						
	Coy M. LaSister (F)						
	Tony Spencer (M)						
	Gloria Jackson (F)						
	Brian O'Dwyer (M)						
	Myra Vaughn (F)						
	Galen D. Kirkland (M)						
	Genevieve J. Hamer (F)						
	Noreen Clark-Smith (F)						
	Charles S. Matthews (M)						
	Robert Rodriquez (M)						
	Betty Hughley (F)						
	Florence Brown (F)						
	Jessie Rademaker (M)						
	Herman D. Farrell, III (M)						
	Milagros Gerena (F)						
	Theresa Johnson (F)						
	Frankye E. Graves (M)						
	Alfred Taylor (M)						
Alternate Delegates to National Convention / Vote for any Two / Delegados Alternos a la Convencion Nacional / Vote por Dos	Leslie Wyech (F)		Eric T. Schneiderman (M)	Mary Hines (F)			
	James Devore (M)		Hilda B. Classon (F)	Christopher Hanford (M)			
	Doris R. Ingrevera (F)						
	Alvin Dionne Turner (M)						
	Angelita Ortega (F)						
	Hilton B. Clark (M)						
	Michael A. Francis (M)						
	Minnie Moore (F)						
	Henry J. Yeager (M)						

NEW YORK 16 CONG. DIST.

Sample

FIGURE 6.1 ***Democratic Party presidential primary ballot, New York City, April 1988.***

applying those formulas, however, can easily be described. The Democratic party's rules favor the most heavily populated states, especially those in the Northeast and the Midwest. The Republican party's rules give greater delegate strength to states in the South, Southwest, and West. Thus the Democratic party generally produces more liberal delegates, while the Republican party produces more conservative ones.

Caucuses and Conventions. In states that do not use primaries, delegates to county conventions are chosen by **caucuses**—meetings of

Residents of Norwood-ville, Iowa, at their presidential caucus in the local fire station in February 1988.

party members at the local or precinct level. The county conventions select delegates to district or state conventions, which in turn select delegates to the national convention. Between 1968 and 1980 the proportion of delegates chosen in states using the caucus system decreased from 42 percent to less than 25 percent. In 1988 only about one-quarter of the delegates were chosen by caucuses.

Traditionally, party caucuses were controlled by the political parties, which were able to have party regulars chosen as delegates. But in recent presidential nominating campaigns candidates have encouraged political activists to attend caucus meetings. Their efforts have been furthered by interest groups such as teachers unions and environmental groups, which also urge their members to attend caucus meetings and support particular candidates.

The Preconvention Campaign

Before the major party conventions meet, each candidate attempts to win the support of a majority of the delegates, or at least enough support to provide a chance of being nominated. Nowadays candidates concentrate on winning state primaries, starting with the first primary, which is held in New Hampshire. A candidate who can win in the early primaries will gain not only delegate support but also national publicity, the support of delegates from states that use a caucus system, increased financial backing, and greater popularity with voters. A series of primary victories, combined with growing popularity in public opinion polls, can produce a "bandwagon effect" in which delegates rally to the support of the candidate they believe is likely to win the nomination.

Candidates also organize and campaign in nonprimary states. In recent presidential campaigns, the Iowa local caucuses have become especially important. These meetings (which were held in early February during the

1988 campaign) provide the first indications of the popularity of the various candidates. Consequently, candidates have put considerable time and effort into gaining support at the Iowa caucuses.

In 1988, for the first time in twenty years, the incumbent President was not seeking reelection. As a result, a large number of candidates entered the race for the presidential nomination in both the Republican and the Democratic parties. The contest in the Republican party was decided fairly quickly. Kansas Senator Robert Dole won an early victory in the Iowa caucus, and public opinion polls showed him ahead in New Hampshire. But Vice President George Bush gained an easy victory in New Hampshire and went on to win most of the contests on "Super Tuesday"—March 8, 1988—the day all the southern states held their primaries. At the end of March, Senator Dole withdrew from the race (a number of other candidates had already done so), and Bush was assured of the Republican party's presidential nomination.

Eight candidates entered the race for the Democratic party's presidential nomination. Many observers believed that no candidate would emerge from the long primary and caucus season with a majority of the delegate votes and that the choice would be made at the national convention. But this analysis proved to be incorrect.

Representative Richard Gephardt of Missouri won the Iowa caucus, but again the outcome in that state did not reflect public sentiment in other parts of the nation. Massachusetts Governor Michael Dukakis won a big victory in New Hampshire, and on "Super Tuesday" he won the two largest southern states, Texas and Florida. The race eventually narrowed to a contest between Dukakis and Rev. Jesse Jackson as the other Democratic candidates withdrew their names from consideration. Although Jackson inflicted a stunning defeat on Dukakis in Michigan, victories in the New York, New Jersey, and California primaries gave the Massachusetts governor the necessary delegate support to guarantee his nomination.

The National Convention

After all the delegates have been selected, the parties prepare to hold their **national conventions.** Several years before the conventions, the national party committees select the cities in which the conventions will be held and the days on which they will meet—sometime between mid-July and mid-August. The main task of the convention is to nominate the party's presidential and vice presidential candidates. But the convention also performs other functions, including the preparation and approval of a party platform.

Adopting a Platform. The first major task of a national convention is to adopt a **party platform.** This consists of a series of statements of general policy, each of which is called a *plank*. It is basically a set of compromises through which the party seeks to unite its many diverse supporters; often the result is a series of vague, general statements about current political issues. If the party is nominating an incumbent President, the platform will reflect his policies; the opposing party's platform will include criticisms of the President's policies and his conduct in office. Although party platforms are often dismissed as meaningless, a comparison of the platforms of the major political parties will often reveal significant differences over major policy issues.

Nominating a Presidential Candidate. The nomination procedure begins with a series of nominating and seconding speeches in which the names of the candidates are proposed to the convention. After all the names have been placed before the delegates, an oral roll call vote of the states is taken and a nominee is chosen.

National party conventions have been held since the early nineteenth century, and it is likely that they will be a feature of American national politics for many years to come. (For lists of the Conventions and nominees since 1900, see Tables 6.1 and 6.2.) But their importance has declined during the past several decades. Today the national conventions simply ratify the choice of a presidential nominee that has already been made in the state primaries. Not since the 1952 Democratic convention has more than one roll call been necessary to select a nominee. And only on rare occasions has a close contest been decided by a convention vote; the case of Ronald Reagan and Gerald Ford at the 1976 Republican convention, in which Ford won by a narrow margin, was an exception to the general pattern.

Conventions also serve as a means of rallying the party faithful. They are also valuable as a way of obtaining television time to publicize the party, its

TABLE 6.1 *Democratic Conventions, 1900–1988*

Year	City	Presidential nominee	Vice presidential nominee
1900	Kansas City	William J. Bryan	Adlai E. Stevenson
1904	St. Louis	Alton S. Parker	Henry G. Davis
1908	Denver	William J. Bryan	John W. Kern
1912	Baltimore	Woodrow Wilson	Thomas R. Marshall
1916	St. Louis	Woodrow Wilson	Thomas R. Marshall
1920	San Francisco	James M. Cox	Franklin D. Roosevelt
1924	New York	John W. Davis	Charles W. Bryan
1928	Houston	Alfred E. Smith	Joseph T. Robinson
1932	Chicago	Franklin D. Roosevelt	John N. Garner
1936	Philadelphia	Franklin D. Roosevelt	John N. Garner
1940	Chicago	Franklin D. Roosevelt	Henry A. Wallace
1944	Chicago	Franklin D. Roosevelt	Harry S Truman
1948	Philadelphia	Harry S Truman	Alben W. Barkley
1952	Chicago	Adlai E. Stevenson	John J. Sparkman
1956	Chicago	Adlai E. Stevenson	Estes Kefauver
1960	Los Angeles	John F. Kennedy	Lyndon B. Johnson
1964	Atlantic City	Lyndon B. Johnson	Hubert H. Humphrey
1968	Chicago	Hubert H. Humphrey	Edmund S. Muskie
1972	Miami Beach	George McGovern	R. Sargent Shriver
1976	New York	Jimmy Carter	Walter Mondale
1980	New York	Jimmy Carter	Walter Mondale
1984	San Francisco	Walter Mondale	Geraldine Ferraro
1988	Atlanta	Michael Dukakis	Lloyd Bentsen

TABLE 6.2 *Republican Conventions, 1900–1988*

Year	City	Presidential nominee	Vice presidential nominee
1900	Philadelphia	William McKinley	Theodore Roosevelt
1904	Chicago	Theodore Roosevelt	Charles W. Fairbanks
1908	Chicago	William H. Taft	James S. Sherman
1912	Chicago	William H. Taft	Nicholas Murray Butler
1916	Chicago	Charles E. Hughes	Charles W. Fairbanks
1920	Chicago	Warren G. Harding	Calvin Coolidge
1924	Cleveland	Calvin Coolidge	Charles G. Dawes
1928	Kansas City	Herbert Hoover	Charles Curtis
1932	Chicago	Herbert Hoover	Charles Curtis
1936	Cleveland	Alfred M. Landon	Frank Knox
1940	Philadelphia	Wendell L. Willkie	Charles L. McNary
1944	Chicago	Thomas E. Dewey	John W. Bricker
1948	Philadelphia	Thomas E. Dewey	Earl Warren
1952	Chicago	Dwight D. Eisenhower	Richard M. Nixon
1956	San Francisco	Dwight D. Eisenhower	Richard M. Nixon
1960	Chicago	Richard M. Nixon	Henry Cabot Lodge
1964	San Francisco	Barry Goldwater	William E. Miller
1968	Miami Beach	Richard M. Nixon	Spiro T. Agnew
1972	Miami Beach	Richard M. Nixon	Spiro T. Agnew
1976	Kansas City	Gerald R. Ford	Robert Dole
1980	Detroit	Ronald Reagan	George Bush
1984	Dallas	Ronald Reagan	George Bush
1988	New Orleans	George Bush	J. Danforth Quayle

candidates, and its platform. The parties have responded to this new reality by organizing the conventions in ways that will appeal to the television viewer.

Nominating a Vice Presidential Candidate. It is customary for the presidential nominee to choose his own running mate, and his selection is always approved by the convention. Presidential nominees have traditionally been concerned primarily with "balancing the ticket" from a geographic and philosophical standpoint. Whereas the President chooses his closest advisers on the basis of personal knowledge and friendships, Vice Presidents are often strangers selected specifically for the purpose of balancing the ticket. Sometimes they are even political opponents of the nominee. For example, in 1960 John F. Kennedy selected Lyndon B. Johnson as his running mate even though there were important philosophical differences between the two men and despite the fact that Johnson had been Kennedy's rival for the Democratic party's presidential nomination.

In 1988 the Democratic presidential nominee, Michael Dukakis, selected Lloyd Bentsen, a conservative Texas senator, as his running mate; the Republican candidate, George Bush, chose Indiana's Dan Quayle, also a conservative senator. In both cases the vice presidential selections provided balance in terms of geography, philosophy, and age.

Although the Vice President has few constitutional and legal powers, the potential importance of the office has been demonstrated on two occasions in the past three decades: the assassination of President Kennedy in 1963 and the resignation of President Nixon in 1974. It is now recognized that it is not enough to select a candidate for the vice presidency merely to balance the ticket. The nominee should also be qualified to serve as the nation's chief executive. Nevertheless, presidential candidates still place their main emphasis on balancing the ticket.

Reform of the National Conventions. In 1968 the Democratic party nominated Senator Hubert Humphrey as its presidential candidate even though he had not entered any of the state primaries. Supporters of the defeated candidates cried foul and criticized the party's convention as undemocratic and unrepresentative. In order to defuse some of the criticism, Humphrey agreed to the formation of a commission to study the party's convention rules and recommend changes. Perhaps the most enduring effect of this episode was the rapid increase in the number of states that choose delegates by means of a primary.[2]

After each of the Democratic party's conventions between 1972 and 1984, new commissions were created to review the party's rules. In each case the commissions proposed important changes. As one observer has concluded, "The major intent of the post-1968 . . . reforms was to open the nomination process in the Democratic Party to broaden participation and thereby make the results more representative."[3] Some of the reforms were short-lived. A 1972 requirement that set specific quotas designed to increase the number of women, minority group members, and younger people in state delegations was soon abandoned. But by 1980 the Democrats had adopted a rule that required that women make up at least 50 percent of each state delegation and that states establish delegate quotas for groups that had been subjected to discrimination in the past—African Americans, Native Americans, and the young.

The Democrats have also outlawed winner-take-all primaries at the state level (they can be used at the district level, and a few states continue to select delegates in this way). Instead, delegates must be selected by a system of proportional representation; for example, a candidate who obtains 25 percent of the vote in the primary must receive 25 percent of the delegates. Under the rules in effect in 1988, a candidate had to receive at least 15 percent of the vote in order to receive delegates.

One consequence of the changes in Democratic party rules during the 1970s was a reduction in the number of party officials and officeholders who attended the national convention. In 1980, for example, only eight out of fifty-nine Democratic senators were present at the party's convention in New York City. To correct this situation the rules were changed again to create so-called *superdelegates*—Democratic governors, members of Congress, and all the members of the party's national committee. As a result of this change, the 1988 Democratic convention was attended by 645 super-delegates—15.5 percent of the total number of convention delegates.[4] Thus, as one political scientist has commented, the Democrats were able "to have reform both ways: mass participation in primaries and caucuses but with party leaders still guaranteed voting rights at the convention."[5]

In the Republican party there has been less pressure for reform, and few significant changes have been made in recent decades. For example, while the national rules of the Democratic party require some form of proportional representation in the choice of delegates, Republican party rules do not. The Republicans also do not have superdelegates attending their convention, and they have no rule mandating that 50 percent of the delegates from each state be women. (Without any change in party rules, 37 percent of the delegates to the 1988 Republican convention were women; the percentage was below 30 in 1980. The number of delegates who were members of minority groups remained very low, however.)

A National Primary? Some critics seek to go beyond these reforms. They favor abolition of the convention system, which would be replaced with a national primary. The idea of a national primary, in which voters would be able to choose among a number of candidates, is not new—President Woodrow Wilson suggested it as early as 1913. Direct nomination of candidates in national primaries would eliminate national conventions, would simplify the nomination system, and might give the people greater control over the nomination process.

The idea of a national primary has never received strong support; moreover, it has several major weaknesses. There would not be enough time for a relatively unknown candidate (e.g., Jimmy Carter in 1976 or Michael Dukakis in 1988) to gain sufficient support to win such a primary. Well-known candidates would have a decided advantage. Under the present system unknown candidates can gradually build support as they move from one state primary or caucus to another. Moreover, if no candidate won more than 50 percent of the vote in a national primary, it would probably be necessary to hold a runoff primary between the two candidates with the highest percentages of the vote to ensure that the final nominee had the support of a majority of the party's voters. Such a system might be confusing to the average voter and reduce turnout for the primary.

■ The Campaign

The American presidential election campaign is the world's most closely watched political event. Aided by campaign managers, media consultants, public relations experts, public opinion poll takers, speechwriters, loyal party members, endless energy, and tireless smiles, the major candidates compete for the chance to govern the nation for the next four years. The winner of the November election will become the most powerful political leader in the democratic world.

The national conventions meet during the summer of a presidential election year, and the campaign begins almost as soon as the two major candidates have been nominated. The speechmaking and banner waving will continue until early November—the longest political campaign in any democratic nation. (In Great Britain, by contrast, national election campaigns last less than a month.)

Today candidates for major political office make extensive use of television advertising, media consultants, and polling, all of which are much more expensive than traditional newspaper, leaflet, and magazine advertising. New methods of publicity have made political campaigning more expensive than ever.

Campaign Financing

Throughout American history, the major parties have obtained the financial support of a relatively small number of wealthy contributors to meet the costs of campaigns. The Republican party has usually been able to outspend the Democrats because far more wealthy people support the Republicans. But the Democrats have also derived much of their campaign support from very wealthy contributors. In addition, the Democrats have been helped by large contributions from the political action committees of labor unions.

The increasing use of television is largely responsible for the skyrocketing costs of political campaigning. (See Figure 6.2.) As the expense of campaigns has increased, the dependence of the parties on the very wealthy has also grown. Big contributors—so-called fat cats—have given even larger amounts of money to pay for the new campaign methods of the television age. In 1972, for example, a Chicago businessman gave an estimated $2 million to the Republican party and its presidential candidate, Richard M. Nixon. For a look at the variety of financial support garnered by Harriet Woods, an unsuccessful Democratic contender for the Senate in 1986, and the way it was spent, see Table 6.3.

The danger that large contributors could influence the policies of the candidates and parties they support has long been a source of concern to observers of American politics. The 1972 presidential campaign dramatized this problem. In that campaign the Republicans alone spent an estimated $61 million. Later it was discovered that some contributors had violated existing campaign spending laws. Dairy producers, for example, had

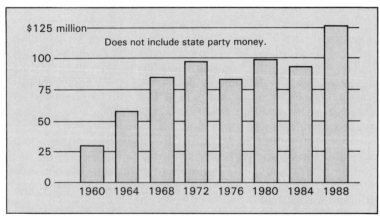

FIGURE 6.2 *Spending on presidential campaigns (in 1960 dollars).*

Source: Citizen's Research Foundation, as reported in *The New York Times*, March 18, 1990, p.1. Copyright © 1990 by the New York Times Company. Reprinted by permission.

NOMINATIONS AND ELECTIONS

TABLE 6.3 *Budget for the Unsuccessful 1986 Senate Campaign of Harriet Woods of Missouri.*

Where the money came from		Where the money went	
Contributions from individuals in Missouri		**Outlays by the Woods campaign**	
St. Louis	$600,000	Television time	$1,900,000
Kansas City	300,000	Production costs	650,000
Rest of state	250,000	Polling	200,000
Subtotal	$1,150,000	Staff	500,000
		Field operations	100,000
Contributions from individuals outside Missouri		Candidate travel	25,000
		General overhead	250,000
New York	$150,000	Subtotal	$3,625,000
California	150,000		
Washington, D.C.	150,000	**Fund-raising costs**	
Other states	150,000	Events	$375,000
Subtotal	$600,000	Mail and phone	
		solicitations	400,000
Contributions from direct mail or phone solicitations	**$1,200,000**	Subtotal	$775,000
		Total spent	**$4,400,000**
Contributions from "bundling" (groups collecting contributions from individuals)			
Emily's List (supports female candidates)	$150,000		
Council for a Livable World (supports a nuclear freeze)	150,000		
Subtotal	$300,000		
Political action committees			
Labor affiliated	$450,000		
Liberal groups	80,000		
Other	270,000		
Subtotal	$800,000		
Funds from Democratic Party	**$350,000**		
Total raised	**$4,400,000**		

Source: The Woods Campaign, as reported in *The New York Times*, May 13, 1990, p. E4. Copyright © 1990 by The New York Times Company. Reprinted by permission.

secretly donated $680,000 to the Nixon campaign and received favorable treatment by his administration. A number of corporate executives also had made illegal contributions. Some of this money had been used to finance the burglary of the Democratic National Committee headquarters at the Watergate apartments in Washington, D.C. The demands for reform that followed these revelations led to the passage of new campaign finance legislation between 1974 and 1979, legislation that greatly changed the way presidential election campaigns are funded.

Reforming Campaign Financing

Before 1971 there had been occasional halfhearted attempts to regulate campaign financing; legislation on this subject was passed as early as 1907. None of these attempts was effective, however, because of major loopholes in the legislation. The Federal Election Campaign Act of 1971 (FECA) set limits on the amount of money that presidential and vice presidential candidates or their families could contribute to their own campaigns. It also required campaign committees and candidates to report the names and addresses of all contributors of amounts over $100. The abuses of the 1972 presidential campaign and the Watergate scandal revealed the inadequacy of this legislation.

In response to this situation, Congress enacted the Federal Election Campaign Act of 1974, which extensively amended the 1971 law. Further changes were made in 1976 and again in 1979. The new legislation established a system for federal financing of presidential campaigns and set limits on the amount of money that could be raised from other sources. It created special funds for presidential primaries, nominating conventions, and the general election campaign. A candidate seeking nomination in a presidential primary is eligible to receive federal money if he or she is able to raise a minimum of $5,000 in each of twenty states, counting only the first $250 of each contribution. Candidates who meet this standard will receive funds equal to the amount of private money they have obtained; only the first $250 of each contribution is matched, however. In order to receive this money, the candidate must accept a ceiling on overall national spending as well as limits on spending for each state campaign. The public funds are supplied out of tax revenues. A box on the individual income tax return permits each taxpayer to earmark $1 of his or her tax payment for this purpose.

In the 1988 presidential primaries, the sixteen candidates—nine Democrats, six Republicans, and a minor-party candidate—raised $213.8 million and spent $210.7 million. Thirty-one percent of this total, or $65.7 million, came from the U.S. government, 66 percent from individuals, and 2 percent from political action committees. The 1988 contenders spent more than three times the amount spent by a similar number of candidates in 1976, the year in which public matching of campaign funds began.[6]

A major political party—that is, one that received 25 percent or more of the vote in the most recent election—is eligible to receive federal funding of the costs of its nominating convention. Moreover, each major-party nominee (not the party or organization) is eligible to receive federal funds to pay for the campaign. In 1976 the parties each received $2.2 million to defray the costs of the nominating conventions, and each candidate received $21.8 million to pay for the campaign. Since federal funding for both conventions and campaigns is adjusted upward every four years to compensate for inflation, the total amounts have risen rapidly. In 1988 the parties received about $9.2 million each for their conventions, and the candidates received about $46.1 million each for their campaigns.

Major-party presidential candidates can receive this public money only if they pledge that they will not spend more than they are entitled to under federal law (i.e., that they will not accept private contributions). But groups such as political action committees can spend additional money in support of a candidate, provided that such spending is kept separate from the candidate's organization and there is no cooperation between the two.

One criticism of the present campaign finance law is that it promotes continued domination of American politics by the existing major political parties. Third-party candidates for President must receive 5 percent of the total popular vote to qualify for retroactive payment of federal funds. If they receive that percentage of the vote, they automatically qualify for federal funds in the next national election. If the 5 percent figure is not reached, the candidate must bear the full cost of the campaign.

FECA also limits political contributions to candidates seeking federal office. An individual contributor is restricted to $1,000 per year for any candidate for the Senate or the House of Representatives in a primary election and to $1,000 per candidate in the general election. The individual is also restricted to $5,000 to political action committees each year and to $20,000 for a national political party committee, with total personal contributions limited to $25,000 in a single year. But this limit is not as restrictive as it appears to be, since each adult member of a family can contribute up to this amount and the limit applies only to candidates for federal offices.

FECA also attempts to control spending by political action committees. PACs may not give more than $5,000 to any candidate for a federal government office. But there are no limits on the total amount a PAC can contribute to all candidates for federal offices. Some PACs spend very large amounts for this purpose.

Finally, FECA contains record-keeping and disclosure provisions. For example, all contributions of $200 or more must be identified and recorded both by candidates and by political organizations. Criminal penalties are provided for violating these parts of the law. Finally, the legislation created a six-person Federal Election Commission to administer the law. The commission's members are appointed by the President with the advice and consent of the Senate.

Congressional Campaigns

The campaign finance legislation just described does not provide for public funding of congressional campaigns. These campaigns are financed by the candidate, either from his or her own resources or, more frequently, with funds obtained from private contributions. The amount of money spent in congressional campaigns has increased greatly in recent years. In 1986, for example, candidates for seats in Congress spent about $450 million—a 500 percent increase over the total spent in 1974.[7]

Much of this money comes from contributions by political action

TABLE 6.4 *Total Spending by Political Action Committees from Jan. 1, 1989 to June 30, 1990*

Group	Amount, in millions
Democratic-Republican Independent Voter Education Committee (International Brotherhood of Teamsters)	$6.4
American Medical Association	3.0
National Association of Realtors	2.7
National Congressional Club (Senator Jesse Helms' political organization)	2.6
American Federation of State, County and Municipal Employees	2.4
Voter Guide (bipartisan Californian group)	2.3
American Telephone and Telegraph Company	2.3
Association of Trial Lawyers of America	2.3
United Automobile Workers	2.0
Committee on Letter Carriers Political Education	1.9
National Rifle Association Political Victory Fund	1.8
American Citizens for Political Action (conservative fund-raising committee)	1.7
National Education Association	1.7
Machinists Non-Partisan Political League	1.6
C.W.A.-COPE Political Contributions Committee (Communications Workers of America)	1.5

Source: Federal Election Commission, as reported in *The New York Times*, August 31, 1990, p. 16. Copyright © 1990 by The New York Times Company. Reprinted by permission.

committees (discussed in Chapter 5). The amount contributed by PACs to congressional campaigns increased dramatically between 1978 and 1988. In 1978, PACs donated a total of $22.9 million to candidates for the House of Representatives; in 1988, they donated $99.7 million.

The pattern of contributions by PACs strongly favors incumbent legislators over challengers. An analysis carried out by the Federal Election Commission for the period between January 1, 1989, and June 30, 1990, showed that PACs had made contributions of $94 million. Of this total, $79 million went to incumbents, while challengers received only $6.5 million ($8.1 million was given to candidates for open seats.) The study also showed that the PACs gave far more money to Democrats—who control both houses of Congress—than to Republicans. The former received $59 million, the latter $34 million during the same eighteen-month period.[8] (Table 6.4 lists the fifteen largest PAC contributors.)

Between campaigns, legislators devote a considerable portion of their time to fund raising. Fund raising by House members, who must seek reelection every two years, is almost continuous. Ironically, most House incumbents face either no opposition or challengers who are poorly financed and have little chance of winning. (As we will see later in the chapter, the reelection rate of House incumbents has been more than 95 percent in recent elections.) Thus the main purpose of the large sums of money amassed by members of Congress between elections is to scare off opponents.

The lack of a system for financing congressional campaigns has become an important issue in recent years. Much concern is expressed over the escalating costs of congressional campaigns. Between 1980 and 1988 the average cost of a successful Senate race rose from about $1.25 million to $3.7 million; the average for a winning House candidate went from under $200,000.00 to $393,000.00 in the same period.[9] Although officials of PACs claim that their contributions give them nothing more than access to legislators, many people believe that their elected representatives are captives of the PACs and that those representatives' votes on legislative issues have been purchased by special interests.

In 1990 Congress made its first serious attempt to reform the campaign financing system. For the first time since the post-Watergate reforms of the 1970s, both the House and the Senate passed legislation dealing with campaign finance reform. The Senate bill would have barred contributions from political action committees; the House version would only have limited them. Both bills proposed voluntary limits on spending in political campaigns. In return for accepting these limits, candidates would receive vouchers to purchase radio and television time for advertising. Neither bill provided any direct payments of public money to cover the costs of campaigns.

Although the Senate bill was the stronger of the two, most critics attacked both plans as inadequate and believed that they would merely

TABLE 6.5 *What Other Countries Do*

	Public financing	*Limits on fund raising or spending*	*Television*
Britain	No	Yes	Free time, allocated according to party's strength in previous election
Denmark	Allowance to parties, based on strength in previous election	No	Parties given equal and free time on public stations
France	Reimbursement to candidates, according to votes received	Yes	Free and equal time to candidates
Italy	Reimbursement to candidates, according to votes received	No	Free and equal time to candidates on state-run stations, but parties control major private stations
Israel	No	No	Parties given equal and free time on public stations
Japan	No	Yes	Candidates given some free time for speeches; no negative advertising
Germany	Reimbursement to parties, according to votes received	No	Free time to candidates on public stations

Source: The New York Times, March 21, 1990, p. A22. Copyright © 1990 by The New York Times Company. Reprinted by permission.

provide additional advantages for incumbent legislators. (The House bill, for example, set a spending limit of $550,000–715,000; however, the average cost of a House race in 1988 was well below these figures.)

The two houses of Congress were not able to resolve their differences, and no legislation was adopted in 1990. But the issue of campaign finance reform continues to be important. Congress will have to confront this vexing problem until it is able to agree on a method of changing the present system. (For a look at how other countries finance campaigns, see Table 6.5.)

Campaign Strategy

Candidates must make plans long before the actual campaign begins. They hire a professional consultant, an opinion research organization, an advertising agency, speechwriters, a direct-mail organization, attorneys, an accounting firm, and similar services. The campaign manager, still a central figure, is aided by the consultant, who generally takes care of opinion surveys, fund raising, budgeting, public relations, advertising, and the like. All of these activities have a single purpose: to create and communicate to the public a favorable image of the candidate and his or her policies.

The two major parties usually adopt different campaign strategies. The Democrats have an advantage over the Republicans in terms of number of registered voters, but those voters are less likely to turn out on election day. The Democrats therefore strive for party unity and stress the importance of voting. The Republicans, by contrast, often try to gain voter support for "the candidate, not the party" in an attempt to gain the votes of Democrats and independents.

The strategies used by candidates vary from one election to the next. The major issues in the campaign and the personalities of the candidates always shape campaign strategy. Incumbent Presidents organize their campaigns differently from nonincumbents. Incumbents often seek to use the prestige of the White House to their advantage. They may choose not to respond to attacks by their opponents and to curtail their campaign trips around the country, insisting that the affairs of the nation are too demanding and important for them to engage in ordinary political campaigning. Instead they engage in activities that are likely to be shown on the nightly television news programs—signing bills, meeting with representatives of foreign governments, and the like. President Richard Nixon used this "White House rose garden" approach successfully in his 1972 bid for reelection. But this strategy does not always work; President Jimmy Carter employed it in his 1980 reelection campaign and was overwhelmingly defeated by Ronald Reagan. And some incumbent Presidents pursue a strategy of active public campaigning. In 1984, for example, President Reagan campaigned extensively throughout the nation.

A candidate who is seeking to defeat an incumbent will inevitably attack the incumbent's record. He will criticize the President's general program, his failure to keep campaign promises, and other mistakes. In 1980 Reagan criticized Carter's record in both domestic and foreign policy. He dramatized this criticism by asking voters the simple question, "Are you better off today than four years ago when Mr. Carter became President?" In the 1984 election the Democratic candidate, Walter Mondale, stressed the "fairness" issue, albeit without success. He sought to portray the Reagan administration as insensitive to the needs of the poor and concerned only with rewarding the affluent.

All candidates, whether incumbent or not, must seek to offset any perceived shortcomings and capitalize on their strong points. In 1960 John F. Kennedy, who was only 43 when he was nominated, had to overcome the unusual problem of being "too young." His campaign stressed vigor and the need for change. In 1976 Carter's problem was that he was almost unknown outside his home state of Georgia. Accordingly, his strategy was to attack the corruption and sheer size of the government in Washington while stressing his "down home" character and moral qualities. In both the 1980 and 1984 elections, Reagan portrayed himself as the representative of traditional American values—patriotism, the family, and religion. During the 1988 presidential campaign George Bush stressed his broad background in foreign affairs and the peace and prosperity experienced by the nation during the Reagan administration. He also criticized Michael Dukakis for being soft on crime and too liberal on other issues.

Candidates for the presidency go to great lengths to make themselves attractive to voters, but they do not attempt to woo the entire voting population. The electoral college system (discussed in the next section)

FIGURE 6.3 *Popular vote cast for President by the two major parties, 1952 to 1988.*

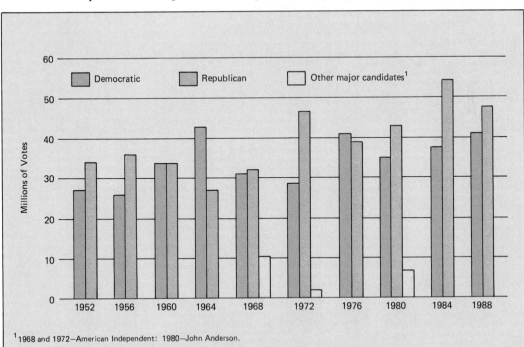

[1] 1968 and 1972—American Independent: 1980—John Anderson.

Source: Statistical Abstract of the United States, 1984, p. 246; updated to include the 1984 and 1988 elections.

requires that a candidate devote much energy to the states with the largest populations and, hence, the greatest number of electoral votes. The candidate's goal is to win a *plurality* (the largest number of votes) of the popular vote in enough states so that his or her total electoral vote will be 270 or more. (For the popular vote in presidential elections, see Figure 6.3.)

In 1988 both George Bush and Michael Dukakis concentrated most of their campaign efforts in states with large populations: California, Illinois, Michigan, Ohio, Pennsylvania, and Texas. (The Republicans largely conceded New York to the Democrats, while the latter made little effort to win in Florida.) President Bush won in each of these large states, for a total of 184 electoral votes, slightly more than two-thirds of the 270 needed to win the presidency. His sweep of the South and his victories in the mountain states and in some midwestern states brought his electoral vote total to 426.

Television Debates

Despite the use of television in presidential campaigns since the 1950s, it took a long time for televised debates between candidates to become an accepted practice. No federal law requires candidates to debate, and for

Candidates George Bush and Michael Dukakis face off at the first presidential debate, September 25, 1988, in Winston-Salem, North Carolina.

NOMINATIONS AND ELECTIONS

many years presidential nominees refused to do so. In 1960 Vice President Nixon appeared in a series of four debates with his Democratic opponent, Massachusetts Senator John F. Kennedy. No other debates took place until 1976, when Gerald R. Ford and Jimmy Carter made three joint television appearances and their running mates also debated. These debates marked the first time an incumbent President (Ford) had faced an opponent on television. Debates have been held in each presidential election campaign since then. In 1988 the presidential candidates held two debates and the vice presidential nominees one.

Debates have become increasingly important during the nomination stage as well as during the general election campaign. In 1988 numerous debates were scheduled in the months preceding the most important early primaries and caucuses. Some were sponsored by newspapers, others by the major television networks and various private organizations. Several debates were carried live on national television or by the Public Broadcasting System and C-SPAN, the cable television public affairs network.

Television debates have sometimes been a crucial factor in a campaign. The narrow victories of John F. Kennedy in 1960 and Jimmy Carter in 1976 may have been due to their television appearances. It was generally believed that Kennedy and Carter had made better presentations than their opponents. The 1980 debate probably contributed to Reagan's landslide victory. During the early weeks of the campaign, Carter attempted to portray Reagan as reckless and warlike, a man who could not be trusted to conduct American foreign and defense policy. On television, however, Reagan gave the impression of a relaxed, genial person. In 1988 it was believed that Michael Dukakis would beat George Bush in the two presidential debates and that Bush would make mistakes and appear weak. But Bush made no serious errors in the first debate and showed strength and confidence in the second. The debates failed to give Dukakis the boost in popular support he had hoped for.

Some observers have criticized the presidential debates on the ground that they are more like press conferences than true debates. The usual format consists of reporters asking questions of the candidates, the candidates' responses to those questions, and a closing statement by each participant. Despite this shortcoming, the joint appearance of presidential candidates on television provides a unique opportunity for millions of Americans (more than 60 million people viewed each of the two 1988 presidential debates) to see the candidates and evaluate their personalities, knowledge of the issues, and ability to handle a difficult situation.

■ The Election

The election of the President, the Vice President, and most other national, state, and local officials takes place on the first Tuesday after the first Monday in November. The procedures used in elections include registration of voters, voting by secret ballot, and counting of the ballots. The election of the President and Vice President involves the constitutionally required procedure for counting electoral votes, a process that occurs during the weeks following election day.

Registration

Registration is a procedure in which a person who wants to vote presents an election official with proof that he or she meets all the legal requirements for voting in the next election. Individuals who have registered do not have to reregister unless they change their name or address or have not voted for a specified number of years. The states adopted registration systems in the early years of the twentieth century to reduce voting fraud—to prevent people from voting more than once on election day, for example.

Critics have argued that the registration system contributes to the relatively low voter turnout in the United States. Registration usually occurs only at certain times of the year and only at designated locations. Many people simply do not know how to go about registering to vote. A few states—Wisconsin, Minnesota, Oregon, and Maine—permit citizens to register on election day at the place where they vote. These states are among those with the highest voter turnouts in the nation.

Balloting

The **ballot** used in the United States was developed in Australia in the mid-nineteenth century and was designed to prevent fraud in elections. The government prints the ballot, which lists all the candidates, and appoints officials to distribute the ballots only at specified polling places on election day. Each qualified voter receives only one ballot, and the vote is secret.

The ballot may be organized in either of two ways. The *office-block* or *Massachusetts ballot* lists all the candidates according to the office for which they are running—the first block may list all the candidates for U.S. senator, the second all the candidates for governor, and so on. This approach encourages *split-ticket* and independent voting, but the voter may get tired and ignore the blocks of candidates at the bottom of the ballot.

The more common *party-column* or *Indiana ballot* lists candidates for all offices in columns according to party. In some states a person can vote a *straight ticket* by marking a box next to the name of the party or, where voting machines are used, by pulling a lever at the top of the party column. In other states the voter must choose a candidate for each office separately. In either case the party-column ballot encourages the voter to vote along party lines rather than considering the merits of each candidate.

The Electoral College

In Article II, as modified by the Twelfth, Twentieth, and Twenty-third Amendments, the Constitution provides for the election of the President and Vice President by an **electoral college.** As mentioned in Chapter 2, this system was devised by the Constitutional Convention as a compromise between the delegates who favored direct popular election of the President and those who wanted Congress to select the President. Under the electoral college system, the voters actually cast their ballots not for the presidential and vice presidential nominees themselves but for slates of electors chosen by the state political parties. Since the position of elector is basically an honorary one, each party normally awards it to people who have been loyal party members.

Each state may select a number of electors equal to its total number of U.S. senators and representatives. In addition, the Twenty-third Amendment, adopted in 1961, gave residents of the District of Columbia the right to choose at least three electors. The party slate that wins the largest number of popular votes is elected in that state. To be elected President by the electoral college, a candidate must receive a majority (270) of the total number of electoral votes (538). This can be achieved by winning a plurality

Does the Electoral College really exist? In November 1988 the majority of Virginia's voters supported the Republican candidates for President and Vice-President. Consequently, on December 19, 1988, that state's Republican electors met in the state capital and cast their votes for George Bush and Dan Quayle.

of the vote in any combination of states whose electoral vote totals at least 270.

The members of the electoral college are elected every four years under procedures established by the legislatures of each state. Early in the nation's history some states provided for the choice of electors by the state legislators, but this system was eventually replaced by one in which electors are selected by popular election. Every state now provides for the popular election of presidential electors. Forty-nine states require the use of a winner-take-all system, in which the presidential candidate who wins the largest number of popular votes in a state gains the state's entire electoral vote.[10]

The winner-take-all system has important consequences. It favors states like California, Florida, Illinois, Michigan, New York, Ohio, Pennsylvania, and Texas, which have the largest populations. Most presidential candidates concentrate their campaign efforts in the dozen or so most populous states. They understand that by winning those states—even by the smallest popular-vote margins—they will gain large blocks of electoral votes and are likely to win the presidency. (See Figure 6.4 for 1988 presidential election results.)

The electors meet in the capital of their state on the first Monday after the second Wednesday in December to cast separate ballots for their party's presidential and vice presidential candidates. The electors almost always support their party's nominees, although there is no way to compel them to do so. Under the existing system they possess the right to exercise independent judgment. Thus occasionally an elector is "faithless" and votes for someone other than his or her party's presidential candidate. But this has happened on fewer than a dozen occasions in the nation's history. The most recent such incident occurred in 1988, when a West Virginia Democratic elector cast her presidential vote for Lloyd Bentsen and her vice presidential vote for Michael Dukakis. (The elector said that she had made the switch as a protest against the electoral college system.)

The results of the voting in each state are sent to the President of the Senate (i.e., the Vice President of the United States). Before a joint session of Congress in early January, he opens the certificates, the electoral votes are counted and announced, and the President and Vice President are formally elected.

If no candidate receives a majority of the electoral votes for President, the President is chosen by the House of Representatives. The Twelfth Amendment sets forth the revised procedure that must be followed in such a case. Voting by states, with each state having one vote, the House must select from among the candidates with the three highest electoral vote totals. It is necessary to obtain a majority of the votes of the fifty states to be elected President.

If no vice presidential candidate receives a majority of the electoral vote, the Senate elects the Vice President. It must choose between the two candidates with the largest number of electoral votes. The person who gets a majority of the votes in the Senate is elected Vice President.

Problems with the Electoral College. The electoral college has the potential to produce results that go against the spirit of a democratic

154

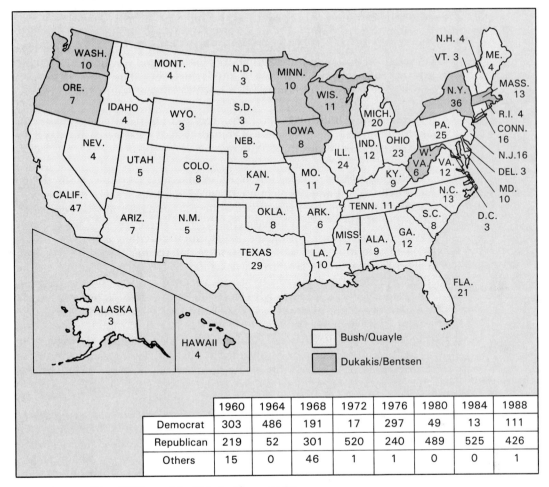

	1960	1964	1968	1972	1976	1980	1984	1988
Democrat	303	486	191	17	297	49	13	111
Republican	219	52	301	520	240	489	525	426
Others	15	0	46	1	1	0	0	1

FIGURE 6.4   *The 1988 presidential election results.*

society. Under this system, for example, it is possible for a person to win the presidency even though he has received fewer popular votes than his opponent. Three Presidents have been elected in this fashion: John Quincy Adams (1824), Rutherford B. Hayes (1876), and Benjamin Harrison (1888). This situation came very close to occurring again in 1976. Jimmy Carter received about 17 million more popular votes than Gerald R. Ford. But a switch of about 4,000 votes in Hawaii and 3,500 votes in Ohio would have given Ford the majority of the electoral votes.

An additional problem with the system arises when no candidate receives a majority of the electoral votes. Since the House of Representatives can choose among the candidates with the three highest electoral-vote totals, it is possible for the candidate of a third or minor party to influence the choice of the President. Such a candidate would be in a position to bargain with the votes of the states he controls and arrange to have them cast for the nominee who promised the most in return. Moreover, under this system it is possible for a minority of the House members to elect the President, since voting is by state and not by individual. Critics contend that this system is undemocratic and should be changed. It should be noted, however, that only twice in the nation's history—1801 and 1825—and under highly unusual circumstances has the House been called upon to elect the President.

Reform or Abolition? A variety of proposals have been offered for changing or abolishing the electoral college system. The five plans that have been discussed most are the following:

1. *Eliminating electors.* This simple proposal would keep the electoral-vote system but eliminate the electors. It would end the threat of the "faithless elector" who votes for a candidate other than the person who received a plurality of the state's popular vote.
2. *Proportional voting.* During the 1950s much attention was given to the idea of adopting a system of proportional voting. Basically, the plan called for electoral votes to be assigned to a candidate in the same proportion as the popular vote he received, thus ending the winner-take-all system. Two candidates who received, for example, 55 percent and 45 percent of the popular vote of a state would receive the same percentage of the state's electoral vote.
3. *The single-member-district plan.* Another plan discussed during the 1950s favored the choice of electors by district. Two electors would be chosen at large to reflect the Senate's portion of the state's electoral vote; the remaining electors would be selected from the districts used for electing members of the House of Representatives.
4. *Changing the procedures in the House of Representatives.* A number of constitutional amendments have been proposed that would change the system for choosing the President when no one candidate receives a majority of votes in the electoral college. Some plans call for the House to vote by individual member and not by state; others advocate election by a joint vote of all the representatives and senators.
5. *Direct popular election.* Most recent proposals for revising the method for electing the President and Vice President call for replacing the electoral college system with direct popular election. Plans for this type of election system usually include a provision that if no candidate received at least 40 percent of the popular vote in the first election, a runoff election would be held between the candidates with the two highest percentages of the vote. The winner of this contest would become President.

The proportional-voting and single-member-district plans could be brought about by changes in state election laws, since the Constitution permits the states to choose their own methods of selecting electors. The other proposals would require a constitutional amendment and therefore be far more difficult to achieve.

The electoral college system is unlikely to be changed in the foreseeable future unless it fails—unless, for example, it elects a candidate who received fewer popular votes than the loser or causes an election to be decided by the House of Representatives. Despite its shortcomings, there is much support for the electoral college system, and strong arguments can be made in its defense. With only a few exceptions in the nineteenth century and none in the twentieth, the electoral-vote system has selected the candidate with the plurality of the popular vote. It maintains the role of the states in a vital political decision. Moreover, the electoral college serves to maintain the stability of the two-party system. It is almost impossible for third parties to have any success in national elections because it is very difficult for them to win electoral votes under the winner-take-all system now used by all of the states. The reform that is discussed most often—direct popular election—would encourage the growth of minor political parties, since they could hope to have more influence under such a system. Direct election might make it difficult for either of the two major parties to win the necessary 40 percent of the popular vote, thus requiring a runoff election.

It is impossible to discuss in abstract terms the merits or demerits of the electoral college or of any proposal designed to alter the method of choosing the President. Each system distributes political advantages to different groups. The present method, for example, generally favors the most populous states. The proportional-voting and single-member-district plans, by contrast, would reduce the influence of those states in presidential elections. The direct-election scheme would eliminate the role of the states in selecting the President; the candidates would seek individual votes without regard to state boundaries.

Congressional Elections

The 435 seats in the House of Representatives, plus one-third of the 100 Senate seats, are up for election every two years. For candidates for seats in the House of Representatives, success in the primary may well mean triumph in the general election because many districts are essentially one-party districts—usually defined as areas in which one political party always wins at least 55 percent of the vote and the other never obtains more than 45 percent. A study conducted by the citizens' group Common Cause during the 1990 congressional elections concluded that of 405 House members who were seeking reelection, 182 went into the election with no major opponent and 300 faced opponents who had raised less than $25,000 in campaign funds. Only about 23 contests could be considered truly competitive.

The competitiveness of House races has declined since the 1930s. In 1936 some 137 House elections were decided by 55 percent of the vote or less. By 1966 this figure had fallen to 72, and it has continued to decline since that time. In 1988 only thirty-seven seats were won with less than 55 percent of the vote; the average margin of victory for House races was almost 73 percent. Senate contests have tended to be more competitive. In the period from 1936 to 1986, an average of 41 percent of Senate elections were decided by majorities of 55 percent or less.[11]

These figures indicate incumbents maintain a tight hold on their seats in the House of Representatives. In 1980, about 90 percent of House

This sign in front of a home in Albany, New York, during the November 1990 campaign indicates voter irritation with incumbents.

members who sought reelection were returned to office. The rate rose to over 98 percent and was 97 percent in the 1990 election; of 407 incumbents seeking reelection, 392 were victorious. (See Figure 6.5.) Reelection rates for incumbent Senators have been much lower than for members of the House, but in 1988 this figure also reached 85 percent.

The explanation for this high reelection rate can be found in a number of factors. Incumbent members of the House have several built-in advantages over their challengers. They are usually better known in their districts, have established a history of providing services to their constituents, and have numerous supporters who can be called upon to work during the

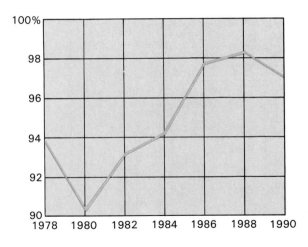

FIGURE 6.5 *Percentage of House members who sought and won reelection, 1978 to 1990.*

campaign. And the *franking privilege* of members of Congress enables them to mail information about their activities to constituents at no cost.

Two other factors provide even more important reasons for the phenomenal success rates of House members. Many House districts have been drawn in a highly irregular way so as to give one political party an advantage over the opposition party in elections. This practice is called **gerrymandering.** (Gerrymandering is discussed in greater detail in Chapter 7.) And as we have already seen, legislative incumbents receive far more financial support, especially from political action committees, than their opponents do. Without adequate financial backing, the parties find it very difficult to attract strong candidates to run against entrenched opponents. (See Figure 6.6.)

One consequence of the high reelection rate of House members is a growing movement to limit the number of terms legislators may serve. The most frequently suggested figure is twelve years—two terms for senators and six for representatives. Such a change would require an amendment to the Constitution, and members of Congress are understandably reluctant to propose a change that would so seriously limit their political power. But public discussion of this proposal may encourage Congress to make changes in the present election system; in particular, it might spur campaign reform legislation that would provide a more level playing field for incumbents and challengers.

In congressional districts and states that are competitive, the presence of a popular President or presidential candidate on the ballot may influence the outcome of legislative elections. This is the so-called **coattail effect**— the ability of a popular candidate to attract and transfer support to other candidates on a party's ticket. A popular presidential candidate may help House and Senate candidates who are running on the same party ballot get elected. The 1980 election illustrates this effect. Ronald Reagan's triumph in the presidential election helped produce a net gain of thirty-three Republicans in the House of Representatives and twelve in the Senate. The Republican victories in the Senate were the largest gain by either party since

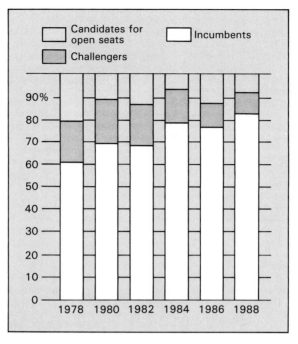

FIGURE 6.6 *Percentage of political action committee contributions to House incumbents and others, 1978 to 1988.*

Source: Congressional Quarterly, as reported in *The New York Times*, March 21, 1990, p. A22. Copyright © 1990 by the New York Times Company. Reprinted by permission.

1958 and created the first Republican majority in the Senate since the 1952 election.

But President Reagan's landslide victory in the 1984 election did not produce a similar result. Although Reagan captured 525 of a possible 538 electoral college votes, the Republican party gained only fourteen seats in the House of Representatives and actually lost two in the Senate. And in 1988 George Bush won the electoral votes of forty states, but the Republican party lost a small number of seats in both houses of Congress. It was the first time in twenty-eight years that the party that captured the presidency had suffered such a loss in the House of Representatives. Indeed, President Bush came to office with the fewest members of his party in the House of any chief executive in the twentieth century.

If congressional candidates believe that their party's presidential candidate will not run a strong race, they will avoid identifying their campaign with that of their party's presidential nominee. Instead, they will stress their own achievements or the shortcomings of their opponents. In the 1984 election, for example, many Democratic candidates for the House and Senate avoided tying their campaigns to that of Walter Mondale, who was believed to have little chance of winning the presidential election.

In an off-year election (one in which a President is not being elected), candidates in competitive districts cannot ride the coattails of a presidential candidate. Even a popular President cannot transfer his popularity when his name is not on the ballot. With only one exception in the twentieth century (1934), the President's party has always lost seats in the House of Representatives during the off-year election. In 1986, for example, the Republicans lost five seats to the Democrats; in 1990, they had a net loss of eight.

■ Summary

Much of American politics is traditional. Long campaigns, speeches, demonstrations, and the like have characterized the nation's political scene since its early years. And the national convention has been in continual use since the 1830s.

Of course, much has also changed, especially in the twentieth century. Instead of trains, jet planes transport candidates around the country. First radio and now television have reduced the importance of personal appearances as the chief means by which candidates communicate with the public. These changes have had clear and important effects on American campaigns and elections.

Since the 1960s there have been other changes in the American election system that are less obvious and not as well understood but have had a profound effect on national politics. Among these are the importance of the primary in the selection of presidential and vice presidential candidates and the reduction of the role of the party convention to that of ratifying choices already made in the primaries; the changes in the rules of the national conventions, especially those of the Democratic party, that make delegates more representative of the American population; and the reform of campaign finance laws for presidential nomination and election campaigns.

The present system for nominating presidential candidates has both defenders and critics. Its defenders argue that it gives the voters a chance to evaluate the various candidates over an extended period. It also gives the candidates a chance to build coalitions of voters who will support them in the state primary elections. And it gives relatively unknown candidates a chance to become much better known and to attract funds and volunteers.

Critics of the existing nomination process argue that it is too long and complex. The process really begins at least two years before the election, when potential candidates visit key primary and caucus states, start raising money, and plan their campaigns. The actual contests extend from early February to mid-June, wearing out the patience and understanding of the public and the physical and mental stamina of the candidates. "It feels so good when you stop. Everybody ought to try it once because every day after it's over is a good day," said Representative Philip M. Crane of Illinois after he dropped out of the Republican primary race in 1980.[12]

The campaign finance laws enacted during the 1970s have had important effects on presidential election campaigns. For one thing, since federal money is available, some candidates who might not have been able to afford to enter and compete in the primaries can now do so. For another, the law encourages candidates to seek relatively small contributions from many voters and rely less on large contributions from a few very wealthy individuals. The legislation has also stimulated the rapid growth of political action committees, a development that has had a number of unforeseen and undesirable consequences.

Campaign finance laws have also played a role in weakening the political parties. The availability of federal funds serves to increase the number of candidates and, consequently, to fragment the parties. Moreover, the candidates, not the parties, receive most of the public funds, and the nominees of the two parties, not the party organizations, control the expenditure of funds during the campaign.[13]

The campaign finance laws have been subjected to some strong criticism. It is claimed that congressional candidates have become more dependent on contributions from interest groups and PACs and that this makes such groups more powerful than ever. PAC money has contributed to the extraordinarily high reelection rates of House members, since most of the money is given to incumbents rather than to challengers. It is also argued that far from making campaign financing more open, the law has given rise to some questionable practices as corporations, unions, and other organizations have sought ways to get around the limits set by existing legislation. Moreover, the Federal Election Commission does not have enough power to enforce the law effectively.

Clearly there are some major problems with current methods of financing congressional campaigns. There is much dissatisfaction with the present system and widespread recognition that change is necessary. But the parties are deeply divided on this issue and have not been able to agree on legislation for reform.

■ Key Terms

convention
primary
runoff primary
closed primary
open primary

blanket primary
presidential primary
caucus
national convention
party platform

registration
ballot
electoral college
gerrymandering
coattail effect

■ Suggested Reading

ABRAMSON, PAUL R., JOHN H. ALDRIDGE, and JOHN W. RHODE. *Change and Continuity in the 1988 Elections.* Washington, D.C.: Congressional Quarterly Press, 1990.

BARTELS, LARRY M. *Presidential Primaries and the Dynamics of Public Choice.* Princeton, N.J.: Princeton University Press, 1988.

FOWLER, LINDA, and ROBERT D. McCLURE. *Political Ambition: Who Decides To Run for Congress.* New Haven, Conn.: Yale University Press, 1989.

HESS, STEPHEN. *The Presidential Campaign.* Washington, D.C.: Brookings Institution, 1988.

JACOBSON, GARY C. *The Politics of Congressional Elections,* 2nd ed. Boston: Little, Brown, 1987.

NELSON, MICHAEL, ed. *The Presidency and the Polit-ical System,* Washington, D.C.: Congressional Quarterly Press, 1990.

PIERCE, NEIL R., and LAWRENCE D. LONGLEY. *The People's President: The Electoral College in American History and the Direct Vote Alternative.* New Haven, Conn.: Yale University Press, 1981.

REICHLEY, A. JAMES, ed. *Elections American Style.* Washington, D.C.: Brookings Institution, 1987.

SHAFER, BYRON E. *Bifurcated Politics: Evolution and Reform in the National Party Convention.* Cambridge, Mass.: Harvard University Press, 1988.

SORAUF, FRANK J. *Money in American Elections.* Glenview, Ill.: Scott, Foresman, 1988.

■ Notes

1. Stephen J. Wayne, *The Road to the White House: The Politics of Presidential Elections*, 3rd ed. (New York: St. Martin's Press, 1988), pp. 14, 90–91.

2. Peverill Squire, "Primaries and the Presidential Nomination Process," *Political Science Teacher*, 1 (Summer 1988), 7.

3. Ibid., p. 8.

4. Wayne, *Road to the White House*, pp. 95–96.

5. Squire, "Primaries and the Presidential Nomination Process," p. 8.

6. Richard L. Berke, "'88 Presidential Candidates Spent $210 Million," *The New York Times*, August 27, 1989, p. 23.

7. Candice J. Nelson, "Campaign Finance in Presidential and Congressional Elections," *Political Science Teacher*, 1 (Summer 1988), 1.

8. Richard L. Berke, "Bulk of $94 Million in Special Interest Gifts Goes to Incumbents," *New York Times*, August 31, 1990, p. 16.

9. Richard L. Berke, "An Edge for Incumbents: Loopholes that Pay Off," *New York Times*, March 20, 1990, pp. A1, A16.

10. Since 1972 Maine has used a district plan for choosing electors: Two electors are chosen on a state-wide basis and one is chosen from each of the state's congressional districts.

11. David E. Rosenbaum, "It's a House of the Same Representatives," *New York Times*, September 25, 1988, sec. 4, p. 1; Warren Weaver, Jr., "More and More House Races Aren't Races But Runaways," *New York Times*, June 15, 1987, pp. A1, B10.

12. Quoted in Saul Pett, "Ex-Candidates on Presidential Race: Mad, Mad Marathon," *New York Times*, August 31, 1980, p. 43.

13. Wayne, *Road to the White House*, pp. 51, 125.

7

Questions for Thought

What are the major nonlegislative functions of Congress?

What constitutional requirements must be met by the states in drawing congressional district lines?

Who are the constitutional officers of the United States Congress? The main political officers?

What are the major types of congressional committees?

Why is the committee system central to the operation of Congress?

What are the main steps in the process by which legislation is adopted by Congress?

Congress

THE framers of the Constitution had divided beliefs about legislative power. On the one hand, they wanted to create a legislature that would have enough authority to govern the new nation effectively. They believed strongly that the legislature established under the Articles of Confederation was inadequate. It lacked the powers they thought necessary for a national legislature—especially the power to regulate interstate commerce and the authority to legislate for individual citizens rather than simply for the state governments.

On the other hand, the nation's founders feared excessive legislative power. They had observed several of the state governments and concluded that the constitutions of those states did not sufficiently limit the legislative branch. Those constitutions, they believed, could not stop the natural tendency of legislatures in a republic to gradually absorb governmental power at the expense of the executive and judicial branches.

The Constitution written in Philadelphia in 1787 reflected these divided beliefs. In Article I, Section 8, it gave significant new powers to the legislative branch of the government, including the power to regulate interstate commerce. But the Constitution also sought to curb the legislature. It established a two-house legislature whose members represented different geographic interests and were elected for different terms of office. Members of one house were to be elected by the people, while those of the second would be chosen by the state legislatures. Through these means the nation's founders believed that Congress would control itself. They did not, however, believe that these restraints were sufficient. So in addition they created a strong President and an independent judiciary that would help curb legislative power.

This chapter will examine the functions and organization of Congress and describe some of the procedures it uses to conduct its work.

■ The Functions of Congress

When we speak of *Congress*, we are really referring to two Congresses: the Congress that enacts legislation for the nation as a whole and the Congress that represents the people of all the states and localities in the nation. Congress, in other words, has a dual nature—it is at once a legislative and a representative body. Its main function, of course, is to enact laws, operating primarily on the basis of its **delegated** (or **expressed** or **enumerated**) **powers** under Article I, Section 8, of the Constitution. But it is not simply a lawmaking body. It is a collection of 535 senators and representatives whose positions depend on the goodwill of voters in San Diego, Kalamazoo, Orlando, Bangor, and thousands of other communities throughout the United States. We therefore begin this chapter with a discussion of these two basic functions of Congress—legislation and representation.

Legislative Functions: Delegated Powers

Taxing and Spending. Congress passes tax laws, which raise money for the government, and appropriations laws, which determine how the money is spent. Taxes are used both to raise money and to regulate the economy. The Constitution requires that all tax bills be introduced in the House of Representatives, where they are handled by the Ways and Means Committee. After they have been passed by the committee, tax measures must be approved by the entire House of Representatives. In the Senate, the Finance Committee handles tax legislation. When it completes its work, the bill is sent to the Senate for final consideration.

Congress also has the constitutional power to make decisions regarding the spending of tax revenues. It does this through a two-step process involving authorizations and appropriations. **Authorization bills** establish specific programs and set limits on the amounts that may be spent on them by the executive branch; **appropriation bills** provide the money itself. (The amount appropriated may be less than the amount authorized.)

The Budget Process. In 1974 Congress passed the Budget and Impoundment Control Act. This legislation was intended to create a new procedure for establishing the annual federal budget. The legislation was motivated by fear of inflation, rapid increases in federal spending and the national debt, and the belief that the executive branch had acquired too much power over government spending.

The 1974 law created budget committees in both houses of Congress, established the Congressional Budget Office to provide Congress with economic information, limited the President's power to *impound* (i.e., not spend) funds appropriated by Congress, and changed the beginning of the federal fiscal year from July 1 to October 1 so as to give Congress more time to consider the budget proposals made by the President in January of each year. The Budget and Impoundment Control Act also established a schedule for the enactment of all tax, authorization, and appropriations legislation. The procedure begins in the spring of each year and is supposed to be completed by October 1.

The President, of course, has his own ideas about the federal budget, and they are likely to be at odds with those of Congress. Thus summer and early fall are times of heated debate between the legislative and executive branches over the final version of the budget. Although all spending bills are supposed to be enacted by October 1, they almost never are, and Congress

An early photo of the Capitol.

usually adopts *continuing resolutions*, or stopgap spending bills that keep the federal agencies running.

In 1985 Congress made a major change in the budget process. It passed the Balanced Budget and Emergency Control Act, also known as the Gramm-Rudman-Hollings Act for its major sponsors. This law was adopted in response to the spiraling federal deficit, which reached $150–220 billion in the late 1980s and remained high during the early 1990s. The deficit was caused by rapid increases in federal defense spending during the 1980s, automatic increases in various federal entitlement programs, and President Ronald Reagan's program of tax reduction coupled with opposition to new taxes. The Gramm-Rudman-Hollings Act established annual targets for the reduction of the deficit until it reached zero. If Congress and the President could not agree on a budget that would accomplish these goals, the power to make the necessary cuts in federal spending was given to a legislative arm of Congress, the General Accounting Office. But the Supreme Court found this system to be a violation of the separation-of-powers system established by the United States Constitution.[1]

The Gramm-Rudman-Hollings law has been revised on several occasions since the 1986 decision of the Supreme Court. The most recent change came in the fall of 1990, when Congress enacted legislation designed to reduce the federal budget deficit in the fiscal years between 1991 and 1995. The new approach no longer focused on a single deficit target for each year. Rather, it provided for the creation of annual caps on spending for the fiscal years 1991, 1992, and 1993 in each of three areas of government activity: defense, domestic programs, and foreign aid. At the close of each fiscal year, the Office of Management and the Budget (see Chapter 9) determines how much money, if any, will be spent in excess of the three spending caps. It then reports this information to the President, who is authorized to issue *sequestration orders*, which will prevent any excess amounts from being spent.

A major problem with the new law is that the main domestic cause of the federal budget deficit has been the rapid growth in *entitlement programs* such as Medicare and Social Security. The spending caps established by the 1990 budget legislation do not apply to these programs, whose costs automatically rise as more people qualify for benefits. Congress has traditionally been unwilling to limit the size of these popular government programs. The new law only specifies that if Congress adds *new* benefit programs, it must pay for them either by raising taxes or cutting other entitlements. (See Figure 7.1.)

Interstate Commerce. A major domestic power of Congress granted by Article I, Section 8, of the Constitution is the authority to regulate interstate commerce. In modern times the Supreme Court has adopted a very broad view of this congressional power. The commerce clause provides the constitutional basis for much of the legislation Congress has passed to control and regulate the American economy. For example, the laws that deal with air traffic, railroads and trucking, radio and television broadcasting, labor-management relations, and the stock exchanges are all based on the commerce clause.

The scope of the commerce clause is not limited to economic issues. Major provisions of the federal criminal code that make certain interstate

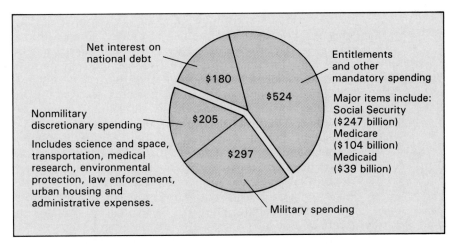

FIGURE 7.1 *Projected federal expenditures for fiscal 1990 (in billions of dollars).*

The bulk of expenditures in the $1.2 trillion budget are mandated by law. Spending is discretionary only to the military, which absorbs 25 percent of the total, and a multitude of programs that together account for 17 percent of the budget.

Source: Congressional Budget Office, as reported in *The New York Times*, January 28, 1990, Section 4, p. 1. Copyright © 1990 by The New York Times Company. Reprinted by permission.

acts illegal (e.g., the interstate shipment of stolen automobiles) are based on it. The commerce clause has also been used to deal with the problem of racial discrimination. The 1964 Civil Rights Act made it a crime for businesses that provide accommodations to interstate travelers (e.g., hotels, motels, and many restaurants) to practice racial discrimination.

Foreign Affairs and Treaties. Although the Constitution gives the President the primary role in foreign affairs, Congress also has significant powers in this area. In Article I, Section 8, the Constitution gives the legislature the power to regulate international commerce, to declare war, and to raise and support both an army and a navy. Congress can also directly affect foreign and military policy through its power over the appropriation of funds.

Article II, Section 2, of the Constitution requires that all treaties made by the President with foreign nations receive the advice and consent of two-thirds of the Senate before they can become effective. The Senate has rejected only about twenty treaties since the Constitution was ratified. But it can also amend proposed treaties or attach reservations to them, and it has exercised this authority on many occasions.

The American constitutional historian Edward S. Corwin described the provisions of the Constitution as "an invitation to struggle for the privilege of directing American foreign policy."[2] Throughout most of American history, this struggle was won by the President. However, in the early 1970s, as the Vietnam War drew to a close, Congress asserted its constitutional powers. The War Powers Resolution of 1973 was the most important attempt to project Congress' authority in foreign and military affairs. The resolution sought to limit the President's freedom to use military forces in combat situations without obtaining the approval of Congress. It requires that the President end the use of military force within sixty days unless Congress declares war or agrees to the continued use of the nation's armed forces; the President can, if necessary, extend the period for an additional thirty days. (See Chapter 8 for a fuller discussion of this legislation.)

Presidents Reagan and Bush have both asserted the power of their office in foreign affairs, and Congress has retreated somewhat from the position it established in the 1970s. During the 1980s Democrats in Congress criticized President Reagan's support of the Contras (opponents of the leftist government) in Nicaragua, and Congress passed legislation that imposed restrictions on the use of federal money to support the Contras. But Reagan's decisions to invade the Caribbean island of Grenada in 1983 and to bomb Libya in 1986 were carried out without advance consultation with Congress. Similarly, President Bush invaded Panama in December 1989 without first consulting with congressional leaders. And in August 1990, in response to Iraq's invasion of Kuwait, he sent a massive American military force into the Middle East to defend against a threatened Iraqi invasion of Saudi Arabia. This was the largest such buildup since the Vietnam War. The initial steps occurred while Congress was on its summer recess and without consultation with congressional leaders. President Bush did, however, notify Congress on the day American troops were sent to the Middle East.

The President continued to add to the number of military personnel in the Persian Gulf during the last months of 1990. Although there were some dissenting voices in the legislature to this policy, Congress took no action to stop the President. Finally, on January 12, 1991, after a lengthy and serious debate, both houses of the Congress voted to give the nation's Chief Executive the right to go to war against Iraq.

Legislative Functions: Implied Powers

After enumerating the powers granted to Congress, Article I, Section 8, of the Constitution concludes by giving the legislature **implied powers:** Congress has the right "to make all Laws which shall be necessary and proper for carrying into Execution the foregoing Powers, and all other Powers vested by this Constitution in the Government of the United States, or in any Department or Officer thereof."

This provision of the Constitution gives Congress a broad range of choices in selecting the means to carry out its expressed powers, as long as the means selected do not violate the Constitution. The necessary and proper clause thus adds significantly to the authority of Congress to act in both the domestic and the international spheres.

Representation

Another important function of Congress—that is, of each of its members—is to represent the people of a particular district or state. This representation takes two basic forms: policy representation and service. *Policy representation* is concerned mainly with attempting to pass legislation that is in the best interests of a senator or representative's constituents. *Service* consists of nonlegislative activities that benefit individuals or groups in the home district or state.

Most members of Congress find that they lack the time to fulfill all the responsibilities of representation. They are required to perform what amounts to a juggling act: Tuesday through Thursday they are busy on Capitol Hill, while the remaining days are spent responding to the demands of constituents. The average representative makes thirty-five trips a year to his or her home district.[3]

Senators and representatives often find that they must choose between meeting the demands of constituents and carrying out their legislative responsibilities. In a survey of House members, representatives were asked about the differences between how they actually spend their time and how they would spend it under ideal circumstances. More than half the respondents stated that solving constituents' problems interferes with lawmaking and other congressional duties.[4]

New legislators are often surprised by the great number of demands made by their constituents. The legislators are asked to carry out such **case work** tasks as helping elderly people obtain their federal pensions and arranging for food stamps for needy constituents. The public seems more interested in such personal services than in current issues or how their representative voted on a major bill. As one member of Congress commented, "I thought I was going to be Daniel Webster and I found that most of my work consisted of personal work for constituents."[5]

Members of Congress devote varying amounts of time to the demands of constituents. But all quickly learn that personal services must be provided and that constituents must be kept in mind at all times:

> Prompt attention should be given to mail from home, district newspapers should be read or scanned regularly, and press coverage of the legislator's office should be supplemented by his own releases publicizing his activities. He should undertake all sorts of projects designed to create a district image of him as an active legislator, informed and concerned about public problems and deeply interested in the opinions and welfare of those he represents.[6]

The new congressman or congresswoman who fails to appreciate this advice is likely to have a short career as a Washington legislator. Indeed, since reelection is a major concern of members of Congress, they are strongly motivated to perform these personal services for voters. This concern is especially pressing for new House members trying to build district support during the first few terms.

Other Constitutional Functions

In addition to its lawmaking authority, Congress performs a variety of nonlawmaking functions assigned to it by the Constitution. Among these are the following:

1. *Watchdog and oversight functions.* Congress is responsible for overseeing the executive branch of the government. Although it is not expressly

A special joint session of Congress on March 2, 1989, on the occasion of the 200th anniversary of the first meeting of Congress.

mentioned in the Constitution, **oversight** is a major function of Congress. It is the power of Congress to watch over the laws it has passed and check on the administrative organizations under its jurisdiction. The oversight function is carried out by the committees of Congress, which may conduct investigations of specific government programs and policies. The most famous recent example is the House and Senate's 1987 investigation of the secret military assistance provided by the Reagan administration to the government of Iran and the Contras in Nicaragua.

2. *Appointments.* According to Article II, Section 2, of the Constitution, presidential nominations of ambassadors and Supreme Court justices and for all other "Offices of the United States"—such as department heads—must receive the "advice and consent" of the Senate. Twenty-eight times in the nation's history the Senate has refused to confirm nominees to the United States Supreme Court. But it is rare for the Senate to reject the President's choice for a position within the executive branch—only one nominee for a Cabinet position has been turned down by the Senate in more than three decades.

3. *Electoral functions.* As mentioned in Chapter 6, if no presidential candidate has received a majority of the electoral votes in the general election, the House of Representatives has the power to elect the President from among the three candidates with the most electoral votes. (In such a situation it votes by states, with each state having one vote.) Similarly, the Constitution assigns the Senate the power to choose the Vice President from the two candidates with the most electoral votes if

no candidate obtains a majority of those votes. In addition, the President of the Senate (i.e., the Vice President of the United States) has the ceremonial duty of counting the electoral votes sent to Congress by the states and announcing the results.[7]

4. *Vice presidential nominations and presidential disability.* The Twenty-fifth Amendment assigns Congress a major role when the office of the Vice President becomes vacant and during times of presidential disability. When a President nominates someone to fill the office of Vice President, both houses of Congress must confirm the nomination by a majority vote. The Twenty-fifth Amendment also gives Congress a role in deciding whether the President is disabled and therefore unable to perform the duties of the office, as well as deciding whether the President is well enough to resume office.

5. *Impeachment.* Congress also plays a role in the **impeachment,** conviction, and removal of the President, Vice President, federal judges, and other civil officers of the United States if it believes those individuals to be guilty of treason, bribery, or other high crimes and misdemeanors. The House of Representatives decides whether to levy formal charges against the official (i.e., to impeach), and it does this by a majority vote. The Senate then determines by a two-thirds vote whether to convict and remove the person from office. The power to impeach has rarely been used; there have been only fifteen impeachment trials in the nation's history (through 1990).

6. *Amendments to the Constitution.* Chapter 2 discussed the procedure set forth by Article V for amending the Constitution. Congress has the power to propose amendments by a two-thirds vote, and it also has the authority to determine whether ratification of the proposed amendment shall be by a three-fourths majority of the state legislatures or by special state conventions. (It has almost always chosen the former method.)

7. *Disciplining and expelling members.* Article I, Section 5, of the Constitution declares that "each House [of Congress] shall be the Judge of the Elections, Returns and Qualifications of its own Members." This clause gives to the Senate and the House of Representatives the power to prevent a newly elected member from taking his or her seat in Congress. The Supreme Court has ruled, however, that this power applies only to the exclusion of individuals who do not meet the constitutional requirements for membership. (A representative must be at least 25 years old, have been a citizen of the United States for at least seven years, and be a resident of the state from which he or she is elected; a senator must be at least 30, have been a citizen at least nine years, and be a resident of the state from which he or she is elected.) Exclusion cannot be based on any other ground.[8]

Article I, Section 5, goes on to state that "Each House may . . . punish its Members for disorderly Behavior, and, with the Concurrence of two thirds, expel a Member." This is the basis for the authority to censure or expel members of Congress who are guilty of misconduct. The Constitution does not specify the kinds of misconduct to which this power may be applied;[9] indeed, Congress has rarely exercised this power. Only fifteen senators have been expelled, none of them since the Civil War, when several were expelled for supporting the rebellion. Only four

The "Keating Five" hearing in the fall of 1990. Senators who faced charges of influence peddling in behalf of Charles H. Keating, Jr., savings and loan owner, appear before the Senate Ethics Committee. In recent years, issues involving financial contributions have plagued Congress.

members of the House of Representatives have been expelled; of these, three were expelled during the Civil War. Votes to censure have also been relatively rare, occurring in response to various forms of misconduct.

■ The Congressional District

Article I, Section 2, of the Constitution provides that House seats shall be assigned to the states mainly on the basis of population. This is done every ten years, when the population of the United States is counted by the Census Bureau. Each state gets at least one seat, but after each census the other seats are apportioned among the states according to population. States whose populations have grown relative to those of other states gain new seats; those that have lost population relative to others have seats taken away from them. Since 1929, however, the total membership of the House has been limited to 435 (except for a brief period during the late 1950s following the admission of Alaska and Hawaii as states, when the figure was 437).

The legislature of each state is responsible for determining the boundaries of the congressional districts within that state as well as those of state legislative districts. Under the process known as **reapportionment,** boundaries are supposed to be changed after each census to reflect population shifts during the preceding ten years, and the resulting districts are to be drawn in such a way as to be equal in population. Until the 1960s, state legislatures were controlled by rural and small-town interests. Following World War II, large numbers of people moved to cities and suburbs, but state legislatures failed to redraw district boundaries to reflect this massive population shift. As a result, people who lived in urban areas were underrepresented in the House of Representatives and in most state legislatures.

The issue of unequal representation reached the Supreme Court in 1964 in a case involving congressional districts in Georgia.[10] The Court ruled that congressional representation must be based "as nearly as practicable" on population. It applied the "one person, one vote" principle to congressional elections and held that congressional districts must be equal in population.

State legislatures can still draw district boundaries in such a way as to give a particular political party an advantage. This practice, known as **gerrymandering,**[11] involves the division of territory into voting districts that give an advantage to the majority party, which draws the boundary lines. To maximize its chances of winning elections, the majority party draws the boundaries so that at least a majority of the voters in the district are its supporters, or supporters of the opposition party are divided among two or more districts. (See Figure 7.2.) For many years the Supreme Court refused to consider cases involving gerrymandering. But in 1986 it held that the federal courts could hear and decide cases involving claims that gerrymandering violates the equal protection clause of the Fourteenth Amendment.[12]

The 1990 national population count conducted by the Census Bureau required changes in the number of seats held in the House of Representatives by twenty-one states. Eight states gained, while thirteen lost one or more representatives (see Table 7.1). In addition, census population figures will also require many states to draw new district lines for the House of Representatives based entirely on the movement of people within the states during the 1980s.

The biggest winners from the 1990 census were California, Florida, and Texas. California, with 52 seats, now has the largest number ever held by a single state, and it possesses almost one-eighth of the votes needed to elect a president in the electoral college.

In general, the states of the South and West gained, and those of the Northeast and Midwest lost political power. This shift should make the House of Representatives more conservative during the 1990s. States like New York, which lost seats, are more liberal; those that gained, like Florida and Texas, are more conservative in their politics.

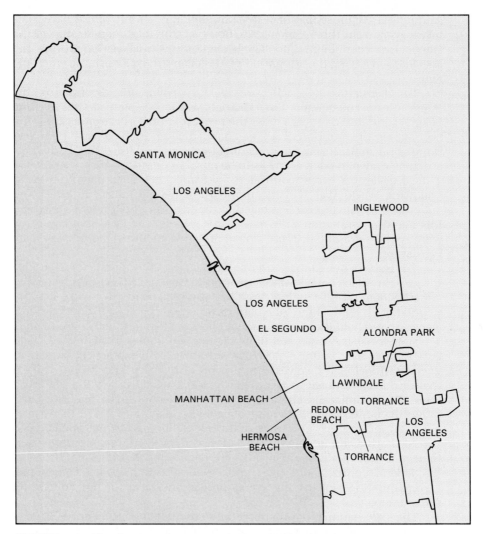

FIGURE 7.2 *The fine art of gerrymandering, California style.*

Gerrymandering reached its height in the California redistricting in the early 1980s. The 27th District is an example. Its two major parts were connected by a thin strip of land along the Pacific Ocean, gathering in as many Democratic voters as possible and excluding Republican areas. These highly irregular district lines enabled the Democrats to win a large majority of California's seats in the House of Representatives.

It is never possible to predict the political consequences of each census. This is especially true when district lines must be redrawn by the legislatures. Even with the present use of modern computer technology, redistricting is a highly political process. But even the most carefully drawn lines sometimes backfire on their designers. Judicial challenges to some plans are likely, which could result in altering the goals set by the politicians.

TABLE 7.1 *Shifting Political Power among the States*

State	Number of seats	Change
Arizona	6	+1
California	52	+7
Florida	23	+4
Georgia	11	+1
Illinois	20	−2
Iowa	5	−1
Kansas	4	−1
Kentucky	6	−1
Louisiana	7	−1
Massachusetts	10	−1
Michigan	16	−2
Montana	1	−1
New Jersey	13	−1
New York	31	−3
North Carolina	12	+1
Ohio	19	−2
Pennsylvania	21	−2
Texas	30	+3
Virginia	11	+1
Washington	9	+1
West Virginia	3	−1

Based on the 1990 Census, 21 states either gained or lost seats in the House of Representatives

■ The Two Houses: Similarities and Differences

The two houses of Congress are equal partners in the lawmaking process. Each must approve a bill before it can become law. In each house, the majority party elects the leader of that house (the Speaker of the House and the President Pro Tempore of the Senate). In addition, in both houses committees are controlled by the majority party, and the important committee chairs are always members of the majority party.

There are, however, certain significant differences between the House and the Senate. The most obvious difference, of course, is size—the Senate has 100 members and the House 435. This factor leads to differences in style. One political scientist has suggested that perhaps "the most striking difference noticed by most visitors to the Capitol is the apparent formality and impersonality in the House chamber as contrasted to the relatively informal and friendly atmosphere in the Senate."[13] Size also influences the procedures followed by the House and the Senate. Senate rules are short and relatively simple; House rules are many and complex. House rules, for example, sharply limit the time in which a member may speak during a debate, whereas senators are not subject to such limits.

Another difference between the two houses of Congress derives from the different terms of office of their members: two years in the House, six in the Senate. Most representatives are therefore campaigning almost all the time, whereas senators have more time before they must seek reelection. As a result, senators can pay more attention to aspects of legislation that do not affect their chances of winning or losing voter support.[14]

A further major difference between the two houses of Congress is the political outlook of their members. Senators have statewide constituencies. As a result, they must keep in mind the interests of a variety of groups. Most representatives have smaller constituencies; each speaks for the residents of a particular district. The representative's concerns, therefore, are often limited to more local issues that are of interest to fewer groups.

■ The Members of Congress

William Mosley ("Fishbait") Miller, the longtime doorkeeper of the House of Representatives, once described the members of Congress as "535 high-school class presidents with a few prom queens thrown in."[15] In a more serious vein, Cabell Phillips admitted that Congress "has its quota of knaves and fools," but added that "it has its fair share of knights. And sandwiched between these upper and nether crusts is a broad and representative slice of upper-middle-class America."[16] Most members of Congress have a college degree; the largest number are lawyers, and the next-largest group consists of people with backgrounds in business and banking. Recently there has been a sharp increase in the proportion of members with backgrounds in politics or public service. On the other hand, very few members of Congress are officials of trade unions (see Table 7.2). The average age of senators in the 102nd Congress (1991–1993) was a little more than fifty-seven years; that of members of the House of Representatives almost fifty-three, the highest average in the past two decades.

Throughout most of American history Congress was composed almost entirely of white Protestant males. Today Congress is no longer overwhelmingly Protestant, but it remains largely male and white. About two-thirds of the members are Protestants; the rest are either Roman Catholic or Jewish. Catholics are now the largest single religious denomination in Congress; more than one-quarter of the members are Roman Catholic.

Although women constitute slightly more than 50 percent of the nation's population, relatively few serve in the national legislature. In the 102nd Congress, there were only two female senators and twenty-eight female representatives, a gain of four from the previous Congress. African-American and Hispanic Americans are also underrepresented in Congress. About 12 percent of the American population is black, but there were no black senators and only twenty-five black representatives in the 102nd Congress. One, Garry Franks of Connecticut, was the first black Republican to serve in the House since 1935. There were eleven Hispanic members of the House and five Pacific Island and Asian legislators in the 102nd Congress.

TABLE 7.2 *Members' Occupations: 102nd Congress*

| | HOUSE | | | SENATE | | | CONGRESS |
	D	R	Total	D	R	Total	Total
Actor/Entertainer	1	1	2	0	0	0	2
Aeronautics	0	1	1	1	0	1	2
Agriculture	11	9	20	3	5	8	28
Business or Banking	77	80	157	15	16	31	188
Clergy	2	0	2	0	1	1	3
Education	37	19	57†	6	4	10	67†
Engineering	4	3	7	0	0	0	7
Journalism	14	10	25†	8	2	10	35†
Labor Officials	3	0	3	0	0	0	3
Law	126	57	183	35	26	61	244
Law Enforcement	4	1	5	0	0	0	5
Medicine	3	2	5	0	0	0	5
Military	0	1	1	0	1	1	2
Professional Sports	2	1	3	1	0	1	4
Public Service/Politics	41	20	61	4	0	4	65

Because some members have more than one occupation, totals are higher than total membership.
†Includes Sanders, I-Vt.

Source: Mike Mills, "Characteristics of Congress," *Congressional Quarterly*, November 10, 1990, p. 3837.

The 1990 elections saw the Democrats extend their long control of the House of Representatives for another two years. The Democratic Party has been the majority party in the lower house of the legislature since 1955 (see Table 7.3 on p. 180).

■ Congressional Leadership

Leadership positions in the two houses of Congress are positions of power. This power is not as great today as it has been in the past, but it is still significant. Congressional leaders, who are elected by their fellow members, often have a major effect on the legislation passed by Congress.

The Speaker of the House

The Constitution provides that the **Speaker of the House**—the presiding officer of the House of Representatives—shall be elected by the entire House. In practice, this means that the candidate of the majority party wins the election and becomes the Speaker. The authority of the Speaker has changed over the course of American history. During much of the nineteenth century the Speaker's powers were shared with the chairs of major standing committees. The office grew in importance, however, and by

TABLE 7.3 *Composition of Congress, by Political Party: 1953 to 1991*

Year	Party and president	Congress	HOUSE Majority party	HOUSE Minority party	HOUSE Other	SENATE Majority party	SENATE Minority party	SENATE Other
1953	R (Eisenhower)	83d	R-221	D-211	1	R-48	D-47	1
1955	R (Eisenhower)	84th	D-232	R-203	—	D-48	R-47	1
1957	R (Eisenhower)	85th	D-233	R-200	—	D-49	R-47	—
1959[1]	R (Eisenhower)	86th	D-284	R-153	—	D-65	R-35	—
1961	D (Kennedy)	87th	D-263	R-174	—	D-65	R-35	—
1963	D (Kennedy)	88th	D-258	R-177	—	D-67	R-33	—
1965	D (Johnson)	89th	D-295	R-140	—	D-68	R-32	—
1967	D (Johnson)	90th	D-247	R-187	—	D-64	R-36	—
1969	R (Nixon)	91st	D-243	R-192	—	D-57	R-43	—
1971[2]	R (Nixon)	92d	D-254	R-180	—	D-54	R-44	2
1973[2,3]	R (Nixon)[4]	93d	D-239	R-192	1	D-56	R-42	2
1975[5]	R (Ford)[4]	94th	D-291	R-144	—	D-60	R-37	2
1977[6]	D (Carter)	95th	D-292	R-143	—	D-61	R-38	1
1979[6]	D (Carter)	96th	D-276	R-157	—	D-58	R-41	1
1981[7]	R (Reagan)	97th	D-242	R-192	1	R-53	D-46	1
1983	R (Reagan)	98th	D-269	R-165	—	R-54	D-46	—
1985	R (Reagan)	99th	D-253	R-182	—	R-53	D-47	—
1987	R (Reagan)	100th	D-258	R-177	—	D-54	R-46	—
1989	R (Bush)	101st	D-262	R-173	—	D-55	R-45	—
1991[8]	R (Bush)	102nd	D-267	R-167	1	D-56	R-44	—

D = Democratic; R = Republican. Data for beginning of first session of each Congress; excludes vacancies at beginning of session.
— Represents zero.
[1] Includes Hawaiian members seated Aug. 1959.
[2] Senate had 1 Independent and 1 Conservative-Republican.
[3] House had 1 Independent-Democrat.
[4] Nixon resigned Aug. 1974.
[5] Senate had 1 Independent, 1 Conservative-Republican, and 1 undecided (New Hampshire).
[6] Senate had 1 Independent.
[7] Senate and House each had 1 Independent.
[8] House had one socialist.

Source: U.S. Department of Commerce, Bureau of the Census, *Statistical Abstract of the United States: 1990*, 110th ed. (Washington, D.C.: U.S. Government Printing Office, 1990), Table 425 p. 255. Updated for November 1990 election.

the turn of the century the Speaker played a dominant role in the House. The Speaker's authority reached its zenith in the years between 1903 and 1910, when Joseph Cannon held the office. Cannon's often arbitrary rule prompted a reaction by the members of the House, and new rules were adopted under which the Speaker lost the right to sit on the House Rules Committee and the power to appoint committee members and chairs.

Today the Speaker's position is very powerful, though not what it was during the Cannon era. The Speaker has the traditional rights of a presiding officer: the right to recognize members for the purpose of speaking and the authority to interpret the rules of the House. With the aid of the parliamentarian, the Speaker assigns new bills to specific committees. The assignment of a bill can be crucial—giving a bill to a friendly or hostile committee can determine its fate. The Speaker's power in this area is limited, however, because the jurisdiction of the various committees is set forth in House rules.

The Speaker's formal powers also include the right to make appointments to some committees, including the conference committees that attempt to resolve differences between the versions of a bill passed by the two houses of Congress. In fact, however, the Speaker usually appoints the candidates whose names have been sent to him by the chair of the committee that considered the legislation.

Several changes made in the mid-1970s by the House Democratic Caucus increased the formal powers of Democratic Speakers. (A **caucus** is composed of all the members of one party in the House or Senate; the Republicans call it a **conference.**) A Democratic Speaker now has the right to appoint members of the Democratic Steering and Policy Committee, which controls the assignment of Democratic representatives to standing committees. Democratic Speakers also have the right to nominate the Democratic members of the all-important House Rules Committee (and, of course, to refuse to renominate uncooperative members). The Speaker's selections are, however, subject to approval by the House Democratic Caucus.

More important than the Speaker's formal authority is his personal influence. As the leader of his party, he strives to unify party members in support of the party's legislative program. He also works with the House **majority leader** and the House Rules Committee to schedule the order in which legislation will be considered by the House. Some Speakers have had more influence than others. Perhaps the most influential Speaker in recent decades was Thomas P. ("Tip") O'Neill, Jr. (D., Mass.), who held the position from 1977 to 1987. O'Neill was popular, colorful, and a forceful spokesperson for the Democratic party during the years he served as Speaker. In the 1980s, with Republican Ronald Reagan in the White House, O'Neill became a national political figure who criticized Reagan's domestic policies and advanced alternative programs for his party.

Senate Leadership

The Constitution makes the Vice President of the United States the presiding officer of the Senate. As **President of the Senate** he may vote to break a tie, but aside from this function he has no significant legislative duties—he is not even permitted to engage in floor debate. The majority party also nominates a **President Pro Tempore** ("for the time being") to help preside over the Senate. (By custom this position is filled by the member of the majority party with the longest record of continual service in the Senate.) The Vice President rarely attends Senate sessions, and the President Pro Tempore rarely presides; neither is a position of great importance in the Senate. The job of presiding over the Senate is usually shared by junior members. While the presiding officer of the Senate has many of the formal powers of the Speaker of the House—such as the right to recognize members who wish to speak and the right to interpret rules—he has little real power or influence.

The Majority Leaders

The **Senate majority leader** is chosen by the majority party in the Senate. His role consists largely of scheduling the work of the Senate and presenting the majority party's position on issues. Perhaps because of the small number of senators and their strong sense of independence, the Senate majority leader has not generally been the equal of the Speaker of the House in power and influence. Howard Baker (R., Tenn.) was the most successful majority leader in recent years. Between 1981 and 1985, when the Republican party controlled the Senate, Baker successfully guided much of President Reagan's often controversial domestic program through the Senate. He worked closely with the President during those years and was a respected leader within the Senate.

The **House majority leader** is second in importance to the Speaker. He, too, is chosen by the majority party, but unlike the Speaker, he is responsible only to his party and is not an officer of the entire House. The job of the majority leader, both in the House and in the Senate, is defined by tradition rather than by congressional or party rules. It consists primarily of serving as the party's principal spokesperson. In addition, majority leaders plan legislative agendas, consult with the President about his legislative proposals, and attempt to influence colleagues to support or defeat particular measures.[17]

Minority Leaders and Floor Whips

The House and Senate **minority leaders** are elected by the minority party in each house. They plan their party's strategy and are expected to examine and criticize the majority party's arguments. The majority and minority leaders are aided by assistant floor leaders, or **whips,**[18] who round up the votes of party members by giving them information for or against a bill that is coming to a vote and persuading them to be present when their votes are needed. The whips thus serve as a liaison between the party leader and the members.

■ The Committee System

Woodrow Wilson once wrote that "Congressional government is Committee government."[19] Although floor debates are necessary in some cases, most of the actual work of Congress is done in committees and subcommittees. These committees are very important to the individual members of Congress. In committee a member can have a direct effect on the shaping of legislation. Moreover, a member's committee assignments can determine his or her effectiveness. A senator from a rural state, for example, can better serve the interests of his or her constituents as a member of the Agriculture Committee than as a member of the Banking, Housing and Urban Affairs Committee.

Types of Committees

The most important committees in Congress are the **standing committees.** These committees do most of the work on legislative proposals. (Each standing committee specializes in a particular field and deals only with bills related to that field.) Thus standing committees can decide the fate of proposed legislation. Only a minority of the bills that are introduced are acted on by the committees. Those that are approved by committees are "reported" to the full House or Senate.

The majority party always holds a majority of the seats on a standing committee, and the chair of the committee is always a member of the majority party. The House of Representatives has twenty-two standing committees; the Senate has sixteen. Legislators serve on a number of committees, but each senator is limited to membership on two major committees, such as Appropriations, Foreign Relations, or Armed Services. In the House, a member must serve on at least one major committee.

Most standing committees are divided into subcommittees that deal with specialized areas of the parent committee's jurisdiction and are created at the discretion of that committee. For example, there are subcommittees of the Appropriations Committees of both houses that handle legislation related to agriculture. Subcommittees have become more numerous as the concerns of the government have grown, and their importance has also increased. In the 101st Congress (1989–1991), there were 137 subcommittees in the House of Representatives and 86 in the Senate (see Tables 7.4 and 7.5).

In addition to the standing committees, there are three other types of congressional committees: select committees, joint committees, and conference committees. **Select** (also called **special) committees** are formed to examine particular issues or new areas of legislation. They have the same powers as standing committees, except that they cannot receive bills or report legislation to the floor of the House or Senate. Most select committees are temporary; they cease to exist when the term of the Congress that created them ends. In 1987, for example, both the Senate and the House established select committees to investigate the Reagan administration's

TABLE 7.4 *Standing Committees in the House of Representatives: 101st Congress (1989–1991)*

Agriculture (8)	Interior and Insular Affairs (6)
Appropriations (13)	Judiciary (7)
Armed Services (7)	Merchant Marine and Fisheries (6)
Banking, Finance, and Urban Affairs (6)	Post Office and Civil Service (7)
Budget (6 Task Forces)	Public Works and Transportation (6)
District of Columbia (3)	Rules (2)
Education and Labor (8)	Science, Space, and Technology (7)
Energy and Commerce (6)	Small Business (6)
Foreign Affairs (8)	Standards of Official Conduct (none)
Government Operations (7)	Veterans (5)
House Administration (7)	Ways and Means (6)

Total: 22 standing committees, 137 subcommittees

The number of subcommittees is in parentheses.

Source: Congressional Directory (Washington, D.C.: U.S. Government Printing Office, 1989).

TABLE 7.5 *Standing Committees in the Senate: 101st Congress*

Agriculture, Nutrition, and Forestry (7)	Finance (8)
Appropriations (13)	Foreign Relations (7)
Armed Services (6)	Governmental Affairs (5)
Banking, Housing, and Urban Affairs (4)	Judiciary (6)
Budget (none)	Labor and Human Resources (6)
Commerce, Science, and Transportation (8)	Rules and Administration (none)
Energy and Natural Resources (5)	Small Business (6)
Environment and Public Works (5)	Veteran's Affairs (none)

Total: 16 standing committees, 86 subcommittees

The number of subcommittees is in parentheses.

Source: Congressional Directory (Washington, D.C.: U.S. Government Printing Office, 1989).

policy of providing covert military aid to Iran and the Nicaraguan Contras. The committees held joint hearings on the subject, a procedure that is rarely used by Congress.

Joint committees are formed by the House and Senate to deal with issues that Congress believes require coordinated action by both houses. In recent years there have been four joint committees: Economic, Taxation, Library, and Printing. Such committees include members of both houses and are permanent, but they are rarely given the right to bring legislation to the floor of either house, only to investigate and make recommendations. Joint committees offer the advantage of coordinating and simplifying congressional procedures, but Congress is reluctant to use this approach. Political rivalries and the fear that they will encroach on the jurisdiction of standing committees are among the factors that make joint committees unpopular. House members are especially fearful of Senate domination of joint committees.

A meeting of the Joint Senate and House Select Committee investigating the Iran-Contra affair in 1987.

Conference committees are joint committees formed to work out a compromise when different versions of a bill have been passed by the House and the Senate. (Bills must pass both houses in exactly the same form before they can be sent to the President.) Conference committees are normally used with major pieces of legislation; differences over less significant legislation are usually resolved without sending a bill to conference.

A conference committee may have from three to nine members; occasionally a larger committee is formed. Members—called *managers* or *conferees*—are drawn from both parties. They are appointed by the Speaker of the House and the presiding officer of the Senate on the basis of suggestions of the chairs and ranking minority members of the committees that reported the measure and are usually members of those committees. Only members who voted for the bill are selected. Both houses normally ask the committee chair and the ranking majority and minority members of the committee to serve on the conference committee.

Differences are ironed out by bargaining over each section of the legislation. The members of the committee vote as representatives of the House and Senate, not as individuals. A majority of the managers from each house must approve a compromise before it can be adopted. If a final agreement is reached by the conference committee, the *conference report* will be sent to the floor of each house. There it cannot be amended, only adopted or rejected. If both houses approve the work of the conference committee, the bill is sent to the President, but if the conference report is rejected by either house, the bill dies. It is possible, however, for the full House and Senate to direct the conference committee to make a further effort to reach an agreement.

Under congressional rules, conference committees are not expected to make any significant changes in the bill being considered. Critics charge, however, that conference committees frequently "exceed their authority, writing virtually new legislation."[20] Indeed, since most important legislation goes to conference committees and the reports of those committees are usually accepted by Congress, it is evident that a small number of legislators often have considerable influence on the passage of laws.

Committee Assignments

Members of all standing committees are elected by the full House or Senate, but these elections are merely ratifications of the choices made by the parties. The size of the standing committees is decided by the majority party leadership in the House and by agreement between the majority and minority leaders in the Senate. In the House, the Democrats have been the majority party continually since 1955; as a result, they have organized the standing committees of the House for almost forty years. It is customary for party representation on a committee to be approximately the same as the percentage of party members in the chamber as a whole.

The Republican Committee on Committees makes its party's assignments to House committees. Since 1910 this committee has consisted of one member from each state that has Republican members in the House. Before 1975 the Democrats' committee assignments were made by the Democratic members of the Ways and Means Committee. In 1975 this power was given to the Steering and Policy Committee of the Democratic Caucus; this committee has about thirty members and is headed by the Speaker.

In the Senate, Republican committee assignments are also made by a Republican Committee on Committees, whose members are appointed by the chair of the Senate Republican Conference (the equivalent of the Democratic Caucus). Democratic committee assignments are made by the Democratic Steering Committee, whose members are appointed by the party leaders.

After each legislative election many changes occur in the membership of committees. Vacancies exist because of retirements and the occasional defeat of an incumbent. New members of Congress must be given places; others seek to change their assignments. There is great demand for assignments to the most important and prestigious committees, and both parties now attempt to appoint newer members of Congress to some of these positions.

Committee Chairs

Until the 1970s the chairs of standing committees had broad power over their committees. They could create and abolish subcommittees, hire the committee's professional staff, and decide when the committee would meet and hold hearings on a bill. A new member of Congress once described this influence as follows:

> I knew committee chairmen were powerful, but I didn't realize the extent of the power or its arbitrary nature. Recently, when my chairman announced he planned to proceed in a particular way, I challenged him to indicate under what rule he was operating. "My rules," he said. That was it.[21]

A series of reforms during the early 1970s changed this situation, reducing the power of committee chairs and increasing the authority of the committee members. Committee chairs still hire the staff, but the time for meetings is set by a vote of the entire committee in consultation with the chair.

In other reforms carried out between 1971 and 1975, the House of Representatives adopted a number of rules that increased the independence and importance of its subcommittees and reduced the authority of committee chairs over these bodies. These reforms also decentralized power within the House by bringing more representatives into positions of authority. The present House rules state that (1) no member of the House can chair more than one subcommittee, (2) senior members of Congress cannot serve on more than one subcommittee of a standing committee, and (3) House committees with more than twenty members must have at least four subcommittees. Senate rules prohibit any committee member from serving as chair of more than one subcommittee.

In 1973 Congress also modified the **seniority system,** under which a committee chairship automatically went to the majority party member with the longest continuous service on that committee. In both houses, committee chairs are now chosen by the party caucuses, although the full Senate and House must formally approve all committee assignments. Seniority continues to be the most important factor in selecting committee chairs. But on a few occasions a party caucus has ousted a senior chair and replaced him with a more junior legislator. Most recently, at the start of the 102nd Congress, the House Democrats removed the chairs of the Public Works and Transportation Committee and the House Administration Committee. While such actions are relatively rare, the 1973 rule change established the important principle that a committee chair is ultimately responsible to the majority of his or her party.

In the Senate, party rules provide that the Republican members of each committee shall elect its chair, subject to the approval of the Republican Conference (i.e., caucus). Democratic senators select committee chairs by secret ballot when one-fifth of the Democrats in the Senate request this procedure. To date, neither party has used these new procedures to deny a committee chairship to a senator who would have received the position under the seniority rule.

As a result of the breakdown of the seniority system and other reforms instituted during the 1970s, it is possible for new members of Congress to influence the legislative process to a much greater extent than before. In the past, "backbenchers" had to serve for a decade or more before they could have a significant effect on legislation. Today it is possible for newly elected members to make a difference within a few years. As one member put it, "You don't have to wait around to have influence. Entrepreneurs do very well."[22]

The Major Committees

Key committees in the Senate include the Appropriations Committee, which considers government expenditures for all programs administered by the departments and agencies of the federal government; the Foreign Relations Committee, which deals with all aspects of American foreign policy, including treaties; the Finance Committee, which reviews proposals having to do with taxes, tariffs, social security, veterans' pensions, and foreign trade agreements; the Armed Services Committee, which deals with military and defense policy; and the Senate Budget Committee, which lists the annual revenues and spending of the federal government.

The major committees in the House of Representatives are Rules, Ways and Means, Appropriations, and Budget. The Rules Committee is important because it determines the order in which all major legislation (except money bills) will be considered by the House as a whole. By granting a special order, or **rule,** that states when and under what conditions a bill will be debated on the House floor, it controls the flow of legislation. By refusing to issue a rule, the Rules Committee can prevent legislation from coming to a vote.

The Ways and Means Committee deals with taxation, tariffs, social security programs, and trade agreements with foreign nations. Unlike other committees, it can report a bill directly to the floor without going through the Rules Committee. The Appropriations Committee recommends specific appropriations for the programs and operations provided for in the federal budget. The House Budget Committee, like its Senate counterpart, obtains budget information and creates a resolution concerned with annual federal revenues and spending.

The Legislative Bureaucracy

Congressional Staff. The members of Congress are assisted by numerous staff aides. These aides mobilize public opinion, advise legislators on how to vote, respond to requests from constituents, and negotiate with lobbyists. Congressional committees also have staff aides. But unlike members' personal staffs, which are concerned primarily with the individual member's reelection, committee staffs focus on legislative policy.[23]

Like most bureaucracies, the personal and committee staffs of Congress have shown a marked tendency to grow. Between 1967 and 1987 the total number of congressional employees swelled from 4,055 to 7,515 in the House and from 1,749 to 4,075 in the Senate. At the same time, the number of committee staff aides grew from 571 to 2,161 in the House and from 509 to 1,040 in the Senate.[24]

What has caused this massive increase? A number of reasons have been suggested. Among them are the greater complexity of the issues facing Congress in the late twentieth century, competition among committees and members, an increase in members' workloads as a result of the demands of constituents, and conflict between the legislative and executive branches. Whatever the cause, there is no doubt that the staff explosion has led to a huge increase in the cost of running Congress. In the 1989 fiscal year, the budget for the legislative branch was approximately $2.2 billion.

Each House member is entitled to hire no more than eighteen full-time and four part-time employees. The average House member's staff totals about fifteen. There is no official limit on the number of personal staff aides that a senator may hire. Senators' personal staffs may range in size from thirteen to seventy-one members. The amount of money given to hire staff aides is determined by the population of a Senator's state.

Some observers of Congress have expressed concern about the influence of congressional staff aides, who are hired, not elected. They feel

Congressman Robert Mrazek (Democrat, N.Y.) meets with members of his staff. In recent years, the number of legislative aides has increased rapidly.

that these individuals actually undercut the lawmaking role of senators and representatives. Often it is staff aides, rather than the members of Congress themselves, who meet to discuss issues and negotiate the content of bills. In such situations it is the aides, rather than elected officials, who determine government policy.[25]

■ The Legislative Process

The legislative process actually begins long before a bill is introduced in the House or Senate. The starting point of legislation is awareness of public problems. As such problems become more prominent, they are increasingly likely to be placed on the **policy agenda,** defined by one political scientist as "the list of subjects to which government officials and those around them are paying serious attention."[26]

Once an issue becomes part of the policy agenda, one or more members of Congress may introduce a bill designed to resolve it. The bill must pass through the legislative process to become law. It is difficult to speak of a "typical" procedure that a bill must follow on the path to either adoption or defeat. Nevertheless, there are certain definite stages that all proposed legislation must go through. Each of these presents an obstacle that could cause the death of the bill. (See Figure 7.3.)

The Introduction of a Bill

Any senator or representative can introduce a bill. A senator can do so by sending the bill to the Senate desk; a representative, by depositing the proposal in the "hopper" located on the floor of the House. To coordinate legislative efforts, a senator and a representative may agree to introduce identical legislation. It should be understood that although any member of

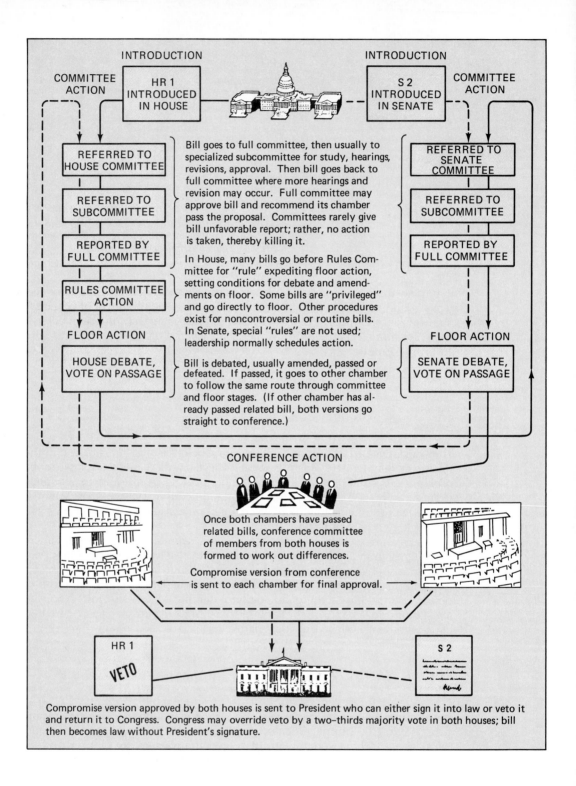

INTRODUCTION

INTRODUCTION

COMMITTEE
ACTION

COMMITTEE
ACTION

HR 1
INTRODUCED
IN HOUSE

S 2
INTRODUCED
IN SENATE

REFERRED TO
HOUSE COMMITTEE

REFERRED TO
SENATE
COMMITTEE

REFERRED TO
SUBCOMMITTEE

REFERRED TO
SUBCOMMITTEE

REPORTED BY
FULL COMMITTEE

REPORTED BY
FULL COMMITTEE

RULES COMMITTEE
ACTION

FLOOR ACTION

FLOOR ACTION

HOUSE DEBATE,
VOTE ON PASSAGE

SENATE DEBATE,
VOTE ON PASSAGE

Bill goes to full committee, then usually to specialized subcommittee for study, hearings, revisions, approval. Then bill goes back to full committee where more hearings and revision may occur. Full committee may approve bill and recommend its chamber pass the proposal. Committees rarely give bill unfavorable report; rather, no action is taken, thereby killing it.

In House, many bills go before Rules Committee for "rule" expediting floor action, setting conditions for debate and amendments on floor. Some bills are "privileged" and go directly to floor. Other procedures exist for noncontroversial or routine bills. In Senate, special "rules" are not used; leadership normally schedules action.

Bill is debated, usually amended, passed or defeated. If passed, it goes to other chamber to follow the same route through committee and floor stages. (If other chamber has already passed related bill, both versions go straight to conference.)

CONFERENCE ACTION

Once both chambers have passed related bills, conference committee of members from both houses is formed to work out differences.

Compromise version from conference is sent to each chamber for final approval.

HR 1

VETO

S 2

Compromise version approved by both houses is sent to President who can either sign it into law or veto it and return it to Congress. Congress may override veto by a two–thirds majority vote in both houses; bill then becomes law without President's signature.

FIGURE 7.3 *How a bill becomes law.*

The process is illustrated by two hypothetical bills: House bill no. 1 (HR 1) and Senate bill no. 2 (S 2). Each bill must be passed by both houses of Congress in identical form before it can become law. The path of HR 1 is traced by a solid line, that of S 2 by a broken line. The figure shows the most typical way proposed legislation is enacted into law; there are more complicated as well as simpler routes, and most bills fall by the wayside and never become law.

Source: Congressional Quarterly Current American Government (Washington, D.C.: Government Printing Office, 1987), p. 140.

Congress can introduce a bill, not every member has an equal chance of having legislation passed. Since Congress is a partisan body, members of the minority party have little or no chance of having their version of a bill enacted into law. Even in the majority party, members are not on an equal footing in terms of ability to influence the passage of legislation. The leaders of the majority party can use their authority to promote the passage of some party members' bills; by not using their influence, they can prevent less favored party members from achieving their goals.

Although a member of Congress must actually introduce a bill, the executive branch is the source of much major legislation. The President's program is announced in the various speeches that he gives at the beginning of each year, especially the annual State of the Union address. Drafts of legislation that embody the President's policies are written in the executive departments and agencies and introduced in Congress by representatives and senators who favor the President's policies.

The Committee Stage

Once a bill has been formally introduced, it is assigned to the appropriate committee for review. If the committee does not want to consider the bill, it is *tabled,* or put aside, and considered dead. This happens to the vast majority of all proposed bills. A **discharge petition** is the only device that can take a bill out of the jurisdiction of a committee. The petition requires the signatures of a majority (218) of the members of the House. Once this is obtained, the House must approve the motion to discharge. Since members of Congress do not like to overrule the standing committees, discharge petitions are very rare. However, the threat of a petition may stimulate a committee to act on a proposed piece of legislation.

If the committee chooses to review the bill, it will be assigned to one of its subcommittees. Subcommittee members often develop considerable knowledge of their subject, which gives them the ability to study a proposed law in depth. On important bills a subcommittee may hold **public hearings** at which individuals testify on the merits or demerits of the bill. These witnesses—technical experts, officials of executive agencies, representatives of organizations, lobbyists, and others—are questioned by members of the committee. In some cases a bill is so controversial that hearings on the subject last for weeks or even months.

After a subcommittee has completed its work, the bill is sent to the full committee for consideration. In the past this was usually done in an *executive session*—a meeting closed to the public and attended only by committee members. But as a result of legislative reforms adopted in 1970, meetings are no longer closed. The committee examines the bill item by item and it is revised, or "marked up." A report explaining the legislation is prepared by the committee. Should there be opposition to the legislation, the report may contain the views of the minority members. If a majority approves the bill, it is "reported out" of the committee. If the majority votes against reporting the bill, the bill dies.

If the standing committee approves the proposal, it is sent to the full House or Senate, where the committee chair manages the debate on the bill. If it is necessary to iron out differences between the versions of a bill passed by the two houses, the chair of the committee that considered the legislation will suggest to the presiding officer of the chamber which members of the committee should serve on the conference committee.

The Calendar

When a bill is reported out of the standing committee, it is placed on a **calendar** in the Senate or the House. The Senate has one calendar that is used for all pending legislation. Routine bills are considered in the order in which they appear on the calendar. In the case of controversial legislation, a time for debate is arranged by the majority leader in consultation with the minority leader, the chair of the committee that considered the bill, and senators who have a special interest in the proposed legislation.

A bill reported to the House is put on one of three major calendars: the *Union Calendar* for appropriations and tax legislation, the *House Calendar* for all other public bills, and the *Private Calendar* for bills dealing with specific individuals, corporations, or localities (e.g., a bill granting citizenship to a particular individual). In addition, the *Consent Calendar* is used for bills that require little or no debate.

The House has special methods for scheduling major bills for floor debate. Bills are not necessarily taken from the two major calendars—the Union and House Calendars—in the order in which they are listed. In the case of money bills on the Union Calendar, the Appropriations Committee can claim priority in floor debate and will arrange a time for debate with the leaders of the House, that is, the Speaker and the majority leader. In the case of nonmoney bills, the House Rules Committee plays a central role in determining the order of debate. When a bill is reported out of committee and placed on the House Calendar, the chair of the committee will request that the Rules Committee assign the bill a rule. The rule takes the bill from the calendar and fixes the time at which it will be considered by the entire House.

Floor Procedure

In the House. When a bill comes up for debate in the House of Representatives, the House usually transforms itself into a Committee of the Whole so that it can operate under more flexible rules of procedure. Only 100 members need be present for the Committee of the Whole to have a quorum, rather than the 218 required under the rules controlling procedure for the House of Representatives. The Committee of the Whole may either reject or approve amendments to the bill it is considering, but any amendments it adopts must receive the consent of the entire House.

In the Senate. Mainly because of its smaller size, the Senate operates under much simpler rules than those governing the House. For example, as already noted, bills are considered on the floor of the Senate either in the order in which they appear on the Senate Calendar or, in the case of more controversial bills, under **unanimous consent agreements,** which are worked out by the Senate leadership and establish terms for consideration of the bill, setting limits on motions, amendments, and debate.

Filibusters. A distinctive feature of Senate procedure is the broad right of each member to speak, a right sharply restricted under the procedures of the House of Representatives. This feature makes possible the Senate **filibuster,** in which one or more senators speak continuously to prevent a bill from coming to a vote. One senator or a group of senators working together can tie up Senate proceedings for days or even weeks. This tactic can be especially effective in the closing weeks of a legislative session.

Filibusters have usually been threatened or actually used on highly controversial subjects. For example, southern conservatives used the filibuster on a number of occasions during the 1950s and 1960s in unsuccessful attempts to block the passage of civil rights legislation. But the filibuster has been used on occasion by Senate liberals as well as conservatives.

A filibuster can be ended only by a **cloture** (or **closure**) **vote.** The Senate adopted its first cloture rule (Rule 22) in 1917. It required a two-thirds vote of the entire Senate membership. In 1959 the rule was changed to two-thirds of those present, and in 1975 it was changed to its present form: when three-fifths (sixty members) of the entire Senate vote to end debate on an issue. After cloture has been voted, the present rules of the Senate require that a final vote be taken after no more than thirty hours of debate.

Before the 1975 rule change, successful cloture votes in the Senate were rare. Between 1917 and 1975 the Senate voted to limit debate on only twenty-one occasions. Filibustering has become more common in the past several decades, but since the adoption of the 1975 rule cloture votes have also become more common and the Senate has acted to restrict debate far more frequently.

Television Coverage. Television coverage of congressional committee hearings began in the late 1940s and 1950s and has continued since that time. The coverage has focused mainly on major committee investigations such as the House Judiciary Committee's consideration of the impeachment of President Richard M. Nixon in 1974 and the Iran-Contra hearings in 1987.

Until the late 1970s, legislative rules prohibited televising floor debates in both houses of Congress. In 1979 the House of Representatives adopted new rules that allowed both radio and television coverage of its proceedings, and the Senate followed suit in 1986. Each house operates its own television cameras and makes signals and videotapes available to the news media. Except when votes are taken, the cameras are required to focus on the speeches and activities occurring at the front of the chamber.

Workers setting up television cameras for the first live broadcast of Senate proceedings in June, 1986. Television now provides regular coverage of floor debates and committee hearings in both houses of Congress.

Voting

Voting is, of course, the most important single act performed by legislators. But how do members of Congress decide how to vote on a bill? There are no easy answers to this question. Political scientists have conducted many studies of legislative voting patterns. In 1975 Donald Matthews and James Stimson conducted an extensive study of the "cue network" in the House. They asked members of Congress to name the person or group from which they seek guidance when called upon to vote on a bill about which they know little. The source that was mentioned most often was the political party. Specifically, the respondents mentioned fellow members of Congress, especially those who are members of the same party and come from the same state, as well as congressional party leaders.[27]

The influence of the party may be seen in the fact that legislators usually try to support their party's program even when it means going against the wishes of their constituents or their own feelings. In one study of Congress, 94 percent of the Democrats and 96 percent of the Republicans answered yes to the question of whether they generally desire to support their party's position on issues. Indeed, 74 percent of the Democrats and 72 percent of the Republicans said that their party's stand is the first factor that affects their position on issues.[28]

While it is true that members of Congress often vote the way one expects them to on the basis of their party affiliation, this does not apply to all of the members all of the time. In fact, **party votes**—in which a large percentage of the Democrats in Congress vote for a bill while a large percentage of the Republicans vote against it, or vice versa—are not very frequent.

Factors other than party enter into the voting decisions of legislators. The influence of constituents is one such factor. A member of Congress may vote according to the wishes of the voters living in his or her district or state (though many voters lack clear views on public issues). Ideology is another force that shapes voting behavior. Although legislators quickly learn that compromise is an essential feature of Congress, some members maintain strong ideological positions, be they liberal or conservative. Still another influence is the President—especially for members of his party, who are often extremely loyal to him. Because of that loyalty, they will sometimes sacrifice their own beliefs in order to vote for the President's policies.

Presidential Approval or Disapproval

If a bill is passed by both houses of Congress, it is signed by the Speaker of the House and the President of the Senate and sent to the President of the United States for his signature. The President may sign the bill, in which case it becomes law, or he can **veto** the bill by returning it with his objections to the house in which it originated. If the President vetoes the bill, Congress may **override** the veto by a two-thirds vote in each house. Since such a vote is hard to achieve, it is relatively rare for a bill to become law over a presidential veto. (See Chapter 8 for a fuller discussion of the veto power.)

■ Summary

The United States Congress produces different reactions in different people. Some are confused by its behavior. After watching several congressional meetings, one visitor from the Soviet Union made the following observation: "Congress is so strange. A man gets up to speak and says nothing. Nobody listens—and then everybody disagrees."

American attitudes toward Congress tend to be negative. Public opinion polls show that a large majority of citizens hold Congress in very low esteem (although they generally have very favorable attitudes toward their own representative and senators). Some of this negativism results from a misunderstanding of the basic nature of any democratically elected legislature. Delay, lengthy debates, and compromise solutions are often viewed harshly by Americans, yet these are an inevitable part of the legislative process.

But public criticism of Congress is also based on some very accurate perceptions. Ethical issues have often cast a cloud over the national legislature. Scandals, particularly scandals involving money, have been all too frequent. The 1989 resignations of Jim Wright, Speaker of the House, and Tony Coelho, majority whip in the House, are recent examples of this problem.

Another problem is campaign financing. As we saw in Chapter 6, Congress has been unable to adopt a satisfactory solution to skyrocketing costs. Legislators often raise huge sums of money to conduct campaigns or to hold in reserve should a challenger present a serious electoral threat. Much of this money is obtained from the political action committees of the many special interest groups that operate in Washington.

Moreover, as we have seen, there is growing public dissatisfaction with the near-impossibility of unseating an incumbent member of Congress. Reelection rates for legislators seeking reelection have been well above 90 percent for more than a decade. This fact has given rise to a movement to limit the number of terms members of the House and Senate can serve.

Despite its shortcomings, Congress is still the governmental center of American democracy. It is the place where policies are freely discussed and where the programs of the President and the activities of the executive branch are examined and criticized. It is also the place where important changes are made in the institutions of society. It has performed these tasks for more than two hundred years and is likely to continue to perform them in the future.

■ Key Terms

delegated powers	Senate majority leader	rule
authorization bill	House majority leader	policy agenda
appropriation bill	President of the Senate	discharge petition
implied powers	President Pro Tempore	public hearings
casework	minority leader	calendar
oversight	whip	unanimous consent agreement
impeachment	standing committee	filibuster
reapportionment	select committee	cloture vote
gerrymandering	joint committee	party vote
Speaker of the House	conference committee	veto
caucus	seniority system	override

■ Suggested Reading

AUERBACH, JOEL D. *Keeping a Watchful Eye: The Politics of Congressional Oversight.* Washington, D.C.: Brookings Institution, 1990.

BACH, STANLEY, and STEVEN S. SMITH. *Managing Uncertainty in the House of Representatives.* Washington, D.C.: Brookings Institution, 1989.

CAIN, BRUCE, JOHN FEREJOHN, and MORRIS FIORINA. *The Personal Vote: Constituency Service and Electoral Independence.* Cambridge, Mass.: Harvard University Press, 1987.

CRABB, CECIL V., JR., and PAT M. HOLT. *Invitation to Struggle: Congress, the President, and Foreign Policy,* 3rd ed. Washington, D.C.: Congressional Quarterly Press, 1989.

CRANFORD, JOHN. *Budgeting for America,* 2nd ed. Washington, D.C.: Congressional Quarterly Press, 1989.

DODD, LAWRENCE C., and BRUCE I. OPPENHEIMER, eds. *Congress Reconsidered,* 4th ed. Washington, D.C.: Congressional Quarterly Press, 1989.

EDWARDS, GEORGE C. *At the Margins: Presidential Leadership of Congress.* New Haven, Conn.: Yale University Press, 1989.

KEEFE, WILLIAM J. *Congress and the American People,* 3rd ed. Englewood Cliffs, N.J.: Prentice-Hall, 1988.

LONGLEY, LAWRENCE D., and WALTER J. OLESZEK. *Bicameral Politics: Conference Committees in Congress.* New Haven, Conn.: Yale University Press, 1989.

SMITH, STEVEN S. *Call To Order: Floor Politics in the House and Senate.* Washington, D.C.: Brookings Institution, 1989.

———, and CHRISTOPHER DEERING. *Committees in Congress,* 2nd ed. Washington, D.C.: Congressional Quarterly Press, 1990.

WORMUTH, FRANCIS D., and EDWIN B. FIRMAGE. *To Chain the Dog of War: The War Power of Congress in History and Law.* Champaign, Ill.: University of Illinois Press, 1989.

■ Notes

1. *Bowsher* v. *Synar,* 478 U.S. 714 (1986).

2. Edward S. Corwin, *The President: Office and Powers,* 4th rev. ed. (New York: New York University Press, 1957), p. 171.

3. Richard F. Fenno, Jr., *Home Style: House Members in Their Districts* (Boston: Little, Brown, 1978), p. 35.

4. House Committee on Administrative Review, *Final Report,* 2 vols., H. Doc. 95–272, 95th Cong., 1st sess., December 31, 1977, 2:875.

5. Quoted in Charles L. Clapp, *The Congressman: His Work as He Sees It* (Garden City, N.Y.: Doubleday, 1964), pp. 51–53.

6. Ibid., p. 13.

7. In 1961 Richard M. Nixon, then President of the Senate and the Republican presidential candidate, had the duty of announcing to Congress the victory of his Democratic opponent, John F. Kennedy. In 1969 the defeated Democratic presidential candidate, Vice President Hubert H. Humphrey, declared the victory of his Republican rival, Richard M. Nixon. And in 1989, then Vice President George Bush announced his own election as President.

8. *Powell* v. *McCormack,* 395 U.S. 486 (1969).

9. Unsuccessful attempts have been made to expel members on charges ranging from dueling to being a Mormon.

10. *Wesberry* v. *Sanders,* 376 U.S. 1 (1964). The Court also applied the "one person, one vote" principle to the state legislatures. See *Reynolds* v. *Sims,* 377 U.S. 533 (1964).

11. Gerrymandering was named for Elbridge Gerry (1744–1814), diplomat, governor of Massachusetts, and Vice President of the United States. While serving as governor, Gerry arranged to have state election districts drawn so as to favor his political party. Because one district's irregular shape resembled that of a salamander, it was dubbed a *gerrymander.*

12. *Davis* v. *Bandemer,* 478 U.S. 109 (1986).

13. Lewis A. Froman, Jr., *The Congressional Process: Strategies, Rules and Procedures* (Boston: Little, Brown, 1967), p. 7.

14. David J. Vogler, *The Politics of Congress,* 4th ed. (Boston: Allyn & Bacon, 1983), p. 204.

15. William Miller, *Fishbait* (New York: Warner Books, 1977), p. 13.

16. Quoted in Committee on House Administration, *History of the United States House of Representatives* (Washington, D.C.: Government Printing Office, 1962), p. 35.

17. Roger H. Davidson and Walter J. Oleszek, *Congress and Its Members,* 3rd ed. (Washington, D.C.: Congressional Quarterly Press, 1990), p. 165.

18. The term *whip* is derived from fox hunting, in which the *whipper-in* keeps the hounds from straying from the pack while chasing the fox.

19. Woodrow Wilson, *Congressional Government* (New York: Meridian Books, 1956). This book was originally published in 1885, almost thirty years before Wilson was elected President of the United States.

20. William J. Keefe and Morris S. Ogul, *The American Legislative Process: Congress and the States,* 6th ed. (Englewood Cliffs, N.J.: Prentice-Hall, 1985), p. 149.

21. Quoted in Clapp, *Congressman,* p. 252.

22. Jeffrey H. Birnbaum, "Backbenchers Like Schumer Leap to the Fore in House Where Seniority Is Sovereign No More," *Wall Street Journal,* June 19, 1987, p. 54.

23. Davidson and Oleszek, *Congress and Its Members,* p. 219.

24. U.S. Bureau of the Census, *Statistical Abstract of the United States, 1990,* 110th ed. (Washington, D.C.: Government Printing Office, 1990), Table 431.

25. Davidson and Oleszek, *Congress and Its Members,* p. 219.

26. John W. Kingdon, *Agendas, Alternatives, and Public Policies* (Boston: Little, Brown, 1984), p. 3.

27. Donald Matthews and James Stimson, *Yeas and Nays: Normal Decision-Making in the U.S. House of Representatives* (New York: John Wiley, 1975), p. 94.

28. Cited in Vogler, *Politics of Congress,* p. 114.

8

Chapter Outline

Selection and Removal of the President
Who May Become President
Succession and Disability
Impeachment and Removal

The President's Roles and Powers
Chief of State
Chief Diplomat
Commander-in-Chief
Chief Administrator
Chief Legislator
Party Leader
National Opinion Leader
Manager of the Economy

Limits on the President's Powers
Judicial Review
The Legislative Veto
The War Powers Resolution
The Budget and Impoundment Control
   Act
The Bureaucracy
The Media
Public Opinion

The Personal Dimension
Beliefs, Motivations, Skills
Presidential Character

The Vice President

Questions for Thought

*What is the problem of presidential
succession, and how does the Constitution
attempt to solve it?*

*Compare the differences and similarities
of a treaty and an executive agreement.*

*Describe the veto power that the
Constitution gives to the President.*

*How does the War Powers Resolution
attempt to limit presidential power?*

*What are the main features of a theory of
a strong president? A weak president?*

*Summarize James David Barber's theory
of presidential character.*

The Presidency

A NEWLY elected President is inaugurated at noon on January 20 in the year following his election. At this time he recites the oath of office: "I do solemnly swear that I will faithfully execute the Office of President of the United States, and will to the best of my Ability, preserve, protect and defend the Constitution of the United States." George Washington, the first President, added the phrase "so help me God," perhaps because he recognized the awesome powers and duties of the presidency.

The Constitution states that "the executive Power shall be vested in a President of the United States of America." With these words it created the presidency, an office unknown under the Articles of Confederation. In a few broad, general statements the Constitution gave the President certain basic powers. Yet the President's power is also limited. It is limited by the

TABLE 8.1 *Presidents and Vice Presidents of the United States*

President and political party	Born	Died	Age at inauguration	Native of	Elected from	Term of service	Vice President
George Washington (F)	1732	1799	57	Va.	Va.	April 30, 1789–March 4, 1793	John Adams
George Washington (F)			61			March 4, 1793–March 4, 1797	John Adams
John Adams (F)	1735	1826	61	Mass.	Mass.	March 4, 1797–March 4, 1801	Thomas Jefferson
Thomas Jefferson (D-R)	1743	1826	57	Va.	Va.	March 4, 1801–March 4, 1805	Aaron Burr
Thomas Jefferson (D-R)			61			March 4, 1805–March 4, 1809	George Clinton
James Madison	1751	1836	57	Va.	Va.	March 4, 1809–March 4, 1813	George Clinton
James Madison			61			March 4, 1813–March 4, 1817	Elbridge Gerry
James Monroe (D-R)	1758	1831	58	Va.	Va.	March 4, 1817–March 4, 1821	Daniel D. Tompkins
James Monroe (D-R)			62			March 4, 1821–March 4, 1825	Daniel D. Tompkins
John Q. Adams (N-R)	1767	1848	57	Mass.	Mass.	March 4, 1825–March 4, 1829	John C. Calhoun
Andrew Jackson (D)	1767	1845	61	S.C.	Tenn.	March 4, 1829–March 4, 1833	John C. Calhoun
Andrew Jackson (D)			65			March 4, 1833–March 4, 1837	Martin Van Buren
Martin Van Buren (D)	1782	1862	54	N.Y.	N.Y.	March 4, 1837–March 4, 1841	Richard M. Johnson
W. H. Harrison (W)	1773	1841	68	Va.	Ohio	March 4, 1841–April 4, 1841	John Tyler
John Tyler (W)	1790	1862	51	Va.	Va.	April 6, 1841–March 4, 1845	
James K. Polk (D)	1795	1849	49	N.C.	Tenn.	March 4, 1845–March 4, 1849	George M. Dallas
Zachary Taylor (W)	1784	1850	64	Va.	La.	March 4, 1849–July 9, 1850	Millard Fillmore
Millard Fillmore (W)	1800	1874	50	N.Y.	N.Y.	July 10, 1850–March 4, 1853	
Franklin Pierce (D)	1804	1869	48	N.H.	N.H.	March 4, 1853–March 4, 1857	William R. King
James Buchanan (D)	1791	1868	65	Pa.	Pa.	March 4, 1857–March 4, 1861	John C. Breckinridge
Abraham Lincoln (R)	1809	1865	52	Ky.	Ill.	March 4, 1861–March 4, 1865	Hannibal Hamlin
Abraham Lincoln (R)			56			March 4, 1865–April 15, 1865	Andrew Johnson
Andrew Johnson (R)	1808	1875	56	N.C.	Tenn.	April 15, 1865–March 4, 1869	
Ulysses S. Grant (R)	1822	1885	46	Ohio	Ill.	March 4, 1869–March 4, 1873	Schuyler Colfax
Ulysses S. Grant (R)			50			March 4, 1873–March 4, 1877	Henry Wilson
Rutherford B. Hayes (R)	1822	1893	54	Ohio	Ohio	March 4, 1877–March 4, 1881	William A. Wheeler
James A. Garfield (R)	1831	1881	49	Ohio	Ohio	March 4, 1881–Sept. 19, 1881	Chester A. Arthur
Chester A. Arthur (R)	1830	1886	50	Vt.	N.Y.	Sept. 20, 1881–March 4, 1885	
Grover Cleveland (D)	1837	1908	47	N.J.	N.Y.	March 4, 1885–March 4, 1889	Thomas A. Hendricks

	Born	Died	Native of	Elected from	Age	Term of Service	Vice President
Benjamin Harrison (R)	1833	1901	Ohio	Ind.	55	March 4, 1889–March 4, 1893	Levi P. Morton
Grover Cleveland (D)	1837	1908			55	March 4, 1893–March 4, 1897	Adlai E. Stevenson
William McKinley (R)	1843	1901	Ohio	Ohio	54	March 4, 1897–March 4, 1901	Garret A. Hobart
William McKinley (R)				Ohio	58	March 4, 1901–Sept. 14, 1901	Theodore Roosevelt
Theodore Roosevelt (R)	1858	1919	N.Y.		42	Sept. 14, 1901–March 4, 1905	
Theodore Roosevelt (R)				N.Y.	46	March 4, 1905–March 4, 1909	Charles W. Fairbanks
William H. Taft (R)	1857	1930	Ohio	Ohio	51	March 4, 1909–March 4, 1913	James S. Sherman
Woodrow Wilson (D)	1856	1924	Va.		56	March 4, 1913–March 4, 1917	Thomas R. Marshall
Woodrow Wilson (D)				N.J.	60	March 4, 1917–March 4, 1921	Thomas R. Marshall
Warren G. Harding (R)	1865	1923	Ohio	Ohio	55	March 4, 1921–Aug. 2, 1923	Calvin Coolidge
Calvin Coolidge (R)	1872	1933	Vt.		51	Aug. 3, 1923–March 4, 1925	
Calvin Coolidge (R)				Mass.	52	March 4, 1925–March 4, 1929	Charles G. Dawes
Herbert Hoover (R)	1874	1964	Iowa	Calif.	54	March 4, 1929–March 4, 1933	Charles Curtis
Franklin D. Roosevelt (D)	1882	1945	N.Y.	N.Y.	51	March 4, 1933–Jan. 20, 1937	John N. Garner
Franklin D. Roosevelt (D)					55	Jan. 20, 1937–Jan. 20, 1941	John N. Garner
Franklin D. Roosevelt (D)					59	Jan. 20, 1941–Jan. 20, 1945	Henry A. Wallace
Franklin D. Roosevelt (D)					63	Jan. 20, 1945–April 12, 1945	Harry S Truman
Harry S Truman (D)	1884	1972	Mo.		60	April 12, 1945–Jan. 20, 1949	
Harry S Truman (D)				Mo.	64	Jan. 20, 1949–Jan. 20, 1953	Alben W. Barkley
Dwight D. Eisenhower (R)	1890	1969	Texas	N.Y.	62	Jan. 20, 1953–Jan. 20, 1957	Richard M. Nixon
Dwight D. Eisenhower (R)				Pa.	66	Jan. 20, 1957–Jan. 20, 1961	Richard M. Nixon
John F. Kennedy (D)	1917	1963	Mass.	Mass.	43	Jan. 20, 1961–Nov. 22, 1963	Lyndon B. Johnson
Lyndon B. Johnson (D)	1908	1973	Texas		55	Nov. 22, 1963–Jan. 20, 1965	
Lyndon B. Johnson (D)				Texas	56	Jan. 20, 1965–Jan. 20, 1969	Hubert H. Humphrey
Richard M. Nixon (R)	1913		Calif.	N.Y.	56	Jan. 20, 1969–Jan. 20, 1973	Spiro T. Agnew
Richard M. Nixon (R)				Calif.	60	Jan. 20, 1973–Aug. 9, 1974	Spiro T. Agnew / Gerald R. Ford
Gerald R. Ford (R)	1913		Neb.	Mich.	61	Aug. 9, 1974–Jan. 20, 1977	Nelson A. Rockefeller
Jimmy Carter (D)	1924		Ga.	Ga.	52	Jan. 20, 1977–Jan. 20, 1981	Walter F. Mondale
Ronald Reagan (R)	1911		Ill.	Calif.	69	Jan. 20, 1981–Jan. 20, 1985	George Bush
Ronald Reagan (R)	1911		Ill.	Calif.	73	Jan. 20, 1985–Jan. 20, 1989	George Bush
George Bush (R)	1924		Mass.	Texas	64	Jan. 20, 1989–	James D. Quayle

Key to abbreviations: (D) Democratic, (D-R) Democrat-Republican, (F) Federalist, (N-R) National Republican, (R) Republican, (W) Whig.

Source: "National Party Conventions 1831–1980," *Congressional Quarterly* (1983): 212. Updated to present.

restraints imposed by the Constitution and by political forces outside the Constitution, as well as by the President's own philosophy, skill, and character and by historical events.

In this chapter we will examine the presidency, its powers, and the limits on that power. But any study of the American presidency requires an examination not only of the nature of the office itself but also of the people who have served as the nation's chief executive. (See Table 8.1.) More than Congress and the courts, the presidency is a product of the individuals who have held the office and the manner in which they have exercised its powers.

■ Selection and Removal of the President

Who May Become President

Under Article II of the Constitution, "No person except a natural born Citizen . . . shall be eligible to the Office of President." The intent of this language was to prevent British loyalists from becoming President. The provision therefore is largely obsolete today. It still creates one potential problem, however; it is not entirely clear whether the phrase "natural born" includes only people born in this country or also people born abroad of parents who are U.S. citizens. Most scholars think it applies to both groups.

The Constitution also states that the candidate must have lived in this country at least fourteen years and must be at least 35 years old. Only a few Presidents—Theodore Roosevelt and John F. Kennedy, for example—were less than 50 years old when they took office. Roosevelt, who became President at the age of 42, was the youngest President in the nation's history. Ronald Reagan, the oldest, was almost 70 when he was inaugurated for his first term in January 1981.

In addition to meeting these simple requirements, a presidential candidate must meet political standards that are more significant than the constitutional ones. Among those standards are holding political offices such as state governor or United States senator, having experience in domestic and foreign affairs, and possessing nationwide popular appeal.

Succession and Disability

Recognizing the unique and important role of the President, the authors of the Constitution included a provision for the transfer of presidential duties if that need should arise. Article II states that "in Case of the Removal of the President from Office, or of his Death, Resignation or Inability to discharge the Powers and Duties of said Office, the same shall devolve on the Vice President." At first it was uncertain whether the Vice President became only the Acting President or actually President. Vice President John Tyler, the first person to acquire the office upon the death of a President (William Henry Harrison in 1841), resolved the matter by insisting that he was legally entitled to the full powers of the presidency.

More difficult problems arise when a President becomes disabled. In 1919 President Woodrow Wilson suffered a stroke and was disabled for more than a year. He remained in office because at the time the Constitution had no provision for declaring a President disabled and hence unable to govern. During the 1950s President Dwight Eisenhower, because of his age and history of serious illnesses, recognized this problem and made an agreement with Vice President Richard Nixon. If the President became disabled, Nixon would assume the duties of the presidency on a temporary basis.

The Twenty-fifth Amendment, ratified in 1967, was designed to solve the problems of presidential succession and disability. It contains detailed provisions for the transfer of power: "The Vice President shall become President" in the event of the "removal of the President from office or of his death or resignation." The amendment also provides for the appointment of a Vice President when that office becomes vacant. The President can nominate a Vice President, but his appointment must be confirmed by a majority vote of both houses of Congress. This provision was used in 1973, when Vice President Spiro Agnew resigned and President Nixon nominated

President Richard Nixon as he appeared on national television to announce his decision to resign from office on August 8, 1974.

Gerald Ford as Vice President. It was used again in 1974, when Ford became President upon Nixon's resignation and nominated Nelson Rockefeller as Vice President. As a result, between August 1974 and January 1977 the United States had both a President and a Vice President who had not been chosen in a national election.

The Twenty-fifth Amendment also provides that if the President becomes disabled he may submit to the Speaker of the House and the President Pro Tempore of the Senate a written declaration that he can no longer fulfill his duties as President. The Vice President then becomes Acting President. In 1985, for example, President Reagan wrote to the officers of Congress to inform them that he was to undergo surgery and would be incapacitated for a brief period. During that time the Vice President, George Bush, served as Acting President.

If the President cannot fulfill his duties adequately but is unwilling or unable to submit such a declaration, the Vice President and a majority of the members of either the Cabinet or an agency established by Congress (e.g., a panel of doctors) can submit to Congress a written statement declaring that the President is disabled. In such a case the Vice President immediately becomes Acting President.

Finally, the Twenty-fifth Amendment provides a method by which the President can regain the office after a period of disability. He reassumes the powers and duties of the presidency upon transmitting to Congress a written statement that the disability no longer exists. But the President's claim can be challenged by the Vice President and a majority of the members of either the Cabinet or a special body created by Congress. Congress must then resolve the conflict. The President regains the office unless Congress decides by a two-thirds vote that he is still unable to perform the duties of the presidency. If a two-thirds vote is obtained, the Vice President remains Acting President.

Impeachment and Removal

The Constitution gives the House of Representatives the power of **impeachment,** that is, the power to indict or formally accuse an official of wrongdoing. This authority applies to the President, the Vice President, federal judges, and other civil offices of the United States and must be based on charges of "Treason, Bribery, or other high Crimes and Misdemeanors." The House first hears evidence about the alleged offenses. If it believes that the evidence warrants the action, it will draft *articles of impeachment* listing the charges. If the articles are adopted by a majority of the House, the named person is impeached. The Senate then sits as a court and conducts a trial of the case. A two-thirds vote of the senators present is required for conviction and removal from office. The Chief Justice of the United States presides in a trial of the President.

Only one President, Andrew Johnson, has ever been impeached by the House, and he escaped conviction by a single vote. President Nixon was not formally impeached for his alleged involvement in the Watergate scandal, but it is very likely that he would have been both impeached and convicted had he not resigned from office in August 1974.

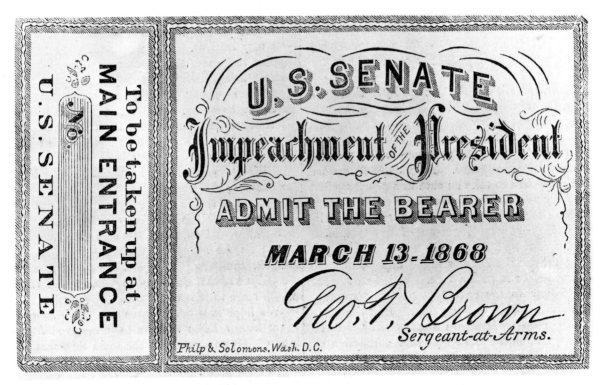

Copy of a ticket of admission to the impeachment trial of President Andrew Johnson.

■ The President's Roles and Powers

"From outside or below, a President is many men or one man wearing many 'hats,' or playing many 'roles.' . . . The President himself plays every 'role,' wears every 'hat' at once."[1] The President's roles are a mixture of constitutional tasks—chief of state, commander-in-chief, and the like—and several roles that are not included in the Constitution but are derived from congressional legislation and precedents set by earlier chief executives; among these are the roles of party leader, public opinion leader, and manager of the economy. In this section we will examine each of the President's roles separately, but it should be kept in mind that these functions are related and often overlap.

Chief of State

The government of the United States is represented by the President, whether he is in Washington, traveling in the United States or abroad, or relaxing at his own home away from the nation's capital. This fact reflects the President's constitutional role as chief of state—the symbolic center of

The official seal of the President of the United States.

the national government. As the spokesperson for more than 250 million Americans, the President represents the nation as a whole. In this role he is expected to stand "above politics" and to unify the country. Thus in his role as chief of state the President serves a function similar to that of the king or queen in a monarchy.

One of the President's duties as chief of state is to serve as the nation's ceremonial head. Whether he is greeting a group of students on the White House lawn, meeting the President of France in the shadow of a jet plane, or laying a wreath on the Tomb of the Unknown Soldier, he is serving as a symbol of American government.

Because ceremonial duties are numerous and time consuming, Presidents assign many ceremonial tasks to the Vice President and other public officials. But all Presidents still devote some time to performing this role. They recognize that, when properly used, the President's role as chief of state can be a source of power and influence.

Chief Diplomat

The Constitution makes the President the main authority in foreign relations, although as we saw in Chapter 7, it also assigns Congress important powers in this area. Article II gives the President several specific powers related to foreign affairs. He has the power to appoint all U.S. ambassadors and other diplomats with the "advice and consent" of the Senate (Article II, Section 2) and the authority to "receive Ambassadors and other public Ministers" from foreign nations (Article II, Section 3). Moreover, the Constitution gives the President the power to make treaties with foreign countries, subject to approval by a two-thirds vote of the Senate (Article II, Section 2).

A dramatic example of the President's authority in foreign affairs was President Richard Nixon's trip to the People's Republic of China in 1972.

Established in 1949, the People's Republic had had no direct diplomatic contacts with the United States for almost a quarter of a century. Nixon's visit to China and his meetings with its political leaders changed this situation. After the trip, diplomatic, commercial, and cultural exchanges between the two countries were begun. It was not until 1979, however, that President Jimmy Carter formally recognized the People's Republic of China through his constitutional power to "receive Ambassadors" from foreign nations.

The President's power to send and receive ambassadors is an important aspect of his authority in foreign affairs. By agreeing to exchange ambassadors with another nation, the President grants *diplomatic recognition* to that country. This means that the two nations are prepared to deal directly with each other through normal and accepted channels of diplomacy.

Treaties and Executive Agreements. Agreements between the United States and other nations can take several forms. The most important of these are treaties and executive agreements. A **treaty** is negotiated by representatives of the President. When negotiations are completed, the Constitution requires that the proposed treaty receive the advice and consent of two-thirds of the Senate before the treaty can go into effect.

The requirement that the Senate give its advice and consent to treaties represents a significant limitation on executive power. Although the Senate usually approves treaties that have been negotiated by the President, it sometimes takes other actions. The Senate can accept the treaty with stated reservations, or it can attach amendments to a treaty, in effect requiring that the President renegotiate the agreement. The Senate can also take no action on a proposed treaty, thereby preventing the agreement from going into effect. Only about twenty treaties have been rejected by the Senate since the Constitution was ratified. The most famous example is the Treaty of Versailles, which ended World War I. President Woodrow Wilson had personally taken part in the negotiation of the treaty, which was intended to settle the problems created by the war. Its most controversial provision called for the creation of a League of Nations. The treaty failed to win the required two-thirds vote of the Senate, largely because of opposition to U.S. membership in the League.

The Constitution says nothing about how treaties can be ended, and the Supreme Court has never resolved this problem. Throughout American history Presidents have claimed that the right to terminate a treaty is an executive one that does not require the advice and consent of two-thirds of the Senate, and the Senate has generally allowed Presidents to exercise this authority.

Executive agreements, though they are not expressly mentioned in the Constitution, are often used by Presidents. They are, in fact, far more common than treaties. An **executive agreement** is an understanding between the President and the chief executive of a foreign nation that does not require the advice and consent of the Senate. In 1937 the Supreme Court clarified the status of executive agreements by holding that they have the same legal force as treaties. Both are the supreme law of the land under the supremacy clause of Article VI of the Constitution.[2]

The decision to use an executive agreement or a treaty is the President's alone. His choice will be based largely on the nature and relative importance of the agreement. Major commitments, such as membership in the United Nations (1945), turning over control of the Panama Canal to Panama (1978), or the 1988 treaty with the Soviet Union eliminating two classes of nuclear missiles, demand a treaty with Senate approval. An agreement involving less important matters will usually take the form of an executive agreement; tariff reductions are an example. Major exceptions to this pattern include the 1940 Lend-Lease Agreement between President Franklin D. Roosevelt and Great Britain (in which the President signed over fifty destroyers in exchange for ninety-nine-year leases on certain British naval bases in the Caribbean), as well as the post–World War II executive agreements made at Yalta and Potsdam by Presidents Franklin D. Roosevelt and Harry Truman. In January 1981, only days before leaving office, President Jimmy Carter made an executive agreement with the Islamic Republic of Iran that provided for the release of fifty-two American hostages seized by Iran in 1979 and created a method for resolving financial claims between the two nations. The Supreme Court upheld the legality of the agreement on the grounds that it was justified by existing laws and by a long history of presidential settlement of claims against foreign nations.[3]

There has been some criticism of the use of executive agreements when they are employed to commit the United States to important international policies. Many senators view executive agreements as a means of bypassing the Senate's constitutional right to decide to concur to international agreements. More important, they prevent the Senate from making amendments and reservations that would require new negotiations by the President. In 1990, for example, President George Bush signed an executive agreement with Soviet leader Mikhail Gorbachev that dealt with the elimination of chemical weapons. The President's action was attacked by Senate leaders from both parties. A letter sent to the President by the chair of the Senate Foreign Relations Committee and the ranking Republican on the committee criticized the President's decision. "We must be unequivocal about the imperative that significant international agreements take treaty form," the letter declared.[4]

The Formulation of Foreign Policy. The scope of foreign policy ranges from recognizing foreign governments and making treaties and agreements with them to sending military forces into combat situations. Presidents are continually called upon to make important foreign policy decisions. In performing this task the President can draw upon information gathered by American embassies and consulates overseas, the Departments of State and Defense, White House staff agencies (the National Security Council and the Central Intelligence Agency), and other executive agencies that are concerned with foreign affairs. (See Chapter 9 for a fuller discussion of the White House staff.)

The Secretary of State is the President's link with the Department of State, but the role of the Secretary varies from one administration to another. Some Presidents have given the Secretary of State broad authority to conduct foreign policy. Others have downgraded the Secretary's role and relied instead on close advisers in the White House Office, especially the National Security Adviser, who is the executive head of the National Security Council.

During the Nixon administration the President's National Security

Adviser, Henry Kissinger, not only advised him on international issues but was also given broad authority to conduct foreign policy. President Reagan also gave his White House advisers the power to make policy decisions. But this arrangement was called into question as a result of the scandal involving an attempt by members of the White House staff to sell arms to Iran and use the profits to support the Nicaraguan Contras. In the Bush administration the National Security Adviser has been limited to an advisory role and the Secretary of State has been given the primary responsibility for the conduct of foreign policy.

Modern Presidents have increasingly become involved in the actual conduct of foreign policy by negotiating with the heads of foreign governments. The ease of international communication and travel has contributed to the growth of this so-called personal diplomacy. In 1978, for example, President Carter met with the President of Egypt and the Prime Minister of Israel at the President's Camp David retreat and successfully negotiated an agreement between the two nations that resolved some of their long-standing differences. Presidents Reagan and Bush have also practiced this form of personal diplomacy. President Reagan met with Mikhail Gorbachev at a number of summit meetings during the 1980s, and President Bush has continued this practice.

World Leader. Some observers view the President as not only the chief diplomat of the United States but as the leader of the democratic world. This role may be looked upon as an extension of the President's constitutional powers as chief of state, commander-in-chief, and chief diplomat. These

President Bush meets with Soviet President Gorbachev at the White House, May 31, 1990.

powers, combined with the political, military, and economic strength of the United States, serve to make the American President a spokesperson for the democratic world. The economic and political collapse of communism in the Soviet Union and Eastern Europe in recent years has contributed to this role of the President. Today no other nation's chief executive can claim to speak with the same authority as the President of the United States.

Commander-in-Chief

According to Article II, Section 2, of the Constitution, "The President shall be Commander in Chief of the Army and Navy of the United States, and of the Militia of the several States, when called into the actual Service of the United States." The President thus has final responsibility for the *conduct* of American military policy. Congress, however, shares with the President the responsibility for determining the *nature* of that policy. It does so, for example, through its power to appropriate money for military purposes.

The President appoints military officers and plans policy with the Secretary of State, the Secretary of Defense, the National Security Council, and other foreign and military policy advisers. The day-to-day operations of the armed forces are left to the Secretary of Defense, the service secretaries in the Defense Department, and the Joint Chiefs of Staff (i.e., the appointed heads of each of the military services).

The authority of the President and the Secretary of Defense over the top officers of the Army and Navy guarantees civilian control of the military. A dramatic example of the principle of civilian control occurred during the Korean War, when President Truman fired General Douglas MacArthur, the commanding officer of the American and Allied forces in Korea. MacArthur was popular in the United States, but his public statements about military policy in Korea were at odds with presidential strategy. More recently, in September 1990, President Bush dismissed the Chief of Staff of the Air Force for revealing to the press military plans for the bombing of Iraq.

Article I, Section 8, of the Constitution gives Congress the power to declare war, and Congress has exercised this power five times. But on more than two hundred occasions the President has taken military action without an official declaration of war by Congress. In close to one-third of these situations Congress authorized the President's action by either appropriating money to support the military action or passing resolutions backing the conduct of the chief executive. But in all the other situations the President has taken military action without any form of congressional support. Recent examples include President Reagan's invasion of the Caribbean island of Grenada in 1983 and his bombing of Libya in 1986.[5]

Many of the military actions undertaken by presidents were of short duration. But a number of major conflicts were fought without a declaration of war, including the American Civil War, the war in Korea during the early 1950s, and the Vietnam conflict. In each of these situations the President claimed that he had a constitutional right as commander-in-chief to commit American military forces to combat, and in each case Congress enacted legislation that sanctioned the President's actions.

In October 1950, during the Korean War, President Harry S Truman and General Douglas MacArthur met on Wake Island. Not long after, Truman, acting as commander-in-chief, dismissed MacArthur as his commanding general because of MacArthur's public criticism of the President's policies on the conduct of the war.

In August 1990, President Bush placed a large military force in the Middle East to protect Saudi Arabia from a threatened attack by Iraq after that nation had invaded neighboring Kuwait. In November 1990, the President more than doubled the size of the military presence in the Persian Gulf, giving the United States and its allies an offensive capability to move against Iraq. The United Nations approved the use of force against Iraq, to begin any time after January 15, 1991, if Iraq did not voluntarily leave Kuwait.

President Bush maintained that as Commander-in-Chief, and with the backing of the United Nations, he had legal authority to commit the military forces of this country to a war with Iraq *without* the consent of Congress. But any potential constitutional conflict between the President and the Congress was avoided when both houses of the legislature voted on January 12, 1991, to authorize the Chief Executive to wage war on Iraq. This step, while not a formal declaration of war, was the equivalent of such an action. On January 16, 1991, war began in the Middle East when President Bush authorized the start of a massive air attack on military targets in Iraq.

Some critics argue that the President lacks the authority to take military action without a declaration of war by Congress. The United States Supreme Court has never decided this question. Several attempts were made during the Vietnam War to obtain a judicial answer to the question, but the Supreme Court refused to hear the cases in which the issue was raised. As we will see later in the chapter, Congress has passed legislation—the War Powers Resolution—that sets limits on the President's ability to conduct military operations without its approval.

Chief Administrator

Article II, Section 2, of the Constitution gives the President the right to make appointments to the executive branch of government with the advice and consent of the Senate.[6] Further, his executive powers have been interpreted by the Supreme Court as including a broad, exclusive right to remove executive officers of the federal government. These powers guarantee that a President can maintain in high executive positions only individuals who are willing to carry out the policies of his administration. And Congress has delegated to the President broad powers to reorganize the executive branch of government, a subject which is discussed more fully later in this chapter.

As chief administrator of the executive branch, the President is responsible for managing the wide variety of departments and agencies that interpret and implement legislation passed by Congress. This relationship looks simple on paper, but in reality it is difficult. The President is in office for a few years, but the agencies are staffed by career civil servants whose primary loyalty is to their organization and its programs. Conflict is almost unavoidable, and although the President is responsible for the activities of the executive branch, he is rarely in full control of them.

Every modern President has complained about the difficulty of serving as the nation's chief administrator. Indeed, some people believe it is impossible for one person to handle this job. The problem is mainly one of numbers—the executive branch has about 3.1 million civilian employees. Obviously, the President cannot control all the activities of this massive bureaucracy, nor can he know very much about its day-to-day functioning. (The federal bureaucracy will be discussed in more detail in Chapter 9.)

Because of these limitations, the President's appointments to high level-positions within the executive branch are extremely important. As one political scientist has argued, "The appointment of the right people as cabinet [and subcabinet] members is fundamental to management control." Appointments should not be made in order to represent the various groups that have supported the President. Rather, it is important to select administrative officials who are "philosophically in tune with the President. . . . Making the right appointments at the outset of a new government is one of the keys for a President in getting a managerial grip on the office."[7]

Chief Legislator

The President's role as chief legislator has developed out of his constitutional power to sign or veto legislation (Article I, Section 7) and his power to advise Congress on the "State of the Union" (Article II, Section 3). It can also be traced to the fact that the President is the only government official who is elected by the nation as a whole. The 535 members of Congress represent people in a large number of different geographic areas, some covering no more than a few square miles. The President, by contrast, represents the entire country. Many Presidents use this fact to gain public support for their legislative programs. Through television speeches and press conferences, Presidents attempt to influence public opinion in the

President George Bush delivering his State of the Union address before a joint session of Congress.

hope that popular support for their policies will convince senators and representatives to back them.

The President has access to all the information gathered by the executive branch and can use this knowledge in proposing policies for the nation. Thus part of the President's job is to design a legislative program. Indeed, when a President does not come up with a legislative program dealing with major public issues, many people complain that he has failed to carry out his duties as President. This view is in sharp contrast to that which prevailed in the nineteenth century, when the separation of powers was viewed in more absolute terms and Presidents did not play a major role in setting the legislative agenda for Congress.

Modern Presidents present their legislative programs through public speeches and written communications. The three main presidential speeches concerned with legislative matters are: (1) the State of the Union message, which is called for by the Constitution and consists of a general statement of policy that is usually delivered in person to a joint session of Congress; (2) the National Budget message, in which the President describes the condition of the economy, his domestic policy goals, and the major expenditures required in the coming year; and (3) the Economic Report of the President, which must be given to Congress each January. In this report the President discusses current economic trends and problems affecting the American economy. In addition to presenting these speeches, Presidents send many written messages to Congress. Those messages state the President's major concerns and are often followed by detailed legislative proposals prepared by legal experts on the President's staff.

Presidents naturally hope Congress will approve their legislative agenda. They realize, however, that merely announcing a program and having bills introduced in the legislature will not accomplish their goals. The President can usually rely on a core of supporters in Congress drawn largely from his own political party. But creating a legislative majority requires convincing doubtful members of his party and reaching out to potential backers in the opposition party.

Presidents use a number of methods to create the needed majority in both houses of Congress. They have traditionally used promises of patronage—judicial appointments, federal construction contracts, campaign support, and favors of various kinds. In addition, Presidents since John F. Kennedy have created a staff position in the White House Office whose purpose is to serve as a liaison with Congress and to oversee the chief executive's legislative program.

Informal contacts with legislators are another means of gaining support for the President's policies. Private meetings, parties, and telephone calls have been used successfully by some Presidents; Lyndon Johnson and Ronald Reagan were especially good with these techniques. Other Presidents, including Richard Nixon and Jimmy Carter, lacked the personal and political skills to employ them effectively.

A President who is faced with opposition in Congress can go over the heads of the legislators and speak directly to the American people. By means of a televised speech the President can attempt to persuade individuals and interest groups to put pressure on their legislators to vote for his policies.[8]

The separation-of-powers system was intended to create some degree of conflict between the executive and legislative branches of government. Presidents must confront this conflict in attempting to have their domestic policies adopted. (Presidents have generally been more successful in achieving their foreign policy objectives.) Normally Presidents achieve their greatest legislative successes during their first years in office. The President's popularity is at its peak in those years, and Congress often finds it difficult to oppose him.

In recent history most Presidents have presided over a government in which Congress was controlled by the opposition party. Four of the last five Presidents, for example, have been Republicans who had to deal with a Congress in which the House of Representatives was controlled by the Democrats and a Senate in which the Democrats maintained a majority for all but six years. In these circumstances, Presidents face additional difficulties in getting their legislative programs enacted into law.

In sum, no President can be a successful legislative leader unless he is, in the words of one political scientist, "an effective politician."[9] He cannot get his programs through Congress without using all his political skills. This means that the President and his major advisers in the executive branch must spend a great deal of time persuading legislators, not commanding them. Over the course of American history, the balance of power between the President and Congress has varied. Sometimes Congress has played the dominant role in shaping legislation; during other periods the President has dominated the legislative process.

The Veto Power. In Article I, Section 7, the Constitution assigns the President a "qualified negative" over acts of Congress in the form of the **veto** power. When a bill is passed by Congress, it is sent to the President for his signature. If he signs it, the bill becomes law. If he does not approve of a particular bill, the Constitution permits him to take one of the following steps:

1. He may keep a bill ten days and not act on it. After ten days, provided that Congress remains in session, an unsigned bill becomes law. The President might allow a bill to become law without signing it if the bill has strong public and congressional support but does not satisfy him personally. This sort of passive disapproval is rare, however.
2. He may veto a bill by sending it back to Congress without his signature. The unsigned bill is accompanied by a statement of the President's objections to it. A veto can be overridden by a two-thirds vote of both houses of Congress, but because such a majority is hard to obtain, presidential vetos are rarely overridden. (See Table 8.2.)
3. He may use the so-called **pocket veto.** If the President does not act on a bill sent to him within ten days of the adjournment of Congress, the proposal dies. By figuratively "putting the bill in his pocket," the president vetoes the measure without giving Congress an opportunity to

TABLE 8.2 *Congressional Bills Vetoed: 1913–1990*

Period	President	Total	Vetoes sustained	Bills passed over veto
1913–1921	Wilson	44	38	6
1921–1923	Harding	6	6	0
1923–1929	Coolidge	50	46	4
1929–1933	Hoover	37	34	3
1933–1945	F. Roosevelt	635	626	9
1945–1953	Truman	250	238	12
1953–1961	Eisenhower	181	179	2
1961–1963	Kennedy	21	21	0
1963–1969	Johnson	30	30	0
1969–1974[a]	Nixon	42	36	6
1974–1977	Ford	72	60	12
1977–1981	Carter	31	29	2
1981–1989	Reagan	78	69	9
1989–1990	Bush	20	20	0

[a] Nixon resignation effective August 8, 1974.

Source: U.S. Department of Commerce, Bureau of the Census, *Statistical Abstract of the United States, 1990.* (Washington, D.C., U.S. Government Printing Office, 1990), Table 425, p. 255. Updated to include the 101st Congress.

override the veto. Pocket vetoes occur fairly frequently because many bills are passed in the days just before Congress adjourns.

Some Presidents have also sought to exercise the pocket veto in the period between the two annual sessions of Congress. During his years in office, President Reagan feuded with Congress over whether he possessed an intersession pocket veto power. But most recent Presidents have not sought to exercise this form of the veto and have worked out an accommodation with Congress whereby the bill is sent back with objections to an officer of the house in which it originated.

The veto power is limited by the fact that the President must approve or reject a bill in its entirety. Unlike most state governors, he does not have the power to use an **item veto,** under which specific provisions can be rejected while the bill as a whole is approved. This restriction encourages members of Congress to attach riders to a bill. **Riders** are legislative additions that are unrelated to the main subject of the bill. This practice is especially common in the Senate, which, unlike the House, has no requirement that an amendment be germane to the proposed legislation. A Senator, for example, might propose a pro-abortion amendment to a bill concerned with agricultural expenditures. If the President favors the bill itself and wants it to become law, he is forced to accept any riders as well.

Presidents have frequently asked Congress to grant them the item veto, although constitutional scholars disagree as to whether this could be done by an act of Congress or would require a constitutional amendment. But Congress has never been willing to provide the President with such a significant increase in his legal authority.

Party Leader

The candidate who wins his party's presidential nomination is called upon to act as party leader. Throughout the campaign and after taking office, he will be the party's national advocate. This role is not mentioned in the Constitution, but it is a source of real political power for the President.

As party leader, the President is expected to appear at party fundraising events, speak at party meetings and rallies, and try to maintain party unity. As part of his role as party leader, he is expected to appoint party members to important diplomatic, administrative, and judicial positions. He is often asked to campaign for his party's candidates for office. During a presidential election year, a popular presidential candidate can attract added support for national, state, and local party candidates and thus help some of them gain election. This is often referred to as the *coattail effect.* In other years, however, Presidents have little chance of transferring their popularity to party candidates. In the 1986 election, for example, President Reagan campaigned actively for Republican senatorial candidates, yet seven incumbent Republican senators lost to Democratic opponents.

The President's control over his party stems from the fact that the party needs him to present its platform to the nation, to raise funds, to get its members elected or appointed, and to push its bills through Congress. The President's influence on Congress is based largely on his role as party leader. In this role he uses the techniques of persuasion and patronage. For example, in return for support of his program, the President can give his backing to a local project that a senator or representative is anxious to obtain.

It should be noted, however, that party members often hold conflicting views that cannot always be changed by the President. The decentralized and varied nature of American parties tends to produce party members who will disagree with some aspects of the President's program. Even the most strenuous efforts by the President may not be enough to persuade such a legislator to change his or her mind.

National Opinion Leader

The President's impact on public opinion depends to a great extent on his skill in using the mass media. His almost unlimited access to radio, television, and the press gives him great potential influence. But he must use the media carefully. Too much exposure can be harmful to the President's image and may even reduce his influence. But if he uses the media wisely and comes across as an effective leader, he can work wonders. "Let him once win the admiration and confidence of the country," President Wilson once said, "and no other single force can withstand him, no combination of forces will easily overpower him. His position takes the imagination of the country."[10]

President John F. Kennedy at a press conference, April 3, 1963. Kennedy was a master of such meetings, and he used them to strengthen his position as national opinion leader.

217

One of the earliest channels used by the President to communicate directly with the public was the White House press conference. President Theodore Roosevelt is said to have invented this technique when he invited reporters to the White House and discussed the issues of the day while having his morning shave. President Wilson made the press conference more formal by scheduling weekly meetings with reporters. Since Wilson's time the number of Washington press correspondents has increased dramatically. With the advent of radio and, later, television, the press conference became a nationwide broadcast, with millions of Americans able to listen to or view its live coverage.

Different Presidents have used the press conference with varying frequency. President Kennedy used it often; President Nixon, by contrast, tried to avoid meeting with reporters and abandoned the use of press conferences during his last troubled years in office. President Reagan rarely held live press conferences during his second term.

The mass media have also been used to gain public support for the President's actions. In his famous "fireside chats" during the depression of the 1930s, President Franklin D. Roosevelt tried to give hope and confidence to radio listeners. Today television gives the President even greater ability to reach the public. President Reagan was perhaps the most skillful recent President in using television to communicate to the American people about his political programs. Indeed, he was often referred to as "the great communicator." Reagan's background as a motion picture and television actor enabled him to use this medium very effectively. Although he often performed poorly at press conferences, his televised speeches were

President Franklin D. Roosevelt delivering one of his famous "fireside chats" to the nation. Roosevelt was the first President to use radio as an effective method of communicating his policies to the American public.

remarkable for their ability to present both his ideas and his personality to the American public.

On other occasions Presidents have been less successful in their attempts to use television. For example, during the Vietnam War President Lyndon Johnson used television to try to persuade Americans that U.S. military activity in Vietnam was justified. Similarly, President Nixon used television to defend his actions in relation to the Watergate affair. Both Presidents failed in these attempts to sway public opinion.

To sum up, in his role as national opinion leader the President has the ability to reach many millions of Americans through radio and television. Effective use of the media is essential to strong leadership. But if the President seeks to "sell" an unpopular position, even the most skillful use of the mass media will not necessarily bring success.

Manager of the Economy

Since the passage of the Employment Act of 1946, the President has been formally responsible for managing the economy, but even before that time he was expected to keep it running smoothly and prevent depressions. Today fiscal policy, inflation, unemployment, the stability of the dollar, foreign trade, and other economic matters are among the President's major concerns, and many people judge him primarily by how well he can cope with them.

Managing the economy is not an easy task. Most economic decisions are made by private individuals and companies, and the President cannot simply tell them what to do. Within the government, some departments are more responsive to the President's directives than others. As we will see in Chapter 9, an important set of agencies—the independent regulatory commissions—are not subject to the President's authority. One such agency, the Federal Reserve Board, has the primary responsibility for determining monetary policy (e.g., raising or lowering interest rates). In short, the President's economic powers do not match his economic responsibilities.

Economic conditions can make or break a President. Whenever the economy slows down, he is under pressure from business, unions, farmers, and the general public to take action. Failure to handle an economic recession adequately can sharply reduce a President's popularity and lead to losses for his party's candidates in the next election. Prosperity generally leads to personal and electoral success both for the President and for his party.

■ Limits on the President's Powers

The powers granted to the President by the Constitution have served as the basis for the development of the modern presidency. In the twentieth century, especially since the 1930s, the office of the President has steadily gained influence in both domestic and international matters. The Vietnam War, however, demonstrated to the American public the great dangers that come with excessive and unrestrained authority.

The framers of the Constitution understood that uncontrolled political power poses a threat to individual liberties and a stable political order, whether the power is executive, legislative, or judicial. Thus, while they sought to create a strong, independent President, they never intended his authority to be unlimited. In this section we will review several important limitations on the President's powers.

Judicial Review

The judicial branch of the government is one source of control over the President. The United States Supreme Court has the right to exercise judicial review over presidential actions and can declare them illegal if it finds that they violate the Constitution. The Court has been reluctant to declare any President's wartime actions illegal, however. During this nation's three largest wars—the Civil War and the two World Wars—the Supreme Court did not declare any step taken by the President unconstitutional. Moreover, it has never been willing to decide on the constitutionality of undeclared wars like the Korean and Vietnam conflicts, which were based in large part on the President's power as commander-in-chief.

Nevertheless, in several significant cases the Supreme Court has curbed presidential authority. Soon after the end of both the Civil War and World War II, the Supreme Court voided presidential policies.[11] In 1952 the Court ruled against President Harry Truman's seizure of the nation's steel industry during a labor-management dispute that occurred while the United States was involved in the Korean War.[12] By a 6-to-3 vote the Court held that Truman had exceeded his powers under Article II of the Constitution, and he was ordered to return the steel mills to their owners.

President Nixon was dealt several setbacks by the Supreme Court. His attempt to prevent the publication by major newspapers of a government study of the Vietnam War—the Pentagon Papers—was rejected by the Court.[13] In 1974 the Court ordered Nixon to turn over to the courts tape recordings of conversations between him and his assistants that were relevant to criminal trials pending against several of his major advisers. The Court rejected Nixon's claim that the tapes were privileged executive materials.[14] This decision led directly to the resignation of the President in August 1974.

The Legislative Veto

The nation's founders relied mainly on conflict between Congress and the President as a means of checking excessive use of power by either branch of the government. Congress is able to control the executive branch through several of its constitutional powers, including its authority to appropriate money for all governmental programs and its right to investigate and oversee the activities of the executive branch. In recent times it has made increasing use of the **legislative veto** as a means of controlling executive power. The Constitution states that every "Order, Resolution, or Vote" that requires the approval of Congress must be submitted to the President for his signature or veto. But by tradition *concurrent resolutions* (those passed by both houses of Congress) and *simple resolutions* (those adopted by only one house) do not have to be sent to the President for his action. Congress has passed approximately two hundred laws that delegate power to the executive branch but allow either or both houses of Congress to adopt a resolution that rejects the use of that power.

One of the first uses of the legislative veto occurred in relation to the President's power to reorganize the executive branch. Historically, any major change in the organization of the federal bureaucracy required the passage of legislation by Congress. Beginning in the 1930s, however, Congress gave the President the right to make changes, subject to rejection by either house of Congress within sixty days after the President presented his plan. This procedure applies to all administrative changes except minor ones like the name of an agency. (Departments cannot be created or abolished without an act of Congress, however.)

The constitutionality of the legislative veto was first considered by the Supreme Court in the 1983 case of *Immigration and Naturalization Service* v. *Chadha*.[15] This case dealt with a provision of the Immigration and Nationality Act that permitted either the Senate or the House, through the adoption of a legislative resolution, to reverse a decision of the Attorney General to suspend the deportation of an alien. The Court held that the legislative veto provision was unconstitutional, basing its decision on an analysis of three provisions of Article I of the Constitution. First, before a bill can become law, it must be "presented" to the President so that he has an opportunity to either sign or veto the proposal. Second, this requirement applies not only to bills but also to "Every Order, Resolution, or Vote to which the Concurrence of the Senate and House of Representatives may be necessary." Third, the Constitution vests all lawmaking authority in a two-house legislature; therefore, before any action can become law it must be passed by both the Senate and the House. The Court concluded that these procedures for passing laws—presentation to the President and passage by both houses of Congress—apply to legislative veto resolutions.[16]

The Chadha decision cast doubt on the legality of the legislative veto provisions found in other statutes, including the 1973 War Powers Resolution.

The War Powers Resolution

Throughout most of American history Congress has limited the President in the domestic sphere while giving him very broad freedom to act in foreign and military matters. This surrender of power in foreign affairs allowed Presidents Kennedy, Johnson, and Nixon to wage an increasingly large-scale war in Southeast Asia. Congressional opposition to the war grew slowly, and only in the early 1970s did it gain sufficient strength to permit Congress to adopt legislation designed to end the fighting in Cambodia and Laos and to control the use of military force by the President.

The War Powers Resolution of 1973 was the most significant piece of legislation passed in this period. This law sought to regulate the future use of American military forces by the President when war has not been declared by Congress. In this way Congress attempted to curb the ability of the President to wage war on the basis of his power as commander-in-chief of the armed forces and his authority to conduct foreign affairs.

The War Powers Resolution requires the President to consult with Congress before American military forces are introduced into hostile situations and to continue this consultation as long as they are engaged in such situations. But the resolution goes beyond this requirement and attempts to establish specific controls on the President's use of American military forces. In the absence of a declaration of war by Congress, the President must send a written report to Congress within forty-eight hours after American soldiers or sailors have been sent into threatened or actual war situations. Within sixty days after the report has been submitted, the President must end the use of American armed forces unless Congress declares war or approves the military action. Congress can extend this period for an additional thirty days if necessary for the safe withdrawal of the troops. The law also provides that Congress can halt the use of the troops before the end of the sixty-day period by adopting a concurrent resolution.

The provisions of the War Powers Resolution have come into play on a number of occasions since the law was enacted. Presidents have sent American military forces into combat or near-combat situations and have used them on rescue missions. On these occasions the President and Congress have responded in different ways to the requirements of the resolution, as can be seen in the following examples:

- In May 1975 President Ford employed Marine and naval forces to free the crew of an American ship that had been captured by Cambodian communists while traveling in international waters. Ford informed Congress several days after the rescue mission had begun, but he did not consult with members of Congress prior to the operation.
- Early in 1980 President Carter informed Congress of the failed attempt to rescue the fifty-two American hostages being held in Iran. He made no attempt at prior consultation, nor did he inform the legislature of his action until several days after the mission had been aborted.
- American Marines were sent into Lebanon early in the fall of 1983 to serve as a peacekeeping force. In September 1983 Congress invoked the War Powers Resolution and set an eighteen-month timetable for their withdrawal. However, President Reagan removed the Marines prior to the expiration of the time set by Congress.
- The invasion of Grenada by American troops in October 1983 was carried out without prior consultation with Congress. Legislative leaders were told of the military action only when the invasion was about to take place. The fighting ended quickly, and American troops were withdrawn before the sixty-day period available to the President had expired. President Reagan maintained that the provisions of the War Powers Resolution did not apply to this situation.

President and Mrs. Bush waving to U.S. Marines and members of the British 7th Armored Brigade in the Saudi desert, November 22, 1990.

■ In 1987 President Reagan sent American naval forces into the Persian Gulf to protect oil shipments from attack by Iran and Iraq. Although there had been numerous raids on cargo ships and much violence in the area, President Reagan claimed that the resolution did not apply, and Congress made no attempt to invoke its provisions.

■ The most extensive deployment of American military power since the Vietnam War came in the summer of 1990, when President Bush sent some 150,000 American military personnel, together with ships, planes, and tanks, to Saudi Arabia and the Persian Gulf to defend these areas from a possible attack by Iraq. The President contended that the American troops had been placed in the region for defensive purposes only and that there were no existing hostilities and no threat of "imminent" hostilities. He therefore believed that the War Powers Resolution did not apply. The President did notify congressional leaders on the day troops were dispatched to the Gulf area and later held meetings with other members of Congress. But he maintained that these steps were taken because he believed in consulting with Congress, not because he was under any legal obligation to do so.

The War Powers Resolution never became a significant issue in the period before the United States went to war against Iraq. Congress never invoked it in the months between August 1990 and January 1991, when President Bush increased the size of the nation's military presence in the Persian Gulf to more than 450,000 men and women. And on January 12, 1991, after the United Nations approved the use of force against Iraq, Congress adopted a resolution that gave the President the authority to wage war against that Middle Eastern nation.

The War Powers Resolution may serve as a symbolic restraint on the President's war-making authority. However, experience with the law does not provide a clear answer as to whether that restraint is effective in practice. Presidents have avoided consulting with Congress before taking military action and have interpreted the resolution's provisions narrowly. Moreover, the War Powers Resolution is not relevant to a nuclear war, since there would not be time to apply its provisions. And the law has yet to be tested in a nonnuclear situation in which the President uses American military power on a large scale or for a long period. Whether the resolution will discourage Presidents from taking such action and whether Congress will refuse to approve them once they have been started are questions that have not yet been answered.

Critics have argued that the War Powers Resolution represents an unwise interference with the President's freedom to act in a crisis and an unconstitutional limitation on his role as commander-in-chief of the armed forces. During outbreaks of hostility the President would be stripped of his constitutional authority as commander-in-chief unless Congress approved the continued use of American military power.[17]

The Budget and Impoundment Control Act

Some modern Presidents have claimed the authority to refuse to spend money that has been appropriated by Congress, a power known as **impoundment.** Although the Constitution does not actually grant the President this authority, since the end of World War II several Presidents have impounded funds on the basis of their power as chief executive. During the early 1970s President Nixon used the power of impoundment as a form of veto, claiming that it was necessary to keep down the rate of inflation. Congress objected strongly, arguing that appropriations are laws and that the President is required to put them into effect.

In 1974 Congress passed the Budget and Impoundment Control Act, which was designed to limit this practice. A President may delay a spending program temporarily unless either house of Congress passes a resolution forbidding that action. If the President wants to cancel a spending program permanently, he must receive the consent of both the House and the Senate within forty-five days. If either house refuses its consent, the President must release the money at the end of the forty-five-day period. (The *Chadha* decision referred to earlier may have rendered this procedure unconstitutional, however.)

The Bureaucracy

Although this was not intended by the nation's founders, the executive bureaucracy also places limits on presidential power. The built-in bureaucratic resistance to change, which can be seen in any large organization, frequently frustrates the goals and policies of the President. President Dwight D. Eisenhower, for example, came to the presidency after a long military career, including many years as a general. He had become accustomed to giving orders and having them carried out. Eisenhower discovered that being President was different. He issued orders, and, he commented sadly, "nothing happened."

We stated earlier that the departments and agencies of the executive branch are not always responsive to the President. This lack of responsiveness has become a major problem for recent Presidents as the federal bureaucracy has grown. It does not mean, however, that the bureaucracy is constantly opposed to the President. Bureaucrats are reasonable people; like the President, they believe their actions are in the best interests of the nation. Thus, even though the bureaucracy and the President may define the national interest differently, both definitions may be reasonable. A President who understands this has a better chance of winning the cooperation of officials in the executive branch.[18]

The Media

The news media—newspapers, magazines, radio, and television—generally serve as a restraint on the power of government. They perform this function by exposing and publicizing facts about the operation of the political system. The authors of the Constitution understood the importance of a free press as a control on government. The First Amendment provides a specific guarantee of freedom of the press to protect it against any attempt by government to regulate and control its operations.

The President and the executive branch are continually under examination by the news media. The information published by the media ranges from the trivial to significant facts about wrongdoing and major policies. The Watergate scandal of the early 1970s showed how the media could help unearth and publicize facts about wrongdoing in the executive branch—including the Executive Office of the President. During 1986 and 1987 the media played an important role in publicizing President Reagan's failed policy of selling arms to Iran to obtain the release of American hostages and then using the anticipated profits to aid the Nicaraguan Contras.

Public Opinion

A final check on the President's power is an informed, alert public. A President who lacks public support may refrain from unwise or unpopular policies. Some Presidents have tried to ignore public opinion, but with little success.

Studies of public attitudes toward the President have found that Presidents are blamed for problems that are beyond their control, whereas a good performance may go unrecognized. Also, public approval of the President tends to decline throughout his years in office. There is a "honeymoon" during the first months in office, but then the opposition party and other groups begin criticizing the President's actions and proposing alternative policies. Thus the President's ability to implement his program normally decreases over time.

The President is also limited by the public's *issue attention cycle*—the

The Oval Office of the President, the White House, Washington, D.C.

fact that the public's attention rarely stays focused on any one issue for very long.[19] More difficult for the President are the times when he is forced to act on an issue on which the public is sharply divided. Whatever he does, he is bound to make enemies; but even when he does not act, he is likely to be criticized by some disappointed supporters.

■ The Personal Dimension

We have seen that the powers of the presidency are limited not only by the checks and balances contained in the Constitution but also by such factors as judicial review and public opinion. What we have not discussed, however, is the role of the President's character and beliefs and their effect on his conduct in office. The powers of the presidency are not the only factors that determine the effectiveness of any President.

The nation's founders created the presidency as a one-person office, and despite the expansion of the executive branch in the twentieth century, it remains, in effect, just that. Since Washington's inauguration in 1789, forty men have served as President of the United States. Each has brought a unique set of beliefs, motivations, and political skills to the office, as well as his own distinct character. These have had important and far-reaching effects on how he has approached his duties as President and how he has used the power of the presidency.

Beliefs, Motivations, Skills

One way to analyze American Presidents is to divide them into two groups: weak and strong. "Weak" Presidents are those who consciously limit their authority; "strong" ones are those who extend their power as far as they feel is necessary, limited only by what the system of checks and balances will not permit. Note that *weak* and *strong* are relative terms, not absolute ones—some Presidents are stronger (or weaker) than others.

The argument for limited presidential power was best stated by President William Howard Taft:

> The true view of the Executive function is, as I conceive it, that the President can exercise no power which cannot be fairly and reasonably traced to some specific grant of power or justly implied and included within such express grant as proper and necessary to its exercise. . . . There is no undefined residuum of power which he can exercise because it seems to him in the public interest.[20]

Taft believed that the President could exercise only the specific powers granted to him by the Constitution or by Congress. This view was shared by Presidents Calvin Coolidge, Herbert Hoover, and Dwight Eisenhower. None of these Presidents believed he should expand the use of executive powers. Eisenhower, for example, believed that

> the principle of separation of powers required the President actually to impose restraints on himself because of the overwhelming power that the Presidency has acquired; and . . . that the incidental influences flowing from the Presidency itself should not be exploited to promote causes beyond those assigned to the President by the Constitution.[21]

Such Presidents, in short, believe that the chief executive should play a less active role within the system of separation of powers.

Perhaps the earliest statement in support of strong presidential leadership was made by Alexander Hamilton in the following passage from *The Federalist:*

> Energy in the executive is a leading character in the definition of good government. It is essential to the protection of the community against foreign attacks; it is not less essential to the steady administration of the laws; to the protection of property against those irregular and high-handed combinations which sometimes interrupt the ordinary course of justice; to the security of liberty against the enterprises and assaults of ambition, of faction and of anarchy. . . . A feeble executive implies a feeble execution of the government. A feeble execution is but another phrase for a bad execution; and a government ill executed, whatever it may be in theory, must be, in practice, a bad government.[22]

Theodore Roosevelt was the first president in this century to articulate a strong theory of his office. He felt that it was his job to do all he could for

Theodore Roosevelt served as President from 1901 to 1909 and was one of the first Presidents to advocate a theory of strong executive powers.

the American people—that he was a steward of the people. To those who criticized him for extending his authority, he replied:

> I did not usurp power, but I did greatly broaden the use of executive power. In other words, I acted for the public welfare, I acted for the common well-being of all our people, whenever and in whatever manner was necessary, unless prevented by direct constitutional or legislative prohibition. I did not care a rap for the mere form and show of power; I cared immensely for the use that could be made of the substance.[23]

Other strong Presidents have included Woodrow Wilson, Franklin D. Roosevelt, Harry Truman, John Kennedy, Lyndon Johnson, Richard Nixon, and Ronald Reagan. President Bush may also be characterized as a strong president. Each of these Presidents had political, economic, and social goals and used the powers of the presidency to achieve his objectives. Strong Presidents all recognize the importance of effective leadership of the executive branch, Congress, and the American public.

Most modern Presidents may be classified as strong. International problems in a nuclear age, as well as domestic economic problems, demand strong executive leadership. Weak Presidents were more common in the nineteenth and early twentieth centuries, and it seems unlikely that any President today would advocate such a restricted view as Taft's of the powers of the nation's chief executive.

Strong and weak Presidents differ not only in their beliefs about the presidency itself but also in the motivations that lead them to seek the office of President. Most strong Presidents have been active in their efforts to win leadership positions and have had the goal of the presidency in mind throughout their political careers. Once in power, they have enjoyed the exercise of that power. Weak Presidents, by contrast, have not been strongly motivated by the desire to be a political leader. Some have been successful in nonpolitical careers (e.g., Taft in law, Herbert Hoover as an engineer) before entering politics.[24]

As might be expected, the differences between weak and strong presidents are expressed in the political skills they bring to the presidency and in the way they put those skills to work. Here the relationship between the President and Congress is all-important. The President must be able to persuade others that his program is desirable, that his actions are justified, and that he deserves their support. A President with the skills and the desire to persuade others to support his goals can accomplish much.[25]

Strong Presidents often have impressive political skills. President Johnson, for example, was famous for his ability to convince members of Congress that things should be done his way. In his first years in office, Johnson was highly successful in getting Congress to adopt much of his domestic reform program in such areas as health care, education, and civil rights. But political skills alone do not make a great President. Johnson's clever use of power on domestic issues was not enough to win widespread support for his Vietnam policies. Nor could President Nixon avoid the consequences of his misdeeds in office, although he managed to fend off the threat of impeachment for more than a year. Political skills, to be effective, must go hand in hand with moral leadership, and morality is an aspect of individual character.

Presidential Character

Some political scientists, historians, and psychologists have tried to analyze the relationship between character, or personality, and politics. This relationship is of particular interest with respect to the President of the United States, not only because of the fascination of the office itself but also because the President is one of the two or three most powerful people in the world. Few individuals, after all, have the power to start a nuclear war, and it would be in the best interests of all of us if a means could be devised to determine what kinds of people would be likely to do so.

James David Barber, a professor of political science at Duke University, has developed a theory of presidential character based on two broad dimensions: active-passive and positive-negative. The first has to do with the amount of energy a person puts into being President; the second deals with how he feels about being President. Using this approach, Barber has devised four categories of presidential character: *active-positive*, *active-negative*, *passive-positive*, and *passive-negative*. He has summarized these general categories as follows:

> The "active-positive" type tends to show confidence, flexibility, and a focus on producing results through rational mastery. The "active-negative" tends to emphasize ambitious striving, aggressiveness, and a focus on the struggle for power against a hostile environment. "Passive-positive" types come through as receptive, compliant, other-directed persons whose superficial hopefulness masks much inner doubt. The "passive-negative" character tends to withdraw from conflict and uncertainty, to think in terms of vague principles of duty and regular procedure.[26]

Among the Presidents whom Barber has classified as active-positive are Franklin D. Roosevelt, Harry Truman, John F. Kennedy, and Jimmy Carter. (President Bush could probably be added to this list.) Active-negatives include Woodrow Wilson, Herbert Hoover, Lyndon Johnson, and Richard Nixon. William Howard Taft, Warren Harding, and Ronald Reagan were passive-positives, and Calvin Coolidge and Dwight Eisenhower were passive-negatives.

At the time of President Bush's inauguration in January 1989, Barber made an interesting and almost prophetic analysis of the character of the new chief executive. He rejected the idea that President Bush would be ". . . a steady middle-of-the-road chairman of the White House team. . . ." Rather, Barber saw the character of the new president as falling in the active-positive category, ". . . a pattern that means that he is ready to learn, to change, to develop in office. . . ." Further, Barber described President Bush as a man who wants "a mission." This need to pursue a mission could lead the President in either of two directions, according to Barber. President Bush might ". . . take on a mission to build a system of peace and justice in the world. . . ." But his ". . . hunger for mission could carry us all over the brink of disaster. . . . The ultimate danger is war."[27] President Bush's attempt to create a new world order following the end of the cold war with the Soviet Union and his leadership in the war against Iraq represent the two alternative missions David Barber foresaw early in 1989.

Many of the nation's greatest Presidents can be classified as active-positive. This is because, in Barber's words,

> active-positive Presidents are more open to evidence because they have less need to deny and distort their perceptions for protective purposes. Their approach is experimental rather than deductive, which allows them to try something else when an experiment fails to pan out, rather than escalate the rhetoric or pursue the villains responsible. Flexibility in style and a world view containing a variety of probabilities are congruent with a character ready for trial and error and furnish the imagination with a wide range of alternatives.[28]

If there is a lesson to be learned from Barber's analysis of presidential character, it is "Beware the active-negative." Active-negatives are often strong leaders with great political ability, but they are motivated by a desire for personal power. They are dangerous because they become inflexible when challenged. The clearest illustrations of this pattern are President Johnson's refusal to change his policies on the Vietnam War despite enormous public pressure to do so and President Nixon's stubborn persistence in attempting to cover up the Watergate scandal—a stubbornness that ended in his resignation from the presidency.

Barber's approach has attracted the attention of politicians as well as political scientists and has been both praised and criticized. Many people have been influenced by his ideas and credit him with developing a useful analytical tool. Others, however, believe that Barber's predictions are vague, that his methods are unscientific, and that the character of anyone who wants to be President is likely to be too complex for analysis. Barber's critics also dislike the concept of character analysis, which, they point out, can easily turn into character assassination.[29]

Whatever the drawbacks of Barber's theory, it has served to focus attention on the personal dimension of the presidency. The style and character of the person who is elected President are important factors in determining how that person will conduct himself in office. These factors are perhaps as significant as the legal powers and limitations of the office and as the candidates' views on political issues. It is therefore important that the American public consider the beliefs and character of candidates for the presidency before going to the polls.

■ The Vice President

The framers of the Constitution created the office of Vice President as an afterthought; almost no discussion was devoted to this matter during the Constitutional Convention. The Constitution simply provides that a Vice President shall be chosen by the electoral college; that he shall be Acting President when a President is temporarily disabled; that he shall assume the office and duties of the President upon the death, resignation, or removal of the President; and that he shall be the President of the Senate, voting only to break a tie on the rare occasions when this occurs. The Vice President, in other words, has little to do as long as the President remains in office. It is for this reason that John Adams, the nation's first Vice President, wrote, "My country has in its wisdom created for me the most insignificant office that ever the invention of man contrived."

Charles G. Dawes, Vice President under President Coolidge, described the position as "the easiest job in the world." He had only two responsibilities, he declared: to sit and listen to the speeches of senators and to examine the morning papers for information about the health of the President. However, nine Vice Presidents have assumed the office of President after the death or resignation of the President; collectively, they have gone on to serve as President for a total of twenty-six years. And four of those who succeeded to the presidency were later elected to that office. Thus, again quoting Adams, "I am Vice President of the United States. In this I am nothing, but I may be everything."

Vice-President Lyndon Johnson taking the oath of office as President following the assassination of President John F. Kennedy on November 22, 1963. At his side is the widow of the slain President, Mrs. Jacqueline Kennedy.

In the past, Presidents have tended to keep the Vice President isolated from decision making, reflecting the fact that their relationship was based largely on political considerations. The Vice President's frequent isolation and lack of influence was perhaps best illustrated by the fact that President Franklin D. Roosevelt, who died in office in 1945, never informed Vice President Truman that the atomic bomb was being developed.

Traditionally, the Vice President has acted as a substitute for the President in performing various ceremonial functions, thereby relieving the President of these time-consuming duties. Recent Presidents have attempted to give their Vice Presidents more important assignments, such as chairing Cabinet committees or White House conferences and making diplomatic trips abroad. They have also sought to keep them better informed about both domestic and foreign policy matters. Thus the office of the Vice President remains a weak and ambiguous one, but the Vice President remains the person who may one day become "everything."

■ Summary

Article II of the Constitution was written in such a way as to permit the presidency to expand to meet the needs of a changing and growing nation. But the nation's founders could not have foreseen how important the presidency would become in response to the demands of twentieth-century society.

The growth of the presidency has been caused in part by the actions of "strong" Presidents, but the economic and social problems of an industrial society have also played a major role in the expansion of presidential powers. The public's expectation that the President will maintain economic growth and avoid recession has increased markedly in the past half-century. The public has also come to expect a high level of service from the national government, and it holds the President largely responsible when its expectations are not met.

Probably the greatest single force contributing to the expansion of the President's power has been war. In this century the two world wars and the wars in Korea and Vietnam greatly increased the scope of the presidency. Aside from the impact of war, the emergence of the United States as a world power has strengthened the office of the President. In the years since the outbreak of World War II, the United States has become involved in a complex web of foreign alliances and commitments that have had the effect of increasing the power of the presidency.

In the years since the close of the Vietnam War, there has been a continuing debate in the United States about the proper roles of the President and Congress in the management of foreign affairs. Some have argued that the Constitution assigns the President the primary role; others have interpreted the powers of the President narrowly and those of Congress broadly. President Bush's actions in invading Panama and sending a large military force to the Middle East have renewed the discussion of the proper balance between the President and Congress.

The framers of the Constitution clearly gave both the President and Congress a role in foreign affairs. But there are areas in which the Constitution is either silent or ambiguous. And it is in this twilight zone that the contest between the President and Congress has been fought. For the most part, the courts have stayed out of this debate. They have viewed the conflict as political, not judicial, and have left the problem to be resolved by the elected branches of the government.

Certainly no President can be allowed to function above the law. However, a return to the nineteenth-century system of weak presidents and dominance by the legislative branch is not possible in today's nuclear age. The system of separation of powers that the nation's founders created two centuries ago provides adequate safeguards against an "imperial" presidency, and strong Presidents can function within the boundaries set by the Constitution and legislative acts. As Supreme Court Justice Robert Jackson wrote in 1952, "With all its defects, delays, and inconveniences, men have discovered no technique for long preserving free government except that the Executive be under the law, and that the law be made by parliamentary deliberations."[30]

■ Key Terms

impeachment	veto	rider
treaty	pocket veto	legislative veto
executive agreement	item veto	impoundment

■ Suggested Reading

BUCHANAN, BRUCE. *The Citizen's Presidency.* Washington, D.C.: Congressional Quarterly Press, 1986.

GLENNON, MICHAEL J. *Constitutional Diplomacy.* Princeton, N.J.: Princeton University Press, 1990.

GOLDSTEIN, JOEL K. *The Modern Vice Presidency.* Princeton, N.J.: Princeton University Press, 1982.

GREENSTEIN, FRED I., ed. *Leadership in the Modern Presidency.* Cambridge, Mass.: Harvard University Press, 1988.

HENKIN, LOUIS. *Constitutionalism, Democracy, and Foreign Affairs.* New York: Columbia University Press, 1990.

HESS, STEPHEN. *Organizing the Presidency,* rev. ed. Washington, D.C.: Brookings Institution, 1988.

JONES, CHARLES O., ed. *The Reagan Legacy.* Chatham, N.J.: Chatham House, 1988.

MILKIS, SIDNEY M., and MICHAEL NELSON. *The American Presidency: Origins and Development, 1776–1990.* Washington, D.C.: Congressional Quarterly Press, 1989.

NELSON, MICHAEL, ed. *The Presidency and the Political System,* 3rd ed. Washington, D.C.: Congressional Quarterly Press, 1990.

ROSE, RICHARD. *The Postmodern Presidency: The White House Meets the World.* Chatham, N.J.: Chatham House, 1988.

SPITZER, ROBERT J. *The Presidential Veto: Touchstone of the American Presidency.* Albany, N.Y.: State University of New York Press, 1988.

THURBER, JAMES A., ed. *Divided Democracy: Cooperation and Conflict between the President and the Congress.* Washington, D.C.: Congressional Quarterly Press, 1990.

■ Notes

1. Richard E. Neustadt, *Presidential Power* (New York: John Wiley, 1960), p. viii.

2. *United States* v. *Belmont,* 301 U.S. 324 (1937).

3. *Dames & Moore* v. *Regan,* 453 U.S. 654 (1981).

4. Quoted in Gerald F. Seib, "Chemical Weapons Agreement with Soviets Spurs Discord as Senators Contend It Should Be a Treaty," *Wall Street Journal,* July 5, 1990, p. A12.

5. L. Gordon Crovitz, "War Powers Resolution Hasn't Saved Saddam Hussein—Yet," *Wall Street Journal,* August 29, 1990, p. A11.

6. For a study of presidential appointments, see James W. Riddelsperger, Jr., and James D. King, "Presidential Appointments to the Cabinet, Executive Office, and White House Staff," *Presidential Studies Quarterly,* 16 (Fall 1986), 691–699.

7. Richard P. Nathan, *The Administrative Presidency* (New York: Wiley, 1983), pp. 88–90.

8. Roger H. Davidson and Walter J. Oleszek, *Congress and Its Members,* 3rd ed. (Washington, D.C.: Congressional Quarterly Press, 1990), pp. 241–242, 245–248.

9. Thomas E. Cronin, *The State of the Presidency,* 2nd ed. (Boston: Little, Brown, 1980), p. 168.

10. Quoted in Erwin C. Hargrove, *Presidential Leadership* (New York: Macmillan, 1966), p. 40.

11. *Ex parte Milligan,* 4 Wall. 2 (1866); *Duncan* v. *Kahanamoku,* 327 U.S. 304 (1946).

12. *Youngstown Sheet and Tube Co.* v. *Sawyer,* 343 U.S. 579 (1952).

13. *New York Times Co.* v. *United States,* 403 U.S. 713 (1971).

14. *United States* v. *Nixon*, 418 U.S. 683 (1974).

15. 103 S.Ct. 2764 (1983).

16. E. Donald Elliott, "INS v. Chadha: The Administrative Constitution, the Constitution, and the Legislative Veto," in *Supreme Court Review 1983* (Chicago: University of Chicago Press, 1984), pp. 131–132.

17. Eugene V. Rostow, "Repeal the War Powers Resolution," *Wall Street Journal*, June 27, 1984, p. 34; Rep. Robert K. Dornan (R., Calif.), letter, *Wall Street Journal*, November 17, 1987, p. 39.

18. Cronin, *State of the Presidency*, p. 334.

19. Ibid., p. 330.

20. William Howard Taft, *Our Chief Magistrate and His Powers* (New York: Columbia University Press, 1925), p. 138.

21. Quoted in Arthur Larsen, *Eisenhower: The President Nobody Knew* (New York: Scribner's, 1968), p. 12.

22. *The Federalist Papers*, no. 70.

23. Theodore Roosevelt, *Theodore Roosevelt: An Autobiography* (New York: Scribner's, 1913), p. 357.

24. Erwin C. Hargrove and Roy Hoopes, *The Presidency: A Question of Power* (Boston: Little, Brown, 1975), pp. 142–143.

25. For an excellent discussion and analysis of this subject, see the influential study by Neustadt, *Presidential Power*.

26. James David Barber, "Analyzing Presidents," *Washington Monthly*, October 1969, p. 34.

27. James David Barber, "George Bush: In Search of a Mission," *New York Times*, January 19, 1989, p. A31.

28. James David Barber, *The Presidential Character*, 3rd ed. (Englewood Cliffs, N.J.: Prentice-Hall, 1985), p. 506.

29. Anthony Ramirez, "Is Ronald Reagan Similar to Coolidge? Should You Care?" *Wall Street Journal*, September 17, 1980, p. 19.

30. *Youngstown Sheet and Tube Co.* v. *Sawyer*, 343 U.S. 579 (1952).

9

Chapter Outline

The Organization of the Executive Branch
Line Agencies
Staff Agencies

The Federal Bureaucrats
The Size of the Bureaucracy
Who Are the Bureaucrats?

Sources of Bureaucratic Power
Size
Expertise
The Agency/Committee/Interest Group
  Triangle
Delegation of Power by Congress

Restraints on the Bureaucracy
The Powers of the President
The Powers of Congress
Whistleblowing
Other Restraints

Questions for Thought

What are the differences between line and staff organizations?

How are the independent regulatory commissions organized, and what function do they perform?

What organizations make up the Executive Office of the President?

In what ways can the President exercise control over the federal bureaucracy?

In what ways can Congress exercise control over the federal bureaucracy?

The Federal Bureaucracy

WHEN we think of a bureaucracy, what usually comes to mind is its darker side: miles of red tape, being "given the runaround," dealing with people who are unsympathetic to our needs. All these things make it seem impossible to get a reasonable response from a large organization. (The organization may be public or private, but public agencies bear the brunt of this criticism.) In reality, though, **bureaucracy** is simply a way of organizing people to achieve a specific goal, that is, to get work done. Ideally, a bureaucracy is efficient and effective. Only when the members of a bureaucracy fail to do their jobs properly or the workloads of bureaucrats become excessive do the problems of delay, red tape, and unresponsiveness appear.

This chapter focuses on the structure and organization of the federal bureaucracy. It also examines the powers of the bureaucracy and some limitations on the bureaucracy's exercise of authority.

237

■ The Organization of the Executive Branch

Within any bureaucracy each unit of organization (department, agency, etc.) falls into one of two broad categories: line and staff. **Line agencies** are those that carry out government policies and provide various types of services. **Staff agencies,** by contrast, neither execute policies nor provide services. Instead, they gather information and make it available to the chief executive officer whenever it is needed. The line agencies of the federal government are the executive departments, the various government agencies and corporations, the independent regulatory commissions, and certain central services and control agencies. The main staff agencies are the Cabinet and the Executive Office of the President.

Line Agencies

The Executive Departments. The organization of the executive branch is based on the principle of division of labor. The basic units are the fourteen Executive or Cabinet **departments:** State, Treasury, Defense, Justice, Interior, Agriculture, Commerce, Labor, Health and Human Services, Housing and Urban Development, Transportation, Energy, Education, and Veterans Affairs. Each department is headed by a *Secretary*, who is a member of the Cabinet. Below the Secretary there are usually an Undersecretary and one or more assistant Secretaries. Each of these officials is appointed by the President with the advice and consent of the Senate and can be removed by the chief executive at his discretion. (See Figure 9.1.)

Although all the departments are organized along the same general lines, they differ greatly in their size and functions. The Department of Defense has a work force of approximately 1.1 million, while the Department of Education has only about 4,400 employees. There are other differences, too. Four of the departments—State, Defense, Treasury, and Justice—perform basic governmental functions. The others are geared toward particular segments of society such as farmers or workers. This factor, together with size, affects the relative importance of the various departments. Thus the Defense and State Departments are considered more important than Education or Housing and Urban Development.

Departments are generally divided into **bureaus,** which are headed by *bureau chiefs.* The bureaus, like the departments, differ widely in their functions. They may be organized according to whom they serve (e.g., the Bureau of Indian Affairs in the Interior Department), what they do (e.g., the Federal Bureau of Investigation in the Justice Department), or the geographic area they serve (e.g., the Africa Bureau in the Department of State).

Most federal bureaus have central offices located in Washington, D.C. These offices often have relatively small staffs and are concerned with setting policy. The majority of a bureau's employees are located in field offices scattered across the nation and in foreign countries. These **field services,** in turn, consist of hundreds of subunits that are responsible for specialized tasks. Examples of field offices include the local Social Security and Internal Revenue Service offices.

                              THE FEDERAL BUREAUCRACY

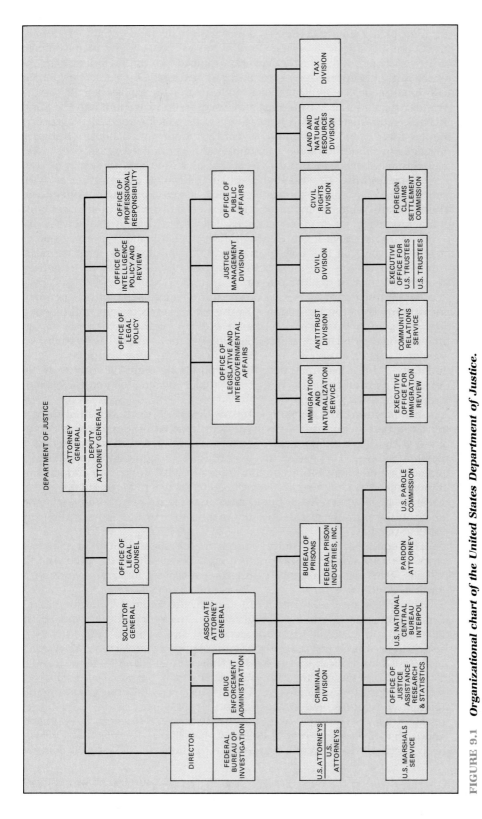

FIGURE 9.1 *Organizational chart of the United States Department of Justice.*

Source: The United States Government Manual, 1989-90 (Washington, D.C.: Government Printing Office, 1990), p. 834.

Agencies. Federal **agencies** are separate from the Cabinet departments but are still under upper-level executive control. The major officials of the forty or so federal agencies are appointed by the President with the advice and consent of the Senate and can be removed by the President at will. Examples of federal agencies include the Environmental Protection Agency, the National Aeronautics and Space Administration, and the Small Business Administration. In general, agencies are formed when a governmental function is too limited to warrant department status. Congress delegates to them the power to administer certain federal programs; some agencies also have the authority to issue rules that have the effect of law.

Corporations. The Federal Deposit Insurance Corporation and the Tennessee Valley Authority are examples of **government corporations.** These organizations combine certain aspects of private businesses with characteristics of government agencies. They are especially useful when the government is providing a service, such as bank deposit insurance or electric power, that can best be run by a corporation free from excessive interference by the President and Congress but still subject to general policies established by Congress.

Each government corporation has a governing board whose members are appointed by the President with the advice and consent of the Senate and serve for a fixed period. The operations of these corporations are financed by long-term congressional appropriations as well as by their own activities (e.g., the selling of electric power by the Tennessee Valley Authority). These features make the corporations quite different from the departments and agencies, which are subject to greater control by both Congress and the President.

Independent Regulatory Commissions. About a dozen **independent regulatory commissions** have been created by Congress and given broad authority to regulate a particular area of the nation's economy. Each regulatory body is headed by a number of commissioners—five is typical—who are appointed by the President with the advice and consent of the Senate. The members serve for fixed but staggered terms of office from three up to fourteen years. Some laws that create commissions also set limits on the number of commissioners who may be members of the same political party.

The commissions are independent in the sense that their members cannot be removed by the President merely because they disagree with his policies. They can be removed only for causes set forth in law, such as criminal conduct.

The Interstate Commerce Commission, the Federal Communications Commission, the Federal Trade Commission, the Federal Reserve Board, the Securities and Exchange Commission, and the National Labor Relations Board are examples of independent regulatory commissions. They make important decisions in the areas that they regulate. The Federal Communications Commission, for example, assigns valuable radio and television licenses to private applicants, and the Federal Trade Commission decides whether companies have engaged in unfair business practices.

Most of the independent commissions were created by Congress during the 1930s, the period of President Franklin D. Roosevelt's New Deal. Their purpose was to free Congress from the task of legislating on complex

Seal of the Federal Trade Commission, one of the independent regulatory commissions of the federal government.

aspects of the American economy. The independent commissions were to be expert regulators that would put into effect the general policy objectives established by Congress.

The independent regulatory commissions are said to exercise all three powers of government—executive, legislative, and judicial. Not only do they enforce the laws passed by Congress, but they also have broad power to establish regulatory policies. In addition, they perform a judicial function in that they settle disputes that arise under their interpretation of the law—subject to review in the federal courts. For this and other reasons, the independent regulatory commissions have been subjected to some criticism. One recent study concluded that the "independent agency is a constitutional sport, an anomalous institution created without regard to the basic principle of separation of powers upon which our government was founded."[1]

Other critics have pointed to the close relationship that develops between the commissions and private interests. It has been argued that some of the independent regulatory commissions tend to identify the well-being of the public with that of the industry or area they are supposed to regulate. The result, according to the critics, is that the regulatory commission is itself "regulated" or controlled by special interests—the Interstate Commerce Commission by the railroads, for example—and that the voice of other groups and of the public is not adequately heard. This criticism may be valid in some cases, but there is considerable variation in the extent to which regulatory commissions are influenced by special-interest groups.

The policies of a regulatory commission depend in part on the views of the people appointed by the President to serve on that commission. Although Presidents cannot fire commissioners because of differences of opinion, they can shape the outlook of a commission through their appointments.

Independent Central Services and Control Agencies. A final set of line agencies handles some of the functions required to keep the government running. Among these agencies are the Office of Personnel Management, which administers the **civil service** (i.e., civilian employees of the federal government), and the General Services Administration, which manages federal buildings and transportation, purchases supplies, and operates institutions such as the National Archives and Records Service.

Staff Agencies

You will recall that staff agencies do not carry out policy but are concerned with gathering information and providing advice. In the executive branch this function is performed partly by the Cabinet but mainly by the Executive Office of the President.

The Cabinet. The President's **Cabinet** is made up of the heads of the fourteen executive departments plus a few other top officials, such as the ambassador to the United Nations. Each of these individuals plays a dual role. He or she is in charge of implementing the President's program in a particular area and at the same time attempts to influence the President's policies in that area. Thus, for example, the Secretary of Defense not only carries out the President's military policy but also tries to shape that policy in ways favored by the Defense Department or by the Secretary himself.

The Cabinet can be seen as divided into an "outer" and an "inner" Cabinet. The inner Cabinet consists of the Secretaries of State, Defense, and Treasury and the Attorney General. Holders of these positions play a "counseling" role in relation to the President. For example, the President's foreign policy decisions are a product of frequent and close consultation with the Secretary of State and other top officials. The same can be said for major defense and economic policies. Members of the outer Cabinet—the Secretaries of Labor, Agriculture, Education, and so forth—have what the political scientist Thomas E. Cronin describes as "advocacy" positions: They represent a specific group of citizens and are involved mainly in carrying out policy and providing services for that sector of society.[2]

In the early years of the nation's history the Cabinet played a major role in governmental decision making. Cabinet meetings were held regularly (as often as twice a week), and all areas of governmental policy were discussed by everyone present. The Cabinet served as an important adviser to the President. In the twentieth century the Cabinet has become much less important as an advisory body. Presidents have found it to be too large and unwieldy to be of much value as a source of guidance. Some recent Presidents have attempted to revive the advisory function of the Cabinet but with little success; the President's personal advisers have played a more significant role than the Cabinet in shaping his policy decisions.

This is not to say that Cabinet members are ignored. As individuals, they play a valuable role as advisers in specific policy areas. Each heads a large bureaucracy with extensive resources for gathering and analyzing information. Individual Cabinet members serve as "the contact points between the President and bureaucracy."[3]

The Executive Office of the President. The Executive Office of the President was created in 1939 after a committee studied the administrative role of the President and concluded that "the President needs help." The Executive Office actually consists of several agencies that provide staff assistance to the President. It includes the White House Office, the Office of Management and Budget, the Council of Economic Advisers, the National Security Council, and several smaller units. Every new President makes some changes in the structure of the Executive Office, but the major units remain unchanged.

THE WHITE HOUSE OFFICE. During the past half-century, as the influence of the Cabinet as a source of advice to the President has declined, that of the White House Office has grown. The White House Office includes a large number of clerical workers and, most important, the President's personal staff. Presidents rely heavily on these assistants for advice and services. Each chief executive organizes his personal staff in a different manner, so it is difficult to generalize about this group. Presidents appoint a variety of assistants for domestic, international, economic, and managerial affairs. Each President has speechwriters, a legal adviser, a liaison officer to deal with Congress, and a press secretary who meets with the news media. All of these assistants share a single purpose: to make the President's job easier. The President appoints them without having to obtain the consent of the Senate and can remove them as he sees fit. They tend to be people whom the President trusts and whose loyalty can be counted on.

The White House Office has grown dramatically in the twentieth century. In the early decades of the century, President Theodore Roosevelt's White House staff consisted of thirty-five people. Just before World War II, President Franklin Roosevelt employed only about fifty people. But the number of people in the White House Office increased to 243 by 1949 under President Harry Truman and reached 606 by 1972 under President Richard Nixon. This upward trend was reversed during the Ford and Carter administrations, when the size of the White House Office was reduced to a little more than 400 people. There were 406 people working in the White House Office in 1980. In 1988 the number was reduced to 366 by President Reagan. During the first year of the Bush administration, 323 people served in the White House Office, which has a budget of almost $28 million.[4]

Different Presidents have organized the White House Office in different ways. As Harold M. Barger has written:

> A White House staff reflects the organizational preferences and personality of the President it serves. Some White House offices have been highly unstructured, with presidential assistants functioning virtually as personal extensions of the President. Others, however, have been structured as tightly as a military command post, with rigid lines of authority linking the President to assistants. . . . Several staffs fell in between these two extremes, with a mix of both structured and free-wheeling relationships between the President and assistants.[5]

President Bush has adopted the more structured approach to organizing the White House Office. In the first years of his administration, the chief of staff, former New Hampshire Governor John Sununu, played an especially important role in controlling access to the President and shaping domestic policy for the administration.

THE OFFICE OF MANAGEMENT AND BUDGET. The most important unit within the Executive Office is the Office of Management and Budget (OMB). The director of OMB, who is nominated by the President with the advice and consent of the Senate, has been a key figure in most recent administrations. OMB performs several functions, including reviewing the budgets and legislative proposals of all the federal departments and agencies. It uses this information to prepare the President's annual budget, which today totals more than one trillion dollars.

Before 1921, Cabinet departments and executive agencies submitted their budget requirements to Congress each year. The House Appropriations Committee analyzed those requests, but it was very difficult for the committee to judge whether the amounts requested were justified. Moreover, the President had no way of making up an executive budget or knowing how money was spent, although under the Constitution he is responsible for the operation of the executive branch of the government. With the passage of the Budget and Accounting Act of 1921, which established the first executive budget office, it became possible to create a more effective executive budget. According to one political scientist, the OMB has become "the most highly developed administrative coordinating and program review unit in the Executive Office; it provides the central institutional mechanism for imprinting . . . presidential will over the government."[6]

OMB's task of serving as a control on the bureaucracy puts it in a peculiar position. On the one hand, it is supposed to be a neutral administrative agency, using its technical expertise in the interests of the nation as a whole. On the other hand, it is almost as important as the White House Office in shaping and implementing the President's policies. On several occasions these roles have come into conflict, and it has been extremely difficult for OMB to maintain a neutral stance.

THE COUNCIL OF ECONOMIC ADVISERS. The Council of Economic Advisers (CEA), created in 1946, consists of a chair and two other economists appointed by the President, plus a permanent staff of about twenty economists who provide technical support. The council's job is to review the state of the economy and advise the President on ways of dealing with such problems as unemployment, inflation, or slow economic growth. The council also prepares the annual *Economic Report of the President* and recommends adjustments in governmental spending and taxation.

In the first twenty-five years of its existence, the council was influential in shaping the government's economic policy; Presidents relied heavily on its advice. For example, the council played an important role in developing President Lyndon Johnson's Great Society program in the mid-1960s. The importance of the council declined over the next few decades; Presidents increasingly turned to the director of OMB and the Secretary of the Treasury for economic advice.[7] President Bush reversed this trend in the first years of his presidency, relying heavily on the council, especially its chair, for advice on domestic economic policy.

THE NATIONAL SECURITY COUNCIL. The National Security Council (NSC) was created in 1947 to advise the President on matters related to national

President Bush meets with his national security advisers.

security. It coordinates domestic, foreign, and military policies, drawing upon experts in the military and civilian bureaucracies. The council consists of the President, the Vice President, the Secretaries of State and Defense, a member of the White House staff (who serves as its director), and the director of the Office of Emergency Preparedness. Its meetings are often expanded to include the chair of the Joint Chiefs of Staff, the ambassador to the United Nations, the director of the Central Intelligence Agency, and other Cabinet officials and members of the White House staff who may be concerned with a particular issue.

Since the 1960s the NSC has become less important as a collective body. At the same time, the National Security Adviser, who heads the NSC, has strongly influenced, and sometimes dominated, the formulation of foreign policy. This top adviser, backed by the permanent staff of the NSC, has become a significant rival to the Secretary of State in terms of influence on presidential decision making. The confused and competitive relationship between the National Security Council and the Department of State has led many observers to suggest that the lines of responsibility between these agencies should be spelled out more clearly. One study recommended that the President "make foreign policy and then delegate to the Department of State the primary responsibility for carrying it out"; at the same time, the advisory role of the NSC should be strengthened.[8]

Figure 9.2 is an organizational chart of the Executive Office of the President. On the chart, the various parts of the Executive Office look neat and orderly, but the reality is anything but orderly. "Instead," says Barger, "there is considerable confusion and intermingling of economic, social,

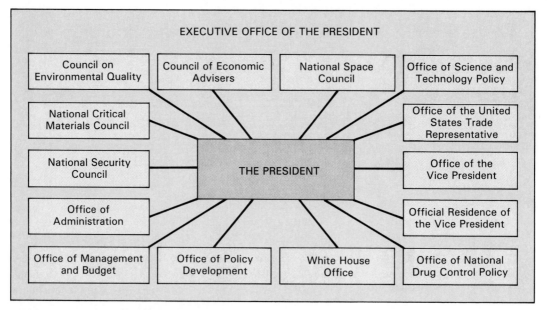

FIGURE 9.2 *Organizational chart of the Executive Office of the President.*

Source: The United States Government Manual, 1989/90 (Washington, D.C.: Government
Printing Office, 1990), p. 86.

budgetary, defense, foreign policy, political, and personal staffs, all of which
are engaged in palace intrigues and court politics."[9]

The Federal Bureaucrats

The Size of the Bureaucracy

"When George Washington's first administration was inaugurated in
1790," one scholar has written,

> it functioned with nine simple executive units and approximately 1,000
> employees. A century later, the 1891 census recorded that over 150,000 civilians
> were working in the Harrison administration. During its first 100 years the
> American government had grown nearly 10 times as fast as the population. By
> 1979 the executive branch employed over 2,800,000 civil servants, divided
> among 12 cabinet departments, 59 independent agencies, and the several
> bureaus of the White House Executive Office. These administrative units in turn
> embraced nearly 1,000 major subunits.[10]

There has been little change in the size of the federal bureaucracy since the
1970s. In fiscal year 1988 the total number of civilian employees in the
executive branch was 3.1 million.[11]

Figure 9.3 presents an organization chart of the federal government as
of 1990. As you can see, the organization of the government is very complex;

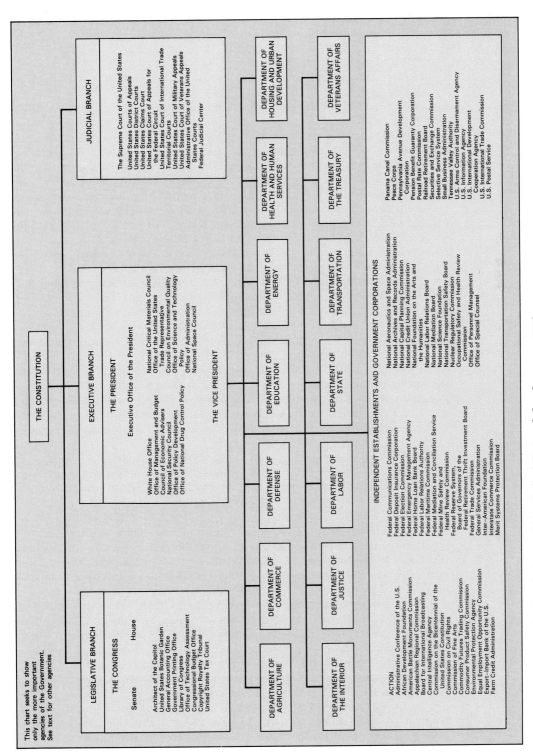

FIGURE 9.3 *Organizational chart of the United States federal government.*

moreover, it changes over time as agencies and bureaus are added, reorganized, or (less often) eliminated.

We tend to think of government bureaucrats as a uniform mass of people sitting behind desks in Washington, D.C., but in reality they are a varied group. Federal government employees include not only administrators and clerks but also lawyers, mechanics, nurses, cooks, economists, wildlife managers, and many other kinds of workers. Only about one out of fourteen federal government employees works in Washington; the rest are in other parts of the United States and the world. A government employee may be a receptionist at the Kalamazoo, Michigan, social security office; a rural development specialist in Nairobi, Kenya; a member of the foreign service in Bangkok, Thailand; an agricultural extension worker in Iowa; or a computer programmer in California. What most of these employees have in common is a view of government or civil service as a career.

The Spoils System. Civil service has not always been considered a career. In the early decades of the nation's history, government jobs were prizes awarded to friends and supporters of each new President when he took office. This practice (which is often linked with President Andrew Jackson though he was not the first to use it) is known as the **spoils system.** It had the virtue of bringing people from many parts of the country and many different backgrounds into government. At the state and local levels the spoils system served as the basis for building and maintaining the political parties. The practice of rewarding loyal supporters with government jobs was defended by George Washington Plunkitt, head of the New York County Democratic party around the turn of the century, as follows:

> First, this great and glorious country was built up by political parties; second, parties can't hold together if their workers don't get offices when they win; third, if the parties go to pieces, the government they built up must go to pieces, too; fourth, then there'll be hell to pay.[12]

The most serious fault of the spoils system was that it encouraged the creation of new jobs and led to the hiring of unqualified people. Much effort was spent in training a new work force after every change of administration, and there was a tendency for government officials to exploit their positions for personal gain.[13]

The spoils system came under fire in the late nineteenth century as part of a general reform movement that was sweeping the country. The goal of the reformers was to replace the spoils system with a merit system, in which people would compete for jobs in the federal government and would be hired on the basis of ability, not party membership. This goal was largely achieved by the passage of the Pendleton Act in 1883, and today the federal government has few, if any, patronage positions.

Today only about 8,000 positions in the federal government are not covered by the merit system. A little more than half are high-level policy-making positions for which civil service would be inappropriate. The remaining positions are part time or honorific in nature or require scientists, doctors, lawyers, and other specialists; examinations for these positions are viewed as unnecessary.

The spoils system remains common, however, in many cities and counties and in some states, including New York, Ohio, Indiana, and Pennsylvania. In a 1990 decision the Supreme Court dealt a major blow to such systems by ruling that party affiliation cannot be used to determine who is hired or promoted for most government jobs. According to the Court, the First Amendment rights of government workers are violated if they are denied a job, promotion, or transfer because of their party affiliation.[14] This ruling is likely to have far-reaching effects on partisan politics throughout the nation. However, it should be noted that there are practical problems associated with enforcing the ruling. It is often very difficult to determine whether a particular personnel action was based on factors other than ability to do the job in question.

The Merit System. The most important feature of the **merit system** is the use of standardized written tests. When people are hired on the basis of test scores, competition is not limited and hiring is related to ability rather than to political beliefs. The civil service tests also serve to weed out unqualified candidates and are easily administered by those who do the hiring. Those who pass a civil service examination will be hired to fill vacant positions and eventually receive tenure—job security during their career in government.

Standardized tests have some drawbacks, however. They may eliminate a few candidates who could do certain jobs but are not good at taking tests, and they may result in the hiring of people who are overqualified for their

Census workers answering telephone calls during the 1990 national census. The Constitution requires that a census be taken every ten years.

positions. They have also been criticized for discriminating against minority groups. The tests, it is claimed, require the kinds of knowledge that are typically possessed by white middle-class Americans and thus discriminate against black and Hispanic candidates.

In 1981, in response to pressure from minority group leaders, the federal government dropped one of its tests, the Professional and Administrative Career Examination. In general, though, federal personnel officers do not want to abandon the use of tests; they believe that testing is the best way to judge the ability of job applicants. Recent court decisions, however, have required employers to prove that their tests are valid indicators of an applicant's ability to handle the job in question. Thus, if the racial, ethnic, or gender makeup of a government agency is very different from that of the labor market in which it hires its employees, it will be called upon to prove that its tests are not discriminatory.

Classification. The Classification Act of 1949 assigned many federal jobs to a general schedule (GS) containing eighteen classes based on job title, duties, and qualifications required. The salaries of government employees are related to those classes. Thus, under the salary schedule in effect in 1988 a GS 1 would earn a minimum of $10,213.00 a year; a GS 9, $23,846.00; and a GS 13, $41,121.00.

In 1978 Congress created a new category of government employees, the Senior Executive Service (SES). This category consists of about 8,000 top administrators who formerly served in GS grades 16–18. Instead of receiving automatic pay raises based on the length of time they have been in the civil service, members of the SES receive cash bonuses for good performance. Their salaries and job tenure also depend on performance. The main goals of the SES are to reward excellence and to encourage the most able employees to remain in the civil service.

Political Executives. As noted earlier, about 8,000 government employees are not part of the civil service system. Of this number, between 4,000 and 5,000 are **political executives** who hold important policy-making positions in government. This category includes department secretaries, undersecretaries, and assistant secretaries, agency heads, ambassadors, and the commissioners of the various independent regulatory agencies.

New Presidents take the appointment of political executives very seriously. They seek people who are highly qualified for these positions and will be loyal as well. It is not easy to find the right people for the many available positions in so short a time. The appointment process therefore often results in choices based on subjective or arbitrary factors and in appointees who are unsuited to their jobs. Or it results in appointees whose opinions and values are so similar to those of the President that they provide little critical appraisal of executive policies.

Another obstacle each President must overcome is obtaining the advice and consent of the Senate. The Senate holds hearings on all major nominations; it is concerned with such issues as whether there are any financial misdeeds in the nominee's record or whether the choice entails any conflict of interest (e.g., whether there is too close a financial connection between a nominee to a regulatory agency and the industry he or she will be regulating).

Presidential nominations almost always receive the Senate's approval.

However, in March 1989 the Senate voted to reject President Bush's nomination of former Texas Senator John Tower as Secretary of Defense. It was the first Senate rejection of a cabinet nomination in thirty years. On occasion a President may withdraw a nomination because of strong opposition to the candidate in the Senate. To avoid the possibility of a withdrawal or actual rejection of a nominee, Presidents often consult privately with Senate leaders about the acceptability of a candidate before making the name public. Thus, even though the power to give advice and consent to executive nominations is rarely used to defeat a President's choice, it must be considered in selecting individuals to fill important positions in the executive branch.

■ Sources of Bureaucratic Power

Size

It has become commonplace to refer to the federal bureaucracy as the "fourth branch" of the government—with good reason. As the part of the government that is responsible for carrying out policies and programs, the bureaucracy has a great deal of power. This power stems from several sources, the most obvious of which is sheer size. The bureaucracy is in charge of administering federal spending—almost $1.2 trillion in the 1990 fiscal year—and directing programs that affect all Americans (and citizens of other nations) in one way or another. As noted earlier, it employs 3.1 million people. It is difficult, if not impossible, to control such a huge organization. Even the President, who is at the head of the federal bureaucracy, cannot be sure that his directives will be carried out.

Expertise

A second source of bureaucratic power is expertise. As we have seen, one of the features of a bureaucracy is specialization or division of labor. Not only is the executive branch divided into departments and agencies that specialize in major areas such as agriculture or commerce, but within each unit of the government there are subunits that are even more specialized, each of which employs experts in various fields for which it is responsible. Thus the Department of the Interior includes the Fish and Wildlife Service. Park biologists, wildlife managers, and other experts are employed by the Park Service to work in the many public parks that are owned and operated by the federal government.

As the complexity of the federal bureaucracy has increased with the creation of more and more specialized units and the funding of increasing numbers of federal programs, its expertise has also grown. As a result, when new programs and policies are being considered, Congress and the President are more likely to listen to experts from the bureau or agency involved than to get information from other sources. In this way the bureaucrats can have an important influence on the programs they will be carrying out.

The Agency/Committee/Interest Group Triangle

Another important but less well understood source of bureaucratic power is the close three-way relationship that often develops among members of the executive agency that administers a program, the congressional committees and subcommittees that appropriate money to it and oversee its operations, and the special-interest groups that are affected by the agency's activities. These relationships, which have been described as "subgovernments,"[15] handle much of the detailed business of government.

To understand the agency/committee/interest group triangle, it is necessary to appreciate the fact that each member of the triangle benefits from the relationship. From the standpoint of the agency, the benefit is more influence. An executive agency with a large and vocal clientele has much more clout with Congress and the White House. If it also has friendly ties with a congressional subcommittee, it has a greater chance of getting its programs approved and funded. The members of the committee benefit from this arrangement by gaining influence over the creation of public policy. For their part, the interest groups gain a greater voice in setting policy through their association with the agency and the subcommittee.

Perhaps the best way to understand the impact of three-way relationships of this kind is through an example. Consider the alliance among the Department of Agriculture, the House and Senate Agriculture Committees, and the American Farm Bureau Federation (along with other interest groups representing farmers). When these three elements are united, they form an "iron triangle" that cannot be overcome by any outside agency.[16]

A classic illustration of this triangle in action is the case of tobacco price supports. All three elements of the "iron triangle" favor the interests of the tobacco industry. (The House Agriculture Committee, for example, is dominated by members from rural districts, whose constituents generally favor farm subsidies. And tobacco-growing states are strongly represented on this standing committee's Subcommittee on Tobacco and Peanuts.) Interest groups opposed to government price supports for tobacco and to the use of tobacco products have been unable to defeat this program. Ironically, the tobacco price support program, administered by the Department of Agriculture, has continued even though another part of the federal government, the Department of Health and Human Services, has for many years issued explicit warnings about the health hazards associated with smoking.

Delegation of Power by Congress

Until the early twentieth century, Congress dominated the federal government. Not only did it make the laws; it also controlled how they were carried out. This control was possible in an earlier, simpler time, before the

The Pentagon, home of the Department of Defense.

government grew into the large, complex organization it is today. Congress now has great difficulty dealing with all the matters in which the government is involved.

But it was not only the complexity of modern government that caused Congress to loosen its hold on the reins of government. Beginning in the late nineteenth century, reformers called for an end to legislative "meddling" with the affairs of the executive branch. And in the early twentieth century more and more people were viewing public administration as a career, and as professionals with training and experience, they were demanding greater freedom from congressional control.

As a result of these forces, Congress delegated broad powers to the executive branch of government and the independent regulatory commissions. It wrote laws in a way that gave much more authority to the agencies responsible for carrying them out. It also passed legislation initiated by the agencies themselves, on the theory that the agency knew more about the subject of the legislation than the legislature did.

The upshot of these trends was a shift away from legislative power toward executive—and bureaucratic—dominance of the federal government. This trend was not reversed until after the Vietnam War and the Watergate scandal of the early 1970s. As a result of those events, members of Congress began calling for a more equitable balance between Congress and the executive branch and began to include in legislation provisions that limited the discretion of executive officials. At the same time, there was growing public concern about the power of administrators to issue numerous regulations—which have the force of law—without congressional approval. Thus in recent decades efforts have been made to limit the power of the bureaucracy. Some examples of those efforts are discussed in the next section.

■ Restraints on the Bureaucracy

To hear some people talk—businesspeople complaining about government "overregulation," liberals who distrust the CIA—the federal bureaucracy is taking over the country. At the same time, there is a common stereotype of bureaucrats as "timid, unimaginative, and reluctant to make decisions" and "paralyzed with indecision when confronted with an opportunity to exercise authority."[17] Neither of these views is accurate. Bureaucrats are not powerless, but their power is not absolute. There are several important restraints on the bureaucracy.

Some of the limitations on the bureaucracy are constitutional and legal. These include the powers of the President, Congress, and the courts. Other limitations are more informal. They include the fact that the bureaucracy must share power and compete with Congress and with private groups. Often intense pressure is placed on governmental agencies by these private organizations. The media also play a role in limiting the power of the bureaucracy, as do the internal restraints that the bureaucracy places on itself. In this section we will discuss both the constitutional and legal checks on the bureaucracy and the more informal restraints on its authority.

The Powers of the President

Since the President is the constitutional head of the executive branch, he is responsible for the bureaucracy. As we have seen, however, it is extremely difficult to control the sprawling organization that the federal bureaucracy has become in the late twentieth century. Still, every President makes some attempt at control.

Appointment Power. The President's effort to control the bureaucracy begins with his appointment power. The more new people (i.e., people who are loyal to him) the President can bring into the bureaucracy, the greater his chance of gaining some control over its operations. The Constitution gives the President the authority to appoint all higher-level members of the executive branch, subject to the "advice and consent" of the Senate. However, the Constitution (Article II, Section 2) also permits Congress to grant the President the power to appoint lower executive officials alone (or to vest such appointments in the courts of law or in the heads of the government departments). The President's appointment power extends to all policy-making positions, including all heads of executive departments and agencies and all Undersecretaries and Assistant Secretaries, but it does not apply to the civil service. It allows the President to select men and women who are in basic agreement with his views on important issues of public policy.

As mentioned earlier, the Senate rarely interferes with the hiring of upper-level executive officials. Its examination of a nominee for such a position is usually brief, and it almost never rejects a candidate suggested by the President. But the President's power to appoint federal officials within a state, as opposed to regional or national officials, is limited by **senatorial courtesy.** Under this unwritten rule the President must clear his nominations with the senior senator of the President's party from the state in question. If the senator declares a particular nominee "personally obnoxious," the Senate will reject the nomination. If neither of the senators from the state in question is a member of the President's party, the President can seek advice from members of his party in the House of Representatives or party leaders in the state.

Removal Powers. In addition to the power of appointment, the President has certain **removal powers.** These powers are not mentioned in the Constitution, but the Supreme Court has stated that the President has the power to remove any executive official and that Congress cannot limit this authority. According to the Court, this power is part of the President's power as chief executive and any attempt by Congress to limit it would be unconstitutional. This power, like the power of appointment, does not apply to civil service positions.[18] The Court has also ruled that members of the independent regulatory commissions may be removed by the President only for causes specified by Congress, since these agencies are not purely executive but have judicial functions and serve chiefly as agents of the legislature.[19]

In removing a member of the executive branch, the President usually acts with care so as to avoid political embarrassment. A top-level official will probably be asked to resign in order to avoid adverse publicity. Rarely is a high government official actually fired by the President.

Power to Reorganize. As mentioned in Chapter 8, the President has the power to reorganize the executive branch, subject to the approval of Congress via a concurrent resolution.

The President's Leadership Role. The President can use the prestige of his office, plus his own leadership ability, to guide the bureaucracy and keep it within certain bounds. The President can set budget and hiring limits and make policy statements, and in many cases the bureaucracy will fall into line. Of course the effectiveness of presidential leadership varies, depending on the character and skills of the President, and there will always be resistance. As Hodding Carter III, an official in the State Department during the Carter administration, has pointed out, the President and the bureaucrats have a different sense of time. The bureaucrats "will be around long after the new wave has fallen back exhausted from their shore."[20] They are not motivated to change the nature of their work—which is, after all, their career—with each new administration.

President Bush speaks to reporters in the White House Rose Garden after a meeting with administrative and congressional budget negotiators in October 1990.

The Powers of Congress

Congress has several important lawmaking powers that serve to set limits on what the bureaucracy can do. Its power to appropriate money is a basic control; to reduce an agency's budget is to limit its ability to function. Congress has the power to delegate to executive agencies and independent regulatory commissions specific authority to regulate and administer programs. And it can, of course, take away or alter this authority. In 1978, for example, Congress deregulated the interstate railroad and trucking industries and thus deprived the Interstate Commerce Commission of powers it had long exercised.

Congress can also eliminate an agency, although it is more difficult to terminate an agency than to end a program, since a single agency may administer a number of programs. Organizations are often able to survive long after their usefulness has ended or their popularity declined. One study found that 148 out of 175 government agencies (85 percent) survived from 1924 through 1973.[21]

Elimination of agencies is rare, but it does occur. On January 1, 1985, the Civil Aeronautics Board went out of existence as a result of congressional action. For many decades the CAB had regulated the fares and flying schedules of the nation's commercial airlines. When Congress deregulated the airline industry in 1978, it also provided for the termination of the CAB. But it took another six years to agree on a specific plan to assign the remaining functions of the CAB to the Department of Transportation and to end the board's existence.

Finally, Congress can pass laws that change the decisions of administrative agencies. It rarely does so, however, mainly because it simply does not have the time. The number of regulations issued by the federal bureaucracy is so great that even if it did nothing else, Congress would be unable to examine them all. Moreover, Congress is more concerned with attempting to solve new problems than with dealing with the consequences of actions it has taken in the past.

In addition to using these powers, Congress has passed specific legislation designed to control the executive branch of the government. These include the Freedom of Information Act of 1966 and the Budget and Impoundment Control Act of 1974. Congress also possesses the basic right to supervise the activities of the federal bureaucracy through its constitutional power of legislative oversight.

The Freedom of Information Act of 1966. In 1966, to the dismay of some federal agencies, Congress enacted a law that requires them to open their files to any person who requests specific documents. The purpose of the Freedom of Information Act is to make available to public scrutiny the decision-making processes of federal agencies. The act contains some significant exceptions, however. Government agencies do not have to make public records that are concerned with national defense and foreign policy; statutes that specifically bar disclosure, such as the 1974 Federal Privacy Act; trade secrets and commercial and financial information obtained on the basis of confidentiality; personnel practices and rules; or the medical and personnel files of federal employees.

Budget Act Controls. We mentioned earlier that Congress delegated control over the budgetary process to the executive branch in the Budget and Accounting Act of 1921. In 1974, however, it regained a role in that process through the Budget and Impoundment Control Act. This act set up a means by which Congress could deal with the budget as a whole instead of one appropriation at a time. As discussed in Chapter 7, it also created the Congressional Budget Office, whose purpose is to keep a watch on the national budget and to report its findings to Congress.

Impoundment Legislation. Chapter 8 also described the action taken by Congress to stop the **impoundment** of funds by the President. This legislation, part of the 1974 act just mentioned, also serves as a restraint on the bureaucracy in that it gives Congress the final say on the spending of federal money.

Legislative Oversight. Oversight (the term means "supervision," not "failure to notice") of bureaucratic activities is an important constitutional power of Congress. It is an aspect of the system of checks and balances, a method by which Congress exercises control over the executive branch.

In general, members of Congress have been reluctant to exercise their oversight function very aggressively. They have been more concerned with two other goals: staying in office and affecting government policy through new legislation.[22] Moreover, to be effective as watchdogs over agency activities, members of Congress have to become experts in the areas in which the agencies are active. In some cases this does happen. As a result of long service on a specific committee, a member of Congress may develop a great deal of expertise in the committee's area of interest. But the three-way relationship described earlier often takes over, making the legislator unwilling to upset the apple cart by scrutinizing the bureaucrats too closely.

There are times, however, when Congress becomes eager to investigate executive units. In 1987 a joint committee of Congress conducted an investigation of the Reagan administration's secret sales of military equipment to Iran and its related policy of using the profits from these sales to aid rebel forces in Nicaragua. And in the early 1990s Congress exercised this power with respect to the banking scandal that rocked the nation's savings and loan institutions.

At a humbler level, members of Congress engage in what is known as casework, that is, helping their constituents deal with government agencies like the Small Business Administration or the Social Security Administra-

United States Department of the Treasury, Washington, D.C.

THE FEDERAL BUREAUCRACY

tion. This also serves as a check on the bureaucracy and can prevent distress and injustice in individual cases, but its effect is limited. This kind of "meddling" is a drop in the bucket compared to the ocean of bureaucratic activity that goes largely unsupervised by Congress.

Judicial Review. With judicial review, the federal courts have the ultimate power to control the decisions and actions of executive agencies and independent regulatory commissions. Legal challenges to the decisions of these bodies can be taken to the federal courts. In recent years, for example, many organizations concerned with environmental issues have brought lawsuits in federal courts seeking to overturn decisions of the Department of the Interior and the Environmental Protection Agency. But legal actions begun in the courts are not the only reason for the importance of judicial review. The mere existence of judicial review serves as a deterrent to arbitrary acts by government agencies.

Although judicial review is a significant check on the illegal use of bureaucratic power, its availability and scope are limited. Normally, federal courts will not hear a case until the challenging party has exhausted all avenues of appeal within the agency itself. Moreover, the courts place considerable weight on the agency's interpretation of federal law and will uphold it as long as it is not unreasonable.

Courts hold administrators accountable by reviewing their actions in two main areas: the procedures used in making decisions and the substance of the decisions themselves. The procedures must meet constitutional standards of due process of law and the requirements of federal statutes, especially the Administrative Procedures Act of 1946. At a minimum the agency must provide the affected party with notice of its decision and an opportunity for a hearing at which the individual can present his or her views on the issue. As for substance, the courts focus on the question of whether there is "substantial evidence" to support the administrative decision. If this standard has been met, the courts will normally affirm the agency's position.[23]

Despite these limitations, the courts are an important source of protection against arbitrary and illegal uses of administrative power. This function is particularly vital in a time when governmental regulations directly affect the lives of Americans in so many ways.

Whistleblowing

Another important limitation on the bureaucracy is provided by **whistleblowers**—employees who "blow the whistle" on waste, fraud, and abuse. Corporate and government employees who reveal the mistakes or misdeeds of their employers are often dealt with harshly; they may be reprimanded, fired, or demoted. An example is the case of Lynn Bruner, a civil servant who became a district director in the Equal Employment Opportunity Commission in 1986. When she arrived at her new position she noticed that there was a large backlog of age-discrimination cases, which must be investigated within two years or they become invalid. She soon reached the conclusion that such cases were intentionally allowed to lapse, and she made a statement on the matter to a major newspaper. She was promptly given a negative job rating and informed that she would be demoted and transferred.[24]

In 1989 Congress acted to protect whistleblowers against arbitrary actions by employers. As one member of the House described it, the Whistleblowers Protection Act is designed to allow employees to "confidently carry out their responsibilities without fear of retribution, of ruined careers, lost jobs, and destroyed families, hopes and dreams." The act provides that a federal agency accused of penalizing a whistleblower must provide "clear and convincing" evidence that the action in question did not stem from the worker's whistleblowing.[25]

Other Restraints

In addition to the powers of Congress, the President, and the courts, there are several other significant restraints on the bureaucracy. The news media play an important role in controlling bureaucratic authority. Since the media both influence and reflect public opinion, executive officials pay attention to the views expressed in the media, especially in major newspapers like the *Washington Post* and the *New York Times*, news magazines such as *Time* and *Newsweek*, and the major television networks. Reporters and correspondents gather information and present it to readers and viewers, who then may question the government's policies.

The media also keep bureaucrats on their toes through the threat of exposure. Not only do reporters make public the personal wrongdoings of bureaucrats, but they also publish information that government agencies might prefer to conceal. A classic example of the latter is the publication by the *New York Times* and the *Washington Post* of the Defense Department's study of the Vietnam War, the so-called *Pentagon Papers*, in 1971. At the same time, the media can sometimes serve as a channel through which executive agencies communicate with the public. Reporters are always looking for news, and the agencies are willing to supply information that will make them look good. There is little danger that the media will become a tool of the bureaucracy, however, since, as one political scientist has pointed out, "The news that reporters commonly seek is information that agencies are reluctant to divulge."[26]

In addition to the media, other outside groups can serve to limit the actions of the bureaucracy. In some cases a private group is an almost permanent opponent of a government agency. Some business groups, for example, do all they can to limit the powers of regulatory commissions. In other cases the relationship between an agency and a private group (e.g., between the Department of Agriculture and farm groups) is a friendly one. Even in these cases, however, the private group limits the bureaucracy in that its views have some influence on what the agency does.

Another set of limitations on bureaucratic power is provided by the bureaucracy itself. For one thing, there is competition within the bureaucracy; various agencies compete for funds, programs, and influence. A good example is the competition among the branches of the armed forces for funding in general and control over weapons systems in particular. There is also competition within executive agencies as different groups of experts present competing solutions to problems like the budget deficit.

The most basic restraint on the bureaucracy is provided by the values of bureaucrats. If bureaucrats believe that they are public servants and that their power must be used for the public good and not for personal gain, abuses of bureaucratic power are less likely. Values like these are taught in the schools and constantly expressed in the media and elsewhere. Thus bureaucrats are always being reminded of their proper role within the governmental system. Indeed, some bureaucrats belong to professional organizations that have established codes of ethics for government employees. Although self-restraint alone cannot be depended on to keep the bureaucracy in line, it must be counted among the factors that prevent bureaucrats from becoming lawbreakers.

Finally, the power of some bureaucratic agencies has been diminished since the 1970s as a result of **deregulation.** Banking, transportation, and communications are among the areas in which Congress has repealed regulatory legislation. It appears, however, that the trend toward deregulation has run its course, and it is unlikely that additional industries will be deregulated. Indeed, there is pressure to increase government regulation in some areas, such as transportation safety and consumer protection.

■ Summary

Many people are concerned about the power of government officials. They feel that the restraints just described are not enough, that nothing is stopping the bureaucrats from overregulating and overtaxing the American people. In reality, however, the power of the bureaucracy is often exaggerated. Government agencies are not free to do whatever they like. They compete with one another; they are limited by Congress, the courts, and private groups; and deregulation has occurred in some areas of the economy.

Nevertheless, it can be argued that the federal bureaucracy has more power than is acceptable in a democratic political system. There is no doubt that the bureaucracy is very large and that its decisions have a significant impact on the lives of citizens. The great size of the bureaucracy is due largely to the actions of Congress: Legislation is drafted in very general terms and must be "translated" into a functioning program by some government agency—either one that already exists or a new one established to carry out the new policy.

When citizens are frustrated by the activities of the bureaucracy (or, often, its lack of activity), they turn to their representatives in Congress for help, not recognizing that Congress was the source of the problem in the first place. As one observer has described the situation, "The bureaucracy serves as a convenient lightning rod for public frustration and a convenient whipping boy for congressmen."[27]

Despite the misplaced public resentment of the bureaucracy, the powerful, if not absolute, role of the federal bureaucracy is unlikely to be challenged in the foreseeable future. As long as members of Congress satisfy voters by continuing existing programs and establishing new ones, the bureaucracy will remain the "fourth branch" of the national government.

■ Key Terms

bureaucracy	government corporation	senatorial courtesy
line agency	independent regulatory commission	removal powers
staff agency	civil service	impoundment
department	Cabinet	oversight
bureau	spoils system	whistleblower
field service	merit system	deregulation
agency	political executive	

■ Suggested Reading

BURKE, JOHN. *Bureaucratic Responsibility*. Baltimore: Johns Hopkins University Press, 1986.

DERTHICK, MARTHA, and PAUL J. QUIRK. *The Politics of Deregulation*. Washington, D.C.: Brookings Institution, 1985.

HARRIS, RICHARD A., and SIDNEY M. MILKIS. *The Politics of Regulatory Change: A Tale of Two Agencies*. New York: Oxford University Press, 1989.

HEYMANN, PHILIP B. *The Politics of Public Management*. New Haven, Conn.: Yale University Press, 1988.

KETTLE, DONALD F. *Government by Proxy: (Mis)-Managing Federal Programs*. Washington, D.C.: Congressional Quarterly Press, 1987.

KNOTT, JACK H., and GARY J. MILLER. *Reforming Bureaucracy: The Politics of Institutional Choice*. Englewood Cliffs, N.J.: Prentice-Hall, 1987.

REAGAN, MICHAEL D. *Regulation: The Politics of Policy*. Boston: Little, Brown, 1986.

RILEY, DENNIS D. *Controlling the Federal Bureaucracy*. Philadelphia: Temple University Press, 1987.

SEIDMAN, HAROLD, and ROBERT S. GILMOUR. *Politics, Position, and Power*, 4th ed. New York: Oxford University Press, 1986.

TOLCHIN, SUSAN J., and MARTIN TOLCHIN. *Dismantling America: The Rush to Deregulate*. New York: Oxford University Press, 1985.

■ Notes

1. Geoffrey P. Miller, "Independent Agencies," in Philip B. Kurland et al., eds., *The Supreme Court Review, 1986* (Chicago: University of Chicago Press, 1987), pp. 96–97.

2. Thomas E. Cronin, *The State of the Presidency*, 2nd ed. (Boston: Little, Brown, 1980).

3. Benjamin I. Page and Mark P. Petracca, *The American Presidency* (New York: McGraw-Hill, 1983), p. 193.

4. William F. Mullen, *Presidential Power and Politics* (New York: St. Martin's Press, 1976), p. 207; U.S. Bureau of the Census, *Statistical Abstract of the United States, 1990*, 110th ed. (Washington, D.C.: Government Printing Office, 1990), Table 519.

5. Harold M. Barger, *The Impossible Presidency: Illusions and Realities of Executive Power* (Glenview, Ill.: Scott, Foresman, 1984), p. 205.

6. Larry Berman, *The New American Presidency* (Boston: Little, Brown, 1987), p. 118.

7. Barger, *Impossible Presidency*, p. 198.

8. Raymond Tatalovich and Byron W. Daynes, *Presidential Power in the United States* (Monterey, Calif.: Brooks/Cole, 1984), p. 274. See also Commission on the Organization of the Government for the Conduct of Foreign Policy, *Final Report* (Washington, D.C.: Government Printing Office, 1975), pp. 5–39.

9. Barger, *Impossible Presidency*, p. 195.

10. Bruce D. Porter, "Parkinson's Law: War and the Growth of American Government," *Public Interest*, Summer 1980, p. 50.

11. *Statistical Abstract, 1990*, Table 521.

12. William L. Riordon, ed., *Plunkitt of Tammany Hall* (New York: E.P. Dutton & Co., 1963), p. 13.

13. Herbert Kaufman, "The Growth of the Federal

Personnel System," in Wallace S. Sayre, ed., *The Federal Government Service* (Englewood Cliffs, N.J.: Prentice-Hall, 1965), pp. 29–31.

14. *Rutan* v. *Republican Party of Illinois*, 110 S. Ct. 2729 (1990).

15. Douglas Cater, *Power in Washington* (New York: Random House, 1964), pp. 17–18.

16. Jack H. Knott and Gary J. Miller, *Reforming Bureaucracy* (Englewood Cliffs, N.J.: Prentice-Hall, 1987), p. 130.

17. Francis E. Rourke, *Bureaucracy, Politics, and Public Policy*, 2nd ed. (Boston: Little, Brown, 1976), p. 166.

18. *Myers* v. *United States*, 272 U.S. 52 (1926); *Bowsher* v. *Synar*, 478 U.S. 714 (1986).

19. *Humphrey's Executor* v. *United States*, 295 U.S. 602 (1935).

20. Hodding Carter III, "The Unequal Bureaucratic Contest," *Wall Street Journal*, January 8, 1981, p. 19.

21. Herbert Kaufman, *Are Government Organizations Immortal?* (Washington, D.C.: Brookings Institution, 1976).

22. Fred A. Kramer, *Dynamics of Public Bureaucracy: An Introduction to Public Management*, 2nd ed. (Cambridge, Mass.: Winthrop, 1981), p. 369.

23. Bernard Rosen, *Holding Government Bureaucrats Accountable* (New York: Praeger, 1982), pp. 108–109.

24. Gillian Sandford, "Reprisals Related by EEOC Worker," *Congressional Quarterly*, March 25, 1989, pp. 643–644.

25. Rep. Gerry Sikorski (D., Minn.), quoted in Macon Morehouse, "'Whistleblower' Protection Bill Cleared Easily by House," *Congressional Quarterly*, March 25, 1989, p. 643.

26. Rourke, *Bureaucracy*, p. 173.

27. Francis E. Rourke, ed., *Bureaucratic Power in National Policy Making*, 4th ed. (Boston: Little, Brown, 1986), p. 230.

10

Chapter Outline

The Law
Criminal and Civil Law
The Adversary System
The Role of the Courts
The Role of the Judge

The Dual Court System
The State Courts
The Federal Courts

The Supreme Court
Oral Arguments
Conferences
Opinions
The Role of the Chief Justice
Bringing a Case before the Court
The Court's Workload

Selection of Federal Judges
Selecting Judges for Lower Federal Courts
The Reagan Appointments
Appointing Supreme Court Justices
Confirmation and Tenure

The Functions of the Judiciary
Judicial Review
Restrictions on the Court
Self-Restraint versus Activism

Questions for Thought

Name and describe five types of law.

Name the main federal courts and their jurisdiction.

What is a writ of certiorari, and what is its importance?

What role does the United States Senate play in the confirmation of judicial nominees?

What is judicial review?

Describe some of the major theories of constitutional interpretation.

The Judiciary

IN a democratic society the law serves both to protect and to restrain the people. "My freedom to swing my arm," Justice Oliver Wendell Holmes once remarked, "stops where the other man's nose begins." When serious disputes arise, there is a need for an impartial third party to settle them. This function is fulfilled by the judiciary, that is, the courts. This chapter focuses on the role of the courts in American society.

The Law

Before we can discuss the courts and how they operate, we need to understand the nature of the law. For our purposes, **law** may be defined as the principles and regulations established by a government, applicable to a people, and enforced by the government. There are five basic types of law: common law, equity, statutory law, constitutional law, and administrative law.

Common law, often called "judge-made" law, is a set of rules that have been created by judges in the course of rendering decisions on court cases. Common law dates from medieval times in England, when the king gave certain officials the authority to travel around the country and settle legal disputes. The decisions of these judges were based on good sense and custom and depended on the facts of the case. Precedent has always been an important force in the development of the common law. Once a rule was adopted in a particular case, it was applied to similar situations and thus became common to the nation. These rules accumulated until they formed a body of judicial rulings that became known as the common law.

The English colonists brought the common law with them to the New World. As new rules were added, American common law evolved. In the United States today judicial practice is guided by common law rules in every state except Louisiana, where the legal system is based on French law.

Common law had some limitations, however. It did not provide a way of dealing with a wrongful act that had not yet occurred. It could not be applied until the act had actually been committed and the case had been brought to court. Moreover, its remedies were confined to awarding money damages to an injured party. **Equity** evolved in response to these weaknesses in the common law. Like common law, equity was based on previous judicial decisions. But it was different in that one of the king's officers, the chancellor, was given the power to prevent an illegal act and to grant remedies other than awards of money. The chancellor's office developed into a separate court—an equity or chancery court—that could issue a court order requiring a person or group to refrain from a particular act.

Consider the following example. Assume that A owns a piece of land on which he is carefully growing his favorite tree. A finds out that B is planning to make a path that will result in the death of his tree. Under common law, A must wait until this act has occurred before suing B for money damages. But under equity he may be able to obtain a court order, called an **injunction,** that requires B to refrain from making her path. If B violates the injunction, she can be punished for contempt of court.

There are no separate equity courts in the federal court system of the United States; equity matters are handled by the regular federal courts. Most states also have an integrated court system in which common law and equity cases are administered by the same courts. A few states, such as Delaware, maintain separate equity courts, however.

Statutory law differs from both common law and equity. A *statute* is a law that has been formally declared by a legislature, in contrast to "judge-made" law. In the twentieth century there has been a shift toward more statutory law and less common law; many areas of law that were once governed by common law are now covered by statutes.

Constitutional law results from the interpretation and application of a national or state constitution. It includes all the statements made by both federal and state courts in interpreting constitutional provisions. Through

The United States Supreme Court building, Washington, D.C.

its decisions, the United States Supreme Court plays an especially important role in defining the meaning and impact of constitutional provisions for the nation as a whole.

Finally, there is a body of law called **administrative law,** which consists of all the regulations that define the powers and procedures of administrative agencies. During the twentieth century executive agencies have grown rapidly in both number and power, largely as a result of increased regulation of the nation's economic and social life by the government. Thus there is now an extensive set of rules, collectively known as administrative law, that have been issued by agencies of the federal, state, and local governments.

Criminal and Civil Law

The law may be divided into two broad areas: criminal and civil. **Criminal law,** which today is almost entirely statutory, deals with acts that endanger the public welfare. Since the government alone enforces criminal law, the government is the **plaintiff** (the party that brings the case to court) in all criminal trials; the party accused of the crime is the **defendant.**

Crimes are usually classified as either **misdemeanors** or **felonies.** These terms are defined differently in the laws of the various states and in federal laws. In general, however, misdemeanors are less serious acts for which punishment may consist of a jail term of up to one year. Felonies are more serious acts for which punishment may involve a jail sentence of more than one year—or death, in states that maintain the death penalty for murder. Some crimes (e.g., violation of national tax laws) are covered by federal law, but most are defined by state laws. Some acts may violate both federal and state law.

Civil law deals primarily with disputes between private individuals or corporations and defines the rights of the parties in the dispute. A divorce suit is a civil case; so is a negligence case in which an accident has caused injury to a person or to property. Sometimes the government is involved in a civil case. Under the Sherman Antitrust Act, for example, the government may sue a corporation that enters into any "contract, combination in the form of trust or otherwise, or conspiracy, in restraint of trade or commerce. . . ." A civil case may also arise when a person or group sues the government, as when an individual is wrongfully injured by an agent of the government.

The Adversary System

Unlike the executive and legislative branches of the government, the judiciary is largely passive. The courts must wait for cases to be brought to them before they can settle disputes. When a case comes to court, it takes the form of a conflict between parties on each side of the dispute. Each side attempts to present a view of the facts that is favorable to its case. Thus, the American legal system is often referred to as an **adversary system,** since it is based on the assumption that truth will emerge from the clash of opposing interests.

The Role of the Courts

Under Article III of the Constitution, the federal courts may hear only "Cases" and "Controversies"; that is, there must be a real conflict of interest—criminal or civil—between the parties. In *Muskrat* v. *United States*, the Supreme Court interpreted cases and controversies as follows: "The term implies the existence of present or possible adverse parties, whose contentions are submitted to the court for adjudication."[1] Moreover, the party bringing a federal suit must demonstrate some form of personal injury, not a general wrong that is shared by the public at large. The party "must distinguish himself from the general citizenry, by showing a personal stake, a particular concrete injury, something more than 'generalized grievances.'"[2]

These principles have a number of important consequences. For example, the federal courts generally will not hear cases brought by individuals solely on the basis of their status as federal taxpayers. Moreover, they will not give advisory opinions. Congress, the President, or a private citizen cannot seek an opinion from the courts on whether a proposed action is constitutional; a case must be brought to a federal court before the court will consider the issue. (In some states, such as Massachusetts and Colorado, the courts do give advisory opinions at the request of the governor or a state legislator.)

The Role of the Judge

The judge is the presiding officer of the court and the expert on all issues of law that arise in court. In a trial court the function of the judge is to maintain a "legal atmosphere," one in which arguments and evidence can be presented according to the rules of judicial procedure. The judge also instructs the jury regarding the law that applies in the case and discusses the possible verdicts it may reach. Finally, the judge pronounces a judgment or a sentence based on the jury's verdict or, in the case of a nonjury trial, on the basis of his or her analysis of the facts.

Laws are written in general terms and are intended to apply to a large number of cases. But the cases to which they apply may be very different. The judge often must decide which law should apply in a given case and then determine the meaning of the legal rule. This process occurs at all levels of the judiciary. A local judge must define the meaning of negligence in a personal injury case, while the Supreme Court will be called upon to clarify the concept of freedom of speech.

Thus it is clear that judges do not simply match the law to the case. If they did, the outcome would always be predictable. The need to interpret the law has the effect of giving judges a certain degree of discretion in the application of the law.

■ The Dual Court System

Having described the general features of the American legal system, we turn our attention to the courts themselves and how they operate. First, however, it should be noted that as a consequence of its federal form of government, the United States has a *dual* court system: a federal court system and fifty state court systems. (The District of Columbia, Puerto Rico, and the U.S. territories also have federal as well as local court systems.) The state systems are separated geographically, of course, but the federal and state systems overlap. The structure of these many systems is established by the constitutions and statutes of the federal government and the various states.

The concept of jurisdiction is basic to understanding the American court system. **Jurisdiction** is the right of a court to hear a particular type of case. This right is granted either by a constitution or by a legislative statute. Without jurisdiction, a court has no authority to decide a dispute. The jurisdiction of state courts is very broad; that of the federal courts is more limited. In a few situations the state and federal courts share jurisdiction and the plaintiff can choose to sue in either court system.

Article III, Section 2, of the Constitution sets forth the jurisdiction of the federal courts. Jurisdiction may be based on either the *subject matter* or the *nature of the parties* in a particular case. Jurisdiction based on subject matter consists of all cases arising under the U.S. Constitution, federal laws, and treaties, as well as certain other areas of law, such as admiralty and maritime cases. Jurisdiction based on the nature of the parties consists of the following:

1. Cases affecting ambassadors, other public ministers, and consuls
2. Cases in which the United States is a party
3. Disputes between two or more states

4. Disputes between citizens in different states
5. Disputes between citizens of the same state who claim lands under grants from different states

A legal dispute must fall within one of these categories to be heard in the federal courts. Not all such cases are heard in federal courts, however; Congress has set certain additional limits on federal jurisdiction. For example, in disputes between citizens of different states—a frequent basis for federal court jurisdiction—the amount involved must be over $50,000. Cases involving smaller amounts must be heard in state courts.

A court's jurisdiction may be original or appellate. Courts that have **original jurisdiction** are trial courts; they determine the facts of the case as well as the law that applies to them. Courts with **appellate jurisdiction** handle appeals; that is, they review the decisions of lower courts. The United States Supreme Court, for example, has both original and appellate jurisdiction. Only rarely, however, does the Supreme Court exercise its original jurisdiction, which is limited to cases affecting ambassadors, other public ministers, and consuls and those in which a state is a party. In all other cases the Court has appellate jurisdiction. Appeals generally go from a federal district court to a court of appeals and then to the Supreme Court. In a case involving the U.S. Constitution, a treaty, or congressional law, an appeal may go directly to the Supreme Court from the highest state court with jurisdiction over the case.

It is important to understand that each court system has the right to make the final interpretation of the law in the cases over which it has jurisdiction. Thus the highest court in each state is the final interpreter of the laws of that state, and the United States Supreme Court is the final interpreter of federal law. If a question of federal law arises in a state court—for example, if a person who has been arrested claims that his or her Fourth Amendment rights have been violated—the United States Supreme Court has the right to rule on the issue.

The State Courts

The various state court systems are organized in different ways, a fact that makes it hard to present a brief description of the state courts. A few generalizations can be offered, however. In some states the lowest level of the court system is the justice of the peace or police court. In many others county, district, or municipal courts are found at the lowest level. (In large cities the local trial courts may be organized in a different—and more complex—way.) In most states the most important trial court is a superior or circuit court (in New York it is the State Supreme Court.) About three-quarters of the states have an appellate court between the trial courts and the highest court in the state. All states have an appellate court of last resort, usually called the Supreme Court (in New York it is called the Court of Appeals and in Maine and Massachusetts the Supreme Judicial Court). Almost all states have special courts that deal with family problems (called domestic relations or family courts) and courts that deal with wills and estates (called probate or surrogate's courts).

The State Supreme Court building in Dover, Delaware. Most civil and criminal cases are heard in state, not federal, courts.

The vast majority of both civil and criminal cases are brought in state courts, which therefore must handle a huge volume of cases. According to the National Center for State Courts, in 1988 (the most recent year for which data are available) the state courts received a total of 98 million new cases, of which 68 million involved violations of traffic laws and local ordinances and more than 30 million were new civil, criminal, and juvenile cases. The number of civil cases increased by 4.3 percent from the 1987 level, while the number of criminal cases rose by more than 5 percent. (Much of the latter increase is attributed to drug-related prosecutions.)[3]

In many state court systems long delays are common, partly because of their heavy workload and partly because of their loose structure. Some states have attempted to centralize their court systems in order to increase their efficiency. Even so, in large cities and metropolitan areas there typically is a large backlog of cases awaiting trial. The National Center for State Courts reports that the number of cases added to state court dockets in 1988 exceeded the number closed by about 5 percent.

The Federal Courts

There are two types of federal courts: constitutional and legislative. The **constitutional courts** are established by Congress under the provisions of Article III, Section 1, of the Constitution, which declares that "the Judicial power of the United States, shall be vested in one supreme Court, and in such inferior Courts as the Congress may from time to time ordain and establish."

The major constitutional courts are the United States district courts, the United States courts of appeals, and the United States Supreme Court. Several other constitutional courts deal with specialized subjects. The Court of International Trade decides disputes arising under the nation's tariff laws (e.g., whether the government has imposed the correct levy on a product imported from another country). The Court of Customs and Patent Appeals reviews decisions of the U.S. Patent Office and some rulings of the U.S. Tariff

Commission and the Court of International Trade. In 1982 Congress created the United States Court of Appeals for the Federal Circuit, which hears appeals from the U.S. Court of Customs and Patent Appeals and from the United States Claims Court. The decisions of these special courts can be appealed to the Supreme Court.

The **legislative courts** are created by Congress under its power in Article I, Section 8, to "constitute Tribunals inferior to the supreme Court" and its various expressed powers to legislate in specific areas. The major legislative courts are the United States Court of Military Appeals, which reviews the decisions of military courts-martial; the United States Tax Court, which settles disputes between taxpayers and the Commissioner of Internal Revenue; the federal territorial courts, which handle cases in Guam, Puerto Rico, the American Virgin Islands, the Canal Zone, and the Mariana Islands; and the United States Claims Court, a trial court that hears financial claims against the federal government.

The main difference between these two types of courts is that judges on constitutional courts have life tenure—they serve during "good behavior"—while judges on legislative tribunals serve for a fixed number of years. Another difference is that legislative courts, unlike federal constitutional courts, may give advisory opinions.

The most important federal constitutional courts are the district courts, the courts of appeals, and the Supreme Court.

United States District Courts. There are eighty-nine district courts in the fifty states, plus one each in the District of Columbia, the Commonwealth of Puerto Rico, and the territories of the United States. Like the state courts, the federal district courts have a large and growing workload—between 1975 and 1988, the number of civil cases begun in each year rose from 117,300 to 239,600. The number of criminal cases remained almost constant, increasing only from 41,000 to 43,500 during the same period.[4]

To reduce the pressure on these courts and decrease the length of time before a case comes to trial, Congress increased the number of federal district court judges in 1978, 1984, and again in 1990, bringing the present total to 649.

The district courts are the trial courts of the federal judicial system; they hear both civil and criminal cases. However, they have only original jurisdiction; that is, they never hear cases on appeal. Each state has at least one district court. The boundary lines for a district never cross state lines, but a state may be divided into two, three, or even four districts (in California, Texas, and New York), depending on such factors as population and the number of cases that must be handled. Each state has at least two federal district judges. The number of judges serving in a district ranges from two to as many as twenty-eight (in the Southern District of New York, which includes part of New York City and its metropolitan area). One observer has described the district courts as follows:

> [They] . . . are the basic trial courts of the federal judiciary. They are primarily concerned with settling *questions of fact* . . . . In that role they are the busiest of the three court layers. From some points of view the work of the trial court is both more interesting and more creative than that found in the two appellate

tiers. The battle of the opposing platoons of counsel . . . takes place here. And it is here that we find the jury, that intriguing, albeit controversial, institution of citizen participation in the judicial process.[5]

United States Courts of Appeals. The thirteen courts of appeals are exclusively appellate courts. Eleven of these courts are regional, covering three or more states. A twelfth court is located in the District of Columbia. The thirteenth, the Court of Appeals for the Federal Circuit, is a national court that hears cases primarily involving patents and tariffs. Except for the latter, the courts of appeals hear both civil and criminal cases. The appeals come from federal district courts within the appellate court's circuit. In addition, about 10 percent of the work of these courts involves appeals from decisions of the federal regulatory agencies such as the Federal Communications Commission and the Federal Trade Commission; most of these appeals come to the appellate court serving the District of Columbia. (See Figure 10.1.)

FIGURE 10.1 *The twelve Federal Circuit Courts of Appeals.*

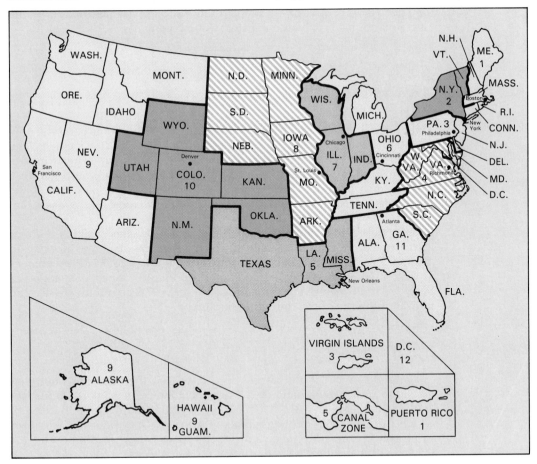

Only a relatively small number of cases are appealed. Even so, the appellate courts have experienced a sharp increase in cases that parallels the increase in cases filed in the district courts. Between 1975 and 1988 the number of cases brought to the courts of appeals rose from 16,658 to 37,524.[6] In order to deal with this problem, Congress increased the number of appeals court judges on three occasions since 1978, bringing the total to its present level of 179.

The courts of appeals have from as few as six to more than thirty judges, depending on the number of cases they must hear. Each case that comes to a court of appeals is normally heard by a panel of three judges. The attorneys for the opposing parties present written arguments, or **briefs,** to the court. They are also allowed a limited time in which to present oral arguments. After hearing these presentations and studying the briefs and the trial records of the case, the judges confer privately before announcing their decision.

The courts of appeals have no choice regarding which cases they will hear. In most situations the losing party in the district court or regulatory agency has a right to appeal. The main exception is that the government may not appeal a loss in a criminal case; such appeals are barred by the Fifth Amendment prohibition against double jeopardy.

■ The Supreme Court

The United States Supreme Court is the nation's highest court and the only one that is actually created by the Constitution (Article III, Section 1). The Supreme Court is the final interpreter of the law on all matters involving the U.S. Constitution, federal laws, and treaties, whether the case began in a federal court or a state court. As such, it has enormous power to shape federal law—especially constitutional law, since most of its cases are concerned with constitutional issues.

The Supreme Court is in session from early October until late June or early July each year. It usually hears oral arguments from Monday to Thursday for two weeks of each month. Fridays are devoted to conferences at which cases are discussed and voted upon and requests for appellate review are considered. The remaining two weeks of each month are devoted to examining the cases and writing opinions.

Oral Arguments

The attorneys for the parties in a case that the Supreme Court has agreed to hear submit carefully written, detailed briefs so that the justices can become familiar with the facts and issues of the dispute. In cases in which the Court allows oral arguments, attorneys may present their views in person. In the early nineteenth century it was not uncommon for the Court to hear several days of argument on a single case. Today, however, its heavy workload no longer permits such a luxury; each case usually receives

The seal of the United States Supreme Court.

one hour (half an hour for the attorney for each side in the dispute). This time restriction is strictly enforced even if an attorney's presentation must be halted in the middle of a sentence. A system of lights on the lectern signals the attorney twice—when there are five minutes remaining and when the time has expired.

The justices may interrupt oral arguments at any time to ask questions, or they may wait until the end of the presentation. In either case this procedure demands a good deal of self-possession and skill on the part of the lawyer. Some justices are gentle in questioning attorneys; others ask difficult and probing questions and seem to enjoy putting the attorneys on the spot.

Conferences

After studying the briefs and hearing oral arguments for several cases, the justices debate the cases in their secret Friday conferences. The doors of the conference room are locked; no one other than the nine justices is present, and no record of the discussion is kept. Although little is known about the Court's informal procedures, it is generally believed that the Chief Justice presents a summary of a case and then asks the other justices, in descending order of seniority, to express their views on the case. A vote is then taken, with the justices now voting in ascending order of seniority. Each case is decided by majority vote, and one of the justices voting with the majority is assigned to write the **majority opinion.**

Opinions

The writer of the majority opinion faces a difficult task. He or she must not only declare the decision of the Court but also create a statement that will satisfy all the justices who voted with the majority. Often justices reach the same decision for different reasons. If such differences are not reconciled, a justice may write a concurring opinion.

The assignment of majority opinions is handled as follows: When the Chief Justice is part of the majority, he either writes the opinion himself (the usual procedure for very important cases) or assigns the case to another justice who has voted with the majority. The assignment may be based on a number of factors, including the legal expertise and philosophy of the individual justices and the desire to equalize the justices' workloads. If the Chief Justice is not part of the majority, the task of making the assignment falls to the member of the majority with the greatest seniority.

Besides the majority opinion, two other kinds of opinions may be written: concurring and dissenting opinions. When justices who voted with the majority feel that the majority opinion does not adequately explain why they voted as they did, they may write **concurring opinions** stating that they agree with the decision on the case but not for the reasons set forth in the majority opinion. A **dissenting opinion** may be written by any justice who voted with the minority. Even though it may have no immediate effect, it serves as a record that may be referred to in the future. As former Chief Justice Charles Evans Hughes stated:

> A dissent in a court of last resort is an appeal to the brooding spirit of the law, to the intelligence of a future day, when a later decision may possibly correct the error into which the dissenting judges believe the court to have been betrayed.[7]

On several days of each month in which the Court is in session—usually Mondays and Tuesdays—decisions are made public. Printed copies of Court opinions are made available to the public and the press. These written opinions are the primary means by which the Supreme Court communicates its ideas to the judiciary, the legal profession, and the public.

The Role of the Chief Justice

The Chief Justice is "first among equals." Like the other eight justices, he has only one vote, but his power to assign the writing of the opinion (if he votes with the majority) gives him some extra authority. Moreover, his presentation of a case to the other justices in the Friday conference could influence the other members of the Court. Finally, the Chief Justice presides over the Court when it is in session and performs certain administrative tasks connected with the federal courts.

Chief Justices have had varying degrees of influence on their colleagues. During the early decades of the nineteenth century, Chief Justice John Marshall dominated the Court with his strong personality and intellect. Among modern Chief Justices, Charles Evans Hughes in the 1930s and Earl Warren in the 1950s and 1960s were very influential. The present Chief Justice, William H. Rehnquist, has received praise for increasing the efficiency of the Court (see Table 10.1).

TABLE 10.1 *Chief Justices of the United States*

Chief Justices	Place of birth	Year of birth	Appointed by	Date oath taken	Date service ended
John Jay	New York	1745	Washington	Oct. 1789	June 1795
John Rutledge*	South Carolina	1739	Washington	**	
Oliver Ellsworth	Connecticut	1745	Washington	Mar. 1796	Dec. 1800
John Marshall	Virginia	1755	Adams	Feb. 1801	July 1835
Roger Brooke Taney	Maryland	1777	Jackson	Mar. 1836	Oct. 1864
Salmon Portland Chase	New Hampshire	1808	Lincoln	Dec. 1864	May 1873
Morrison Remick Waite	Connecticut	1816	Grant	Mar. 1874	Mar. 1888
Melville Weston Fuller	Maine	1833	Cleveland	Oct. 1888	July 1910
Edward Douglass White*	Louisiana	1845	Taft	Dec. 1910	May 1921
William Howard Taft	Ohio	1857	Harding	July 1921	Feb. 1930
Charles Evans Hughes*	New York	1862	Hoover	Feb. 1930	June 1941
Harlan Fiske Stone*	New Hampshire	1872	F. Roosevelt	July 1941	Apr. 1946
Frederick Moore Vinson	Kentucky	1890	Truman	June 1946	Sept. 1953
Earl Warren	California	1891	Eisenhower	Oct. 1953	June 1969
Warren Earl Burger	Minnesota	1907	Nixon	June 1969	June 1986
William H. Rehnquist*	Arizona	1924	Reagan	Oct. 1986	—

*Also served as an Associate Justice of the Supreme Court.
**Rutledge served a 4 month recess appointment. The Senate refused to approve his nomination.

Bringing a Case before the Court

Almost all the cases heard by the Supreme Court fall within its appellate jurisdiction;[8] that is, they are appeals from lower court decisions. These cases reach the Court by means of a writ of certiorari. A **writ of certiorari** (made more certain) is an order directing a lower court to send the record of a case to the Supreme Court for review. It is a discretionary writ; that is, it enables the Court to decide which cases are important enough for it to consider. The procedure begins when the losing party in a federal court of appeals, or the highest state court with jurisdiction over the case, petitions the Supreme Court for a writ of certiorari. If at least four of the justices agree that "there are special and important reasons" for the Court to hear the case, the writ will be issued.

The Court's Workload

Despite its broad power to control the number and type of cases it will hear through the writ of certiorari, the Court's caseload grew dramatically during the 1950s and 1960s and at a more moderate rate during the 1970s and 1980s. There has also been a shift in the nature of the Court's caseload. Whereas in the past it consisted largely of civil cases, today more than half the cases are criminal, involving provisions of the Bill of Rights and the Fourteenth Amendment (see Chapter 11).

Until recently the Supreme Court heard oral arguments for between 150 and 185 cases during each term. But in the past few years the Court's docket has actually declined. During the 1989–1990 term the Court decided 129 cases. In the previous term (1988–1989) it heard 145, and five years earlier it heard 156. The reasons for this decline in the Court's workload are not clear, but both the justices themselves and observers outside the Court believe this trend is favorable and that the Court previously was deciding too many cases.[9]

■ Selection of Federal Judges

Choosing federal judges is one of the most important responsibilities of the President. The President's power to appoint federal judges enables him to shape the character of the judiciary. Because they serve during "good behavior," the individuals he selects will continue to influence the American legal system for years, perhaps decades, after the President has left office.

Selecting Judges for Lower Federal Courts

Lower court judges are formally nominated by the President with the advice and consent of the Senate.[10] But although the President has the constitutional power to make judicial nominations, he does not usually participate directly in this process. Such participation would not be practical because of the large number of vacancies at any given time. Moreover, under the long-established tradition of **senatorial courtesy,** the judges in a particular state are selected jointly by the President and the senior senator from that state who belongs to the President's party. Thus, during a Republican administration candidates for lower court judgeships are approved by the Republican senator from the state in which the judge is to serve. If there are no Republican senators, the President is free to consult with Republican representatives from that state, with the state governor (if he or she is a Republican), or with state party officials. In effect, senatorial courtesy gives senators who belong to the President's party the right to veto nominations for judgeships in their state.

Senatorial courtesy applies to both district and appeals court judgeships, but it operates most fully in the case of district court vacancies.[11] Most senators play an active role in the selection of judges for their state; they actually designate the person to be nominated. A few simply submit a list of acceptable candidates to the Justice Department, leaving the choice to the President's staff. The candidates are evaluated by the Federal Bureau of Investigation, and officials in the Justice Department evaluate the FBI's report. In addition, a committee of the American Bar Association evaluates all judicial nominees and rates their qualifications.

The members of the Senate Judiciary Committee also participate in the nomination process. Although most choices are routinely approved, the

Sandra Day O'Connor, Associate Justice of the United States Supreme Court. The first woman to serve on the nation's highest court, Justice O'Connor was appointed by President Reagan in 1981.

committee occasionally holds hearings at which supporters and opponents of a particular candidate present arguments for or against the nomination. The Judiciary Committee can also delay approval of the President's choices by slowing the pace of nomination hearings.

The Reagan Appointments

The importance of the President's power to appoint judges can be seen in the impact of former President Ronald Reagan's judicial appointments on the composition of the federal judiciary—an impact that is likely to continue into the next century. During his two terms in office, Reagan appointed a stunning total of 344 federal jurists: 258 district court judges, 76 circuit court judges, 6 special court judges, and 4 Supreme Court justices. He filled about half of all lower court judgeships, more than any other President since Franklin Roosevelt. Like those of other Presidents, Reagan's appointments were partisan in nature; but Reagan went further and chose Republicans who were generally quite conservative in their legal philosophy.

The judges appointed during the Reagan administration are predominantly young white males who had already established a reputation for legal conservatism. Few women, African-Americans, or members of other minority groups were appointed. Almost 10 percent of the appellate judges appointed by Reagan were under the age of 40 at the time that they were appointed; the average age of district court judges was under 50. Approximately 90 percent had prior judicial or prosecutorial experience. They generally came from wealthy upper-class backgrounds; close to half had a net worth of more than $500,000.

Although the Justice Department claimed that the religious orientation of nominees was not considered, a larger percentage of Catholics was appointed than had been the case in previous administrations—including two Supreme Court justices. It is possible that the increased tendency to appoint Catholic judges was due in part to the Justice Department's preference for opponents of abortion. In any case, there can be no doubt that the judges appointed by Reagan are more conservative than those appointed by his predecessors and that this outlook will be reflected in federal court decisions for the foreseeable future.[12]

President Bush's appointments to the federal courts have generally followed the pattern established by his predecessor. They have largely been conservative, prosperous, white male Republicans.

Appointing Supreme Court Justices

The appointment of a Supreme Court justice may be the most significant act a President can perform. Since justices have life tenure, the appointee will most likely serve on the Court for many years after the President has left office. For this reason, Presidents give careful thought to the task of filling a vacancy on the Supreme Court.

TABLE 10.2 Occupations[a] of Supreme Court Designees at Time of Appointment[b]

Federal officeholder in executive branch	22
Judge of inferior federal court	24
Judge of state court	23
Private practice of law	18
U.S. senator	8
U.S. representative	4
State governor	3
Professor of law	3
Associate Justice of U.S. Supreme Court[c]	3
Justice of the Permanent Court of International Justice	1

[a]Many of the appointees held a variety of federal or state offices, or even both, prior to their selection.
[b]In general, the appointments from state office are clustered at the beginning of the Court's existence; those from federal office are more recent.
[c]Justices White, Stone, and Rehnquist were promoted to the Chief Justiceship in 1910, 1930, and 1986, respectively.

Source: Henry J. Abraham, *The Judicial Process: An Introductory Analysis of the Courts of the United States, England and France,* 5th ed., (New York: Oxford University Press, 1988) p. 63. Copyright © 1988 by Oxford University Press, Inc. Reprinted by permission. Updated to include the appointment of Justice David H. Souter in 1990.

TABLE 10.3 *Members of the United States Supreme Court, 1990–1991 Term*

	Home state	Year of birth	Year of appointment and President who appointed
Chief Justice			
William H. Rehnquist	Ariz.	1924	1986–Reagan
Associate Justices			
Byron R. White	Colo.	1917	1962–Kennedy
Thurgood Marshall*	N.Y.	1908	1967–Johnson
Harry A. Blackmun	Minn.	1908	1970–Nixon
John Paul Stevens	Ill.	1920	1975–Ford
Sandra Day O'Connor	Ariz.	1930	1981–Reagan
Antonin Scalia	N.J.	1936	1986–Reagan
Anthony M. Kennedy	Calif.	1936	1988–Reagan
David H. Souter	N.H.	1939	1990–Bush

*Resigned June 1991.

The President takes into account a wide variety of factors in selecting a Supreme Court justice. Among those factors are age, religion, race, place of residence, political party, legislative, executive or judicial experience, and judicial philosophy. No African-American served on the Court until 1967, when President Lyndon Johnson appointed Thurgood Marshall, and no woman served on the Court until 1981, when President Reagan appointed Sandra Day O'Connor (see Tables 10.2 and 10.3).

The nominee's political party and judicial beliefs are especially important in the appointment of a Supreme Court justice. The President will almost always appoint a member of his own party whose judicial philosophy matches his own. Thus all the justices appointed by President Reagan—Sandra Day O'Connor in 1981, William H. Rehnquist and Antonin Scalia in 1986, and Anthony M. Kennedy in 1988—are Republicans with generally conservative judicial views.

Confirmation and Tenure

The same basic procedure is followed in confirming nominations to the Supreme Court as in confirming appointments to the lower federal courts. The major difference is that senatorial courtesy does not apply; the President is entirely free to make the initial selection of a nominee. Once that choice has been made, the nomination is sent to the Senate, which must approve the candidate by a majority vote.

Twenty-eight presidential nominees have been denied Senate confirmation since the nation's founding. Many of the senators' rejections took place in the nineteenth century, and almost half were the choices of lame-duck presidents—those serving in their least year or two in office.[13]

In the past several decades the Senate has once again asserted its power over appointments to the Supreme Court; it has blocked five presidential nominations. In 1968, President Johnson attempted to elevate Associate

Justice Abe Fortas to the position of Chief Justice. The nomination was withdrawn when it became clear that Fortas lacked sufficient support in the Senate. In 1969 and 1970, two successive nominees selected by President Nixon were rejected by the Senate. President Reagan's nomination of Robert Bork in 1987 was also voted down, making Bork the twenty-seventh person to be denied Senate confirmation. Soon afterward Douglas Ginsberg became the twenty-eighth when President Reagan withdrew his name because it was clear that the Senate would not confirm the choice—largely because it had become known that Ginsberg had smoked marijuana earlier in his life.

The Senate Judiciary Committee plays a key role in considering presidential nominees to the Supreme Court. Its practices have varied over the years. Many noncontroversial choices have been approved rapidly, with as little as a single day spent on hearings at which the candidate testifies. But the process is likely to be more prolonged when the President selects controversial candidates. In 1916 the Judiciary Committee held hearings over a four-month period before approving President Woodrow Wilson's choice of Louis Brandeis. More recently, during the 1987 hearings on the nomination of Robert Bork committee members questioned the candidate for five days. And the fall 1990 hearings on President George Bush's first nomination to the Supreme Court, David H. Souter, lasted five days, with three of those days devoted to the testimony of the nominee.

Recent experience indicates that longer hearings and more intense examination of nominees have become more common. The Bork hearings were almost unprecedented in the nation's history. Witnesses testified in both support of and opposition to Bork's nomination, and senators quizzed him relentlessly about legal ideas he had expressed earlier in his career as a law professor and federal judge. Bork's opponents also conducted an extensive advertising campaign in the mass media.

The stakes involved in recent Supreme Court nominations have been very high. For many years the Court has been almost evenly divided between liberal and more conservative jurists. On some controversial constitutional questions, such as church-state relations, affirmative action programs, and abortion, the liberal members of the Court have usually been

Robert Bork testifying before the Senate Judiciary Committee in the fall of 1987. Bork's nomination to be an associate justice of the United States Supreme Court was rejected after a long, bitter confirmation debate.

Supreme Court nominee David Souter appears before the Senate Judiciary Committee at a confirmation hearing in September 1990.

able to produce a slender majority in favor of their position. But conservative nominations by Republican presidents have gradually changed the balance, and conservatives now command a majority of votes on the Court.

Recent confirmation hearings have raised some important issues concerning the proper role of the Senate in questioning nominees. It is agreed that professional qualifications and possible ethical problems in a nominee's background are legitimate areas of inquiry. Most observers also agree that it is not proper to ask a nominee how he or she would decide a specific case. Such questions constitute interference with the independence of the judiciary and tend to cast doubt on a candidate's ability to make decisions on the basis of the facts and law of actual cases.

The controversy centers on whether senators should ask questions about a nominee's legal philosophy. By obtaining answers about an individual's legal philosophy, one may be able to infer his or her views on specific issues. For example, an answer to the question of whether a nominee believes in a constitutional right to privacy may serve as an indicator of that person's views on the subject of abortion.

The use of a nominee's prior writings as a basis for questioning has also generated controversy. Use of such material permits senators to refer to a person's past opinions in attempting to gauge how that person would decide cases. This procedure penalizes individuals whose positions have required them to express opinions on constitutional topics—law professors and federal judges, for example. One unintended result of this form of questioning has been the selection of nominees who have not written or spoken on national issues. Certainly one of the reasons President Bush chose David H. Souter in 1990 was that he had little in the way of a written record that could be examined by the Senate. Souter's career as a state prosecutor and judge in New Hampshire provided no insight into his views on such issues as abortion or affirmative action. One might ask whether the nation benefits from the elimination of candidates who have expressed themselves on important national issues in the past.

Once appointed, a federal judge who sits on a constitutional court serves for life or, in the words of the Constitution, during "good Behavior" (Article III, Section I). A judge may be removed only by means of **impeachment** and conviction for "Treason, Bribery, or other high Crimes and Misdemeanors" (Article II, Section 4). The House of Representatives decides whether to impeach by a simple majority vote; conviction and removal, however, require a two-thirds vote of the Senate. Only one Supreme Court justice has been impeached—Samuel Chase in 1805—but the Senate did not find him guilty of the charges against him. There have been eleven impeachment trials of federal judges, of which four ended in acquittal and seven in conviction and removal. Until 1986 there had not been an impeachment trial of any federal government official since 1936, but between 1986 and 1989 three federal judges were impeached by the House of Representatives and convicted by the Senate.

■ The Functions of the Judiciary

The main functions of the judiciary in general and the Supreme Court in particular are the interpretation of statutes and constitutional provisions and the exercise of judicial review. Statutory interpretation involves deciding the meaning and intent of a statute enacted by the legislature. Courts are also called upon to determine the meaning of various provisions of the Constitution, such as "due process of law" in the Fifth and Fourteenth Amendments and the power of Congress to regulate interstate and foreign commerce in Article I, Section 8. The United States Supreme Court is primarily a constitutional court, but each term it decides a significant number of cases that involve the interpretation of statutes. Only rarely do courts exercise their ultimate power: judicial review.

Judicial Review

The American judiciary has the power to decide whether the acts of the executive and legislative branches of government are in conflict with the Constitution and, if so, to declare them void. This is the power of **judicial review,** and it is this power that makes the courts, especially the Supreme Court, important actors in the American governmental system.

The legal basis of the Supreme Court's authority to review the decisions of state courts is Article VI of the Constitution. Not only does this article state that the Constitution and all federal statutes and treaties "shall be the supreme Law of the Land"; it also states that "Judges in every State shall be bound thereby, any Thing in the Constitution or Laws of any State to the Contrary notwithstanding."

The power to exercise judicial review over acts of Congress or the President is not expressly stated in the Constitution. It is based primarily on the Supreme Court's ruling in the case of *Marbury v. Madison* (1803).[14] Chief Justice John Marshall's opinion in that case established the precedent under which the federal courts could use the power of judicial review to declare an act of Congress unconstitutional.

Marbury v. *Madison* arose out of an unusual situation. The Federalist party had been defeated in the election of 1800. Eager to maintain its influence in the federal judiciary, the Federalist-controlled Congress enacted legislation to create a number of new judicial positions. The outgoing President, John Adams, appointed loyal members of the Federalist party to fill these offices. William Marbury, one of the new appointees, was to become a justice of the peace for the District of Columbia. His appointment had been approved, and his commission to hold office had been prepared and signed. But the commission had not yet been delivered to him when Adams' term expired and the new Republican President, Thomas Jefferson, took office.

The new Secretary of State, James Madison, acting on instructions from Jefferson, refused to deliver the commission to Marbury. Marbury began a legal action in the United States Supreme Court to have the Court compel the delivery of the document by issuing a **writ of mandamus**—a court order to a public official to perform an act that is legally required.

The immediate issue in the case was the authority of the Supreme Court to issue a writ of mandamus. Chief Justice Marshall began has opinion by agreeing with Marbury that he had a legal right to the judicial office in question and that mandamus was the proper remedy for the wrong he had suffered. But the Chief Justice went on to declare that the Supreme Court could not issue the writ of mandamus. He ruled as unconstitutional a provision of the Judiciary Act of 1789 that permitted cases involving mandamus to be heard by the federal courts. According to Marshall, it violated Article III, Section 2, of the Constitution, which restricts the original jurisdiction of the Supreme Court to several specific types of cases, not including disputes involving writs of mandamus.

Marbury v. *Madison* contains a closely reasoned argument defending the right of a court to declare acts of Congress unconstitutional. Briefly, Marshall contended that written constitutions are adopted to define and limit the power of government and are intended to serve as the fundamental law of the nation. If an act of the legislature could violate this basic law, written constitutions would serve no meaningful purpose. They can be significant only if their provisions control legislative acts. Marshall went on to conclude that it is the duty of the judicial branch of government to decide issues involving conflicts between the U.S. Constitution and the laws passed by Congress:

> It is emphatically the province and duty of the judicial department to say what the law is. Those who apply the rule to particular cases, must of necessity expound and interpret that rule. If two laws conflict with each other, the courts must decide on the operation of each.

So if a law be in opposition to the constitution; if both the law and the constitution apply to a particular case, so that the court must either decide that case conformably to the law, disregarding the constitution; or conformably to the constitution, disregarding the law; the court must determine which of these conflicting rules governs the case. This is of the very essence of judicial duty.

If, then, the courts are to regard the constitution, and the constitution is superior to any ordinary act of the legislature, the constitution, and not such ordinary act, must govern the case to which they both apply.

Over the course of American history, some observers of the American governmental system have criticized the use of judicial review by the federal courts. These critics have based their arguments on several grounds: (1) The Constitution did not expressly assign this power to the courts; (2) the mistakes of the legislative and executive branches of the government are best corrected by those two branches themselves, and if they are not, the people will replace the officials involved at election time; and (3) judicial review violates the principle of majority rule because it puts supreme power over the Constitution and official acts in the hands of nine justices who are appointed for life.

These arguments have not been sufficient to overturn the principle established in *Marbury*, and the United States governmental system has operated under this principle for almost two centuries. One writer on the subject offers the following explanation of the significance of the case:

> The Marshall opinion denying Marbury his commission covers seventeen pages in the official reports of the Supreme Court. But its breadth cannot be measured in pages. It must be admired for its assertion that all men, even Presidents, must adhere to the law. . . . It must be admired primarily, however, for establishing a rule of law, a procedure for settling disputes without the sword.[15]

Despite the significance of *Marbury*, judges are generally reluctant to exercise the power of judicial review, especially to acts of Congress. Through 1988 only 124 federal statutes had been declared unconstitutional by the Supreme Court. Indeed, between 1803, when *Marbury* was decided, and 1857, no federal law was declared unconstitutional by the Supreme Court. (In 1857, in the infamous *Dred Scott* decision,[16] the Court upheld the legality of slavery.) A recent example of judicial review came in 1988 when the Supreme Court voided an act of Congress that prohibited the display within the District of Columbia of any sign within 500 feet of a foreign embassy if the sign brought the foreign government into "public odium" or "public disrepute." The law, the Court held, violated the First Amendment guarantee of freedom of speech.[17]

Judicial review has become more common in the twentieth century, but it is still unusual for acts of the national legislature and the President to be pronounced void. The power of judicial review is exercised far more frequently against state laws and practices. Thus judicial review is more significant as a control on the states than as a control on Congress and the President.

THE JUDICIARY

The Constitution places some restrictions on the power of the Supreme Court and the federal judiciary. As we have already seen, federal judges can be impeached and, if convicted by the Senate, removed from office. But Congress has other legal powers over the courts. It can, in theory, alter or abolish all of the Supreme Court's appellate jurisdiction,[18] change the jurisdiction of all other federal courts, reduce the pay of future federal judges, cut appropriations to pay for the operation of the courts, and increase the number of federal judges.

During the early 1980s a number of bills were introduced to prevent the federal courts from hearing cases concerning such issues as abortion and prayer in public schools. Bills were also introduced that would have denied the Supreme Court the right to hear appeals in cases involving these controversial issues. None of these proposals was passed by Congress, however. Even though Congress possesses broad powers to shape the federal judiciary, it has almost never used them for the purpose of restricting or punishing the courts. When Congress has changed the jurisdiction of the courts or increased the number of judges, for example, it has done so in order to increase the efficiency of the federal courts.

One of the most famous attempts to limit the power of the Supreme Court was made in 1937, when President Franklin D. Roosevelt proposed the so-called court-packing bill. Roosevelt faced a hostile, conservative Supreme Court that had declared major portions of his New Deal program unconstitutional. He therefore asked Congress to pass a law providing for the addition to the Supreme Court of one new appointee for every sitting

Associate Justice David Souter signing the documents of office after being sworn in as the newest member of the Supreme Court. Left to right are Chief Justice William Rehnquist, Associate Justices Antonin Scalia, Sandra Day O'Connor, Thurgood Marshall, Anthony Kennedy, Harry Blackmun, and John Paul Stevens. On June 27, 1991, Justice Marshall resigned for reasons of health.

justice over the age of 70, up to a maximum of fifteen. Had the legislation passed, the President would have gained the right to appoint six people who were sympathetic to the New Deal and would have voted to support his legislative policies.[19] During the spring of 1937, while Congress was debating Roosevelt's plan, several members of the Court began to take a different view of the government's power to regulate the economy. As a result, in a series of narrowly decided cases the Court sustained the right of the national and state governments to enact regulatory measures.[20]

The legislation proposed by President Roosevelt was within the constitutional power of Congress, but it represented unwise political interference with the independence of the Supreme Court. Largely for this reason, the heavily Democratic Congress, which usually favored Roosevelt's proposals, refused to adopt the court-packing plan. Still, the incident illustrates the fact that congressional laws can be used to limit and control judicial power.

Another restriction on the authority of the Supreme Court arises when it makes a decision on a highly controversial issue. The Court's decisions do not enforce themselves; their effectiveness depends on the public's willingness to accept them. On a few occasions there has been significant resistance to Supreme Court rulings. A well-known example is the Court's ruling, in *Brown* v. *Board of Education of Topeka* (1954),[21] that public schools must be desegregated. There was much public opposition to this decision in the South, and in several instances federal troops had to be used to enforce court orders to desegregate public schools in the region. There has also been considerable resistance to the Court's rulings in the early 1960s concerning prayer in public schools. Many communities have not complied with those decisions, which held that government-authorized prayers or Bible reading in public schools are in violation of the First Amendment.[22]

Finally, decisions of the Supreme Court can be changed by legislation or constitutional amendment. If the Court decides a case involving a federal law on statutory grounds, Congress can overturn the ruling by passing new legislation. When it decides a case on a constitutional basis, however, only an amendment to the Constitution can reverse the ruling. There have been many attempts to reverse unpopular decisions by constitutional amendment, but most have been unsuccessful. In 1990, for example, the House of Representatives could not muster the necessary two-thirds vote to initiate an amendment to alter the Supreme Court's decision that the First Amendment protects the right to burn an American flag. A few constitutional amendments have changed Supreme Court rulings; they include the Eleventh Amendment, Section 1 of the Fourteenth Amendment, and the Sixteenth, Twenty-fourth, and Twenty-sixth Amendments.

Self-Restraint versus Activism

The Supreme Court also places certain restraints on itself. The idea of **judicial self-restraint** holds that judges should exercise great self-control in using their judicial power and should generally defer to the policies of the elected branches of the government. The doctrine of judicial self-restraint is accepted in varying degrees by different justices. Some justices, however, reject a limited role for the judiciary and favor a policy of **judicial activism.** Advocates of this philosophy are more likely to declare actions of the other branches unconstitutional and are more inclined to have the courts set policy for the nation.

It is important to note that the difference between restrainers and activists is not absolute. The activists do believe in some limits, and those who favor self-restraint do use their judicial power in some situations. The difference between the activists and the self-restrainers is basically a disagreement over when the Court should say no.[23]

■ Summary

The federal court system of this nation began in humble circumstances. The framers of the Constitution provided for the establishment of a Supreme Court, but they left to the discretion of Congress whether there would be lower federal courts. The framers also only sketched in broad outline what jurisdiction the federal courts would possess, but again left the details to Congress. Finally, they were entirely silent on the most important question about the powers of the judicial branch of government: whether it would have the right of judicial review.

In 1789 the first Congress of the United States answered some of the questions the framers had left open. It created a system of district tribunals for the original thirteen states, which would serve as the basic trial courts of the federal judicial system. The Judiciary Act of 1789 also provided these courts with the authority to hear specific types of cases. This original system of district courts provided the model for the extension of the federal court system as the nation expanded and new states were admitted into the Union.

The early years of the Supreme Court gave no indication of the important role it was eventually to play in the American governmental system. In its first decade, it had few cases and little prestige. One associate justice—John Rutledge—thought his position to be so unimportant that he resigned from the court to become the Chief Justice of the state court system of South Carolina.

It was Chief Justice John Marshall who contributed most to the early development of the legal authority, prestige, and independence of the Supreme Court. During his thirty-five years as Chief Justice (1801–1835), Marshall's many opinions established the Court as a co-equal branch of the federal government. His most important contribution was to establish as precedent the right of the federal court to exercise the power of judicial review over acts of Congress and also to assert its right to review the actions of state governments.

The power of judicial review gradually led to the emergence of the Supreme Court as a major force in the nation's governmental system. In its present form, judicial review has been interpreted by the nation's highest court to mean that the court is the final interpreter of the United States Constitution. This view of our constitutional system has now generally been accepted by the Congress, the President, the state governments, and the American people.

Over the course of American history, the Supreme Court has dealt with many constitutional problems. The proper relationship between the states and the central government and the extent of national powers were issues that dominated the work of the Court for about a century and a half. But in the past fifty years, cases involving the Bill of Rights and the Fourteenth Amendment have become the most important areas of the Supreme Court's work. The Court decisions interpreting these parts of the Constitution have had a major impact on Americans, since they clarify their freedom from illegal and arbitrary governmental action. This point will become clear in the next two chapters, which analyze the role of the Supreme Court in defining the civil liberties and civil rights of Americans.

■ Key Terms

law	misdemeanor	majority opinion
common law	felony	concurring opinion
equity	civil law	dissenting opinion
injunction	adversary system	writ of certiorari
statutory law	jurisdiction	senatorial courtesy
constitutional law	original jurisdiction	impeachment
administrative law	appellate jurisdiction	judicial review
criminal law	constitutional court	writ of mandamus
plaintiff	legislative court	judicial self-restraint
defendant	brief	judicial activism

■ Suggested Reading

ABRAHAM, HENRY J., *The Judicial Process: An Introductory Analysis of the Courts of the United States, England and France*, 5th ed. New York: Oxford University Press, 1988.

———. *Justice and Presidents*, 2nd ed. New York: Oxford University Press, 1985.

BALL, HOWARD. *Courts and Politics: The Federal Judicial System*, 2nd ed. Englewood Cliffs, N.J.: Prentice Hall, 1987.

CANNON, MARK W. and DAVID M. O'BRIEN., eds. *Views From the Bench: The Judiciary and Constitutional Politics*, Chatham, N.J.: Chatham House, 1985.

CARP, ROBERT A., and RONALD STIDHAM. *Judicial Process in America*. Washington, D.C.: Congressional Quarterly Press, 1989.

———, and ———. *The Federal Courts*. 2nd ed. Washington, D.C.: Congressional Quarterly Press, 1990.

ELY, JOHN HART. *Democracy and Distrust: A Theory of Judicial Review*. Cambridge, Mass.: Harvard University Press, 1980.

GATES, JOHN B., and CHARLES A. JOHNSON, EDS. *American Courts: A Critical Assessment*. Washington, D.C.: Congressional Quarterly Press, 1990.

LASSER, WILLIAM. *The Limits of Judicial Power: The Supreme Court in American Politics*. Chapel Hill, N.C.: University of North Carolina Press, 1989.

MURPHY, WALTER F., and C. HERMAN PRICHETT. *Judges and Politics: An Introduction to the Judicial Process*, 4th ed. New York: Random House, 1986.

O'BRIEN, DAVID M. *Storm Center: The Supreme Court in American Politics*, 2nd ed. New York: Norton, 1990.

STEAMER, ROBERT J. *Chief Justice: Leadership and the Supreme Court*. Columbia, S.C.: University of South Carolina Press, 1986.

Notes

1. *Muskrat* v. *United States*, 219 U.S. 346 (1911).

2. *Schlesinger* v. *Reservists Committee to Stop the War*, 418 U.S. 208 (1974).

3. Edward Felsenthal and Wade Lambert, "Workload of State Courts Surged by 98 Million in 1988," *Wall Street Journal*, May 31, 1990, p. B11.

4. U.S. Bureau of the Census, *Statistical Abstract of the United States, 1990*, 110th ed. (Washington, D.C.: Government Printing Office, 1990), Table 313.

5. Henry J. Abraham, *The Judiciary: The Supreme Court in the Governmental Process*, 8th ed. (Dubuque, Iowa: Wm. C. Brown, 1991), p. 11.

6. *Statistical Abstract, 1990*, Table 312.

7. Charles E. Hughes, *The Supreme Court of the United States* (New York: Columbia University Press, 1928), p. 68.

8. In its entire history the Supreme Court has heard only about 160 cases under its original jurisdiction. See Abraham, *Judiciary*, p. 19.

9. Stephen Wermiel, "High Court Docket Shrinks, But No One Understands Why," *Wall Street Journal*, June 4, 1990, p. B9A.

10. This discussion is based on Stephen L. Wasby, *The Supreme Court in the Federal Judicial System*, 3rd ed. (Chicago: Nelson-Hall Publishers, 1988), pp. 100–107.

11. Since appeals courts serve several states, it is more difficult to determine which senator should suggest a candidate for any given state. Here again, tradition plays a major role, with certain vacancies "belonging" to particular states.

12. David M. O'Brien, "The Reagan Judges: His Most Enduring Legacy?" in Charles O. Jones, ed., *The Reagan Legacy: Promise and Performance* (Chatham, N.J.: Chatham House, 1988), pp. 60, 75–78.

13. Lawrence Baum, *The Supreme Court*, 3rd ed. (Washington, D.C.: Congressional Quarterly Press, 1989), pp. 46–47.

14. 1 Cranch 137 (1803).

15. Leonard Baker, *John Marshall: A Life in Law* (New York: Macmillan, 1974), pp. 408–409.

16. *Dred Scott* v. *Sandford*, 19 Howard 393 (1857).

17. *Boos* v. *Barry*, 485 U.S. 312 (1988).

18. "The Supreme Court shall have appellate Jurisdiction, both as to Law and Fact, with such Exceptions and under such Regulations as the Congress shall make" (Article III, Section 2).

19. Congress has changed the number of Supreme Court justices several times. The original Court consisted of six justices. In 1801 the number was reduced to five; from 1807 to 1837 there were seven; from 1837 to 1863, nine; from 1863 to 1866, ten; and from 1866 to 1869, seven. Since 1869 the Court has consisted of nine justices.

20. Alfred H. Kelly, Winfred A. Harbison, and Herman Belz, *The American Constitution*, 6th ed. (New York: Norton, 1983), pp. 500–502.

21. 347 U.S. 483.

22. See Chapter 11 for further discussion of *Engel* v. *Vitale*, 370 U.S. 421 (1962), and *Abington School District* v. *Schempp*, 374 U.S. 203 (1963).

23. Abraham, *Judiciary*, p. 72.

11

Chapter Outline

Applying the Bill of Rights to the States

Freedom of Religion
The Free Exercise Clause
The Establishment Clause

Freedom of Speech, Press, Assembly, and Petition
No Prior Restraint
Sedition: Advocacy of Illegal Acts
Symbolic Speech
Commercial Speech
Protecting Public Order: The First Amendment in Public Places
Protecting Public Morals: Obscenity
Libel and Slander
Free Press and Fair Trial
Freedom of the Press and the Rights of Reporters
The Right of Association

The Rights of the Criminally Accused
Search and Seizure
Freedom from Self-Incrimination
Indictment by a Grand Jury
Double Jeopardy
The Right to Counsel
Confessions
The Right of Confrontation
The Eighth Amendment
Plea Bargaining

Questions for Thought

Does the Bill of Rights apply to both the national government and the states? Explain.

What are the major exceptions to the First Amendment's guarantees of freedom of speech and the press?

What is the meaning and importance of the doctrine of no prior restraint?

Miranda v. Arizona established what constitutional rights for persons in the custody of the police?

What is plea bargaining?

What is the exclusionary rule of evidence?

Civil Liberties

T HE Bill of Rights was designed to protect citizens against arbitrary use of power by the national government. It is, in effect, a charter of civil liberties. Its guarantees include freedom of speech, press, and assembly, as well as protection against arbitrary procedures in criminal prosecutions.

Civil liberties may be defined as the individual rights that are guaranteed by the Constitution, especially in the Bill of Rights and the due process clause of the Fourteenth Amendment. The **due process clause** asserts that no state ". . . shall . . . deprive any person of life, liberty, or property without due process of law. . . ." Civil liberties are not the same as civil rights, which are concerned with protection against discrimination and are derived from the equal protection clause of the Fourteenth Amendment and from statutes passed by federal or state legislatures. The **equal**

protection clause declares: "No State shall . . . deny to any person within its jurisdiction the equal protection of the laws." (Civil rights are discussed in Chapter 12.)

The courts, especially the Supreme Court, have the task of interpreting civil liberties and civil rights, that is, defining the rights of the individual that are protected against the power of government. Since the end of World War II, civil liberties and civil rights have been by far the most important areas of concern for the Supreme Court.

■ Applying the Bill of Rights to the States

In 1833 the Supreme Court held that the limitations on government set forth in the Bill of Rights applied only to the national government and not to the states.[1] Its ruling was based on the view that the Bill of Rights had been added to the Constitution because the people feared the power of the national government and that it was not intended to apply to the actions of the states. This decision has never been overruled, but under the due process clause of the Fourteenth Amendment, ratified in 1868, nearly all the limitations contained in the Bill of Rights have been extended to the states. In a long series of decisions that began in 1925, the Court has used the various provisions of the Bill of Rights as the standard for defining the term "liberty" in the due process clause, and has incorporated almost all of these provisions into the Fourteenth Amendment. (It should be noted that the Bill of Rights does not limit the actions of private individuals, only those of government and its agents.)

Today the constitutional rights of individuals are practically uniform throughout the nation. Only a few guarantees contained in the Bill of Rights have not been applied to the states by the Supreme Court. They include the following:

■ The Fifth Amendment requirement of indictment by a grand jury
■ The Second Amendment freedom to keep and bear arms
■ The Third Amendment protection against quartering of soldiers
■ The Seventh Amendment requirement of trial by jury in common law cases involving more than $20
■ The Sixth Amendment right to be tried in the district where the crime was committed
■ The Fifth Amendment due process clause (which is not applied because the Fourteenth Amendment, which limits the states, contains a similar provision)

The issue of whether the remaining provisions of the Bill of Rights should be incorporated into the Fourteenth Amendment is not an important one today, since all the major rights have already been applied to the states. The important problems center on the specific meaning of the various protections of individual liberties found in the Bill of Rights. The Supreme Court is often faced with cases that raise difficult and often highly controversial issues concerning the nature and extent of the liberties enjoyed by American citizens.

Freedom of Religion

Freedom of religion is the first guarantee contained in the Bill of Rights. The First Amendment states that "Congress shall make no law respecting an establishment of religion, or prohibiting the free exercise thereof." This statement puts two limitations on the government with respect to religion. The first, the **establishment clause,** prohibits many forms of association between church and state. The second, the **free exercise clause,** prohibits the government from limiting the right to hold and express religious beliefs and, as long as criminal conduct is avoided, to practice one's religion.

The Free Exercise Clause

In interpreting the free exercise clause, the Supreme Court has held that although religious beliefs are not subject to government control, certain religious practices may be forbidden. The first major case to deal with freedom of religion was *Reynolds v. United States* (1878).[2] Reynolds, a Mormon, had violated a congressional statute that outlawed polygamy. The Supreme Court upheld the conviction of Reynolds and the constitutionality of the statute, even though polygamy was permitted under Mormon religious doctrine. The Court decided that although religious freedom includes the right to *believe* anything, it does not include the right to commit unlawful acts. It refined this opinion in *Davis v. Beason* (1890), noting that religious freedom is allowed "provided always the laws of society, designed to secure its peace and prosperity, and the morals of its people are not interfered with."[3]

In recent cases, however, the Court has extended the free exercise clause to most forms of religious conduct that conflict with governmental policy. The Court balances the claim of religious freedom against the government's interest. Only if that interest is compelling, and no other type of regulation would serve that purpose, will the claim of religious freedom be rejected. This approach makes it quite difficult for the government to sustain its position. Thus, for example, the Supreme Court upheld the right of a member of the Seventh-Day Adventist church to receive state unemployment benefits after she had been dismissed from her job for refusing to work on Friday evenings and Saturdays. The state of Florida had failed to show a compelling interest sufficient to overcome the free exercise claim of the church member.[4] On the other hand, the Court has recently upheld the right of a state government to prosecute the use of illegal drugs as part of a religious ceremony. Thus Native Americans who use peyote for sacramental purposes are not protected from criminal prosecution under a state's narcotics law.[5]

The Supreme Court has also held that the free exercise clause includes the right to disbelieve as well as to believe. This ruling occurred in the case of Roy Torcaso, an atheist who had been appointed a notary public in Maryland. Torcaso was denied his commission because he refused to declare that he believed in the existence of God, a statement that was required by the Maryland constitution as part of the oath of office. The Court ruled that the Maryland law infringed on Torcaso's rights under the free exercise clause because it placed the state of Maryland on the side of "one particular belief," namely, belief in the existence of God. Neither a state nor the federal government can force a person "to profess a belief or disbelief in any religion." Nor can it pass laws or impose requirements that aid all religions as against individuals who do not hold religious beliefs.[6]

The Establishment Clause

The establishment clause has been a subject of more heated and continual debate than the free exercise clause. This debate has centered on three major issues: aid to religious or parochial schools, prayers and Bible reading in public schools, and religious displays on public property.

Aid to Parochial Schools. When the issue of aid to parochial schools first arose during the 1940s, the Supreme Court interpreted the establishment clause as requiring a "wall of separation" between church and state. This test seemed to create an absolute standard that would permit no contact between religion and government. However, the Court soon began making exceptions: It allowed some forms of public aid to parochial schools, such as government paying the costs of transporting children to such schools.[7]

Pressure to expand the amount and kind of state aid to parochial schools grew during the 1960s as the cost of operating those schools—most of which are Roman Catholic—rose sharply. State legislatures responded by passing aid programs in such areas as teachers' salaries, special education, administrative help, construction and repair costs, tax deductions and credits, and tuition. The Supreme Court, however, has taken a stand against most of these laws. It developed a three-part test to determine whether a law violates the establishment clause. First, the law must have a secular purpose. Second, the primary effect of the program must not be to either promote or interfere with religion. Third, the government's policy must not result in "excessive entanglement" of church and state.

Using these standards, the Court has found most forms of public aid to religious schools unconstitutional. In 1985, for example, it voided a state program that used public funds to pay the salaries of government employees providing remedial and guidance services to children in parochial school classrooms.[8] However, the Court has found a few government programs that aid parochial schools to be constitutional. It has accepted the legality of textbook loan programs on the theory that they benefit the child and are not a form of direct aid to nonpublic schools.[9] And it has upheld most forms of government assistance to church-related colleges and universities.[10]

School Prayer. In 1962 a storm of controversy arose over the Supreme Court's decision in *Engel* v. *Vitale*. This case dealt with the constitutionality

A rally in support of prayer in the public schools. There has been strong opposition to the Supreme Court decision outlawing such prayer.

of New York State's so-called Regents' prayer, a short nondenominational prayer that had been approved by the New York State Board of Regents. In a 6-to-1 decision the Court ruled that the prayer was an unconstitutional establishment of religion. According to Justice Hugo Black, conducting a religious exercise in a public school violates the establishment clause of the First Amendment, which applies to the states through the due process clause of the Fourteenth Amendment.[11] The Court has also held that Bible reading in public schools is unconstitutional.[12]

A few states adopted legislation designed to avoid the Court's original school prayer decisions, but these efforts have not been successful. For example, an Alabama law that authorized a period of silence in public schools "for meditation or voluntary prayer" was found to be an unconstitutional establishment of religion because its main purpose was to promote religious observance.[13] On a related issue, the Court declared unconstitutional a Louisiana statute that required public schools that teach the theory of evolution also to teach biblical creationism as a science. The Court held that the purpose of the law was to promote religion.[14]

Religious Displays on Public Property. The Supreme Court has decided a number of cases involving the display of religious symbols on public property. It is difficult to summarize the Court's actions in this area because the facts of each case have been quite different. In 1989, for example, the Court held that it is unconstitutional for the government to display a nativity scene that included the Latin words for "Glory to God in the Highest." Such a display had been placed on the main staircase of the county courthouse in Pittsburgh, Pennsylvania. The Court found that the display violated the establishment clause because it clearly endorsed the creche's religious message. On the other hand, the Court upheld the display on public property of a Chanukah menorah that had been placed next to a large Christmas tree with a sign stating that they were part of the city's salute to liberty. In this case the Court reasoned that the presence of the menorah was simply a way of showing that Christmas is not the only way to celebrate the winter holiday. Moreover, the sign linking the tree and the menorah to liberty emphasized the secular purpose of the display.[15]

CIVIL LIBERTIES

■ Freedom of Speech, Press, Assembly, and Petition

The First Amendment states that "Congress . . . shall make no law abridging the freedom of speech, or of the press." But the Supreme Court has never interpreted this freedom as absolute. It has held that in certain very limited circumstances the government does have a right to restrict freedom of speech. A 1942 Court ruling set forth some of the general limits on freedom of expression:

> There are certain well-defined and narrowly limited classes of speech, the prevention and punishment of which have never been thought to raise any Constitutional problem. These include the lewd and obscene, the profane, the libelous, and the insulting or "fighting" words—those which by their very utterance inflict injury or tend to incite an immediate breach of the peace. It has been well observed that such utterances are no essential part of any exposition of ideas, and are of such slight social value as a step to truth that any benefit that may be derived from them is clearly outweighed by the social interest in order and morality.[16]

In this section we examine these exceptions as well as other First Amendment issues that have been considered by the Court. Although we deal separately with issues related to freedom of speech, press, assembly, and petition, it is important to note that the boundaries among these different rights are not always clear in practice. The right to hold a rally and make speeches in front of a public building, for example, involves the guarantees of speech, assembly, and petition.

No Prior Restraint

The concept of **no prior restraint** is basic to the interpretation of the First Amendment. Prior restraint means restraining or censoring material before it is spoken or published. The Supreme Court has prohibited all forms of prior restraint on the ground that government censorship in advance of publication constitutes an especially serious threat to First Amendment guarantees because it denies the public total access to ideas and information.

The no-prior-restraint doctrine was established in *Near* v. *Minnesota* (1931), in which the Supreme Court declared unconstitutional a state law that allowed police officials to prevent the publication of newspapers containing defamatory statements. In ruling on the case, Chief Justice Charles Evans Hughes stated that "liberty of the press has meant . . . immunity from previous restraints or censorship."[17]

Perhaps the most important Supreme Court case involving prior restraint was the Pentagon Papers dispute of 1971. Formally titled *History of the U.S. Decision-Making Process on Viet Nam Policy*, the document was a "classified" or secret government study of the Vietnam War. When two newspapers began to print parts of this classified material, the Nixon administration sought a court injunction to halt further publication. The case came before the Supreme Court, which ruled that the prior restraint sought by the government was unjustified and upheld the newspapers' right to publish the papers. In a short opinion six members of the Court agreed that

> any system of prior restraints of expression comes to this Court bearing a heavy presumption against its constitutional validity; the Government thus carries a heavy burden of showing justification for imposition of such a restraint. The district court . . . held that the Government had not met that burden. We agree.[18]

Another example of prior restraint of the press is the use of so-called *gag orders,* which bar the press and other news media from publishing certain facts about a pending criminal case. During the first half of the 1970s such orders, which had been almost unknown before that time, suddenly became quite frequent. They were issued by judges to protect defendants against adverse pretrial publicity that might injure their right to a fair trial and an impartial jury. In 1976, however, the Supreme Court unanimously declared that a gag order issued by the Nebraska courts in an ugly multiple-murder case was a prior restraint of the press and hence was void under the First Amendment.[19]

Sedition: Advocacy of Illegal Acts

Sedition may be defined as speech or writing that advocates or incites discontent or rebellion against government. Although the First Amendment

The New York Times *begins publication of the Pentagon Papers.*

restricts the right of the government to punish the expression of seditious ideas, it places no restraint on the power to regulate overt acts directed at the overthrow of lawful authority. Only a few sedition laws have been adopted since the nation's founding. In 1798 Congress passed the first such law, but it was repealed within a few years. Congress did not pass another sedition law until <u>1918</u>. That law was used to convict political dissenters for seditious speaking and writing during and just after World War I. The third national sedition law, the Smith Act, was passed shortly before the United States entered World War II. Under this act, advocating violent overthrow of the government, organizing any group with such intentions, or conspiring to do either of these was defined as a crime.

Dennis v. United States (1951) was the first major test of the Smith Act. The Supreme Court found the law constitutional and ruled that the leaders of the American Communist party could be convicted under its provisions. The Court interpreted the statute as prohibiting only "advocacy, not discussion" and held that the convictions of the Communist party leaders could be upheld even though there was no evidence that the defendants had made any specific plans to overthrow the government.[20]

In *Brandenburg v. Ohio* the Supreme Court set forth its present standard for deciding on the constitutionality of prosecutions for sedition. The power of government in this area was narrowed. Under the *Dennis* decision, only abstract advocacy of forcible action was protected by the First Amendment; a demand for revolutionary change, even in the distant future, was not protected. In *Brandenburg* the Court held that the First Amendment requires the showing of imminent danger and the likelihood that the danger will actually occur:

> The constitutional guarantees of free speech and free press do not permit a State to forbid or proscribe advocacy of the use of force or of law violation except where such advocacy is directed to inciting imminent lawless action and is likely to incite or produce such action.[21]

Symbolic Speech

Freedom of speech is not confined to words; it includes some forms of **symbolic speech**—acts that dramatize a person's beliefs, such as flying a banner or wearing an armband. Not all symbolic activity is protected by the First Amendment, however. In 1984, for example, the Supreme Court held that the right to engage in some forms of symbolic speech did not include the right of demonstrators to sleep in Lafayette Park and on the Mall in Washington, D.C., in an effort to call public attention to the plight of homeless people. The Court upheld the right of the National Park Service to prohibit camping in these public places.[22]

Perhaps the most controversial free speech issue of recent years has been that of whether the First Amendment protects the right to burn or deface an American flag. In 1989 the Supreme Court, by a 5-to-4 vote, declared unconstitutional a Texas law that punished desecration of the flag.[23] In the wake of this decision, Congress quickly enacted a law that made it a federal crime to burn or deface the American flag. In June 1990 the Court, again by a 5-to-4 vote, invalidated this legislation.[24] Opponents

Demonstrators opposed to the United States war in Iraq burn an American flag in downtown Chicago on January 14, 1991. The Supreme Court has held that such acts are a form of expression that is protected by the First Amendment to the Constitution.

of the Court's ruling, with the support of President George Bush, placed pressure on Congress to initiate a constitutional amendment that would have given both Congress and the states the "power to prohibit the physical desecration of the Flag of the United States." However, the proposed amendment failed to obtain the required two-thirds vote in the House of Representatives.

Commercial Speech

Until the 1970s the Supreme Court refused to grant First Amendment protection to purely commercial expression. But in a number of decisions during the past two decades the Court has declared that certain forms of truthful **commercial speech** are protected from government control by the First and Fourteenth Amendments. Thus a state may not prevent pharmacies from advertising the prices of prescription drugs,[25] nor may it prevent the advertising of fees charged by lawyers, doctors, and other professionals for performing certain basic services.[26] Such advertising provides members of society with important information that enables them to make more informed decisions on subjects that arise in the course of everyday life. Moreover, First Amendment rights apply to corporations as well as individuals.[27]

But the Court has held that the First Amendment protection of commercial speech is not as broad as the protection granted to noncommercial forms of speech. Commercial speech, for example, can be restricted if it is false or misleading or if it promotes unlawful conduct. The Supreme Court has also held that a state may prohibit corporations from directly using corporate money to help finance political campaigns.[28]

Protecting Public Order: The First Amendment in Public Places

A variety of problems arise in connection with the right of individuals and groups to use public places to hold political rallies, distribute literature, and the like. The right to use public streets and other places to express political views is very broad, but it is not absolute. Most public places—streets, parks, courthouses, the grounds of state and local legislatures—may be used for demonstrations. Exceptions may be made when a public place is reserved for a particular use. Governments may, for example, prohibit demonstrations near schools during class hours if they interfere or threaten to interfere with school activities.[29]

In general, in protecting public order governments may enforce laws related to traffic control and safety. Neutral regulations regarding the time, place, and manner in which streets may be used have been upheld. Governments may also prevent the blocking of entrances to public buildings. But a government may not discriminate in the enforcement of its traffic and safety laws. It may not, for example, grant a right to one individual or group and deny it to another. And it may not prevent groups from exercising their First Amendment rights in public places by, for example, denying them a permit; this would constitute an illegal prior restraint.

An example of the government's legal right to establish neutral rules regarding traffic control can be seen in the case of *Heffron* v. *International Society for Krishna Consciousness, Inc.* A regulation required that solicitation of funds and distribution of literature at the Minnesota State Fair be conducted only at designated places within the fairgrounds. The Krishna

Should the First Amendment protect racists and enemies of democracy, such as these members of the American Nazi movement? This is one of the most difficult problems the courts must resolve in interpreting the guarantees of the First Amendment.

group challenged the rule because it prevented members of the organization from walking about the grounds selling literature and raising money. The Supreme Court upheld the state regulation as a valid "time, place, manner" rule: It applied to all groups, served a valid governmental purpose (preventing congestion and promoting the safe movement of people), and permitted the Krishna group to sell literature at booths and to present its views anywhere on the fairgrounds.[30]

Protecting Public Morals: Obscenity

Another controversial area involving freedom of speech and the press concerns material that is alleged to be obscene. It is difficult to establish a clear definition of obscenity, however, since what is obscene to one person might not be to another, and moral standards change over time and differ from one community to another.

Since the 1950s the Supreme Court has repeatedly tried to set standards for judging whether a film, book, play, or other published material is obscene. In *Roth* v. *United States* (1957) it held that sex and obscenity are not synonymous: "The portrayal of sex . . . in art, literature, and scientific works, is not itself sufficient reason to deny material the constitutional protection of freedom of speech and press." Obscenity, on the other hand, "is not protected by the freedom of speech and press." The Court also established a test for determining whether a particular item is obscene. An item was to be judged obscene if to the average person, applying contemporary community standards, the dominant theme of the material taken as a whole appeals to the prurient interest."[31] The key terms in this test are *average person* (which excludes children and other highly susceptible people) and *dominant theme* (which requires that the item be judged in its entirety; thus, a book cannot be declared obscene because of a few scattered passages).

In 1973, after more than a decade of legal confusion over the meaning of obscenity, the Supreme Court made another attempt to clarify the law in this area. In *Miller* v. *California* the Court restated the basic tests of obscenity:

> (a) whether "the average person, applying contemporary community standards," would find that the work, taken as a whole, appeals to the prurient interest; (b) whether the work depicts or describes, in a patently offensive way, sexual conduct specifically defined by the applicable state law; and (c) whether the work, taken as a whole, lacks serious literary, artistic, political, or scientific value.

The Court made clear that in applying the community standard test, a jury need not consider a national standard but is free to consult local tastes.[32]

The *Miller* case failed to resolve the problem of defining obscenity. Despite this restatement of the law, which appeared to increase the ability of government to punish those who publish and sell obscene materials, prosecutors still find it very difficult to obtain convictions in obscenity cases.[33] The Supreme Court has, however, upheld the right of communities to use their zoning power to regulate the location of businesses that show

Many communities require that newsstands show only the title of magazines displaying sexually explicit material.

or sell sexually explicit materials.[34] Moreover, the Court has held that the standards used to define obscenity do not apply to the sale or distribution of sexually oriented materials to minors[35] and that child pornography is not protected by the First Amendment.[36]

The Supreme Court has also found that the First Amendment protects the right of an individual to possess obscene material for private use in the home. But in 1990 the Court modified its position on this subject. It held that a state may make it a crime to possess in one's home pornographic pictures of children.[37]

Libel and Slander

Although the First Amendment's protection of freedom of speech and press has been interpreted broadly, it does not guarantee the freedom to use speech or language that is slanderous or libelous. **Slander** refers to spoken words that are false and hold an individual up to public ridicule and contempt; **libel** refers to defamation by written word.

The Supreme Court has made it very difficult for a public official to sue successfully for **defamation.** In a famous case, *New York Times Co.* v. *Sullivan* (1964), it ruled that an advertisement in the *Times* criticizing officials of Birmingham, Alabama, for their treatment of blacks was not libelous. For a statement about a public official to be considered libelous, the plaintiff must prove that the statement was made with *actual malice,* "that is, with the knowledge that it was false or with reckless disregard of whether it was false or not."[38]

The Supreme Court soon extended the actual malice rule of the *Sullivan* case to individuals who have become "public figures," such as movie and sports celebrities. But the Court has generally defined this category quite narrowly. It has held, for example, that an attorney in a publicized lawsuit was not a public figure, but rather a private one, and therefore did not have to prove actual malice to win a libel case. He had "not accepted public office or assumed an 'influential role in ordering society.' "[39]

The Supreme Court has said that the Constitution affords greater protection to private individuals against defamatory statements than is granted to public figures since private individuals have not voluntarily surrendered their privacy and have less access to the media to respond to criticism. Private individuals, therefore, only have to prove some degree of fault by the defendant—for example, that the statement in question was made negligently—and that they have sustained some type of injury (e.g., the loss of a job or friends) as a result of the statement. Private persons, unlike public ones, do not need to prove actual malice to be successful in a libel case.

Historically, the law of defamation applied only to statements of fact, not to opinions. It was assumed, for example, that a person reading a newspaper editorial or movie review understood that the published statements represented the personal views of the editor or reviewer. Only factual statements that were false and held a person up to the contempt of the community could be considered defamatory. But in 1990 the Supreme Court held that the First Amendment does not automatically protect all opinions. Opinions have full constitutional protection from defamation actions only if they do not contain "a provably false factual connotation."[40]

The number of libel suits brought against newspapers, magazines, and television stations increased greatly during the 1970s and 1980s. Many cases are either dismissed or settled before they go to trial. But plaintiffs win a very high percentage of cases that are actually tried, and juries often award large sums of money in damages. Many cases are reversed on appeal, however, or the amount of money awarded by the jury is substantially reduced by the appellate court.

Free Press and Fair Trial

There are a few situations in which certain provisions of the Bill of Rights come into conflict. The most important of these is the clash between the First Amendment guarantee of freedom of the press and the Sixth Amendment right of a person accused of a crime to a fair trial and an impartial jury. Sixth Amendment rights are threatened when the news media give extensive coverage to a crime. The vast majority of cases receive little or no press coverage, but the difficulty arises in the relatively few sensational cases receiving widespread media attention that may be prejudicial to the accused person.

A number of procedures can be used to deal with this problem. The Supreme Court has held that it is permissible for a trial judge to control the effects of pretrial publicity by changing the location of the trial, postponing the trial, instructing the jury to ignore press reports about the case, or even *sequestering* (locking up) the jury during the trial. The Court has also held that the trial judge may control the flow of information to the news media by using the contempt-of-court power to restrict statements made by parties, witnesses, lawyers, and court officials connected with the case.[41] But as noted earlier, attempts to use gag orders have been declared unconstitutional. The Supreme Court has also held that the right of the press and the public to attend criminal trials is protected by the First Amendment and that a trial judge may not exclude the press from such proceedings.[42] Similarly, the press and the public have the right of access to a court when jurors are being selected for a criminal case.[43]

Freedom of the Press and the Rights of Reporters

In the early 1970s reporters for the news media raised a constitutional argument regarding press freedom that had not previously been tested in the courts. The reporters claimed that the First Amendment guarantee of freedom of the press protects them from being forced to reveal confidential sources of information to the government. The Supreme Court dealt with this problem for the first time in *Branzburg* v. *Hayes* (1972). This case concerned a reporter who had published an article in a Louisville, Kentucky, newspaper about the selling of narcotics. He was subpoenaed by a county grand jury but refused to identify the people about whom the story had been written. In a 5-to-4 decision the Supreme Court rejected Branzburg's argument that the First Amendment protects the confidential nature of news sources and held that "the great weight of authority is that newsmen are not exempt from the normal duty of appearing before a grand jury and answering questions relevant to a criminal investigation."[44]

Although the Supreme Court has refused to extend First Amendment protection to reporters with regard to the confidentiality of their sources, about half of the states have passed so-called *shield laws*. These laws grant reporters a statutory right not to reveal their sources to governmental bodies such as grand juries.

The Right of Association

The right of association is not expressly stated in the Constitution, but the Supreme Court has held that it is derived from the freedoms of the First Amendment. The Court formally recognized this right for the first time in the case of *NAACP v. Alabama* (1958), which arose during the period of civil rights protests in the South. The Court ruled that the National Association for the Advancement of Colored People could not be required to give its membership lists to the state of Alabama. Making public the names of members of the NAACP could subject those individuals to physical and economic harassment and thus interfere with their right to join together in an association designed to express their beliefs.[45] In 1982 the Court held that the right of association also includes the right of individuals to join together in a nonviolent economic boycott of businesses that practice racial discrimination.[46]

■ The Rights of the Criminally Accused

Movies and television shows about crime and criminals are commonplace. Crimes and arrests of criminals make headlines in newspapers and are featured on local television news programs. But despite all the attention to crime, criminal justice procedures are not generally understood by Americans, nor are the constitutional rights of accused persons.

The Constitution contains several provisions limiting the powers of the government in relation to people accused of crimes. For example, it bars both the national and state governments from passing **ex post facto laws,** laws that impose a penalty for committing an act that was not considered criminal when it was committed or increase the punishment for a crime after it has been committed. This is a fundamental protection of individual rights that has rarely, if ever, been violated.

The Constitution also prohibits the enactment of bills of attainder. A **bill of attainder** is an act of a legislature that singles out specific people or groups and orders that they be punished without judicial trial. Only three legislative acts have been struck down by the Supreme Court as bills of attainder. The most recent of these cases occurred in 1965, when the Court declared void an act of Congress that made it a crime for a member of the American Communist party to be an employee or officer of a trade union.[47]

Most of the rights of the criminally accused are contained in the Bill of Rights. They were intended to protect citizens against certain types of conduct by law enforcement authorities and judges. Their purpose was to prevent people from being wrongly convicted, even though a few of the guilty might go free. We will discuss the major rights of the criminally accused under the Fourth, Fifth, Sixth, and Eighth Amendments and the due process clause of the Fourteenth Amendment.

Search and Seizure

The Fourth Amendment declares that

> The right of the people to be secure in their persons, houses, papers, and effects, against unreasonable searches and seizures, shall not be violated, and no Warrants shall issue, but upon probable cause, supported by Oath or affirmation, and particularly describing the place to be searched, and the persons or things to be seized.

This provision reflects the common law rule that "a man's home is his castle," and it imposes important restrictions on government. In attempting to make an arrest or obtain evidence of criminal acts, the government must follow certain procedures. The general rule set forth by the Fourth Amendment is that searches and seizures may be conducted only after a search warrant has been issued by a judge or magistrate. To justify the warrant, the law enforcement officer must show the judge, in a written affidavit, sufficient information to establish "probable cause." The affidavit must also specifically describe the place to be searched and the things to be

Police questioning occupants of an automobile. The courts have held that warrantless searches of automobiles are constitutional.

seized. This requirement was intended to prevent general searches of homes and neighborhoods and general seizures of people and property.

The Fourth Amendment does not require that *all* searches and seizures be based on warrants. In fact, because of the urgency of much police work, most searches and seizures occur without warrants. The language of the Fourth Amendment indicates that the nation's founders understood this fact; it recognizes that in some situations warrantless searches and seizures are reasonable and therefore valid.

The courts have created a number of exceptions to the warrant requirement of the Fourth Amendment: searches based on consent, searches incident to a lawful arrest, evidence that is in "plain view" of police officers, and searches of automobiles when there is probable cause that the vehicle contains illegal items. The Supreme Court has recently held that police officers may stop drivers at roadside check points to determine whether they have been drinking.[48]

Under the common law a court could permit the use of any item of evidence at a trial regardless of the methods used by the police to obtain it. In 1914, however, the Supreme Court ruled that evidence obtained as a result of illegal search and seizure could not be used against the accused in a federal criminal case.[49] This rule, the so-called **exclusionary rule of evidence,** is intended to deter illegal searches and seizures by the police. The rule was not binding on the states until the 1961 decision of the Supreme Court in *Mapp* v. *Ohio*. In his majority opinion on that case, Justice Tom Clark wrote, "We hold that all evidence obtained by searches and seizures in violation of the Constitution is, by that same authority, inadmissible in a state court."[50]

The exclusionary rule has been the subject of much criticism and is an important issue in criminal law. Critics have contended that the exclusionary rule permits people who have committed crimes to go free because trial juries are denied access to reliable evidence of an incriminating nature. Some opponents of the exclusionary rule have called for its abolition. Others would modify the rule, allowing illegally obtained evidence to be introduced in criminal trials under certain conditions.

The Supreme Court has accepted some of the criticisms of the exclusionary rule and has created several exceptions to the rule. In *Nix* v. *Williams* it held that illegally obtained evidence is admissible in a criminal trial if the government can establish that the evidence would "inevitably" have been found by the police through the use of lawful methods.[51] And in

United States v. *Leon* it ruled that evidence obtained by the police is admissible when they have acted in "good faith" reliance on a warrant issued by a magistrate, even if that warrant was later found to be defective.[52]

Another challenge to the Fourth Amendment has arisen as a result of technological advances. When the Fourth Amendment was adopted in 1791, its authors could not have foreseen the development of electronic listening devices, which make it unnecessary to enter a home or place of business to conduct a search or seizure. The development of increasingly sophisticated methods of electronic surveillance has forced the courts to reexamine the Fourth Amendment. Initially, the Supreme Court refused to apply the warrant requirements of the Fourth Amendment to telephone tapping and other electronic listening devices. It was not until 1967, in *Katz* v. *United States*, that the Court extended the scope of the Fourth Amendment to include electronic eavesdropping. The amendment protects "people, not places," the Court declared. It extends to situations in which a person has a "reasonable expectation of privacy."

> What a person knowingly exposes to the public, even in his own home or office, is not a subject of Fourth Amendment protection. . . . But what he seeks to preserve as private, even in an area accessible to the public, may be constitutionally protected.[53]

In 1968, after many years of considering such legislation, Congress passed the Omnibus Crime Control and Safe Streets Act. This act legalized electronic surveillance by federal, state, and local police, but it placed them under the limitations of the Fourth Amendment. The law requires that police officers obtain a warrant from a magistrate when they intend to use a wiretap, and its provisions have been upheld by the courts.

As noted earlier, the Supreme Court's 1967 decision in *Katz* v. *United States* established that the warrant requirement of the Fourth Amendment applied to situations in which a person has a "reasonable expectation of privacy." The Court has periodically been called upon to interpret this phrase in reference to particular situations. It has held that a person can reasonably expect privacy while talking to someone in a home or a place of business. But the right of privacy does not extend to garbage placed in front of a home for collection.[54] Nor can one reasonably expect privacy for a partially covered greenhouse in which marijuana has been observed by police officers in a helicopter.[55]

Freedom from Self-Incrimination

The Fifth Amendment provides that no person "shall be compelled in any Criminal Case to be a witness against himself." In a criminal case, therefore, the government must establish the guilt of a person by presenting evidence obtained from sources other than the accused person. This protection applies not only to people who are actually suspected of criminal wrongdoing but also to people who testify before investigatory groups such as grand juries and congressional committees. Although this protection against **self-incrimination** has always limited the federal government, it was not made fully binding on the states until 1964 in the case of *Malloy v. Hogan*, in which the Supreme Court ruled that "the Fourteenth Amendment secures against state invasion the same privilege that the Fifth Amendment guarantees against federal infringement—the right of a person to remain silent."[56]

The Fifth Amendment requires that the silence of an accused person not be interpreted as an indication of guilt. Thus, when defendants in criminal trials choose not to take the stand in their own defense, the jury must be warned by the judge not to interpret this decision as evidence of guilt.

Indictment by a Grand Jury

The Fifth Amendment declares that "no person shall be held to answer for a capital, or otherwise infamous crime, unless on a presentment or indictment of a Grand Jury." A *capital crime* is one that is punishable by death. An *"infamous" crime* refers to serious violations of the law, or felonies.

Unlike a trial or *petit* jury, a **grand jury** does not render a verdict of guilty or innocent. Rather, it determines whether the government, represented by the prosecuting attorney, has evidence to warrant a criminal trial on the charges made against the accused person. If the grand jury believes that the government has enough evidence, it returns an **indictment** or **true bill**. An indictment is a written accusation charging the person named in it with doing an act which is, by law, punishable as a crime. While the main purpose of the grand jury is to protect the accused against unjustified criminal trials, in practice grand juries return indictments in more than 90 percent of the cases they hear.

Indictment by a grand jury is one of the few procedural guarantees of the Bill of Rights that is not binding on the states. Thus, while some states use the grand jury because of their own constitution and laws, a majority do not. Instead, they employ the **bill of information** in felony cases. This is a written affidavit filed by a prosecutor and presented to a court to show that there is enough evidence to justify a trial. (The same device is used by

The right to counsel and to a jury trial are guaranteed by the Sixth Amendment to defendants in criminal cases.

governments throughout the United States to charge individuals with misdemeanor crimes.)

Double Jeopardy

Protection against **double jeopardy** is guaranteed by the Fifth Amendment: "Nor shall any person be subject for the same offence to be twice put in jeopardy of life or limb." In 1969 the Supreme Court held that the guarantee against double jeopardy applied to the states under the Fourteenth Amendment.[57]

The protection against double jeopardy basically means that once a person has been tried for a particular crime and the trial has ended in a verdict of not guilty, that person cannot be tried again for the same crime. The double jeopardy provision does not, however, prevent a defendant from being tried again for the same offense if the jury cannot arrive at a verdict and there is a *mistrial.* Moreover, if the defendant has been convicted but the verdict has been set aside after a successful appeal, the government may retry that defendant for the same offense.

The Right to Counsel

"In all criminal prosecutions, the accused shall enjoy the right . . . to have the Assistance of Counsel for his defence." This Sixth Amendment guarantee was designed to ensure that accused people are represented by a lawyer, someone who understands the law and court procedures. The right to counsel becomes an issue in cases involving defendants who cannot afford to hire a lawyer.

In *Powell* v. *Alabama* (1932) the right to counsel was applied to the states through the Fourteenth Amendment in cases involving the death penalty,[58] and since 1938 the Supreme Court has applied an absolute rule requiring that attorneys be appointed for all indigent defendants in federal cases. This right, Justice Hugo Black wrote, "is necessary to insure fundamental human rights of life and liberty."[59] It was not until 1963, in *Gideon* v. *Wainwright,* that the right to counsel was applied to the states in cases that do not involve the death penalty. In this decision the Court held that the Sixth Amendment right to have an attorney applies to all state felony trials.[60] In 1972 it extended the *Gideon* ruling to include misdemeanor cases in which a person might be imprisoned: In the absence of "a knowing and intelligent waiver, no person may be imprisoned for any offense, whether classified as petty, misdemeanor, or felony, unless he was represented by counsel at his trial."[61]

The *Gideon* case left unanswered the question of the precise point in the criminal process at which a person's right to counsel begins. This question was answered in *Escobedo* v. *Illinois* (1964). Escobedo had repeatedly requested an attorney while he was being questioned by police, but none was provided. Statements he had made during the questioning had later been used to convict him of murder. The Supreme Court reversed the conviction, holding that the right to counsel begins when police

The Scottsboro case was a major criminal trial that attracted worldwide attention. In this 1933 photo, four of the nine young, poorly educated black defendants, who were accused of raping two white women, are marched to the courthouse. Their convictions were later overturned by the United States Supreme Court.

conduct is no longer investigatory but accusatory.[62] In this case, the police activity had centered on Escobedo and the questions had been designed to produce a confession to a crime.

Confessions

The use of confessions in criminal cases raises two important constitutional questions. One is whether statements obtained by the police from people accused of crimes violate the Fifth Amendment protection against self-incrimination. The other is whether an accused person should have a Sixth Amendment right to counsel when being questioned by the police.

The police view confessions as a vital and speedy method of solving crimes. But confessions can be obtained through coercion and are subject to abuse by law enforcement officials. Since the 1930s the Supreme Court has heard many cases involving confessions and has formulated standards designed to reconcile the interests of the police and the rights of the accused. The first test used by the Court in such cases was whether the confession had been given voluntarily, but since 1966 the Court has imposed more specific controls regarding confessions.

In *Miranda v. Arizona* (1966) the Supreme Court set forth the procedural rules the police must follow before questioning anyone. The person must

be warned prior to any questioning that he has the right to remain silent, that anything he says can be used against him in a court of law, that he has the right

A police officer reads the Miranda warnings to a person who has been arrested.

to the presence of an attorney, and that if he cannot afford an attorney one will be appointed for him prior to any questioning if he so desires. Opportunity to exercise the rights must be afforded to him throughout the interrogation. After such warnings have been given, and such opportunity afforded him, the individual may knowingly and intelligently waive these rights and agree to answer questions or make a statement. But unless and until such warnings and waiver are demonstrated by the prosecution at trial, no evidence obtained as a result of interrogation can be used against him.[63]

These constitutional rules apply when a person has been taken into custody or otherwise significantly deprived of freedom of movement by the police. They are necessary, in the view of the Court, to guarantee the Fifth Amendment protection against self-incrimination. Without these rules, there is too much danger that the police could obtain statements and confessions that are not truly voluntary.

The *Miranda* decision has never been overruled by the Supreme Court, and its basic principles still govern in-custody interrogations by the police. But the Court has refused to extend *Miranda* to related situations, and it has made important exceptions to its application. It has held, for example, that a witness before a grand jury need not be informed of his constitutional rights even though he is suspected of criminal wrongdoing.[64] It has also created a "public safety" exception to the *Miranda* rules. In *New York* v. *Quarles* the police had pursued a suspected rapist who was thought to be armed. The man was found in a supermarket, but no gun was discovered. Without giving him the *Miranda* warning, the officer asked him where the gun was and the suspect pointed toward an empty carton. The Supreme Court ruled that the evidence was admissible, holding that public safety was threatened by the existence of the concealed gun and that protection of the public supersedes the need for strict application of the *Miranda* rules.[65] And in 1990 the Court held that a confession is admissible at a criminal trial even though it was obtained from an inmate by a law enforcement officer who posed as a prisoner and did not give the *Miranda* warning to the inmate.[66]

The Right of Confrontation

The Sixth Amendment provides that in all criminal prosecutions the accused person has a right "to be confronted with the witnesses against him." The Supreme Court has held that this right is part of the liberty protected by the due process clause of the Fourteenth Amendment, and it has applied it to state criminal proceedings. It has also held that the right to cross-examine witnesses, though not expressly mentioned in the Sixth Amendment, is "a primary interest" protected by the **confrontation clause.**[67]

Issues related to the confrontation clause have come before the Supreme Court on relatively few occasions. But in 1990 the Court decided two important cases that raised novel questions related to this Sixth Amendment right. Both involved individuals accused of child abuse, a type of crime that has become more common in the United States in recent years and has produced a number of sensational trials. In one case the Court, by a 5-to-4 vote, upheld a Maryland law that allowed child victims to testify on closed-circuit television rather than having to face the accused person in the courtroom. The Sixth Amendment does not require an actual face-to-face encounter at trial in every instance, the Court declared.[68] But the Court restricted the right of a state to permit a physician to testify about statements made by a child, an example of so-called hearsay testimony. It found that such statements violate the confrontation clause because they lack sufficient reliability and trustworthiness.[69]

The Eighth Amendment

The two major provisions of the Eighth Amendment are the prohibitions against "excessive bail" and "cruel and unusual punishments."

Excessive Bail. *Bail* is money or other property given to the government as security by an accused person in order to be released from jail. Its sole purpose is to guarantee the appearance of that person at the time of the trial. Bail gives the accused a greater chance to prepare a defense and is a recognition of the basic legal principle that a person is innocent until proved guilty.

The Eighth Amendment limitation on "excessive bail" applies both to legislative acts that regulate bail and to the decisions of judges in setting bail in particular cases. This provision places no specific financial restrictions on the government. The Supreme Court has held, however, that bail is excessive when it is fixed "at a figure higher than an amount reasonably calculated" to ensure that the defendant will appear at the time of the trial.[70]

The Supreme Court has upheld the controversial Bail Reform Act of 1984, which requires federal courts to deny bail to individuals charged with serious felonies if the government can show that this action is necessary to protect the safety of others. By a 6-to-3 vote the Court rejected challenges to this so-called preventive detention law based on the bail provision of the Eighth Amendment and the due process clause of the Fifth Amendment.[71]

Cruel and Unusual Punishment. Historically, the Eighth Amendment prohibition of cruel and unusual punishment has rarely been used as a basis for challenging acts of governments. But in the past two decades it has been raised on a large number of occasions to challenge the constitutionality of the death penalty. Since 1972 the Supreme Court has said that the death penalty is not in itself a cruel and inhuman punishment when applied to someone who has been convicted of murder (though it may not be imposed for other crimes). Nevertheless, it has held that the Eighth and Fourteenth Amendments require that the state death penalty laws meet certain standards. For example, the determination of guilt or innocence and the sentencing of a guilty person in a capital case must take place in separate proceedings. The Court has also held that in making the decision on whether to impose the death penalty, the sentencing court must be able to consider both mitigating and aggravating factors. The death penalty cannot be imposed automatically once a defendant has been convicted; nor can a court be allowed to use uncontrolled discretion in making this decision. The court must be able to consider specific mitigating factors, such as the age of the defendant, prior convictions, and whether the crime was committed under the influence of drugs or alcohol, and also aggravating factors such as the amount of violence used in the killing.[72]

The present Supreme Court has generally upheld state death penalty laws against various constitutional challenges, though usually by narrow 5-to-4 votes. In this area of law, the Court has shown great deference to the judgments of state governments. It has, for example, rejected a claim that statistical evidence shows that the death penalty is applied disproportionately to black defendants. The Court found that such evidence is not sufficient to establish unconstitutional discrimination. A defendant "must prove that the decision makers in *his* case acted with discriminatory purpose."[73]

The Supreme Court has also upheld the right of a state to execute youths who were less than 18 years of age at the time that they committed murder.[74] And it has held that the Eighth Amendment does not in and of itself prohibit the execution of a mentally retarded person.[75] During the Court's 1989–1990 term, it continued to uphold provisions of state death penalty laws against various constitutional challenges.[76]

Supporters of the death penalty have often criticized the legal system for allowing long delays in carrying out the sentence. The delays—which have lasted for more than a decade in some cases—are the result of numerous appeals made in both the state and federal courts. Prisoners have been able to make repeated requests for writs of habeas corpus in the federal courts. A **writ of habeas corpus** is a court order that protects people from arbitrary imprisonment by requiring that public officials bring a prisoner to court and establish the legal reasons for holding that person. But during its 1989–1990 term the Supreme Court limited the authority of the federal courts to review constitutional challenges by means of writs of habeas corpus appeals.[77] The Court imposed these new limitations in several death penalty cases, but the restrictions placed on the federal courts apply to habeas corpus appeals in all types of criminal cases.

Capital punishment was once quite common in the United States, reaching a peak during the 1930s and 1940s, when more than one hundred people were executed annually. Public support for the death penalty declined during the 1950s, and many states repealed their death sentence laws. Between 1967 and 1977 no executions occurred in the United States.

But the dramatic increase in crime throughout the nation led to renewed public support for capital punishment, and the Supreme Court's decisions on the death sentence gave constitutional support to public demands for reinstatement of this form of punishment. Today about two-thirds of the states have laws providing for capital punishment in cases of aggravated murder. (See Figure 11.1.)

FIGURE 11.1 *Capital punishment in the United States.*

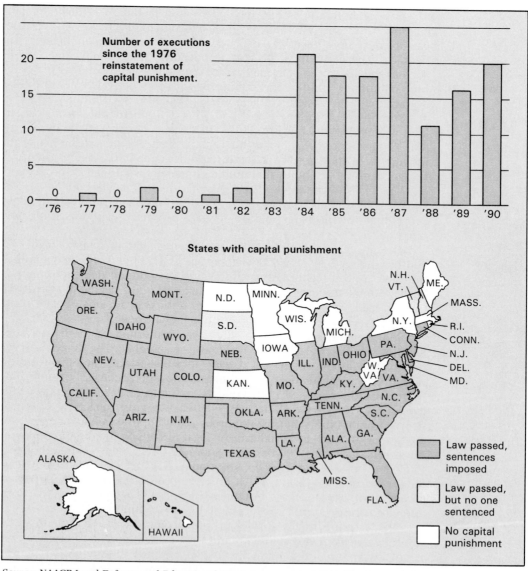

Source: NAACP Legal Defense and Educational Fund, Inc., as reported in *The New York Times,* October 13, 1990. Copyright © 1990 by The New York Times Company. Reprinted by permission.

The number of executions has increased since the Supreme Court upheld the legality of the death penalty in the 1970s. Between 1976 and December of 1990, 143 people had been put to death in the United States, and more than 2,200 people were on death row awaiting this punishment. The Court's growing impatience with appeals in death penalty cases, along with its willingness to approve the penalty, suggests that the number of executions will increase in coming years.

Plea Bargaining

It is important to understand that most people who are accused of crimes never actually stand trial. Their cases are resolved by means of a procedure called **plea bargaining.** A plea bargain is an agreement between an individual and the attorney for the government in which the former agrees to enter a guilty plea to a lesser criminal charge in return for the government's dismissal of more serious charges, or its recommendation to the court that it will accept a certain sentence, or that it will take both of these steps. As a consequence of the plea, the defendant in effect agrees to surrender various constitutional rights, such as the right to a trial by jury. The constitutionality of plea bargaining has been upheld in the courts, provided that the plea is made voluntarily and the accused person understands the meaning and consequences of the guilty plea.[78] Plea bargaining is an especially important feature of criminal procedure in large metropolitan areas. Its use enables the government to resolve the large number of cases that flood the courts; for the accused, it removes the threat of a conviction for a more serious crime. For better or worse, plea bargaining is a reality of the nation's criminal justice system today.

■ Summary

The positions taken by the Supreme Court are influenced by the personal philosophies of the justices. During the 1960s, the Court handed down many decisions based on a broad interpretation of the individual liberties guaranteed by the Bill of Rights. During the 1970s and 1980s, the nation's highest court became more conservative on some issues of individual rights. This change was largely a result of the appointment of more conservative justices by Republican Presidents—Richard Nixon and Ronald Reagan.

The present Supreme Court's more conservative orientation is not generally reflected in issues related to the First Amendment protections of freedom of religion, speech, and press. In these areas the Court has continued to define these liberties broadly. But in the area of criminal procedure the Court has become increasingly conservative. While it has not actually overruled any of the landmark decisions from the 1960s, it has narrowed their application and created new rules that generally favor the government. This trend is clearly illustrated by the results of the criminal cases decided during the Court's 1989–1990 term. Of thirty-five such cases, twenty-seven were decided in favor of the government.

Some observers see signs of a decrease in the overall level of protection of civil liberties in the United States. The chief cause of this trend is the war on drugs, which has generated a variety of new techniques that invade the privacy of citizens. Among these are urine testing, questioning of passengers at airports, roadblocks, and helicopter searches. These actions, which have the support of many Americans, may be subtly eroding the constitutional guarantees of individual liberties. In the view of some legal scholars and other experts, these encroachments on the Constitution, especially the Fourth Amendment, are not especially serious when viewed one at a time. But taken as a whole, they are creating an increasingly authoritarian atmosphere that may have a major impact on the nature of American society.[79]

Regardless of how one views the government's efforts to combat drugs, there can be little doubt that the scope of individual liberty in the United States is extensive. Political and religious freedom flourishes almost without restriction, and individuals accused of crimes enjoy a degree of protection that is unmatched in any other society. In upholding the constitutional guarantees of civil liberties, the Supreme Court has played a major role in limiting the power of the government and protecting the rights of citizens. In so doing, it has acted to strengthen democracy by guaranteeing the liberties of the American people.

■ Key Terms

civil liberties
due process clause
equal protection clause
establishment clause
free exercise clause
no prior restraint
sedition
symbolic speech

commercial speech
slander
libel
defamation
ex post facto law
bill of attainder
exclusionary rule of evidence

self-incrimination
indictment
bill of information
double jeopardy
confrontation clause
writ of habeas corpus
plea bargaining

■ Suggested Reading

ALLEY, ROBERT S. *The Supreme Court on Church and State.* New York: Oxford University Press, 1988.

ABRAHAM, HENRY J. *Freedom and the Court: Civil Rights and Liberties in the United States,* 5th ed. New York: Oxford University Press, 1988.

BOLLINGER, LEE C. *The Tolerant Society: Free Speech and Extremist Speech in America.* New York: Oxford University Press, 1986.

CURTIS, MICHAEL KENT. *No State Shall Abridge: The Fourteenth Amendment and the Bill of Rights.* Durham, N.C.: Duke University Press, 1986.

FRIENDLY, FRED W. *Minnesota Rag.* New York: Random House, 1981. (About *Near* v. *Minnesota*)

LABUNSKI, RICHARD. *Libel and the First Amendment.* New Brunswick, N.J.: Transaction Publishers, 1989.

LEWIS, ANTHONY. *Gideon's Trumpet.* New York: Random House, 1964. (About *Gideon* v. *Wainwright*)

McCLOSKY, HERBERT, and ALIDA BRILL. *Dimensions of Tolerance: What Americans Believe about Civil Liberties.* New York: Russell Sage Foundation, 1983.

VAN ALSTYNE, WILLIAM W. *Interpretations of the First Amendment.* Durham, N.C.: Duke University Press, 1984.

WITT, ELDER. *The Supreme Court and Individual Rights,* 2nd ed. Washington, D.C.: Congressional Quarterly Press, 1988.

■ Notes

1. *Barron v. Baltimore,* 7 Peters 243 (1833).
2. 98 U.S. 145 (1878).
3. 133 U.S. 33 (1890).
4. *Hobbie v. Unemployment Appeals Commission of Florida,* 480 U.S. 136 (1987).
5. *Employment Division v. Smith,* 110 S. Ct. 1595 (1990).
6. *Torcaso v. Watkins,* 367 U.S. 488 (1961).
7. *Everson v. Board of Education of the Township of Ewing,* 330 U.S. 1 (1947).
8. *Aguilar v. Felton,* 473 U.S. 402 (1985). See also *Grand Rapids School District v. Bell,* 473 U.S. 373 (1985).
9. *Meek v. Pittenger,* 421 U.S. 349 (1975).
10. *Roemer v. Maryland Public Works Board,* 426 U.S. 736 (1976).
11. 370 U.S. 421 (1962). The Regents' prayer was this: "Almighty God, we acknowledge our dependence upon Thee, and we beg Thy blessings upon us, our parents, our teachers and our country."
12. *Abington School District v. Schempp,* 374 U.S. 203 (1963).
13. *Wallace v. Jaffree,* 472 U.S. 38 (1985).
14. *Edwards v. Aguillard,* U.S. 482 U.S. 578 (1987).
15. *Allageny County v. ACLU,* 109 S. Ct. 3086 (1990).
16. *Chaplinsky v. New Hampshire,* 315 U.S. 568, 571–572 (1942).
17. 283 U.S. 697 (1931).
18. *New York Times Co. v. United States,* 403 U.S. 713 (1971).
19. *Nebraska Press Association v. Stuart,* 427 U.S. 539 (1976).
20. 341 U.S. 494 (1951).
21. 395 U.S. 444 (1969).
22. *Clark v. Community for Creative Non-Violence,* 468 U.S. 288 (1984).
23. *Texas v. Johnson,* 109 S. Ct. 2533 (1989).
24. *United States v. Eichman,* 110 S. Ct. 2404 (1990).
25. *Virginia State Board of Pharmacy v. Virginia Citizens Consumer Council,* 425 U.S. 748 (1976).
26. *Bates v. State Bar of Arizona,* 433 U.S. 350 (1977).
27. *Central Hudson Gas and Electric Corporation v. Public Service Commission,* 447 U.S. 557 (1980).
28. *Austin v. Michigan Chamber of Commerce,* 110 S. Ct. 1391 (1990).
29. *Grayned v. City of Rockford,* 408 U.S. 104 (1972).
30. 452 U.S. 640 (1981).
31. 354 U.S. 476 (1957).
32. 413 U.S. 15 (1973).
33. See, e.g., *Jenkins v. Georgia,* 418 U.S. 153 (1974).
34. *Young v. American Mini Theatres, Inc.,* 427 U.S. 50 (1976); *Renton v. Playtime Theatres, Inc.,* 475 U.S. 41 (1986).
35. *Ginsberg v. New York,* 390 U.S. 629 (1968).
36. *New York v. Ferber,* 458 U.S. 747 (1982).
37. *Stanley v. Georgia,* 394 U.S. 557 (1969); *Osborne v. Ohio,* 110 S. Ct. 1691 (1990).
38. 376 U.S. 254 (1964).
39. *Gertz v. Robert Welch, Inc.,* 418 U.S. 323 (1974).
40. *Milkovich v. Lorain Journal,* 110 S. Ct. 2695 (1990).
41. *Sheppard v. Maxwell,* 384 U.S. 333 (1966).
42. *Richmond Newspapers, Inc. v. Virginia,* 448 U.S. 555 (1980).
43. *Press-Enterprise Co. v. Superior Court,* 464 U.S. 501 (1984).
44. 408 U.S. 665 (1972).
45. 357 U.S. 449 (1958).
46. *NAACP v. Claiborne Hardware Co.,* 458 U.S. 886 (1982).
47. *United States v. Brown,* 381 U.S. 437 (1965).
48. *Michigan Dept. of State Police v. Sitz,* 110 S. Ct. 2481 (1990).
49. *Weeks v. United States,* 232 U.S. 383 (1914).
50. 367 U.S. 643 (1961).
51. 467 U.S. 431 (1984).
52. 468 U.S. 897 (1984).
53. 389 U.S. 347 (1967).
54. *California v. Greenwood,* 486 U.S. 35 (1988).
55. *Florida v. Riley,* 488 U.S. 445 (1989).
56. 378 U.S. 1 (1964).
57. *Benton v. Maryland,* 395 U.S. 784 (1969).
58. 287 U.S. 45 (1932).
59. *Johnson v. Zerbst,* 304 U.S. 458 (1938).
60. 372 U.S. 335 (1963).
61. *Argersinger v. Hamlin,* 407 U.S. 25 (1972).
62. 378 U.S. 478 (1964).
63. 384 U.S. 436 (1966).
64. *United States v. Mandujano,* 425 U.S. 564 (1976).
65. 467 U.S. 649 (1984).
66. *Illinois v. Perkins,* 110 S. Ct. 2394 (1990).
67. *Pointer v. Texas,* 380 U.S. 400 (1965); *Douglas v. Alabama,* 380 U.S. 415 (1965).
68. *Maryland v. Craig,* 110 S. Ct. 3157 (1990).
69. *Idaho v. Wright,* 110 S. Ct. 3139 (1990).
70. *Stack v. Boyle,* 342 U.S. 1 (1951).
71. *United States v. Salerno,* 481 U.S. 738 (1987).
72. *Gregg v. Georgia,* 428 U.S. 153 (1976); *Roberts v. Louisiana,* 428 U.S. 325 (1976); *Woodson v. North Carolina,* 428 U.S. 280 (1976).
73. *McClesky v. Kemp,* 107 S. Ct. 1756 (1987).
74. *Stanford v. Kentucky* and *Wilkens v. Missouri,* 109 S. Ct. 2969 (1989).
75. *Penry v. Lynaugh,* 109 S. Ct. 2934 (1989).
76. See, e.g., *Blynstone v. Penna,* 110 S. Ct. 1078 (1990).
77. See, e.g., *Butler v. McKellar,* 110 S. Ct. 1212 (1990).
78. *Brady v. United States,* 397 U.S. 742 (1970).
79. Joseph B. Treaster, "Is the Fight on Drugs Eroding Civil Rights?" *New York Times,* May 6, 1990, sec. 4, p. 5.

12

Chapter Outline

The Rights of Nonwhite Americans
Voting Rights
School Desegregation
Equality in Public Facilities
Equality in Employment

Women's Rights
Legislation to End Sex Discrimination
The Constitution and Women's Rights

The Civil Rights of the Disabled

Affirmative Action

Questions for Thought

What is meant by strict scrutiny of a constitutional provision?

What are the major provisions of the Civil Rights Act of 1964?

How did the southern states attempt to deny blacks their constitutional right to vote?

What are the main arguments for and against affirmative action plans?

What test is used by the Supreme Court to decide whether a law based on gender is unconstitutional?

What rules regarding a woman's right to an abortion were established in the case of Roe *v.* Wade?

Civil Rights

A S mentioned in Chapter 11, *civil rights* are not the same as *civil liberties.* Civil rights are often confused with the Bill of Rights. As we have seen, however, the Bill of Rights is basically a list of civil liberties. When we speak of the **civil rights** of a particular group, such as Hispanics or the disabled, we are not referring to their First Amendment freedom to believe what they choose or to express unpopular opinions. We are referring to their right not to be discriminated against because of some characteristic, such as national origin or disability.

Various provisions of the Constitution provide a basis for the protection of civil rights: the equal protection clause of the Fourteenth Amendment; the Thirteenth, Fifteenth, Nineteenth, and Twenty-fourth Amendments; the due process clause of the Fifth Amendment; and, as will be seen, the power of Congress to pass civil rights legislation, which is based on its power to regulate interstate commerce and to enforce the various constitutional amendments that are concerned with discrimination.

In this chapter we will explore the past and present application of these sections of the Constitution, focusing on the problem of discrimination against nonwhite Americans, discrimination based on sex, and the rights of the disabled. We will also discuss the problem of voting rights and consider significant court decisions having to do with civil rights.

The problem of civil rights for black Americans has been a major issue in the domestic life of this nation for most of its history; the question of civil rights for women, Hispanic Americans, and other minority groups, as well as for the disabled, is of more recent origin. Governments at all levels as well as the private sector have been forced to reexamine and change their policies toward these and other groups. Such change is especially urgent in the case of Hispanic and Asian Americans, the fastest-growing groups in American society today.

■ The Rights of Nonwhite Americans

Many people believe that the most severe challenge to American democracy lies in the struggle for equality. Early in this century the African-American historian W. E. B. Du Bois, the founder of the National Association for the Advancement of Colored People, wrote that the racial issue was the major problem of the twentieth century. But racial prejudice in America began in the seventeenth century, when Native Americans and Europeans first met. The Native Americans were driven from their lands and denied access to European culture as it was taking root in American soil. Race relations in the colonies were further complicated by the arrival of captive African blacks.

At first slavery was not confined to the South. Black slaves were brought to the northern colonies, but the smaller northern farms did not need a large work force and had nothing for slaves to do during the long winters. The southern plantations, by contrast, depended on slavery. By the first half of the nineteenth century, slavery was well established in the United States, and even free blacks were often deprived of their civil rights. As time went by, the difference between the South and the North became more and more pronounced, and the issue of slavery became explosive.

As the new nation expanded westward, the question of whether slavery should be permitted in the new territories served as a focus for the differences between northerners and southerners. The matter first arose in 1819, when a bill to admit Missouri to the Union came before the House of Representatives. To the surprise and indignation of southern members, Representative James Tallmadge of New York proposed an amendment banning the further entry of slaves into Missouri. The amendment passed in the House but was defeated in the Senate. When Congress again took up the question, in January 1820, a compromise was reached. Missouri was admitted as a slaveholding state, but slavery was not permitted in U.S. territories north of Missouri's southern boundary.

A slave auction in the South before the Civil War. Slavery flourished during the first six decades of the nineteenth century. It was finally outlawed by the Thirteenth Amendment, adopted in 1865.

For a generation the Missouri Compromise resolved the legal issue of whether slavery would be permitted in the territories and new states of the American West. It did not, however, deal with the moral issue of whether it was right for one person to own another. *Abolitionists*—people who sought to have slavery abolished—continued to speak out against slavery and to agitate for an end to the practice. One of the leading abolitionists was a New England minister, William Ellery Channing, who wrote:

> [A man] cannot be property in the sight of God and justice, because he is a Rational, Moral, Immortal Being; because created in God's image, and therefore in the highest sense his child; because created to unfold godlike faculties, and to govern himself by a Divine Law written on his heart, and republished in God's Word. His whole nature forbids that he should be seized as property. From his very nature it follows, that so to seize him is to offer an insult to his Maker and to inflict aggravated social wrong.[1]

In 1857 the United States Supreme Court attempted to resolve the slavery issue, but its efforts only served to anger large segments of American society and aggravate existing tensions. In the infamous *Dred Scott* decision, the Court sided with the supporters of slavery by ruling that slaves were not citizens, upholding the right of slave owners to possess human property, and declaring the Missouri Compromise unconstitutional.[2]

The slavery issue was finally decided on the battlefields of the Civil War in the early 1860s. The Emancipation Proclamation of 1863 freed the slaves in the states that had taken part in the rebellion against the United States, and in 1865 the Thirteenth Amendment permanently outlawed slavery. After the war the Fourteenth and Fifteenth Amendments were passed in an attempt to give the freed slaves the full rights of citizenship.

During the decade of Reconstruction following the war, Congress enacted a number of civil rights laws designed to enforce the principles set forth in the Civil War amendments. But after the presidential election of 1876, support for extending civil rights to black Americans declined quickly, and the South became a racially segregated society.

The movement away from racial equality was clearly reflected in two major decisions by the United States Supreme Court during the last decades of the nineteenth century: the *Civil Rights Cases* and *Plessy* v. *Ferguson.* In the *Civil Rights Cases* of 1883, the Court declared unconstitutional the main provisions of the Civil Rights Act of 1875. This law had made it both a crime and a civil wrong for any person to deny another "the full and equal enjoyment of any of the accommodations, advantages, facilities and privileges of inns, public conveyances on land or water, theaters, and other places of public amusement." The Court took a narrow view of the Fourteenth Amendment, holding that since the amendment bars only discrimination by government, Congress could remedy only governmental, not private, acts of discrimination. "It is state action of a particular character that is prohibited. Individual invasion of individual rights is not the subject-matter of the Amendment," the Court declared.[3]

The Court's decision in *Plessy* v. *Ferguson* (1896) was the next step in the movement away from true racial equality. This decision established the **separate-but-equal doctrine** as a valid interpretation of the Fourteenth

Dred Scott was a black slave whose owner took him from the slave state of Missouri to Illinois and the Minnesota Territory, where slavery was forbidden. After Scott was returned to Missouri, he brought suit in the federal courts to gain his freedom, claiming that his years of residence in free areas made him a free man. After losing in the lower courts, Scott appealed to the United States Supreme Court. Its proslavery decision in Dred Scott v. Sanford *produced a storm of opposition in the North and contributed to the coming of the Civil War several years later.*

Segregation extended to all phases of life in the South before the 1960s—even to bathrooms and drinking fountains.

Amendment's statement that no state can deprive any person of the equal protection of the laws. The case involved a Louisiana state law that required whites and nonwhites to occupy separate railway cars. The law was challenged on the ground that the state had violated the equal protection clause of the Fourteenth Amendment. The Supreme Court ruled that as long as facilities for whites and nonwhites were equal, the Fourteenth Amendment had not been violated even though the facilities were separate.[4] The Court thus gave constitutional protection to a wide variety of so-called **Jim Crow laws,** which segregated people of different races in most public and private institutions and facilities in the southern states.

But the problem of racial inequality is not unique to the South. Before World War I the vast majority of blacks lived in the South, though even in the nineteenth century many northern cities had small black communities. America's entry into World War I in 1917 resulted in a significant migration of blacks to northern industrial centers like New York, Philadelphia, and Chicago. World War II produced an even larger movement of blacks in search of the jobs created by the war. During the 1950s and 1960s the migration of rural blacks to the large northern and western cities continued at a rapid pace. The growing use of machinery in southern agriculture eliminated the need for much farm labor, which had been the main source of employment for rural blacks. By the 1960s blacks and rural Hispanic people, who had left Mexico, Puerto Rico, the Caribbean islands, and the countries of Central and South America to settle in the United States, made up a large percentage of the population of some of America's major cities, where they faced discrimination in employment, housing, and other areas of social life.

One response to discrimination is the creation of organizations designed to protect and advance the interests of minority groups. The first important organization of this kind, the National Association for the Advancement of Colored People (NAACP) was founded in 1909 by W. E. B. Du Bois and other prominent African-American civil rights leaders of that period. The NAACP is not only the oldest but also the largest of the organizations dedicated to achieving civil rights for minority groups. Although it engages in a wide variety of activities, its greatest successes have come through the many court actions that it has brought in an effort to achieve racial equality and justice.

African Americans have also organized other groups dedicated to furthering civil rights. These range from the moderate Urban League to more militant black nationalist groups. Many of these organizations have worked to strengthen racial consciousness. As a result, in recent years African Americans have developed great interest and pride in their history. Most recently, self-help groups at the community level have been organized to address such problems as poor housing, drugs, and unemployment, which affect many black Americans.

Other minority groups, such as Puerto Ricans and Hispanic Americans, have also organized and become more vocal in their demands for equality. The Puerto Rican Legal Defense and Education Fund, the League of United Latin American Citizens, and the Mexican American Legal Defense and Education Fund are examples of these civil rights organizations.

Voting Rights

One of the first efforts by the federal government to enforce the voting rights of nonwhites came with the passage of the Fifteenth Amendment, which barred the states from denying any citizen the right to vote on the basis of race, color, or previous condition of servitude. But the political power of southern whites made the battle for racial equality at the polls very difficult. Various devices—including literacy tests, grandfather clauses, the white primary, and poll taxes—were used to keep blacks from voting. Violence and intimidation were also used to maintain white control of southern politics.

The use of **literacy tests** as a requirement for voting began in the mid-nineteenth century and was common in many states. At first the tests simply required the would-be voter to demonstrate some basic knowledge of reading and writing. But later they were used in the South to disqualify blacks from voting. By insisting that voters be able to read, understand, and interpret the national or state constitution, the southern states were able to deny the vote to a very large portion of their black population. It was a simple matter for white voting registrars to administer these tests in a discriminatory fashion; they would allow even illiterate whites to pass the tests, while failing blacks who were educated and obviously literate.

Some southern states tried to get around the requirement that whites as well as blacks pass a literacy test by adding grandfather clauses to their voting laws. **Grandfather clauses** allowed persons or their descendants who had voted before January 1, 1867, to register without having to pass a literacy test. Since blacks had not been permitted to vote before that date,

Frederick Douglass (1817-1895). After escaping from slavery in 1838, Douglass became a leading abolitionist. He lectured on the subject, published an abolitionist newspaper, and aided fugitive slaves who escaped from the South. During the Civil War he recruited blacks into the Union army, and supported the emancipation of blacks and their right to vote. Douglass backed the post-Civil War reconstruction policies of the Congress and was an active supporter of the Republican Party. Douglass was also an early champion of the rights of women. Toward the end of his life he held several federal appointments, including Minister to Haiti.

they had to pass the test to vote, whereas most whites did not. In 1915 the Supreme Court ruled that Oklahoma's grandfather clause was a violation of the Fifteenth Amendment.[5] The Court stated that although the grandfather clause in Oklahoma's voting laws did not mention race or color, it was clearly discriminatory because the only reason for setting the date at 1867 was to deny blacks the right to vote.

During the 1930s and 1940s an important device used in the South to keep blacks from voting was the so-called **white primary,** in which only white citizens could vote for party nominees. In the heavily Democratic South, the primary became the key election; the candidate who won the primary was assured victory on election day. The white primary was finally declared unconstitutional in 1944, when the Supreme Court held that it violated the Fifteenth Amendment.[6]

For more than one hundred years **poll taxes** were a major obstacle for millions of poor voters, both white and black, in many southern states. In 1964, with the ratification of the Twenty-fourth Amendment, poll taxes were abolished in national elections, but several southern states retained them for state elections. In 1966 the Supreme Court declared that these taxes were an unconstitutional denial of equal protection of the law.[7]

After the white primary, poll taxes, and other devices had been declared unconstitutional, there remained one last, very effective barrier to be overcome before blacks could vote: the literacy test. It took federal legislation, especially the Civil Rights Acts of 1965, 1970, and 1975, to eliminate the literacy test once and for all.

In 1964 almost 3 million African Americans of voting age were not registered to vote. Only 32 percent were registered in Louisiana, 23 percent in Alabama, and 6.7 percent in Mississippi.[8] The literacy test remained the greatest barrier to black voting, especially in the rural areas of the South. In response to civil rights protests across the nation, Congress passed the Voting Rights Act of 1965. Through this legislation the use of literacy tests or other such devices was to be suspended in any state or county of the nation in which less than 50 percent of the eligible voting-age population had been registered on November 1, 1964, or had voted in the presidential election of November 1964. Local registrars were required to register voters without regard to their literacy. The executive branch was given the power to appoint federal examiners to register voters in case local officials refused to do so. Moreover, states covered by the act—there were eighteen as of 1990—must submit all proposed changes in their election laws to the Attorney General or the Federal District Court in Washington, D.C., for approval.

In 1970 Congress finally enacted legislation that completely outlawed the use of literacy tests by the states. In 1975 it expanded the Voting Rights Act to protect "language minorities," that is, groups whose members neither speak nor write English. The law now provides that any state or political subdivision in which at least 5 percent of the population cannot speak or understand English well enough to participate in elections must print ballots and other voting materials in both English and the second language. (The most widely used second language is Spanish, particularly in the southwestern states and in large cities like Los Angeles and New York.)

Puerto Rican citizens register to vote at sidewalk registration tables in New York City. The federal Voting Rights Act protects "language minorities" and requires elections in some areas to be conducted bilingually.

Several states and about two hundred counties in various parts of the nation must now conduct elections using bilingual ballots and instructions.

In 1982 Congress extended the Voting Rights Act for another ten years. The 1982 law included a provision that makes it easier for civil rights groups to prove that a state or local government has engaged in discriminatory practices. A violation of the voting rights law can be established by showing that the *result* of a particular practice or procedure is discriminatory; it is no longer necessary to establish that the government *intended* to discriminate.

The Voting Rights Act of 1965 had an enormous impact on the political life of the South. The protection provided by the federal law led to massive voter registration drives by African Americans during the late 1960s and early 1970s. More than 4 million blacks were registered to vote during the decade following the passage of the 1965 law. Open appeals to race and support for segregation rapidly disappeared from southern politics. The example of Mississippi is illustrative. With the largest black population of any state, it had the lowest percentage of voting by black citizens. It also experienced perhaps the worst turmoil over the issue of voting rights. The head of the state chapter of the NAACP was killed in 1963, and three civil rights workers were murdered in 1964 while attempting to encourage voting by blacks. Today more African Americans have been elected to public office in Mississippi than in any other state, and blacks register and vote in approximately the same percentages as whites.

School Desegregation

As we have seen, beginning in 1896 the Supreme Court used the principle of "separate but equal" as the rule for interpreting the Fourteenth Amendment. The doctrine was originally employed in cases involving transportation, but in the early twentieth century it was extended to public education. By the late 1930s, however, the Court began to edge away from the separate-but-equal doctrine. Ironically, during the 1940s and early 1950s it used the principle to declare various forms of segregation unconstitutional. For example, in *Sweatt v. Painter* (1950) the University of Texas Law School had refused admission to a qualified black man on the ground that a separate state law school had been created for blacks. The Supreme Court declared the system unconstitutional on the ground that the state had not provided truly equal facilities for black students. It found that the two law schools were unequal in such factors as library facilities and the quality of faculty, as well as in such intangible factors as reputation and prestige.[9]

But it was not until the historic case of *Brown v. Board of Education of Topeka* (1954) that the separate-but-equal doctrine was rejected by the Supreme Court as the governing principle in cases involving public education. The case began when Oliver Brown sued the Board of Education of Topeka, Kansas, to allow his daughter to attend a public school near his home instead of a black school farther away. The case attracted intense national interest when it and several other similar suits were accepted for decision by the Supreme Court. The Court's decision would affect more than 3 million black children in segregated schools across the nation. The

Court listened to arguments on the case during its 1952–1953 and 1953–1954 terms. The final arguments for *Brown* were presented by Thurgood Marshall, then counsel for the NAACP and later a justice of the Supreme Court. On May 17, 1954, the Court announced its decision. Again it had examined intangible factors—this time the harmful psychological effect of segregation on black children:

> Does segregation of children in public schools solely on the basis of race, even though the physical facilities and other "tangible" factors may be equal, deprive the children of the minority group of the equal educational opportunities? We believe that it does. . . .

> We conclude that in the field of public education the doctrine of "separate but equal" has no place. Separate educational facilities are inherently unequal. Therefore, we hold that the plaintiffs and others similarly situated for whom the actions have been brought are, by reason of the segregation complained of, deprived of the equal protection of the laws guaranteed by the Fourteenth Amendment.[10]

In a companion case decided on the same day, the Court also declared that it was unconstitutional for the federal government to segregate children in the public schools of the District of Columbia. Although the Constitution contains no equal protection clause that applies to the national government, the Court held that the due process clause of the Fifth Amendment places similar restrictions on the exercise of federal power and thus bars segregation in education.[11]

A year later the Supreme Court issued an order setting forth standards for desegregating public schools. It declared that local public school districts must end segregation "with all deliberate speed." The task of supervising this process was assigned to the federal district courts in the affected areas.[12]

School desegregation took place relatively quickly in border states such as Maryland and Delaware and in the District of Columbia. But it occurred at a snail's pace in the deep South. Frequently local school boards either did nothing or proposed plans that required only minimal changes in the existing system. When lawsuits were brought to achieve desegregation, the federal district courts—staffed by judges from the area—often frustrated the objectives of the *Brown* decisions.

A major crisis in the battle for school desegregation was the 1957 confrontation between Governor Orville Faubus of Arkansas and President Dwight D. Eisenhower. When the governor used the State Guard to stop black children from entering a Little Rock school that was to be desegregated, the President sent federal troops to support the court order for desegregation. In response to the claim that state officials could nullify a federal court order, the Supreme Court stated that

> the constitutional rights of children not to be discriminated against in school admission . . . can neither be nullified openly and directly by state legislators or state executive or judicial officers, nor nullified indirectly by them through evasive schemes. . . . Article 6 of the Constitution makes the Constitution the supreme law of the land. . . . The federal judiciary is supreme in the exposition of the law of the Constitution. . . . No state legislator or executive or judicial

A black high school student is jeered as she walks down a line of national guardsmen in an attempt to integrate Central High School, Little Rock, Arkansas, September 1957. The guardsmen blocked the door of the building and prevented her from entering. Later the state guardsmen were placed under federal control by President Eisenhower and were used to achieve the integration of the school.

officer can war against the Constitution without violating his undertaking to support it.[13]

The situation in the South did not change significantly until Congress passed the Civil Rights Act of 1964. Title VI of that act permitted the executive branch of the government to cut off federal financial aid to local and state governments that discriminated on the basis of race. The following year Congress enacted the first major law that provided federal financial aid for public education. Southern communities that badly needed the assistance would lose the money if they continued to practice segregation in their schools. The results were dramatic. In 1963 fully 98 percent of nonwhite students in the South attended schools whose enrollments were entirely nonwhite. In 1968 the figure had fallen to 68 percent, and in 1972 it was 9 percent.[14]

In the North, segregation of African Americans and other minority groups has most often taken the form of **de facto** ("in fact") **segregation.** This segregation results largely from housing patterns and the decisions of private citizens, rather than from the actions of government, which result in **de jure** ("by law") **segregation.** De facto segregation is especially prevalent in the nation's public schools. Children normally attend schools that are located in their neighborhoods, regardless of the makeup of the school. The result is that schools in neighborhoods where nonwhites predominate have all-nonwhite students.

The Supreme Court has not held that de facto segregation violates the Fourteenth Amendment. It still requires proof that the government helped create the segregated situation. In 1973, however, it found for the first time that the school board of a major city outside the South—Denver,

Colorado—had "practiced deliberate racial segregation in schools attended by over one-third of the Negro school population."[15]

The problem of ending legal segregation in education is great, especially in large school districts. School buildings cannot be moved, neighborhood housing patterns are already established, and the number of school-age children may be very large. The Supreme Court has authorized the federal district courts to use a variety of devices to desegregate such schools. They can change the attendance zones of schools within the district. Racial quotas can be used; for example, if 50 percent of the students in the district are white and 50 percent are black, the courts can use these figures as goals for integrating each school in the district. Finally, the courts can order the busing of children from their neighborhood to a school in another part of the district.[16]

The use of school busing as a remedy for de jure segregation has long been a controversial one. Busing has been voluntarily adopted by some school districts; in others it has been imposed by court order after a finding that the local public schools had been illegally segregated. Such mandatory school busing has continued in some areas for many years. In an important 1991 decision, the Supreme Court set forth some general standards for

Busing children to achieve racial integration was highly controversial when judges and school boards adopted this method of desegregating schools. Boston, Massachusetts was the scene of a prolonged struggle over busing in the early 1970s. Here police stand by as black students board buses to be transported to schools that had been largely white.

establishing when a community's school system could be released from court-ordered busing. The court held that the order could be lifted after a school district had taken all "practicable" steps to end the history of segregation in the area. The fact that new one-race schools had again appeared did not bar the removal of the order so long as those schools emerged as a consequence of private housing decisions, and not government policies. Such one-race schools were not "vestiges" of illegal de jure segregation, the Court declared. But the high court did not define what it meant by taking all "practicable" steps to end segregation or when the "vestiges" of that illegal practice had been ended.[17]

The task of desegregating the public schools in many northern cities is a particularly difficult, if not impossible, one. The majority of students in cities like New York and Detroit are nonwhite. Many white families have moved outside the central cities and into other school districts, and school enrollments in those areas are likely to be mostly white. Some proponents of school integration have argued that the courts should ignore the political boundary lines between city and suburban school districts and exchange students among those districts. But the Supreme Court has held that such plans are illegal unless it can be shown that racial discrimination was practiced by the state government or by suburban officials as well as by the inner-city government.[18]

Ironically, the states that have been most successful in integrating public schools are the southern states that formerly practiced de jure segregation. Today most of the school systems in which nonwhite students predominate are located in northern states with long-established patterns of de facto segregation.

The number of cities that are attempting to desegregate their public school systems has declined in recent years. Although the issue remains important in some communities, it is now rarely discussed in large cities like New York, Chicago, Los Angeles, Philadelphia, and Washington, whose school enrollments are predominantly black and Hispanic. One expert has said that the country "is floating on the desegregation issue. It's a status quo situation, with a few steps backward in some places offset by a few steps forward elsewhere."[19]

Equality in Public Facilities

Equal access to public facilities such as restaurants, buses, theaters, hospitals, and parks was another major goal of the civil rights movement. Segregation in public facilities was not seriously challenged until 1955, when blacks in Montgomery, Alabama, led by Rev. Martin Luther King, Jr., boycotted the local bus company for a year. The company lost much of its business and was forced to cut back schedules, lay off drivers, and raise fares. Finally the company and the civil rights group reached a settlement: The company agreed not only to end segregation on the buses but also to hire black drivers. This breakthrough led to others. The Interstate Commerce Commission banned segregation of interstate passengers, and the Supreme Court ordered that restaurants in a bus terminal serving interstate travelers must be desegregated.[20]

President Lyndon Johnson signs into law the 1968 open housing bill, one of several major civil rights laws enacted during his presidency.

Protests against other forms of racial discrimination in public (but privately owned) facilities followed the Montgomery victory. The first lunch counter sit-in took place in Greensboro, North Carolina, on February 1, 1960. During *sit-ins* black protestors would occupy seats, request service, and prevent normal business from being carried on by refusing to leave when they were not served. By 1963 sit-ins had become the most popular and often the most effective means of protesting racial discrimination in public facilities. In that year the Supreme Court reversed the convictions of black protesters in Greenville, South Carolina, who had refused to leave an all-white lunch counter. It ruled that a Greenville city ordinance requiring segregated eating facilities violated the equal protection clause of the Fourteenth Amendment.[21]

Demonstrations, marches, sit-ins, violence against blacks and civil rights supporters in the South, and perhaps most important, the 1963 civil rights march on Washington—all led to the passage of the Civil Rights Act of 1964. Title II of that law forbids discrimination in public facilities because of race, color, religion, or national origin. The act applies to such facilities as motels, hotels, and restaurants that engage in interstate business, and the Justice Department has the power to enforce the law.

The 1964 law was based on Article I, Section 8, of the Constitution, which gives Congress the power to regulate interstate commerce. Congress contended that it was exercising this power in order to remove a burden on interstate commerce—the burden of segregation, which discouraged nonwhites from traveling because of the difficulty of finding restaurant and hotel accommodations. The Supreme Court upheld the validity of Title II of the law in the case of *Heart of Atlanta Motel v. United States.*[22]

The Civil Rights Act of 1964, like the Voting Rights Act passed the following year, was extremely successful. Within a relatively short period accommodations in hotels and restaurants became generally available without regard to race. The fierce opposition to desegregation that had prevailed until the 1960s gradually gave way to a spirit of acceptance and tolerance.

Equality in Employment

Equal opportunity for all people to obtain jobs that offer self-respect and a decent wage did not become a major issue in Congress until the early 1960s. Title VII of the 1964 Civil Rights Act forbids discrimination in employment on the basis of race, color, religion, sex, or national origin. The law established the Equal Employment Opportunity Commission (EEOC), which has the power to investigate complaints of discrimination and to resolve disputes through conciliation. If these methods are not effective, EEOC can bring lawsuits in the federal courts against private employers. (The Justice Department enforces Title VII against government agencies.) People who feel that they have been discriminated against can also bring **class action** suits. These are legal actions brought by one or more persons as representatives of a group of similarly situated persons. For example, an employee could sue an employer on behalf of other workers who have allegedly been victims of discriminatory hiring or promotion policies.

All intentional acts of employment discrimination are illegal under Title VII of the Civil Rights Act of 1964. The question soon arose as to whether the law also applies to situations in which there is no proof that the employer acted intentionally, yet a particular business practice (e.g., an educational requirement) has the effect of preventing qualified women or members of minority groups from obtaining employment. In 1971 the Supreme Court held that Title VII applies not only to intentional forms of discrimination but also to "practices that are fair in form, but discriminatory in operation."[23]

Problems of equal opportunity arise in government employment as well as in the private sphere. A high percentage of lower-level positions in government are held by members of minority groups, but these groups are underrepresented in top managerial and policy-making positions.

Discrimination can also occur in companies that do business with the government. Presidents since Franklin Roosevelt have issued executive orders prohibiting discrimination in hiring by such companies. These requirements have resulted in significant increases in the employment of minority group members by companies that do work for the government.

Serious problems still exist in employment opportunities for African Americans and other minorities, some of them a result of continued

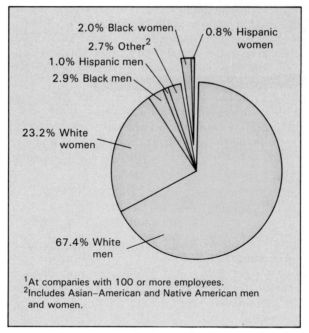

2.0% Black women

2.7% Other[2]

1.0% Hispanic men

2.9% Black men

0.8% Hispanic women

23.2% White women

67.4% White men

[1]At companies with 100 or more employees.
[2]Includes Asian–American and Native American men and women.

FIGURE 12.1 *Percentages of management jobs held by black and Hispanic women compared to others (1988 data).*

Source: U.S. Employment Opportunity Commission, as reported in *The Wall Street Journal*, July 25, 1990, p. B1. Copyright © 1990 by Dow Jones & Company, Inc. All rights reserved worldwide.

discrimination. For example, a 1988 study by the EEOC found that only 4.9 percent of management jobs with companies that employ more than one hundred persons were held by African Americans and only 1.8 percent by Hispanics. More than 90 percent of such positions were held by white men and women. (See Figure 12.1).

■ Women's Rights

The women's rights movement has a long history in the United States. Its formal beginning can be traced to a convention held in Seneca Falls, New York, in 1848. Under the leadership of Elizabeth Cady Stanton and Lucretia Mott, the convention adopted resolutions that called for equality of rights for women regarding property, contracts, marriage, and business. The Seneca Falls convention also took the then-controversial step of supporting the right to vote for women.

Women were also active in the antislavery movement prior to the American Civil War and in a variety of other reform causes. But the right to vote became the main objective of women at the end of the nineteenth century. In 1890 the National American Suffrage Association was formed under the leadership of Carrie Chapman Catt and Anna Howard Shaw. By

1900 four states—Colorado, Idaho, Utah, and Wyoming—had granted women the right to vote. By 1914, seven more states were added to this list.

Change was occurring, but at too slow a pace for many supporters of women's suffrage. The more militant suffragists turned their attention to Washington and away from the states. The Congressional Union was formed, and under the leadership of Alice Paul its members began parading through the streets of the nation's capital and demonstrating in front of the White House. President Wilson finally gave his backing to the cause, and in 1916 both major parties endorsed the right to vote for women. In 1919 Congress passed the women's suffrage amendment. It was quickly ratified by the required number of states, and in 1920 became the Nineteenth Amendment to the Constitution.

Leaders of today's women's movement point out that women have been discriminated against, given inferior roles in society, and denied educational and employment opportunities equal to those enjoyed by men. For example, women who work outside the home generally receive less pay than men, regardless of whether they are factory or clerical workers or are employed in management or professional positions.

For many generations single women have worked to support themselves, but since the 1970s there has been a sharp rise in the number of married women in the labor force. The increased cost of living and the desire for greater personal fulfillment have been the main causes of this trend. Many working women have small children, and a majority of women with school-age children work outside the home, usually full time. In addition, in recent years there has been a rapid increase in the number of unmarried and divorced women with children to support. These developments have made such issues as employment discrimination, job opportunities, and availability of child care facilities the major focus of the women's movement.

Spurred by the success of the civil rights movement, women have organized to fight for their civil rights. One of the oldest and most influential women's rights groups is the National Organization for Women (NOW). In 1967 its first national conference on women's rights in Washington, D.C., listed its demands in the form of a Bill of Rights for women. Included in the document were

> demands for the development of child–care centers to facilitate the entrance of women into the labor force and to allow for increased education; the extension of maternity leaves, social security benefits, and tax deductions for child–care expenses as a means for encouraging women to stay in the labor force; and the availability of birth control and abortion on demand to allow women to control their reproductive lives and to decide when and if they want to assume parental responsibilities.[24]

NOW and other women's rights groups have continued to promote this agenda through public education programs and by lobbying at all levels of government. They have also called for the enactment and enforcement of laws intended to outlaw discrimination based on sex. In addition, women have instituted many lawsuits against both public and private organizations that discriminate against women in employment, education, and other areas of social life.

Affordable child care has been part of the program of women's organizations for several decades and is a major political and social issue today.

As we will see shortly, women have won many legal and political battles since the 1960s. But there was one major defeat; the states were unwilling to ratify a constitutional amendment that would have guaranteed equal rights for members of both sexes. The proposed Equal Rights Amendment (ERA) read as follows:

Section 1. Equality of rights under the law shall not be denied or abridged by the United States or by any State on account of sex.

Section 2. The Congress shall have the power to enforce, by appropriate legislation, the provisions of this article.

Section 3. This amendment shall take effect two years after the date of ratification.

The ERA was approved by the necessary two-thirds vote of both houses of Congress in 1972 and forwarded to the states for ratification. The original deadline for ratification was March 22, 1979, but this was extended by Congress to June 30, 1982. By that time only thirty-five of the states had ratified the amendment—three short of the three-fourths required for it to become part of the Constitution.

Several factors led to the defeat of the ERA. It was not entirely clear what legal changes would be required by the amendment, and many Americans believed that there was a valid basis for maintaining some legal gender distinctions. The failed effort to adopt the ERA led its supporters to rely on the equal protection clause of the Fourteenth Amendment and antidiscrimination laws to bring about an end to bias against women.

Legislation To End Sex Discrimination

The political activities of the women's movement, together with its intensive efforts to educate and inform the public, have produced significant legislative victories. Many state and local governments have enacted legislation that forbids discrimination against women. Several federal laws also deal with this problem. As noted earlier, Title VII of the Civil Rights Act of 1964, as amended by the Equal Employment Opportunities Act of 1972, prohibits discrimination in employment based on sex. Title VII permits only bona fide occupational qualifications to serve as an exception to the prohibition against sex-based discrimination in employment. This narrow exception would apply, for example, in cases in which privacy requires a member of a particular sex, as in the hiring of a restroom attendant, or in which authenticity requires a member of a particular sex, as in the hiring of a fashion model.

In an important 1984 decision the Supreme Court interpreted Title VII to apply to partnerships. A woman attorney had been hired by a large Atlanta law firm as an associate. Seven years later the firm decided not to make her a partner and ended her employment. She sued under Title VII, charging that the firm's decision had been motivated by sex discrimination. The Court held that partnerships are covered by the civil rights law and ordered a trial of the case so that the woman could attempt to prove her claim.[25]

Another important federal civil rights law is Title IX of the Education Amendment of 1972, which makes it illegal for all schools—elementary, secondary, college, or university—that receive federal financial aid to discriminate on the basis of sex. The 1972 law does, however, allow schools to maintain separate living facilities for men and women, and it permits public and private colleges that have traditionally admitted only members of one sex to continue this practice.

The Constitution and Women's Rights

Women's rights groups have been active in the courts. A major constitutional victory of the women's movement was the Supreme Court's decision in the case of *Roe v. Wade* (1973). In this ruling the Court declared a Texas abortion law unconstitutional on the ground that it violated a liberty protected by the due process clause of the Fourteenth Amendment—the liberty to make a decision about the ending of a pregnancy. The Texas law was typical of abortion statutes in more than forty states in that it made abortion illegal except to save the life of the mother. According to the Court, such laws failed to balance the constitutional rights of the individual against the interests of society. It summarized its decision as follows:

> A state criminal abortion statute of the current Texas type, that excepts from criminality only a *life saving* procedure on behalf of the mother, without regard to pregnancy stage and without recognition of the other interests involved, is violative of the Due Process Clause of the Fourteenth Amendment.

(a) For the stage prior to approximately the end of the first trimester, the abortion decision and its effectuation must be left to the medical judgment of the pregnant woman's attending physician.

(b) For the stage subsequent to approximately the end of the first trimester, the State, in promoting its interest in the health of the mother, may, if it chooses, regulate the abortion procedure in ways that are reasonably related to maternal health.

(c) For the stage subsequent to viability the State, in promoting its interest in the potentiality of human life, may, if it chooses, regulate, and even proscribe, abortion except where it is necessary, in appropriate medical judgment, for the preservation of the life or health of the mother.[26]

The *Roe* decision has been both applauded and denounced, and in the twenty years since the Court's ruling, abortion has been the most controversial domestic issue in the United States. Supporters of the *Roe* decision have praised it as a recognition of the constitutional right of women to control their own bodies; opponents have denounced it for its failure to recognize the right to life of the unborn fetus and have criticized the decision as an abuse of the Court's judicial power.

In the years between 1973 and 1989, opponents of the *Roe* decision made many, largely unsuccessful, attempts to overturn or modify the decision. A proposed constitutional amendment to permit the states to restrict abortions never obtained the necessary two-thirds vote in Congress. Some states passed legislation designed to limit the scope of the *Roe* ruling, and a few such laws were upheld by the Supreme Court. For example, the Court accepted a Virginia law requiring that second-trimester abortions be performed only in licensed clinics.[27] But laws that would have had a more

Abortion has been a divisive issue in the United States since the 1973 decision of the Supreme Court in Roe v. Wade, *which held that the Fourteenth Amendment to the Constitution grants women the right to an abortion.*

direct effect on the rules set forth in the *Roe* decision were found unconstitutional. In 1986, for example, the Court voided the provisions of a Pennsylvania law that placed a variety of restrictions on the right of women to have abortions, including reporting requirements for doctors, a provision that informational material must be given to women seeking abortions, and a requirement that a second doctor be present whenever there is a chance that the fetus might be viable.[28]

During the 1980s the membership of the Supreme Court changed. Retiring members—some of whom had supported the original *Roe* decision—were replaced with more conservative jurists. In the 1989 case of *Webster* v. *Reproductive Health Services* the Court, by a 5-to-4 vote, upheld a Missouri law that imposed a number of significant restrictions on women's right to have abortions. For the first time the Court indicated that it was willing to give the states greater freedom to control access to abortions.[29] A year later the Court upheld the right of the states to require teenagers to give notice to both parents before obtaining an abortion as long as the law provides the alternative of a judicial hearing for young women who do not wish to inform their parents.[30] (See Figure 12.2.)

Unlike *Roe* and other abortion-related cases, which involve the meaning of the due process clause of the Fourteenth Amendment, most court challenges to sex-based discrimination have been brought under the equal protection clause of that amendment. In 1971 the Supreme Court for the first time declared unconstitutional on equal protection grounds a state law that discriminated against women. The case of *Reed* v. *Reed* was a simple one. A young child died and left a small estate. Both parents petitioned the Idaho court to be selected as the administrator of the estate. The father was selected because Idaho law required that in such a situation the court must automatically appoint the father. The Court unanimously held that the law was arbitrary and irrational and therefore violated the equal protection clause.[31]

Since 1971 the Supreme Court has heard a large number of cases involving claims of illegal sex-based discrimination. The unanimity shown in the *Reed* case quickly disappeared, however, and the Court has been divided over the proper standard to use in cases involving claims of sex discrimination. Some members of the Court want to consider laws based on sex as **suspect classifications,** which would place them in the same category as laws that discriminate on the basis of race. The concept of a suspect category evolved from the post–World War II series of Supreme Court cases dealing with laws based on race. In those cases the Court abandoned its traditional test of the equal protection clause, which was to ask whether the law in question was **reasonable**. Instead, the Court placed race-based laws in a suspect class and subjected them to strict scrutiny. It did not make the usual assumption that the law in question was constitutional, and it demanded a very high standard of proof—demonstration of "a compelling governmental interest"—to justify laws based on race. Using this reasonableness approach, the Court has found all such laws to be unconstitutional.

Thus far, however, a majority of the Supreme Court justices have refused to place laws based on sex in the suspect category, while also refusing to apply the traditional test of reasonableness. Instead, the Court

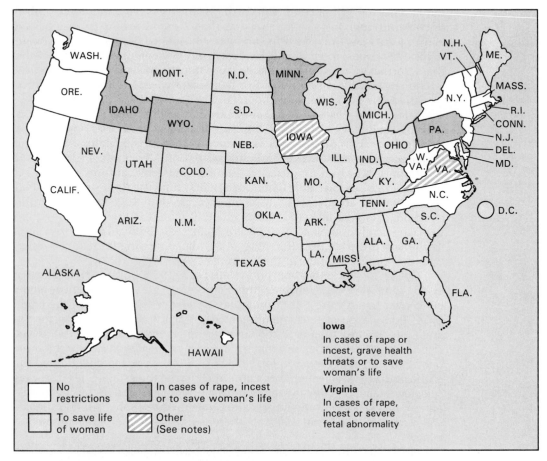

FIGURE 12.2 *Availability of public financing for abortions.*

The Supreme Court has held that women have a constitutional right to abortion. But it has also found that poor women do not have a constitutional right to require that government pay for this medical procedure. The fifty states have adopted different legislative policies regarding public financing of abortions for poor women.

Source: *The New York Times*, June 25, 1989, p. 20. Copyright © 1990 by The New York Times Company. Reprinted by permission.

has created an intermediate standard, the **substantiality test:** "To withstand constitutional challenge . . . classifications by gender must serve important governmental objectives and must be substantially related to achievement of those objectives."[32]

The results of this approach have been mixed. The Court has found some laws that discriminate against women unconstitutional. For example, women cannot be barred from employment because of arbitrary weight or height standards.[33] Nor can an employer pay women lower retirement benefits than men, even though on the average women live longer than men.[34] The Court has also declared unconstitutional some laws that discriminate against men. It ruled, for example, that a state-supported nursing school denied a male applicant the equal protection of the law when it refused to admit him because of his sex.[35] On the other hand, the Court has upheld a federal law that requires military draft registration for men but not for women[36] and a state law that punishes males, but not females, for the crime of statutory rape.[37]

The Supreme Court has also upheld the right of the states to legislate against sex discrimination. Thus a state may make it illegal for a private club to exclude women from membership.[38] And in a case of great significance both to employers and to working women, the Court upheld the right of the state of California to require companies to give up to four months of unpaid leave to employees who are unable to work because of pregnancy, childbirth, or related medical problems.[39]

■ The Civil Rights of the Disabled

Until recently, the disabled were largely excluded from the mainstream of society, both by overt discrimination and by physical barriers such as steps, curbs, and narrow doorways. However, like women, African Americans, and other minority groups, the disabled have organized to put pressure on public and private agencies to grant them equal treatment with other groups in society and to improve their access to public facilities. In

Representative Steny Hoyer (D. Md.), Senator Orrin Hatch (R. Utah), Justin Dart, head of the president's commission on employing persons with disabilities, and others show their emotions while celebrating the adoption of the new civil rights bill for disabled Americans, July 1990.

response to such pressure, Congress passed the Rehabilitation Act of 1973, which bars discrimination against the disabled by the federal government and by contractors receiving federal funds. The Education for All Handicapped Children Act of 1975 requires that handicapped children be provided with a "free appropriate public education" in the least restrictive environment suitable to their needs. But the most far-reaching legislation affecting people with physical and mental disabilities is the Americans with Disabilities Act, which was passed in 1990.

The 1990 act may be compared to the Civil Rights Act of 1964 in its scope; it bars discrimination against the disabled in employment, transportation, public accommodations, and telecommunications. The act requires employers who receive federal funds to provide equal opportunity for employment and for participation in programs and services to otherwise qualified people with disabilities. Employers must make reasonable accommodations to the disabilities of those individuals; that is, they must make facilities physically accessible, restructure job duties and modify work schedules, purchase or modify equipment, and provide readers, interpreters, or other support services. (Businesses that can demonstrate that such changes would be too costly or disruptive or would substantially alter the way they do business may be exempted from these requirements.) In addition, public accommodations must be made accessible to people in wheelchairs, and telephone companies must provide relay services allowing hearing- or voice-impaired people to place and receive calls.

Perhaps the greatest impact of the new law will be felt in the area of transportation. The act requires operators of railroads, intercity and intracity bus lines, mass transit systems, and school bus companies to ensure that all new vehicles are accessible to people with physical disabilities. Within five years all trains and subways must have at least one car that is accessible to the disabled. Public mass transit systems must provide alternative transportation for people who cannot board buses or subways. Key subway and railway stations must be modified so as to be accessible to the disabled.

The act defines a disability as a condition that "substantially limits" a "major life activity" such as walking or reading. People infected with the AIDS virus are covered, as are recovering alcoholics and drug abusers; in fact, the act will affect an estimated 43 million Americans. Compliance with the requirements of the act will cost private businesses many millions of dollars annually. The actual cost will depend on the precise regulations accompanying the legislation and the legal penalties businesses will face for violations; these will be drafted within eighteen months after passage of the act.

■ Affirmative Action

A device designed to improve the situation of minority groups in employment and in other areas of social life such as college and professional school admissions is known as affirmative action. **Affirmative**

Affirmative action plans have enabled women to obtain employment in positions once held almost entirely by men. Law enforcement is one area where the number of women holding jobs has increased sharply in recent years.

action refers to a variety of policies and programs that seek to advance the position of African Americans, Hispanics, Asian Americans, women, and other minority groups who have been the victims of past discrimination. Since the late 1960s many affirmative action programs have been adopted by national, state, and local governments, by public institutions such as state colleges and universities, and by some private employers and organizations.

Originally these programs involved attempts to increase the number of women and minority group members attending college or employed by business and government. They took the form of increased recruitment activity or special training and education programs. Later some programs began giving special preference or advantages to members of certain defined groups. Other programs used quotas, reserving a fixed percentage of total admissions, hirings, or promotions for members of minority groups.

Affirmative action programs, particularly those using quota systems, have been extremely controversial. Supporters of such programs maintain that they are necessary in order to reverse the economic, educational, and psychological effects of past discrimination. Moreover, it is argued that the nation's economic and social life will be advanced by improving the condition of minority groups and that quotas do not violate the Constitution.

Opponents of quota-based affirmative action plans contend that these plans tend to aid members of minority groups who are able to advance on their own ability while doing little to help those who are most in need of assistance. There is also a danger, especially in professions such as medicine and law, that less-qualified individuals will be providing important services to the public. Opponents also maintain that quotas are psychologically damaging to members of minority groups because they know that other people doubt their qualifications for particular positions and feel they have not attained success as a result of their own talents. Finally, opponents argue that quotas based on race, nationality, or sex constitute a form of discrimination that has been illegal since the Supreme Court's 1954 decision in *Brown v. Board of Education.*

The Supreme Court first ruled on the constitutionality of affirmative action programs in 1978 in the case of *Regents of the University of California v. Bakke.*[40] Allan Bakke, a white student, had applied to the University of California Medical School at Davis. His application was rejected twice. During the same period the school accepted a specific number of Mexican-American and African-American students whose qualifications were lower than Bakke's. The school set aside a quota of sixteen out of one hundred places for minority students and considered their applications separately. Bakke argued that this procedure denied him the equal protection of the laws guaranteed by the Fourteenth Amendment.

In a 5-to-4 decision the Supreme Court ordered that Bakke be admitted to the Davis Medical School. The Court held that it was illegal for a public university to use a rigid quota-based admissions policy, at least in the absence of evidence that the school had engaged in discriminatory practices in the past. But the Court upheld the right of a university to consider race as a factor in its admissions program. Such consideration was valid because it served the legitimate purpose of creating diversity in the student body.

The affirmative action issue has continued to divide the Supreme Court since the *Bakke* decision. Many of the Court's decisions in these cases have involved 5-to-4 or 6-to-3 votes, usually in support of such programs. The Court has upheld the legality of voluntary programs that were a product of collective bargaining between an employer and a trade union.[41] It has also given its support to affirmative action plans that have been enacted by Congress. In a 1980 decision, for example, it rejected by a 6-to-3 vote a challenge to a provision of the Public Works Employment Act that required that 10 percent of the money appropriated under the law be given to construction companies owned by members of minority groups.[42] And in 1990, by a 5-to-4 vote, the Court upheld the right of Congress to adopt "benign race-conscious measures" designed to increase the number of minority-held radio and television licenses issued by the Federal Communications Commission.[43] The Court has also defended the right of a federal district court to require that Alabama use a strict racial quota in promoting state troopers (one black for one white) to correct a history of discrimination against blacks in such positions.[44]

The Court has been less sympathetic toward preferential treatment programs adopted by state and local governments. In a 1989 decision that affected the policies of some 36 states and close to two hundred local governments, it declared unconstitutional a Richmond, Virginia, program requiring that 30 percent of all money appropriated for public works in the city be directed to minority-owned construction companies. By a 6-to-3 vote, the Court held that the law violated the constitutional right of white businessmen and women to the equal protection of the laws.[45]

The Supreme Court has also considered affirmative action plans designed to benefit women. The Court has generally been willing to accept sex-based government policies that seek to help women overcome past economic and social disadvantages. For example, in 1987 it upheld a gender-based affirmative action plan adopted by a California county agency. The plan permitted the agency to consider sex in making appointments to job positions in which women were traditionally underrepresented. The Court recognized the existence of an imbalance in the job category in question and found that it was not a violation of the Civil Rights Act for the government agency to consider an applicant's sex in order to correct such imbalances.[46]

■ Summary

In the past three decades much progress has been made toward guaranteeing the civil rights of all Americans. Race relations in the United States have changed greatly since the Supreme Court decided the case of *Brown* v. *Board of Education* in 1954. The system of separate and unequal treatment of African Americans that existed in the South for generations has been ended. The legal rights of African Americans and other minority groups have been made more secure by subsequent Court decisions and by legislative and executive actions. Long denied the right to vote, African Americans have become more politically active and are an increasingly powerful force in American politics. Despite these gains, however, major difficulties still confront nonwhite Americans. Unemployment, substandard housing, poor education and job skills, teenage pregnancy, and high rates of welfare dependency are far more serious problems for these groups than they are for white Americans. And they are harder to solve than the problem of legal discrimination.

There has also been progress toward achieving greater equality between the sexes. Women's rights advocates have won many notable legal and political successes during the past quarter-century, despite the defeat of the proposed Equal Rights Amendment. However, the constitutional right of a woman to obtain an abortion, which was established in *Roe* v. *Wade* in 1973, appears in danger of being overturned by the Supreme Court. The appointment of more conservative justices by Presidents Ronald Reagan and George Bush seems likely to create a new Court majority that will give state legislatures the freedom to regulate abortions. While a majority of the states will probably continue to grant women the freedom to choose to have abortions, some more conservative states will probably impose restrictions on this right.

Change in the membership of the Supreme Court is also likely to affect the legality of affirmative action programs. While the Court has not always upheld the constitutionality of such programs, in the majority of cases it has supported their use. But there are growing doubts as to whether the present Supreme Court will continue to permit that use.

The United States has recently made a major commitment to ensuring equal rights for disabled citizens. The passage of the 1990 Americans with Disabilities Act can be expected to bring about far-reaching changes in American society. At present, however, it is still too early to envision all its possible consequences.

■ Key Terms

civil rights
separate-but-equal doctrine
Jim Crow laws
literacy test
grandfather clause

white primary
poll tax
de facto segregation
de jure segregation
class action

suspect classification
reasonableness test
substantiality test
affirmative action

■ Suggested Reading

CRITES, LAURA L., and WINIFRED L. HEPPERLE. *Women, the Courts, and Equality.* Newbury Park, Calif.: Sage Publications, 1987.

FLEXNER, ELEANOR. *Century of Struggle: The Women's Rights Movement in the United States.* New York: Atheneum, 1968.

GRAHAM, HUGH DAVIS. *The Civil Rights Era: Origins and Developments of National Policy, 1960–1972.* New York: Oxford University Press, 1990.

KLUGER, RICHARD. *Simple Justice: The History of* Brown *v.* Board of Education *and Black America's Struggle for Equality.* New York: Knopf, 1976.

LOFGREN, CHARLES A. *The Plessy Case: A Legal-Historical Interpretation.* New York: Oxford University Press, 1987.

MANSBRIDGE, JANE J. *Why We Lost the ERA.* Chicago: University of Chicago Press, 1986.

NIEMAN, DONALD G. *Promises to Keep: African-Americans and the Constitutional Order, 1776 to the Present.* New York: Oxford University Press, 1990.

SCHWARTZ, BERNARD. *Swann's Way: The School Busing Case and the Supreme Court.* New York: Oxford University Press, 1986.

SOWELL, THOMAS. *Preferential Policies: An International Perspective.* New York: Morrow, 1990.

TAKAKI, RONALD, ed. *From Different Shores: Perspectives on Race and Ethnicity.* New York: Oxford University Press, 1987.

THERNSTROM, ABIGAIL M. *Whose Vote Counts? Affirmative Action and Voting Rights.* Cambridge, Mass.: Harvard University Press/Twentieth Century Fund, 1987.

WOODWARD, C. VANN. *The Strange Career of Jim Crow,* 3rd rev. ed. New York: Oxford University Press, 1974.

■ Notes

1. William Ellery Channing, *Works* (Boston: George G. Channing, 1849), pp. 26–27.

2. *Dred Scott* v. *Sandford,* 19 Howard 393 (1857).

3. 109 U.S. 3 (1883).

4. 163 U.S. 537 (1896).

5. *Guinn* v. *United States,* 238 U.S. 347 (1915).

6. *Smith* v. *Allwright,* 321 U.S. 649 (1944).

7. *Harper* v. *Virginia State Board of Elections,* 383 U.S. 663 (1966).

8. U.S. Commission on Civil Rights, *Political Participation* (Washington, D.C.: Government Printing Office, 1968), pp. 227, 243, 246.

9. 339 U.S. 629 (1950).

10. 347 U.S. 483 (1954).

11. *Bolling* v. *Sharpe,* 347 U.S. 497 (1954).

12. *Brown* v. *Board of Education,* 349 U.S. 294 (1955).

13. *Cooper* v. *Aaron,* 358 U.S. 1 (1958).

14. Harrell R. Rodgers, Jr., "The Supreme Court and School Desegregation: Twenty Years Later," *Political Science Quarterly,* 89 (1974), 751, 753.

15. *Keyes* v. *Denver School District No. 1,* 413 U.S. 189 (1973).

16. *Swann* v. *Charlotte-Mecklenburg Board of Education,* 402 U.S. 1 (1971).

17. *Board of Education* v. *Dowell,* 111 S.Ct. 630 (1991).

18. *Milliken* v. *Bradley,* 418 U.S. 717 (1974).

19. Gary Orfield, quoted in Lee A. Daniels, "The Winning Ways To Desegregate the Schools," *New York Times,* December 17, 1989, sec. E, p. 4.

20. *Boynton* v. *Virginia,* 364 U.S. 454 (1960).

21. *Peterson* v. *City of Greenville,* 373 U.S. 244 (1963).

22. 379 U.S. 241 (1964).

23. *Griggs* v. *Duke Power Co.,* 401 U.S. 424 (1971).

24. Quoted in Ethel Klein, *Gender Politics* (Cambridge, Mass.: Harvard University Press, 1984), p. 47.

25. *Hishon* v. *King and Spalding,* 467 U.S. 69 (1984).

26. 410 U.S. 113 (1973).

27. *Simopoulos* v. *Virginia,* 462 U.S. 506 (1983).

28. *Thornburgh* v. *American College of Obstetricians and Gynecologists,* 476 U.S. 747 (1986).

29. 109 S.Ct. 3040 (1989).

30. *Hodgson* v. *Minnesota,* 110 S.Ct. 2926 (1990).

31. 404 U.S. 71 (1971).

32. *Craig* v. *Boren,* 429 U.S. 190 (1976).

33. *Dothard* v. *Rawlinson,* 433 U.S. 321 (1977).

34. *Arizona Governing Committee* v. *Norris,* 463 U.S. 1073 (1983).

35. *Mississippi University for Women* v. *Hogan,* 458 U.S. 718 (1982).

36. *Rostker* v. *Goldberg,* 453 U.S. 57 (1981).

37. *Michael M.* v. *Superior Court,* 450 U.S. 464 (1981).

38. *Board of Directors of Rotary International* v. *Rotary Club of Duarte,* 481 U.S. 537 (1987).

39. *California Federal Savings and Loan* v. *Guerra,* 479 U.S. 272 (1987).

40. 438 U.S. 265 (1978).

41. *United States Steel Workers* v. *Weber,* 443 U.S. 193 (1979). No constitutional issue was raised in this case because the plan involved two private organizations and did not involve the government.

42. *Fullilove* v. *Klutznick,* 448 U.S. 448 (1980).

43. *Metro Broadcasting* v. *FCC,* 110 S.Ct. 2997 (1990).

44. *United States* v. *Paradise,* 480 U.S. 149 (1987). See also *Sheet Metal Workers* v. *EEOC,* 478 U.S. 421 (1986).

45. *City of Richmond* v. *J. A. Croson Co.,* 488 U.S. 469 (1989).

46. *Johnson* v. *Santa Clara County,* 480 U.S. 616 (1987).

The Declaration of Independence

When in the course of human events, it becomes necessary for one people to dissolve the political bands which have connected them with another, and to assume among the Powers of the earth, the separate and equal station to which the Laws of Nature and of Nature's God entitle them, a decent respect to the opinions of mankind requires that they should declare the causes which impel them to the separation.

We hold these truths to be self-evident, that all men are created equal, that they are endowed by their Creator with certain unalienable Rights, that among these are Life, Liberty and the pursuit of Happiness.—That to secure these rights, Governments are instituted among Men, deriving their just powers from the consent of the governed. That whenever any Form of Government becomes destructive of these ends, it is the Right of the People to alter or to abolish it, and to institute new Government, laying its foundation on such principles and organizing its powers in such form, as to them shall seem most likely to effect their Safety and Happiness. Prudence, indeed, will dictate that Governments long established should not be changed for light and transient causes; and accordingly all experience hath shown, that mankind are more disposed to suffer, while evils are sufferable, than to right themselves by abolishing the forms to which they are accustomed. But when a long train of abuses and usurpations, pursuing invariably the same Object, evinces a design to reduce them under absolute Despotism, it is their right, it is their duty, to throw off such Government, and to provide new Guards for their future security.—Such has been the patient sufferance of these Colonies; and such is now the necessity which constrains them to alter their former Systems of Government. The history of the present King of Great Britain is a history of repeated injuries and usurpations, all having in direct object the establishment of an absolute Tyranny over these States. To prove this, let Facts be submitted to a candid world.

He has refused his Assent to Laws, the most wholesome and necessary for the public good.

He has forbidden his Governors to pass Laws of immediate and pressing importance, unless suspended in their operation till his Assent should be obtained; and when so suspended, he has utterly neglected to attend to them.

He has refused to pass other Laws for the accommodation of large districts of people, unless those people would relinquish the right of Representation in the Legislature, a right inestimable to them and formidable to tyrants only.

He has called together legislative bodies at places unusual, uncomfortable, and distant from the depository of their Public Records, for the sole purpose of fatiguing them into compliance with his measures.

He has dissolved Representative Houses repeatedly, for opposing with manly firmness his invasions on the rights of the people.

He has refused for a long time, after such dissolutions, to cause others to be elected; whereby the Legislative Powers, incapable of Annihilation, have returned to the People at large for their exercise; the State remaining in the mean time exposed to all the dangers of invasion from without, and convulsions within.

He has endeavoured to prevent the population of these States; for that purpose obstructing the Laws of Naturalization of Foreigners, refusing to pass others to encourage their migration hither, and raising the conditions of new Appropriations of Lands.

He has obstructed the Administration of Justice, by refusing his Assent to Laws for establishing Judiciary Powers.

He has made Judges dependent on his Will alone, for the tenure of their offices, and the amount and payment of their salaries.

He has erected a multitude of New Offices, and sent hither swarms of Officers to harass our People, and eat out their substance.

He has kept among us, in times of peace, Standing Armies without the Consent of our legislature.

He has affected to render the Military independent of and superior to the Civil Power.

He has combined with others to subject us to a jurisdiction foreign to our constitution, and unacknowledged by our laws giving his Assent to their acts of pretended legislation:

For quartering large bodies of armed troops among us:

For protecting them, by a mock Trial, from Punishment for any Murders which they should commit on the inhabitants of these States:

For cutting off our Trade with all parts of the world:

For imposing taxes on us without our Consent:

For depriving us in many cases, of the benefits of Trial by Jury:

For transporting us beyond Seas to be tried for pretended offences:

For abolishing the free System of English Laws in a neighboring Province, establishing therein an Arbitrary government, and enlarging its Boundaries so as to render it at once an example and fit instrument for introducing the same absolute rule into these Colonies:

For taking away our Charters; abolishing our most valuable Laws, and altering fundamentally the Forms of our Governments:

For suspending our own Legislature, and declaring themselves invested with Power to legislate for us in all cases whatsoever.

He has abdicated Government here, by declaring us out of his Protection and waging War against us.

He has plundered our seas, ravaged our Coasts, burnt our towns, and destroyed the lives of our people.

He is at this time transporting large armies of foreign mercenaries to compleat the works of death, desolation and tyranny, already begun with circumstances of Cruelty & perfidy scarcely paralleled in the most barbarous ages, and totally unworthy the Head of a civilized nation.

He has constrained our fellow Citizens taken Captive on the high Seas to bear Arms against their Country, to become the executioners of their friends and Brethren, or to fall themselves by their Hands.

He has excited domestic insurrections amongst us, and has endeavoured to bring on the inhabitants of our frontiers, the merciless Indian Savages, whose known rule of warfare, is an undistinguished destruction of all ages, sexes and conditions.

In every stage of these Oppressions We have Petitioned for Redress in the most humble terms: Our repeated Petitions have been answered only by repeated injury. A Prince, whose character is thus marked by every act which may define a Tyrant, is unfit to be the ruler of a free People.

Nor have We been wanting in attention to our British brethren. We have warned them from time to time of attempts by their legislature to extend an unwarrantable jurisdiction over us. We have reminded them of the circumstances of our emigration and settlement here. We have appealed to their native justice and magnanimity, and we have conjured them by the ties of our common kindred to disavow these usurpations, which, would inevitably interrupt our connections and correspondence. They too have been deaf to the voice of justice and of consanguinity. We must, therefore, acquiesce in the necessity, which denounces our Separation, and hold them, as we hold the rest of mankind, Enemies in War, in Peace, Friends.

We, therefore, the Representatives of the united States of America, in General Congress, Assembled, appealing to the Supreme Judge of the world for the rectitude of our intentions, do, in the Name, and by Authority of the good People of these Colonies, solemnly publish and declare, that these United Colonies are, and of Right ought to be Free and Independent States; that they are Absolved from all allegiance to the British Crown, and that all political connection between them and the State of Great Britain, is and ought to be totally dissolved; and that as Free and Independent States, they have full Power to levy War, conclude Peace, contract Alliances, establish Commerce, and to do all other Acts and Things which Independent States may of right do. And for the support of this Declaration, with a firm reliance on the Protection of Divine Providence, we mutually pledge to each other our Lives, our Fortunes and our sacred Honor.

B The Articles of Confederation

To all to whom these Presents shall come, we the under signed Delegates of the States affixed to our Names send greeting. Whereas the Delegates of the United States of America in Congress assembled did on the fifteenth day of November in the Year of our Lord One Thousand Seven Hundred and Seventy seven, and in the Second Year of the Independence of America agree to certain articles of Confederation and perpetual Union between the States of Newhampshire, Massachusetts-bay, Rhodeisland and Providence Plantations, Connecticut, New York, New Jersey, Pennsylvania, Delaware, Maryland, Virginia, North-Carolina, South-Carolina and Georgia in the Words following, viz, "Articles of Confederation and perpetual Union between the States of Newhampshire, Massachusetts-bay, Rhodeisland and Providence Plantations, Connecticut, New-York, New-Jersey, Pennsylvania, Delaware, Maryland, Virginia, North-Carolina, South-Carolina and Georgia.

Article I. The Stile of this confederacy shall be "The United States of America."

Article II. Each state retains its sovereignty, freedom and independence, and every Power, Jurisdiction and right, which is not by this confederation expressly delegated to the United States, in Congress assembled.

Article III. The said states hereby severally enter into a firm league of friendship with each other, for their common defence, the security of their Liberties, and their mutual and general welfare, binding themselves to assist each other, against all force offered to, or attacks made upon them, or any of them, on account of religion, sovereignty, trade, or any other pretence whatever.

Article IV. The better to secure and perpetuate mutual friendship and intercourse among the people of the different states in this union, the free inhabitants of each of these states, paupers, vagabonds and fugitives from Justice excepted, shall be entitled to all privileges and immunities of free citizens in the several states; and the people of each state shall have free ingress and regress to and from any other state, and shall enjoy therein all the privileges of trade and commerce, subject to the same duties, impositions and restrictions as the inhabitants thereof respectively, provided that such restriction shall not extend so far as to prevent the removal of property imported into any state, to any other state of which the Owner is an inhabitant; provided also that no imposition, duties or restriction shall be laid by any state, on the property of the united states, or either of them.

If any Person guilty of, or charged with treason, felony, or other high misdemeanor in any state, shall flee from Justice, and be found in any of the united states, he shall upon demand of the Governor or executive power, of the state from which he fled, be delivered up and removed to the state having jurisdiction of his offence.

Full faith and credit shall be given in each of these states to the records, acts and judicial proceedings of the courts and magistrates of every other state.

Article V. For the more convenient management of the general interests of the united states, delegates shall be annually appointed in such manner as the legislature of each state shall direct, to meet in Congress on the first Monday in November, in every year, with a power reserved to each state, to recal its delegates, or any of them, at any time within the year, and to send others in their stead, for the remainder of the Year.

No state shall be represented in Congress by less than two, nor by more than seven Members; and no person shall be capable of being a delegate for more than three years in any term of six years; nor shall any person, being a delegate, be capable of holding any office under the united states, for which he, or another for his benefit receives any salary, fees or emolument of any kind.

Each state shall maintain its own delegates in a meeting of the states, and while they act as members of the committee of the states.

In determining questions in the united states, in Congress assembled, each state shall have one vote.

Freedom of speech and debate in Congress shall not be impeached or questioned in any Court, or place out of Congress, and the members of congress shall be protected in their persons from arrests and imprisonments, during the time of their going to and from, and attendance on congress, except for treason, felony, or breach of the peace.

Article VI. No state without the Consent of the united states in congress assembled, shall send any embassy to, or receive any embassy from, or enter into any conference, agreement, alliance or treaty with any King prince or state; nor shall any person holding any office of profit or trust under the united states, or any of them, accept of any present, emolument, office or title of any kind whatever from any king, prince or foreign state; nor shall the united states in congress assembled, or any of them, grant any title of nobility.

No two or more states shall enter into any treaty, confederation or alliance whatever between them, without the consent of the united states in congress assembled, specifying accurately the purposes for which the same is to be entered into, and how long it shall continue.

No state shall lay any imposts or duties, which may interfere with any stipulations in treaties, entered into by the united states in congress assembled, with any king, prince or state, in pursuance of any treaties already proposed by congress, to the courts of France and Spain.

No vessels of war shall be kept up in time of peace by any state, except such number only, as shall be deemed necessary by the united states in congress assembled, for the defence of such state, or its trade; nor shall any body of forces be kept up by any state, in time of peace, except such number only, as in the judgment of the united states, in congress assembled, shall be deemed requisite to garrison the forts necessary for the defence of such state; but every state shall always keep up a well regulated and disciplined militia, sufficiently armed and accoutred, and shall provide and constantly have ready for use, in public stores, a due number of field pieces and tents, and a proper quantity of arms, ammunition and camp equipage.

No state shall engage in any war without the consent of the united states in congress assembled, unless such state be actually invaded by enemies, or shall have received certain advice of a resolution being formed by some nation of Indians to invade such state, and the danger is so imminent as not to admit of a delay,

THE ARTICLES OF CONFEDERATION

till the united states in congress assembled can be consulted: nor shall any state grant commissions to any ships or vessels of war, nor letters of marque or reprisal, except it be after a declaration of war by the united states in congress, assembled, and then only against the kingdom or state and the subjects thereof, against which war has been so declared, and under such regulations as shall be established by the united states in congress assembled, unless such state be infested by pirates, in which case vessels of war may be fitted out for that occasion, and kept so long as the danger shall continue, or until the united states in congress assembled shall determine otherwise.

Article VII. When land-forces are raised by any state for the common defence, all officers of or under the rank of colonel, shall be appointed by the legislature of each state respectively by whom such forces shall be raised, or in such manner as such state shall direct, and all vacancies shall be filled up by the state which first made the appointment.

Article VIII. All charges of war, and all other expences that shall be incurred for the common defence or general welfare, and allowed by the united states in congress assembled, shall be defrayed out of a common treasury, which shall be supplied by the several states, in proportion to the value of all land within each state, granted to or surveyed for any Person, as such land and the buildings and improvements thereon shall be estimated according to such mode as the united states in congress assembled, shall from time to time direct and appoint. The taxes for paying that proportion shall be laid and levied by the authority and direction of the legislatures of the several states within the time agreed upon by the united states in congress assembled.

Article IX. The united states in congress assembled, shall have the sole and exclusive right and power of determining on peace and war, except in the cases mentioned in the sixth article—of sending and receiving ambassadors—entering into treaties and alliances, provided that no treaty of commerce shall be made whereby the legislative power of the respective states shall be restrained from imposing such imposts and duties on foreigners, as their own people are subjected to, or from prohibiting the exportation or importation of any species of goods or commodities whatsoever—of establishing rules for deciding in all cases, what captures on land or water shall be legal, and in what manner prizes taken by land or naval forces in the service of the united states shall be divided or appropriated— of granting letters of marque and reprisal in times of peace—appointing courts for the trial of piracies and felonies committed on the high seas and establishing courts for receiving and determining finally appeals in all cases of captures, provided that no member of congress shall be appointed a judge of any of the said courts.

The united states in congress assembled shall also be the last resort on appeal in all disputes and differences now subsisting or that hereafter may arise between two or more states concerning boundary, jurisdiction or any other cause whatever; which authority shall always be exercised in the manner following. Whenever the legislative or executive authority or lawful agent of any state in controversy with another shall present a petition to congress stating the matter in question and praying for a hearing, notice thereof shall be given by order of congress to the legislative or executive authority of the other state in controversy, and a day assigned for the appearance of the parties by their lawful agents, who shall then be directed to appoint by joint consent, commissioners or judges to constitute a court for hearing and determining the matter in question: but if they cannot agree, congress shall name three persons out of each of the united states, and from the list of such persons each party shall alternately strike out one, the petitioners beginning, until the number shall be reduced to thirteen; and from that number no less than seven, nor more than nine names as congress shall direct, shall in the presence of congress be drawn out by lot, and the persons whose names shall be so drawn or any five of them, shall be commissioners or judges, to hear and finally determine the controversy, so always as a major part of the judges who shall hear the cause shall agree in the determination: and if either party shall neglect to attend at the day appointed, without shewing reasons, which congress shall judge sufficient, or being present shall refuse to strike, the congress shall proceed to nominate three persons out of each state, and the secretary of congress shall strike in behalf of such party absent or refusing; and the judgment and sentence of the court to be appointed, in the manner before prescribed, shall be final and conclusive; and if any of the parties shall refuse to submit to the authority of such court, or to appear or defend their claim or cause, the court shall nevertheless proceed to pronounce sentence, or judgment, which shall in like manner be final and decisive, the judgment or sentence and other proceedings being in either case transmitted to congress, and lodged among the acts of congress for the security of the parties concerned: provided that every commissioner, before he sits in judgment, shall take an oath to be administered by one of the judges of the supreme or superior court of the state, where the cause shall be tried, "well and truly to hear and determine the matter in question, according to the best of his judgment, without favour, affection or hope of reward:" provided also that no state shall be deprived of territory for the benefit of the united states.

All controversies concerning the private right of soil claimed under different grants of two or more states, whose jurisdictions as they may respect such lands, and the states which passed such grants are adjusted, the said grants or either of them being at the same time claimed to have originated antecedent to such settlement of jurisdiction, shall on the petition of either party to the congress of the united states, be finally determined as near as maybe in the same manner as is before prescribed for deciding disputes respecting territorial jurisdiction between different states.

The united states in congress assembled shall also have the sole and exclusive right and power of regulating the alloy and value of coin struck by their own authority, or by that of the respective states—fixing the standard of weights and measures throughout the united states—regulating the trade and managing all affairs with the Indians, not members of any of the states, provided that the legislative right of any state within its own limits be not infringed or violated—establishing and regulating post-offices from one state to another, throughout all the united states, and exacting such postage on the papers passing thro' the same as may be requisite to defray the expences of the said office—appointing all officers of the land forces, in the service of the united states, excepting regimental officers—appointing all the officers of the naval forces, and commissioning all officers whatever in the service of the united states—making rules for the government and regulation of the said land and naval forces, and directing their operations.

The united states in congress assembled shall have authority to appoint a committee, to sit in the recess of congress, to be denominated "A Committee of the States," and to consist of one delegate from each state; and to appoint such other committees and civil officers as may be necessary for managing the general affairs of the united states under their direction—to appoint one of their number to preside, provided that no person be allowed to serve in the office of president more than one year in any term of three years; to ascertain the necessary sums of Money to be raised for the service of the united states, and to appropriate and apply the same for defraying the public expences—to borrow money, or emit bills on the credit of the united states, transmitting every half year to the respective states an account of the sums of money so borrowed or emitted,—to build and equip a navy—to agree upon the number of land forces, and to make requisitions from each state for its quota, in proportion to the number of white inhabitants in such state; which requisition shall be binding, and thereupon the legislature of each state shall appoint the regimental officers, raise the men and cloath, arm and equip them in a soldier like manner, at the expence of the united states, and the officers and men so cloathed, armed and equipped shall march to the place appointed, and within the time agreed on by the united states in congress assembled: But if the united states in congress assembled shall, on consideration of circumstances judge proper that any state should not raise men, or should raise a smaller number than its quota, and that any other state should raise a greater number of men than the quota thereof, such extra number shall be raised, officered, cloathed, armed and equipped in the same manner as the quota of such state, unless the legislature of such state shall judge that such extra number cannot be safely spared out of the same, in which case they shall raise officer, cloath, arm and equip as many of such extra number as the judge can be safely spared. And the officers and men so cloathed, armed and equipped, shall march to the place appointed, and within the time agreed on by the united states in congress assembled.

The united states in congress assembled shall never engage in a war, nor grant letters of marque and reprisal in time of peace, nor enter into any treaties or alliances, nor coin money, nor regulate the value thereof, nor ascertain the sums and expences necessary for the defence and welfare of the united states, or any of them, nor emit bills, nor borrow money on the credit of the united states, nor appropriate money, nor agree upon the number of vessels of war, to be built or purchased, or the number of land or sea forces to be raised, nor appoint a commander in chief of the army or navy, unless nine states assent to the same: nor shall a question on any other point, except for adjourning from day to day be determined, unless by the votes of a majority of the united states in congress assembled.

The congress of the united states shall have power to adjourn to any time within the year, and to any place within the united states, so that no period of adjournment be for a longer duration than the space of six Months, and shall publish the Journal of their proceedings monthly, except such parts thereof relating to treaties, alliances or military operations, as in their judgment require secresy; and the yeas and nays of the delegates of each state on any question shall be entered on the Journal, when it is desired by any delegate; and the delegates of a state, or any of them, at his or their request shall be furnished with a transcript of the said Journal, except such parts as are above excepted, to lay before the legislatures of the several states.

Article X. The committee of the states, or any nine of them, shall be authorized to execute, in the recess of congress, such of the powers of congress as the united states in congress assembled, by the consent of nine states, shall from time to time think expedient to vest them with; provided that no power be delegated to the said committee, for the exercise of which, by the articles of confederation, the voice of nine states in congress of the united states assembled is requisite.

Article XI. Canada acceding to this confederation, and joining in the measures of the united states, shall be admitted into, and entitled to all the advantages of this union: but no other colony shall be admitted into the same, unless such admission be agreed to by nine states.

Article XII. All bills of credit emitted, monies borrowed and debts contracted by, or under the authority of congress, before the assembling of the united states, in pursuance of the present confederation, shall be deemed and considered as a charge against the united states, for payment and satisfaction whereof the said united states, and the public faith are hereby solemnly pledged.

Article XIII. Every state shall abide by the determinations of the united states in congress assembled, on all questions which by this confederation are submitted to them. And the Articles of this confederation shall be inviolably observed by every state, and the union shall be perpetual; nor shall any alteration at any time hereafter be made in any of them; unless such alteration be agreed to in a congress of the united states, and be afterwards confirmed by the legislatures of every state.

And Whereas it hath pleased the Great Governor of the World to incline the hearts of the legislatures we respectively represent in congress, to approve of, and to authorize us to ratify the said articles of confederation and perpetual union. Know Ye that we the undersigned delegates, by virtue of the power and authority to us given for that purpose, do by these presents, in the name and in behalf of our respective constituents, fully and entirely ratify and confirm each and every of the said articles of confederation and perpetual union, and all and singular the matters and things therein contained: And we do further solemnly plight and engage the faith of our respective constituents, that they shall abide by the determinations of the united states in congress assembled, on all questions, which by the said confederation are submitted to them. And that the articles thereof shall be inviolably observed by the states we respectively represent, and that the union shall be perpetual. In Witness whereof we have hereunto set our hands in Congress. Done at Philadelphia in the state of Pennsylvania the ninth Day of July in the Year of our Lord one Thousand seven Hundred and Seventy-eight, and in the third year of the independence of America.

C

The Antifederalists

Statement by George Mason to the Philadelphia Convention

George Mason, a delegate from Virginia to the Philadelphia Convention, was one of only three delegates who refused to sign the completed draft of the proposed constitution. The other two were Elbridge Gerry of Massachusetts and Edmund Randolph, also of Virginia. A statement summarizing the views of the three men and written by Mason was presented to the Convention on September 15, 1787, just two days before that body met for the last time.

There is no Declaration of Rights, and the laws of the general government being paramount to the laws and constitution of the several States, the Declarations of Rights in the separate States are no security. Nor are the people secured even in the enjoyment of the benefit of the common law.

In the House of Representatives there is not the substance but the shadow only of representation; which can never produce proper information in the legislature, or inspire confidence in the people; the laws will therefore be generally made by men little concerned in, and unacquainted with their effects and consequences.

The Senate have the power of altering all money bills, and of originating appropriations of money, and the salaries of the officers of their own appointment, in conjunction with the president of the United States, although they are not the representatives of the people or amenable to them.

These with their other great powers, viz.: their power in the appointment of ambassadors and all public officers, in making treaties, and in trying all impeachments, their influence upon and connection with the supreme Executive from these causes, their duration of office and their being a constantly existing body, almost continually sitting, joined with their being one complete branch of the legislature, will destroy any balance in the government, and enable them to accomplish what usurpations they please upon the rights and liberties of the people.

The Judiciary of the United States is so constructed and extended, as to absorb and destroy the judiciaries of the several States; thereby rendering law as tedious, intricate and expensive, and justice as unattainable, by a great part of the community, as in England, and enabling the rich to oppress and ruin the poor.

The President of the United States has no Constitutional Council, a thing unknown in any safe and regular government. He will therefore be unsupported by proper information and advice, and will generally be directed by minions and favorites; or he will become a tool to the Senate—or a Council of State will grow out of the principal officers of the great departments; the worst and most dangerous of all ingredients for such a council in a free country; From this fatal defect has arisen the improper power of the Senate in the appointment of public officers, and the alarming dependence and connection between that branch of the legislature and the supreme Executive.

Hence also sprung that unnecessary officer the vice president, who for want of other employment is made president of the Senate, thereby dangerously blending the executive and legislative powers, besides always giving to some one of the States an unnecessary and unjust pre-eminence over the others.

The President of the United States has the unrestrained power of granting pardons for treason, which may be sometimes exercised to screen from punishment those whom he had secretly instigated to commit the crime, and thereby prevent a discovery of his own guilt.

By declaring all treaties supreme laws of the land, the Executive and the Senate have, in many cases, an exclusive power of legislation; which might have been avoided by proper distinctions with respect to treaties, and requiring the assent of the House of Representatives, where it could be done with safety.

By requiring only a majority to make all commercial and navigation laws, the five Southern States, whose produce and circumstances are totally different from that of the eight Northern and Eastern States, may be ruined, for such rigid and premature regulations may be made as will enable the merchants of the Northern and Eastern States not only to demand an exhorbitant freight, but to monopolize the purchase of the commodities at their own price, for many years, to the great injury of the landed interest, and impoverishment of the people; and the danger is the greater as the gain on one side will be in proportion to the loss on the other. Whereas requiring two-thirds of the members present in both Houses would have produced mutual moderation, promoted the general interest, and removed an insuperable objection to the adoption of this government.

Under their own construction of the general clause, at the end of the enumerated powers, the Congress may grant monopolies in trade and commerce, constitute new crimes, inflict unusual and severe punishments, and extend their powers as far as they shall think proper; so that the State legislatures have no security for the powers now presumed to remain to them, or the people for their rights.

There is no declaration of any kind, for preserving the liberty of the press, or the trial by jury in civil causes; nor against the danger of standing armies in time of peace.

The State legislatures are restrained from laying export duties on their own produce.

Both the general legislature and the State legislature are expressly prohibited making *ex post facto* laws; though there never was nor can be a legislature but must and will make such laws, when necessity and the public safety require them; which will hereafter be a breach of all the constitutions in the Union, and afford precedents for other innovations.

This government will set out a moderate aristocracy: it is at present impossible to foresee whether it will, in its operation, produce a monarchy, or a corrupt, tyrannical aristocracy; it will most probably vibrate some years between the two, and then terminate in the one or the other.

The general legislature is restrained from prohibiting the further importation of slaves for twenty odd years; though such importations render the United States weaker, more vulnerable, and less capable of defence.

"Brutus": *Essay No. 1*

During the debates over the ratification of the Constitution, the opponents of the document produced a large body of printed works. They ranged in quality from hysterical to serious. Perhaps the most carefully reasoned essays opposing the adoption of the Constitution were those that appeared between October 1787 and April 1788 in the New York Journal *under the pseudonym "Brutus." "Brutus" was probably Robert Yates, a New York judge and a delegate to the Philadelphia Convention. His* Essay No. 1, *excerpted here, attacks the idea of a large consolidated republic, which he believed would be created by the Constitution.*

The first question that presents itself on the subject is, whether a confederated government be the best for the United States or not? Or in other words, whether the thirteen United States should be reduced to one great republic, governed by one legislature, and under the direction of one executive and judicial; or whether they should continue thirteen confederated republics, under the direction and control of a supreme federal head for certain defined national purposes only?

This enquiry is important, because, although the government reported by the convention does not go to a perfect and entire consolidation, yet it approaches so near to it, that it must, if executed, certainly and infallibly terminate in it.

This government is to possess absolute and uncontrolable power, legislative, executive and judicial, with respect to every object to which it extends, for by the last clause of section 8th, article 1st, it is declared "that the Congress shall have power to make all laws which shall be necessary and proper for carrying into execution the foregoing powers, and all other powers vested by this constitution, in the government of the United States; or in any department or office thereof." And by the 6th article, it is declared "that this constitution, and the laws of the United States, which shall be made in pursuance thereof, and the treaties made, or which shall be made, under the authority of the United States, shall be the supreme law of the land; and the judges in every state shall be bound thereby, any thing in the constitution, or law of any state to the contrary notwithstanding." It appears from these articles that there is no need of any intervention of the state governments, between the Congress and the people, to execute any one power vested in the general government, and that the constitution and laws of every state are nullified and declared void, so far as they are or shall be inconsistent with this constitution, or the laws made in pursuance of it, or with treaties made under the authority of the United States.—The government then, so far as it extends, is a complete one, and not a confederation. It is as much one complete government as that of New York or Massachusetts, has as absolute and perfect powers to make and execute all laws, to appoint officers, institute courts, declare offences, and annex penalties, with respect to every object to which it extends, as any other in the world. So far therefore as its powers reach, all ideas of confederation are given up and lost. It is true this government is limited to certain objects, or to speak more properly, some small degree of power is still left to the states, but a little attention to the powers vested in the general government, will convince every candid man, that if it is capable of being executed, all that is reserved for the individual states must very soon be annihilated, except so far as they are barely necessary to the organization of the general government. The powers of the general legislature extend to every case that is of the least importance—there is nothing valuable to human nature, nothing dear to free men, but what is within its power. It has authority to make laws which will affect the lives, the liberty, and property of every man in the United States; nor can the constitution or laws of any state, in any way prevent or impede the full and complete execution of every power given. The legislative power is competent to lay taxes, duties, imposts, and excises— there is no limitation to this power, unless it be said that the clause which directs the use to which those taxes, and duties shall be applied, may be said to be a limitation: but this is no restriction of the power at all, for by this clause they are to be applied to pay the debts and provide for the common defence and general welfare of the United States; but the legislature have authority to contract debts at their discretion; they are the sole judges of what is necessary to provide for the common defence, and they only are to determine what is for the general welfare; this power therefore is neither more nor less, than a power to lay and collect taxes, imposts, and excises, at their pleasure; not only [is] the power to lay taxes unlimited, as to the amount they may require, but it is perfect and absolute to raise them in any mode they please. No state legislature, or any power in the state governments, have any more to do in carrying this into effect, than the authority of one state has to do with that of another. In the business therefore of laying and collecting taxes, the idea of confederation is totally lost, and that of one entire republic is embraced. It is proper here to remark, that the authority to lay and collect taxes is the most important of any power that can be granted; it connects with it almost all other powers, or at least will in process of time draw all other after it; it is the great means of protection, security, and defence, in a good government, and the great engine of oppression and tyranny in a bad one. This cannot fail of being the case, if we consider the contracted limits which are set by this constitution, to the late [state?] governments, on this article of raising money. No state can emit paper money—lay any duties, or imposts, on imports, or exports, but by consent of the Congress; and then the net produce shall be for the benefit of the United States: the only mean therefore left, for any state to support its government and discharge its debts, is by direct taxation; and the United States have also power to lay and collect taxes, in any way they please. Every one who has thought on the subject, must be convinced that but small sums of money can be collected in any country, by direct taxes, when the federal government begins to exercise the right of taxation in all its parts, the legislatures of the several states will find it impossible to raise monies to support their governments. Without money they cannot be supported, and they must dwindle away, and, as before observed, their powers absorbed in that of the general government.

It might be here shown, that the power in the federal legislative, to raise and support armies at pleasure, as well in peace as in war, and their control over the militia, tend, not only to a consolidation of the government, but the destruction of liberty—I shall not, however, dwell upon these, as a few observations upon the judicial power of this government, in addition to the preceding, will fully evince the truth of the position.

The judicial power of the United States is to be vested in a supreme court, and in such inferior courts as Congress may from time to time ordain and establish. The powers of these courts are very extensive; their jurisdiction comprehends all civil causes, except such as arise between citizens of the same state; and it extends to all cases in law and equity arising under the constitution. One inferior court must be established, I presume, in each state, at least, with the necessary executive officers appendant thereto. It is easy to see, that in the common course of things, these courts will eclipse the dignity, and take away from the respectability, of the state courts. These courts will be, in themselves, totally independent of the states, deriving their authority from the United States, and receiving from them fixed salaries; and in the course of human events it is to be expected, that they will swallow up all the powers of the courts in the respective states.

D

The Federalist

NUMBER 10

The Size and Variety of the Union as a Check on Faction

To the People of the State of New York:

Among the numerous advantages promised by a well-constructed Union, none deserves to be more accurately developed than its tendency to break and control the violence of faction. The friend of popular governments never finds himself so much alarmed for their character and fate, as when he contemplates their propensity to this dangerous vice. He will not fail, therefore, to set a due value on any plan which, without violating the principles to which he is attached, provides a proper cure for it. The instability, injustice, and confusion introduced into the public councils, have, in truth, been the mortal diseases under which popular governments have everywhere perished; as they continue to be the favorite and fruitful topics from which the adversaries to liberty derive their most specious declamations. The valuable improvements made by the American constitutions on the popular models, both ancient and modern, cannot certainly be too much admired; but it would be an unwarrantable partiality, to contend that they have as effectually obviated the danger on this side, as was wished and expected. Complaints are everywhere heard from our most considerate and virtuous citizens, equally the friends of public and private faith, and of public and personal liberty, that our governments are too unstable, that the public good is disregarded in the conflicts of rival parties, and that measures are too often decided, not according to the rules of justice and the rights of the minor party, but by the superior force of an interested and overbearing majority. However anxiously we may wish that these complaints had no foundation, the evidence of known facts will not permit us to deny that they are in some degree true. It will be found, indeed, on a candid review of our situation, that some of the distresses under which we labor have been erroneously charged on the operation of our governments; but it will be found, at the same time, that other causes will not alone account for many of our heaviest misfortunes; and, particularly, for that prevailing and increasing distrust of public engagements, and alarm for private rights, which are echoed from one end of the continent to the other. These must be chiefly, if not wholly, effects of the unsteadiness and injustice with which a factious spirit has tainted our public administrations.

By a faction, I understand a number of citizens, whether amounting to a majority or minority of the whole, who are united and actuated by some common impulse of passion, or of interest, adverse to the rights of other citizens, or to the permanent and aggregate interests of the community.

There are two methods of curing the mischiefs of faction: the one, by removing its causes; the other, by controlling its effects.

There are again two methods of removing the causes of faction: the one, by destroying the liberty which is essential to its existence; the other, by giving to every citizen the same opinions, the same passions, and the same interests.

It could never be more truly said than of the first remedy, that it was worse than the disease. Liberty is to faction what air is to fire, an aliment without which it instantly expires. But it could not be less folly to abolish liberty, which is essential to political life, because it nourishes faction, than it would be to wish the annihilation of air, which is essential to animal life, because it imparts to fire its destructive agency.

The second expedient is as impracticable as the first would be unwise. As long as the reason of man continues fallible, and he is at liberty to exercise it, different opinions will be formed. As long as the connection subsists between his reason and his self-love, his opinions and his passions will have a reciprocal influence on each other: and the former will be objects to which the latter will attach themselves.

The diversity in the faculties of men, from which the rights of property originate, is not less an insuperable obstacle to a uniformity of interests. The protection of these faculties is the first object of government. From the protection of different and unequal faculties of acquiring property, the possession of different degrees and kinds of property immediately results; and from the influence of these on the sentiments and views of the respective proprietors, ensues a division of the society into different interests and parties.

The latent causes of faction are thus sown in the nature of man; and we see them everywhere brought into different degrees of activity, according to the different circumstances of civil society. A zeal for different opinions concerning religion, concerning government, and many other points, as well of speculation as of practice; an attachment to different leaders ambitiously contending for preeminence and power; or to persons of other descriptions whose fortunes have been interesting to the human passions, have, in turn, divided mankind into parties, inflamed them with mutual animosity, and rendered them much more disposed to vex and oppress each other than to co-operate for their common good. So strong is this propensity of mankind to fall into mutual animosities, that where no substantial occasion presents itself, the most frivolous and fanciful distinctions have been sufficient to kindle their unfriendly passions and excite their most violent conflicts. But the most common and durable source of factions has been the various and unequal distribution of property. Those who hold and those who are without property have ever formed distinct interests in society. Those who are creditors, and those who are debtors, fall under a like discrimination. A landed interest, a manufacturing interest, a mercantile interest, a moneyed interest, with many lesser interests, grow up of necessity in civilized nations, and divide them into different classes, actuated by different sentiments and views. The regulation of these various and interfering interests forms the principal task of modern legislation, and involves the spirit of party and faction in the necessary and ordinary operations of the government.

No man is allowed to be a judge in his own cause, because his interest would certainly bias his judgment, and, not improbably, corrupt his integrity. With equal, nay with greater reason, a body of men are unfit to be both judges and parties at the same time; yet what are many of the most important acts of legislation, but so many judicial determinations, not indeed concerning the rights of single persons, but concerning the rights of large bodies of citizens? And what are the different classes of legislators but advocates and parties to the causes which they determine?

Is a law proposed concerning private debts? It is a question to which the creditors are parties on one side and the debtors on the other. Justice ought to hold the balance between them. Yet the parties are, and must be, themselves the judges; and the most numerous party, or, in other words, the most powerful faction must be expected to prevail. Shall domestic manufactures be encouraged, and in what degree, by restrictions on foreign manufactures? are questions which would be differently decided by the landed and the manufacturing classes, and probably by neither with a sole regard to justice and the public good. The apportionment of taxes on the various descriptions of property is an act which seems to require the most exact impartiality; yet there is, perhaps, no legislative act in which greater opportunity and temptation are given to a predominant party to trample on the rules of justice. Every shilling with which they overburden the inferior number is a shilling saved to their own pockets.

It is in vain to say that enlightened statesmen will be able to adjust these clashing interests, and render them all subservient to the public good. Enlightened statesmen will not always be at the helm. Nor, in many cases, can such an adjustment be made at all without taking into view indirect and remote considerations, which will rarely prevail over the immediate interests which one party may find in disregarding the rights of another or the good of the whole.

The inference to which we are brought is, that the *causes* of faction cannot be removed, and that relief is only to be sought in the means of controlling its *effects*.

If a faction consists of less than a majority, relief is supplied by the republican principle, which enables the majority to defeat its sinister views by regular vote. It may clog the administration, it may convulse the society; but it will be unable to execute and mask its violence under the forms of the Constitution. When a majority is included in a faction, the form of popular government, on the other hand, enables it to sacrifice to its ruling passion or interest both the public good and the rights of other citizens. To secure the public good and private rights against the danger of such a faction, and at the same time to preserve the spirit and the form of popular government, is then the great object to which our inquiries are directed. Let me add that it is the great desideratum by which this form of government can be rescued from the opprobrium under which it has so long labored, and be recommended to the esteem and adoption of mankind.

By what means is this object attainable? Evidently by one of two only. Either the existence of the same passion or interest in a majority at the same time must be prevented, or the majority, having such coexistent passion or interest, must be rendered, by their number and local situation, unable to concert and carry into effect schemes of oppression. If the impulse and the opportunity be suffered to coincide, we well know that neither moral nor religious motives can be relied on as an adequate control. They are not found to be such on the injustice and violence of individuals, and lose their efficacy in proportion to the number combined together, that is, in proportion as their efficacy becomes needful.

From this view of the subject it may be concluded that a pure democracy, by which I mean a society consisting of a small number of citizens, who assemble and administer the government in person, can admit of no cure for the mischiefs of faction. A common passion or interest will, in almost every case, be felt by a majority of the whole; a communication and concert result from the form of government itself; and there is nothing to check the inducements to sacrifice the weaker party or an obnoxious individual. Hence it is that such democracies have ever been spectacles of turbulence and contention; have ever been found incompatible with personal security or the rights of property; and have in general been as short in their lives as they have been violent in their deaths. Theoretic politicians, who have patronized this species of government, have erroneously supposed that by reducing mankind to a perfect equality in their political rights, they would, at the same time, be perfectly equalized and assimilated in their possessions, their opinions, and their passions.

A republic, by which I mean a government in which the scheme of representation takes place, opens a different prospect, and promises the cure for which we are seeking. Let us examine the points in which it varies from pure democracy, and we shall comprehend both the nature of the cure and the efficacy which it must derive from the Union.

The two great points of difference between a democracy and a republic are: first, the delegation of the government, in the latter, to a small number of citizens elected by the rest; secondly, the greater number of citizens, and greater sphere of country, over which the latter may be extended.

The effect of the first difference is, on the one hand, to refine and enlarge the public views, by passing them through the medium of a chosen body of citizens, whose wisdom may best discern the true interest of their country, and whose patriotism and love of justice will be least likely to sacrifice it to temporary or partial considerations. Under such a regulation, it may well happen that the public voice, pronounced by the representatives of the people, will be more consonant to the public good than if pronounced by the people themselves, convened for the purpose. On the other hand, the effect may be inverted. Men of factious tempers, of local prejudices, or of sinister designs, may, by intrigue, by corruption, or by other means, first obtain the suffrages, and then betray the interests, of the people. The question resulting is, whether small or extensive republics are more favorable to the election of proper guardians of the public weal; and it is clearly decided in favor of the latter by two obvious considerations:

In the first place, it is to be remarked that, however small the republic may be, the representatives must be raised to a certain number, in order to guard against the cabals of a few; and that, however large it may be, they must be limited to a certain number, in order to guard against the confusion of a multitude. Hence, the number of representatives in the two cases not being in proportion to that of the two constituents, and being proportionally greater in the small republic, it follows that, if the proportion of fit characters be not less in the large than in the small republic, the former will present a greater option, and consequently a greater probability of a fit choice.

In the next place, as each representative will be chosen by a greater number of citizens in the large than in the small republic, it will be more difficult for unworthy candidates to practise with success the vicious arts by which elections are too often carried; and the suffrages of the people being more free, will be more likely to centre in men who possess the most attractive merit and the most diffusive and established characters.

It must be confessed that in this, as in most other cases, there is a mean, on both sides of which inconveniences will be found to lie. By enlarging too much the number of electors, you render the representative too little acquainted with all their local circumstances and lesser interests; as by reducing it too much, you render him unduly attached to these, and too little fit to comprehend and pursue great and national objects. The federal Constitution forms a happy combination in this respect; the great and aggregate interests being referred to the national, the local and particular to the State legislatures.

The other point of difference is, the greater number of citizens and extent of territory which may be brought within the compass of republican than of democratic government; and it is this circumstance principally which renders factious combinations less to be dreaded in the former than in the latter. The smaller the society, the fewer probably will be the distinct parties and interests composing it; the fewer the distinct parties and interests, the more frequently will a majority be found of the same party; and the smaller the number of individuals composing a majority, and the smaller the compass within which they are placed, the most easily will they concert and execute their plans of oppression. Extend the sphere, and you take in a greater variety of parties and interests; you make it less probable that a majority of the whole will have a common motive to invade the rights of other citizens; or if such a common motive exists, it will be more difficult for all who feel it to discover their own strength, and to act in unison with each other. Besides other impediments, it may be remarked that, where there is a consciousness of unjust or dishonorable purposes, communication is always checked by distrust in proportion to the number whose concurrence is necessary.

Hence, it clearly appears, that the same advantage which a republic has over a democracy, in controlling the effects of faction, is enjoyed by a large over a small republic,—is enjoyed by the Union over the States composing it. Does the advantage consist in the substitution of representatives whose enlightened views and virtuous sentiments render them superior to local prejudices and to schemes of injustice? It will not be denied that the representation of the Union will be most likely to possess these requisite endowments. Does it consist in the greater security afforded by a greater variety of parties, against the event of any one party being able to outnumber and oppress the rest? In an equal degree does the increased variety of parties comprised within the Union, increase this security. Does it, in fine, consist in the greater obstacles opposed to the concert and accomplishments of the secret wishes of an unjust and interested majority? Here, again, the extent of the Union gives it the most palpable advantage.

The influence of factious leaders may kindle a flame within their particular States, but will be unable to spread a general conflagration through the other States. A religious sect may degenerate into a political faction in a part of the Confederacy; but the variety of sects dispersed over the entire face of it must secure the national councils against any danger from that source. A rage for paper money, for an abolition of debts, for an equal division of property, or for any other improper or wicked project, will be less apt to pervade the whole body of the Union than a particular member of it; in the same proportion as such a malady is more likely to taint a particular county or district, than an entire State.

In the extent and proper structure of the Union, therefore, we behold a republican remedy for the diseases most incident to republican government: And according to the degree of pleasure and pride we feel in being republicans, ought to be our zeal in cherishing the spirit and supporting the character of Federalists.

Publius
(James Madison)

NUMBER 51

Checks and Balances

To the People of the State of New York:

To What expedient, then, shall we finally resort, for maintaining in practice the necessary partition of power among the several departments, as laid down in the Constitution? The only answer that can be given is, that as all these exterior provisions are found to be inadequate, the defect must be supplied, by so contriving the interior structure of the government as that its several constituent parts may, by their mutual relations, be the means of keeping each other in their proper places. Without presuming to undertake a full development of this important idea, I will hazard a few general observations, which may perhaps place it in a clearer light, and enable us to form a more correct judgment of the principles and structure of the government planned by the convention.

In order to lay a due foundation for that separate and distinct exercise of the different powers of government, which to a certain extent is admitted on all hands to be essential to the preservation of liberty, it is evident that each department should have a will of its own; and consequently should be so constituted that the members of each should have as little agency as possible in the appointment of the members of the others. Were this principle rigorously adhered to, it would require that all the appointments for the supreme executive, legislative, and judiciary magistracies should be drawn from the same fountain of authority, the people, through channels having no communication whatever with one another. Perhaps such a plan of constructing the several departments would be less difficult in practice than it may in contemplation appear. Some difficulties, however, and some additional expense would attend the execution of it. Some deviations, therefore, from the principle must be admitted. In the constitution of the judiciary department in particular, it might be inexpedient to insist rigorously on the principle: first, because peculiar qualifications being essential in the members, the primary consideration ought to be to select that mode of choice which best secures these qualifications; secondly, because the permanent tenure by which the appointments are held in that department, must soon destroy all sense of dependence on the authority conferring them.

It is equally evident, that the members of each department should be as little dependent as possible on those of the others, for the emoluments annexed to their offices. Were the executive magistrate, or the judges, not independent of the legislature in this particular, their independence in every other would be merely nominal.

But the great security against a gradual concentration of the several powers in the same department, consists in giving to those who administer each department the necessary constitutional means and personal motives to resist encroachments of the others. The provision for defence must in this, as in all other cases, be made commensurate to the danger of attack. Ambition must be made to counteract ambition. The interest of the man must be connected with the constitutional rights of the place. It may be a reflection on human nature, that such devices should be necessary to control the abuses of government. But what is government itself, but the greatest of all reflections on human nature? If men were angels, no government would be necessary. If angels were to govern men, neither external nor internal controls on government would be necessary. In framing a government which is to be administered by men over men, the great difficulty lies in this: you must first enable the government to control the governed; and in the next place oblige it to control itself. A dependence on the people is, no doubt, the primary control on the government; but experience has taught mankind the necessity of auxiliary precautions.

This policy of supplying, by opposite and rival interests, the defect of better motives, might be traced through the whole system of human affairs, private as well as public. We see it particularly displayed in all the subordinate distributions of power, where the constant aim is to divide and arrange the several offices in such a manner as that each may be a check on the other—that the private interest of every individual may be a sentinel over the public rights. These inventions of prudence cannot be less requisite in the distribution of the supreme powers of the State.

But it is not possible to give to each department an equal power of self-defence. In republican government, the legislative authority necessarily predominates. The remedy for this inconveniency is to divide the legislature into different branches; and to render them, by different modes of election and different principles of action, as little connected with each other as the nature of their common functions and their common dependence on the society will admit. It may even be necessary to guard against dangerous encroachments by still further precautions. As the weight of the legislative authority requires that it should be thus divided, the weakness of the executive may require, on the other hand, that it should be fortified. An absolute negative on the legislature appears, at first view, to be the natural defence with which the executive magistrate should be armed. But perhaps it would be neither altogether safe not alone sufficient. On ordinary occasions it might not be exerted with the requisite firmness, and on extraordinary occasions it might be perfidiously abused. May not this defect of an absolute negative be supplied by some qualified connection between this weaker department and the weaker branch of the stronger department, by which the latter may be led to support the constitutional rights of the former, without being too much detached from the rights of its own department?

If the principles on which these observations are founded be just, as I persuade myself they are, and they be applied as a criterion to the several State constitutions, and to the federal Constitution, it will be found that if the latter does not perfectly correspond with them, the former are infinitely less able to bear such a test.

There are, moreover, two considerations particularly applicable to the federal system of America, which place that system in a very interesting point of view.

First. In a single republic, all the power surrendered by the people is submitted to the administration of a single government; and the usurpations are guarded against by a division of the government into distinct and separate departments. In the compound republic of America, the power surrendered by the people is first divided between two distinct governments, and then the portion allotted to each subdivided among distinct and separate departments. Hence a double security arises to the rights of the people. The different governments will control each other, at the same time that each will be controlled by itself.

Second. It is of great importance in a republic not only to guard the society against the oppression of its rulers, but to guard one part of the society against the injustice of the other part. Different interests necessarily exist in different classes of citizens. If a majority be united by a common interest, the rights of the minority will be insecure. There are but two methods of providing against this evil: the one by creating a will in the community independent of the majority— that is, of the society itself; the other, by comprehending in the society so many separate descriptions of citizens as will render an unjust combination of a majority of the whole very improbable, if not impracticable. The first method prevails in all governments possessing an hereditary or self-appointed authority. This, at best, is but a precarious security; because a power independent of the society may as well espouse the unjust views of the major, as the rightful interests of the minor party, and may possibly be turned against both parties. The second method will be exemplified in the federal republic of the United States. Whilst all authority in it will be derived from and dependent on the society, the society itself will be broken into so many parts, interests and classes of citizens, that the rights of individuals, or of the minority, will be in little danger from interested combinations of the majority. In a free government the security for civil rights must be the same as that for religious rights. It consists in the one case in the multiplicity of interests, and in the other in the multiplicity of sects. The degree of security in both cases will depend on the number of interests and sects; and this may be presumed to depend on the extent of country and number of people comprehended under the same government. This view of the subject must particularly recommend a proper federal system to all the sincere and considerate friends of republican government, since it shows that in exact proportion as the territory of the Union may be formed into more circumscribed Confederacies, or States, oppressive combinations of a majority will be facilitated; the best security, under the republican forms, for the rights of every class of citizens, will be diminished; and consequently the stability and independence of some members of the government, the only other security, must be proportionally increased. Justice is the end of government. It is the end of civil society. It ever has been and ever will be pursued until it be obtained, or until liberty be lost in the pursuit. In a society under the forms of which the stronger faction can readily unite and oppress the weaker, anarchy may as truly be said to reign as in a state of nature, where the weaker individual is not secured against the violence of the stronger; and as, in the latter state, even the stronger individuals are prompted, by the uncertainty of their condition, to submit to a government which may protect the weak as well as themselves; so, in the former state, will the more powerful factions or parties be gradually induced, by a like motive, to wish for a government which will protect all parties, the weaker as well as the more powerful. It can be little doubted that if the State of Rhode Island was separated from the Confederacy and left to itself, the insecurity of rights under the popular form of government within such narrow limits would be displayed by such reiterated oppressions of factious majorities that some power altogether independent of the people would soon be called for by the voice of the very factions whose misrule had proved the necessity of it. In the extended republic of the United States, and among the great variety of interests, parties, and sects which it embraces, a coalition of a majority of the whole society could seldom take place on any other principles than those of justice and the general good; whilst there being thus less danger to a minor from the will of a major party, there must be less pretext, also, to provide for the security of the former, by introducing into the government a will not dependent on the latter, or, in other words, a will independent of the society itself. It is no less certain than it is important, notwithstanding the contrary opinions which have been entertained, that the larger the society, provided it lie within a practical sphere, the more duly capable it will be of self-government. And happily for the *republican cause*, the practicable sphere may be carried to a very great extent, by a judicious modification and mixture of the *federal principle*.

Publius
(James Madison)

E The Constitution of the United States of America*

We the People of the United States, in Order to form a more perfect Union, establish Justice, insure domestic Tranquility, provide for the common defence, promote the general Welfare, and secure the Blessings of Liberty to ourselves and our Posterity, do ordain and establish this Constitution for the United States of America.

ARTICLE I

Section 1

(General Legislative Powers)

All legislative Powers herein granted shall be vested in a Congress of the United States, which shall consist of a Senate and House of Representatives.

Section 2

(House of Representatives, Elections, Qualifications, Officers, and Impeachment Power)

The House of Representatives shall be composed of Members chosen every second Year by the People of the several States, and the Electors in each State shall have the Qualifications requisite for Electors of the most numerous Branch of the State Legislature.

No Person shall be a Representative who shall not have attained the Age of twenty-five Years, and been seven Years a Citizen of the United States, and who shall not, when elected, be an Inhabitant of that State in which he shall be chosen.

Representatives and direct Taxes shall be apportioned among the several States which may be included within this Union, according to their respective Numbers, *which shall be determined by adding to the whole Number of free Persons, including those bound to Service for a Term of Years, and excluding Indians not taxed, three fifths of all other Persons.* The actual Enumeration shall be made within three Years after the first Meeting of the Congress of the United States, and within every subsequent Term of ten Years, in such Manner as they shall by Law direct. The Number of Representatives shall not exceed one for every thirty Thousand, but each State shall have at least one Representative; and until each enumeration shall be made, the State of New Hampshire shall be entitled to chuse three, Massachusetts eight, Rhode-Island and Providence Plantations one, Connecticut five, New-York six, New Jersey four, Pennsylvania eight, Delaware one, Maryland six, Virginia ten, North Carolina five, South Carolina five, and Georgia three.

When vacancies happen in the Representation from any State, the Executive Authority thereof shall issue Writs of Election to fill such Vacancies.

The House of Representatives shall chuse their Speaker and other Officers; and shall have the sole Power of Impeachment.

---

*Provisions in italics have been repealed or modified by subsequent amendment.

Section 3
(The Senate: Election, Qualifications, Officers, and Impeachment Trials)

The Senate of the United States shall be composed of two Senators from each State, *chosen by the Legislature thereof*, for six Years; and each Senator shall have one Vote.

Immediately after they shall be assembled in Consequence of the first Election, they shall be divided as equally as may be into three Classes. The Seats of the Senators of the first Class shall be vacated at the Expiration of the second Year, of the second Class at the Expiration of the fourth Year, and of the third Class at the Expiration of the sixth Year, so that one third may be chosen every second Year; *and if Vacancies happen by Resignation, or otherwise, during the Recess of the Legislature of any State, the Executive thereof may make temporary Appointments until the next Meeting of the Legislature, which shall then fill such Vacancies.*

No person shall be a Senator who shall not have attained to the Age of thirty Years, and been nine Years a Citizen of the United States, and who shall not, when elected, be an inhabitant of that State for which he shall be chosen.

The Vice President of the United States shall be President of the Senate, but shall have no Vote, unless they be equally divided.

The Senate shall chuse their other Officers, and also a President pro tempore, in the Absence of the Vice President, or when he shall exercise the Office of President of the United States.

The Senate shall have the sole Power to try all Impeachments. When sitting for that Purpose, they shall be on Oath or Affirmation. When the President of the United States is tried, the Chief Justice shall preside: And no Person shall be convicted without the Concurrence of two thirds of the Members present.

Judgment in Cases of Impeachment shall not extend further than to removal from Office, and disqualification to hold and enjoy any Office of honor, Trust or Profit under the United States; but the Party convicted shall nevertheless be liable and subject to Indictment, Trial, Judgment and Punishment, according to Law.

Section 4
(State Regulation of Congressional Elections)

The Times, Places and Manner of holding Elections for Senators and Representatives, shall be prescribed in each State by the Legislature thereof; but the Congress may at any time by Law make or alter such Regulations, except as to the Places of chusing Senators.

The Congress shall assemble at least once in every Year, *and such Meeting shall be on the first Monday in December, unless they shall by Law appoint a different Day.*

Section 5
(Congressional Rules and Procedures)

Each House shall be the Judge of the Elections, Returns and Qualifications of its own Members, and a Majority of each shall constitute a Quorum to do Business; but a smaller Number may adjourn from day to day, and may be authorized to compel the Attendance of absent Members, in such Manner, and under the Penalties as each House may provide.

Each House may determine the Rules of its Proceedings, punish its Members for disorderly Behavior, and, with the Concurrence of two thirds, expel a Member.

Each House shall keep a Journal of its Proceedings, and from time to time publish the same, excepting such Parts as may in their Judgment require Secrecy; and the Yeas and Nays of the members of either House on any question shall, at the Desire of one fifth of the present, be entered on the Journal.

Neither House, during the Session of Congress, shall, without the Consent of the other, adjourn for more than three days, nor to any other Place than that in which the two Houses shall be sitting.

Section 6
(Congressional Pay, Privileges, and Restrictions)

The Senators and Representatives shall receive a Compensation for their Services, to be ascertained by Law, and paid out of the Treasury of the United States. They shall in all Cases, except Treason, Felony and Breach of the Peace, be privileged from Arrest during their Attendance at the Session of their respective Houses, and in going to and returning from the same; and for any Speech or Debate in either House, they shall not be questioned in any other Place.

No Senator or Representative, shall, during the time for which he was elected, be appointed to any civil Office under the authority of the United States, which shall have been created, or the Emoluments whereof shall have been encreased during such time; and no Person holding any Office under the United States, shall be a Member of either House during his Continuance in Office.

Section 7
(Legislative Procedures)

All Bills for raising Revenue shall originate in the House of Representatives; but the Senate may propose or concur with Amendments as on other Bills.

Every Bill which shall have passed the House of Representatives and the Senate, shall, before it become a Law, be presented to the President of the United States; if he approve he shall sign it, but if not he shall return it, with his Objections to that House in which it shall have originated, who shall enter the Objections at large on their Journal, and proceed to reconsider it. If after such Reconsideration two thirds of that House shall agree to pass the Bill, it shall be sent, together with the Objections, to the other House, by which it shall likewise be reconsidered, and if approved by two thirds of that House, it shall become a Law. But in all such Cases the Votes of both Houses shall be determined by Yeas and Nays, and the Names of the Persons voting for and against the Bill shall be entered on the Journal of each House respectively. If any Bill shall not be returned by the President within ten Days (Sundays excepted) after it shall have been presented to him, the Same shall be a Law, in like Manner as if he had signed it, unless the Congress by their Adjournment prevent its Return, in which Case it shall not be a Law.

Every Order, Resolution, or Vote to which the Concurrence of the Senate and House of Representatives may be necessary (except on a question of Adjournment) shall be presented to the President of the United States; and before the Same shall take Effect, shall be approved by him, or being disapproved by him, shall be repassed by two thirds of the Senate and House of Representatives, according to the Rules and Limitations prescribed in the Case of a Bill.

Section 8
(Powers of Congress)

The Congress shall have Power

To lay and collect Taxes, Duties, Imposts and Excises, to pay the Debts and provide for the common Defence and general Welfare of the United States; but all Duties, Imposts and Excises shall be uniform throughout the United States;

To borrow Money on the Credit of the United States;

To regulate Commerce with foreign Nations, and among the several States, and with the Indian Tribes;

To establish an uniform Rule of Naturalization, and uniform Laws on the subject of Bankruptcies throughout the United States;

To coin Money, regulate the Value thereof, and of foreign Coin, and fix the Standard of Weights and Measures;

To provide for the Punishment of counterfeiting the Securities and current Coin of the United States;

To establish Post Offices and post Roads;

To promote the Progress of Science and useful Arts, by securing for limited Times to Authors and Inventors the exclusive Right to their respective Writings and Discoveries,

To constitute Tribunals inferior to the supreme Court,

To define and Punish Piracies and Felonies committed on the high Seas, and Offences against the Law of Nations;

To declare War, grant Letters of Marque and Reprisal, and make Rules concerning Captures on Land and Water;

To raise and support Armies, but no Appropriation of Money to that Use shall be for a longer Term than two Years;

To provide and maintain a Navy;

To make Rules for the Government and Regulation of the land and naval forces;

To provide for calling for the Militia to execute the Laws of the Union, suppress Insurrections and repel Invasions;

To provide for organizing, arming, and disciplining, the Militia, and for governing such Part of them as may be employed in the Service of the United States, reserving to the States respectively, the Appointment of the Officers, and the Authority of training the Militia according to the discipline prescribed by Congress;

To exercise exclusive Legislation in all Cases whatsoever, over such District (not exceeding ten Miles square) as may, by Cession of particular States, and the Acceptance of Congress, become the Seat of the Government of the United States, and to exercise like Authority over all Places purchased by the Consent of the Legislature of the State in which the Same shall be, for the Erection of Forts, Magazines, Arsenals, dock-Yards, and other needful Buildings;—And

To make all Laws which shall be necessary and proper for carrying into Execution the foregoing Powers, and all other Powers vested by this Constitution in the Government of the United States, or in any Department or Officer thereof.

Section 9
(Restrictions on Congressional Power)

The Migration or Importation of such Persons as any of the States now existing shall think proper to admit, shall not be prohibited by the Congress prior to the Year one thousand eight hundred and eight, but a Tax or Duty may be imposed on such Importation, not exceeding ten dollars for each Person.

The privilege of the Writ of Habeas Corpus shall not be suspended, unless when in Cases of Rebellion or Invasion the public Safety may require it.

No Bill of Attainder or ex post facto Laws shall be passed.

No Capitation, or other direct, Tax shall be laid, unless in Proportion to the Census or Enumeration herein before directed to be taken.

No Tax or Duty shall be laid on Articles exported from any State.

No Preference shall be given by any Regulation of Commerce or Revenue to the Ports of one State over those of another; nor shall Vessels bound to, or from, one State, be obliged to enter, clear, or pay Duties in another.

No Money shall be drawn from the Treasury, but in Consequence of Appropriations made by Law; and a regular Statement and Account of the Receipts and Expenditures of all public Money shall be published from time to time.

No Title of Nobility shall be granted by the United States; And no Person holding any Office of Profit or Trust under them, shall, without the Consent of the Congress, accept of any present, Emolument, Office, or Title, or any kind whatever, from any King, Prince, or foreign State.

Section 10
(Restriction on the Powers of the States)

No State shall enter into any Treaty, Alliance, or Confederation; grant Letters of Marque and Reprisal; coin Money; emit Bills of Credit; make any Thing but gold and silver Coin a Tender in Payment of Debts; pass any Bill of Attainder, ex post facto Law, or Law impairing the Obligation of Contracts, or grant any Title of Nobility.

No State shall, without the Consent of the Congress, lay any Imposts or Duties on Imports or Exports, except what may be absolutely necessary for executing its inspection Laws: and the net Produce of all Duties and Imposts, laid by any State on Imports or Exports, shall be for the Use of the Treasury of the United States; and all such Laws shall be subject to the Revision and Control of the Congress.

No State shall, without the Consent of Congress, lay any Duty of Tonnage, keep Troops, or Ships of War in time of Peace, enter into any Agreement or Compact with another State, or with a foreign Power, or engage in War, unless actually invaded, or in such imminent Danger as will not admit of Delay.

ARTICLE II

Section 1
(Presidential Power, Election, and Qualifications)

The executive Power shall be vested in a President of the United States of America. He shall hold his Office during the Term of four Years and, together with the Vice President, chosen for the same Term, be elected as follows:

Each State shall appoint, in such Manner as the Legislature thereof may direct, a Number of Electors, equal to the whole Number of Senators and Representatives to which the State may be entitled in the Congress: but no Senator or Representative, or Person holding an Office of Trust or Profit under the United States, shall be appointed an Elector.

The electors shall meet in their respective States, and vote by ballot for two Persons, of whom one at least shall not be an Inhabitant of the same State with themselves. And they shall make a List of all the Persons voted for, and of the Number of Votes for each; which List they shall sign and certify, and transmit sealed to the Seat of the Government of the United States, directed to the President of the Senate. The President of the Senate shall, in the Presence of the Senate and House of Representatives, open all the Certificates, and the Votes shall then be counted. The Person having the greatest Number of Votes shall be the President, if such Number be a Majority of the whole Number of Electors appointed; and if there be more than one who have such Majority and have an equal Number of Votes, then the House of Representatives shall immediately chuse by Ballot one of them for President; and if no person have a Majority, then from the five highest on the List the said House shall in like Manner chuse the President. But in chusing the President, the Votes shall be taken by States, the Representation from each State having one Vote; A quorum for this Purpose shall consist of a Member or Members from two-thirds of the States, and a Majority of all the States shall be necessary to a Choice. In every Case, after the Choice of the President, the person having the greatest Number of Votes of the Electors shall be the Vice President. But if there should remain two or more who have equal vote, the Senate shall chuse from them by Ballot the Vice President.

The Congress may determine the Time of chusing the Electors, and the Day on which they shall give their Votes; which Day shall be the same throughout the United States.

No person except a natural born Citizen, or a Citizen of the United States, at the time of the Adoption of this Constitution, shall be eligible to the Office of President; neither shall any Person be eligible to that Office who shall not have attained to the Age of thirty-five Years, and been fourteen Years a Resident within the United States.

In Case of the Removal of the President from Office, or of his Death, Resignation, or Inability to discharge the Powers and Duties of the said Office, the same shall devolve on the Vice President, and the Congress may by Law provide for the Case of Removal, Death, Resignation, or Inability, both of the President and Vice President, declaring what Officer shall then act as President, and such Officer shall act accordingly, until the Disability be removed, or a President shall be elected.

The President shall, at stated Times, receive for his Services, a Compensation, which shall neither be encreased nor diminished during the Period of which he shall have been elected, and he shall not receive within that Period any other Emolument from the United States, or any of them.

Before he enter on the Execution of his Office, he shall take the following oath or Affirmation:—"I do solemnly swear (or affirm) that I will faithfully execute the Office of President of the United States, and will to the best of my Ability, preserve, protect and defend the Constitution of the United States."

Section 2
(Powers of the President)

The President shall be the Commander in Chief of the Army and Navy of the United States, and of the Militia of the several States, when called into the actual Service of the United States, he may require the Opinion, in writing, of the principal Officer in each of the executive Departments, upon any Subject relating to the Duties of their respective Offices, and he shall have the Power to grant Reprieves and Pardons for Offences against the United States, except in Cases of Impeachment.

He shall have Power, by and with the Advice and Consent of the Senate to make Treaties, provided two thirds of the Senators present concur; and he shall nominate, and by and with the Advice and Consent of the Senate, shall appoint Ambassadors, other public Ministers and Consuls, Judges of the Supreme Court, and all other Offices of the United States, whose Appointments are not herein otherwise provided for, and which shall be established by Law: but the Congress may by Law vest the Appointment of such inferior Offices, as they think proper, in the President alone, in the Courts of Law, or in the Heads of Departments.

The President shall have Power to fill up all Vacancies that may happen during the Recess of the Senate, by granting Commissions which shall expire at the End of their next Session.

Section 3
(Presidential/Congressional Relationship)

He shall from time to time give to the Congress Information of the State of the Union, and recommend to their Consideration such Measures as he shall judge necessary and expedient; he may, on extraordinary Occasions, convene both Houses, or either of them, and in Case of Disagreement between them, with Respect to the Time of Adjournment, he may adjourn them to such Time as he shall think proper; he shall receive Ambassadors and other public Ministers; he shall take Care that the Laws be faithfully executed, and shall Commission all the Officers of the United States.

Section 4
(Impeachment)

The President, Vice President and all civil Officers of the United States, shall be removed from Office on Impeachment for, and Conviction of, Treason, Bribery, or other high Crimes and Misdemeanors.

ARTICLE III

Section 1
(Structure of the Judiciary)
The judicial Power of the United States, shall be vested in one supreme Court, and in such inferior Courts as the Congress may from time to time ordain and establish. The Judges, both of the supreme and inferior Courts, shall hold their Offices during good Behavior, and shall, at stated Times, receive for their Services, a Compensation, which shall not be diminished during their Continuance in Office.

Section 2
(Jurisdiction of Federal Courts)
The judicial Power shall extend to all Cases, in Law and Equity, arising under this Constitution, the Laws of the United States, and Treaties made, or which shall be made, under their Authority;—to all Cases affecting Ambassadors, other public Ministers and Consuls;—to all Cases of admiralty and maritime Jurisdiction;—to Controversies to which the United States shall be a party;—*between a State and Citizens of another state*;—between Citizens of different States;—between Citizens of the same State claiming Lands under Grants of different States, and between a State, or the Citizens thereof, and foreign States, Citizens, or Subjects.

In all Cases affecting Ambassadors, other public Ministers and Consuls, and those in which a State shall be Party, the supreme Court shall have original Jurisdiction. In all the other Cases before mentioned, the supreme Court shall have appellate Jurisdiction, both as to Law and Fact, with such Exceptions, and under such Regulations as Congress shall make.

The Trial of all Crimes, except in Cases of Impeachment, shall be by Jury; and such Trial shall be held in the State where the said Crimes shall have been committed; but when not committed within any State, the Trial shall be at such Place or Places as the Congress may by Law have directed.

Section 3
(Treason)
Treason against the United States, shall consist only in levying War against them, or in adhering to their Enemies, giving them Aid and Comfort.

No Person shall be convicted of Treason unless on the Testimony of two Witnesses to the same overt Act, or on Confession in open Court.

The Congress shall have Power to declare the Punishment of Treason, but no Attainder of Treason shall work Corruption of Blood, or Forfeiture except during the Life of the Person attainted.

ARTICLE IV

Section 1
(Faith and Credit Among States)
Full Faith and Credit shall be given in each State to the public Acts, Records, and judicial Proceedings of every other State. And the Congress may by general Laws prescribe the Manner in which such Acts, Records and Proceedings shall be proved, and the Effect thereof.

Section 2
(Privileges and Immunities)
The Citizens of each State shall be entitled to all Privileges and Immunities of Citizens in the several States.

A person charged in any State with Treason, Felony or other Crime, who shall flee from Justice, and be found in another State, shall on Demand of the executive Authority of the State from which he fled, be delivered up to be removed to the State having jurisdiction of the Crime.

No person held to Service or Labour in one State, under the Laws thereof, escaping into another, shall, in Consequence of any Law or Regulation therein, be discharged from such Service or Labour, but shall be delivered up on Claim of the Party to whom such Service or Labour may be due.

Section 3
(Admission of New States)
New States may be admitted by the Congress into this Union; but no new State shall be formed or erected within the Jurisdiction of any other State; nor any State be formed by the Junction of two or more States, or Parts of States, without the Consent of the Legislatures of the States concerned as well as of the Congress.

The Congress shall have Power to dispose of and make all needful Rules and Regulations respecting the Territory or other Property belonging to the United States; and nothing in this Constitution shall be so construed as to Prejudice any Claims of the United States, or of any particular State.

Section 4
(The States as Republican Governments)
The United States shall guarantee to every State in this Union a Republican Form of Government, and shall protect each of them against Invasion; and on Application of the Legislature, or of the Executive (when the Legislature cannot be convened) against domestic Violence.

ARTICLE V
(Amending the Constitution)
The Congress, whenever two thirds of both Houses shall deem it necessary, shall propose Amendments to this Constitution, or, on the Application of the Legislatures of two thirds of several States, shall call a Convention for proposing Amendments, which, in either Case, shall be valid to all Intents and Purposes, as Part of this Constitution, when ratified by the Legislatures of three fourths of the several States, or by Conventions in three fourths thereof, as the one or the other Mode of Ratification may be proposed by the Congress; Provided that no Amendment which may be made prior to the Year One thousand eight hundred and eight shall in any Manner affect the first and fourth Clauses in the Ninth Section of the first Article; and that no State, without its Consent, shall be deprived of its equal Suffrage in the Senate.

ARTICLE VI
(Debts, Supremacy, and Oath)
All Debts contracted and Engagements entered into, before the Adoption of this Constitution, shall be as valid against the United States under the Constitution, as under the Confederation.

This Constitution, and the Laws of the United States which shall be made in Pursuance thereof; and all Treaties made, or which shall be made, under the Authority of the United States, shall be the supreme Law of the Land; and the Judges in every State shall be bound thereby, any Thing in the Constitution or Laws of any State to the Contrary notwithstanding.

The Senators and Representatives before mentioned, and the Members of the several State Legislatures, and all executive and judicial Officers, both of the United States and of the several States, shall be bound by Oath or Affirmation, to support this Constitution; but no religious Test shall ever be required as a Qualification to any Office or public Trust under the United States.

ARTICLE VII
(Ratification)
The Ratification of the Conventions of nine States, shall be sufficient for the Establishment of this Constitution between the States so ratifying the Same.

Done in Convention by the Unanimous Consent of the States present the Seventeenth Day of September in the Year of our Lord one thousand seven hundred and Eighty seven and of the Independence of the United States of America the Twelfth. In Witness whereof We have hereunto subscribed our Names.

G:⁰ WASHINGTON—Presidt, and Deputy from Virginia

New Hampshire	{ John Langdon Nicholas Gilman
Massachusetts	{ Nathaniel Gorham Rufus King
Connecticut	{ Wm Saml Johnson Roger Sherman
New York	Alexander Hamilton
New Jersey	{ Wil: Livingston David Brearley Wm Paterson Jona: Dayton
Pennsylvania	{ B Franklin Thomas Mifflin Robt Morris Geo. Clymer Thos. FitzSimons Jared Ingersoll James Wilson Gouv Morris

Delaware	Geo Read Gunning Bedfor Jun John Dickinson Richard Bassett Jaco: Broom	North Carolina	Wm Blount Richd Dobbs Spaight Hu Williamson
Maryland	James McHenry Dan of St Thos. Jenifer Danl Carroll	South Carolina	J. Rutledge Charles Cotesworth Pinckney Charles Pinckney Pierce Butler
Virginia	John Blair— James Madison Jr.	Georgia	William Few Abr Baldwin

Amendments to the Constitution

(The first ten amendments, known as the Bill of Rights, were ratified and adopted on December 15, 1791.)

AMENDMENT I

(Freedom of Religion, Speech, Press, Assembly, and Petition)

Congress shall make no law respecting an establishment of religion, or prohibiting the free exercise thereof; or abridging the freedom of speech, or of the press; or the right of the people peaceably to assemble, and to petition the Government for a redress of grievances.

AMENDMENT II

(Freedom to Keep and Bear Arms)

A well regulated Militia, being necessary to the security of a free State, the right of the people to keep and bear Arms, shall not be infringed.

AMENDMENT III

(Quartering of Soldiers)

No Soldier shall, in time of peace be quartered in any house, without the consent of the Owner, nor in time of war, but in manner to be prescribed by law.

AMENDMENT IV

(Security from Unreasonable Searches and Seizures)

The right of the people to be secure in their persons, houses, papers, and effects, against unreasonable searches and seizures, shall not be violated, and no Warrants shall issue, but upon probable cause, supported by Oath or affirmation, and particularly describing the place to be searched, and the persons or things to be seized.

AMENDMENT V

(Rights of Accused Persons in Criminal Cases)

No person shall be held to answer for a capital, or otherwise infamous crime, unless on a presentment or indictment of a Grand Jury, except in cases arising in the land or naval forces, or in the Militia, when in actual service in time of War or in public danger; nor shall any person be subject for the same offence to be twice put in jeopardy of life or limb; nor shall be compelled in any Criminal Case to be a witness against himself, nor be deprived of life, liberty, or property, without due process of law; nor shall private property be taken for public use, without just compensation.

AMENDMENT VI

(Additional Rights of the Accused)

In all criminal prosecutions, the accused shall enjoy the right to a speedy and public trial, by an impartial jury of the State and district wherein the crime shall have been committed, which district shall have been previously ascertained by law, and to be informed of the nature and cause of the accusation; to be confronted with the witnesses against him; to have compulsory process for obtaining Witnesses in his favor, and to have the Assistance of Counsel for his defence.

AMENDMENT VII

(Rights in Common Law Suits)

In suits at common law, where the value in controversy shall exceed twenty dollars, the right of trial by jury shall be preserved, and no fact tried by a jury shall be otherwise re-examined in any Court of the United States, than according to the rules of the common law.

AMENDMENT VIII

(Bails, Fines, and Punishments)

Excessive bail shall not be required, nor excessive fines imposed, nor cruel and unusual punishments inflicted.

AMENDMENT IX

(Retention of Rights of the People)

The enumeration in the Constitution, of certain rights, shall not be construed to deny or disparage others retained by the people.

AMENDMENT X

(Reservation of Powers to the States or People)

The powers not delegated to the United States by the Constitution, nor prohibited by it to the States, are reserved to the States respectively, or to the people.

AMENDMENT XI

(Ratified on January 8, 1798.)
(Restriction of Judicial Power)

The Judicial power of the United States shall not be construed to extend to any suit in law or equity, commenced or prosecuted against one of the United States by Citizens of another State, or by Citizens or Subjects of any Foreign State.

AMENDMENT XII

(Ratified on September 25, 1804.)
(Election of President and Vice-President)

The Electors shall meet in their respective states, and vote by ballot for President and Vice-President, one of whom, at least, shall not be an inhabitant of the same state with themselves; they shall name in their ballots the person voted for as President, and in distinct ballots the person voted for as Vice-President, and they shall make distinct lists of all persons voted for as President, and of all persons voted for as Vice-President, and of the number of votes for each, which lists they shall sign and certify, and transmit sealed to the seat of the government of the United States, directed to the President of the Senate;—The President of the Senate shall, in presence of the Senate and House of Representatives, open all the certificates and the votes shall then be counted;—The person having the greatest number of votes for President, shall be the President, if such number be a majority of the whole number of Electors appointed; and if no person have such majority, then from the persons having the highest numbers not exceeding three on the list of those voted for as President, the House of Representatives shall choose immediately, by ballot, the President. But in choosing the President, the votes shall be taken by states, the representation from each state having one vote; a quorum for this purpose shall consist of a member or members from two thirds of the states, and a majority of all states shall be necessary to a choice. And if the House of Representatives shall not choose a President whenever the right of choice shall devolve upon them, *before the fourth day of March next following*, then the Vice-President shall act as President, as in the case of the death or other constitutional disability of the President. The person having the greatest number of votes as Vice-President, shall be the Vice-President, if such a number be a majority of the whole numbers of Electors appointed, and if no person have a majority, then from the two highest numbers on the list, the Senate shall choose the Vice-President; a quorum for the purpose shall consist of two-thirds of the whole number of Senators, and a majority of the whole number shall be necessary to a choice. But no person constitutionally ineligible to the office of President shall be eligible to that of Vice-President of the United States.

AMENDMENT XIII

(Ratified on December 18, 1865.)

Section 1
(Abolition of Slavery)

Neither slavery nor involuntary servitude, except as a punishment for crime whereof the party shall have been duly convicted, shall exist within the United States, or any place subject to their jurisdiction.

Section 2

Congress shall have power to enforce this article by appropriate legislation.

AMENDMENT XIV

(Ratified on July 28, 1868.)

Section 1
(Rights of Citizenship)

All persons born or naturalized in the United States, and subject to the jurisdiction thereof, are citizens of the United States and of the State wherein they reside. No State shall make or enforce any law which shall abridge the privileges or immunities of citizens of the United States; nor shall any State deprive any person of life, liberty, or property, without due process of law; nor deny to any person within its jurisdiction the equal protection of the laws.

Section 2
(Representation in Congress)

Representatives shall be apportioned among the several States according to their respective numbers, counting the whole number of persons in each State, excluding Indians not taxed. But when the right to vote at any election for the choice of electors for President and Vice-President of the United States, Representatives in Congress, the Executive and Judicial officers of a State, or the members of the Legislature thereof, is denied to any of the male inhabitants of such State, being twenty-one years of age, and citizens of the United States, or in any way abridged, except for participation in rebellion, or other crime, the basis of representation therein shall be reduced in the proportion which the number of such male citizens shall bear to the whole number of male citizens twenty-one years of age in such State.

Section 3
(Restriction on Eligibility to Hold Office)

No person shall be a Senator or Representative in Congress, or elector of President and Vice-President, or hold any office, civil or military, under the United States, or under any State, who, having previously taken an oath, as a member of Congress, or as an officer of the United States, or as a member of any State legislature, or as an executive or judicial officer of any State, to support the Constitution of the United States, shall have engaged in insurrection or rebellion against the same, or given aid or comfort to the enemies thereof. But Congress may by a vote of two-thirds of each House, remove such disability.

Section 4
(Definition of Public Debts)

The validity of the public debt of the United States, authorized by law, including debts incurred for payment of pensions and bounties for services in suppressing insurrection or rebellion, shall not be questioned. But neither the United States nor any State shall assume or pay any debt or obligation incurred in aid of insurrection or rebellion against the United States, or any claim for the loss or emancipation of any slave; but all such debts, obligations and claims shall be held illegal and void.

Section 5

The Congress shall have power to enforce, by appropriate legislation, the provisions of this article.

AMENDMENT XV

(Ratified on March 30, 1870.)

Section 1
(Black Suffrage)

The right of citizens of the United States to vote shall not be denied or abridged by the United States or by any State on account of race, color, or previous condition of servitude.

Section 2

The Congress shall have power to enforce this article by appropriate legislation.

AMENDMENT XVI

(Ratified on February 25, 1913.)
(Personal Income Taxes)

The Congress shall have power to lay and collect taxes on incomes, from whatever source derived, without apportionment among the several States, and without regard to any census or enumeration.

AMENDMENT XVII

(Ratified on May 31, 1913.)
(Popular Election of Senators)

The Senate of the United States shall be composed of two Senators from each State, elected by the people thereof, for six years; and each Senator shall have one vote. The electors in each State shall have the qualifications requisite for electors of the most numerous branch of the State Legislature.

When vacancies happen in the representation of any State in the Senate, the executive authority of such State shall issue writs of election to fill such vacancies; Provided, That the Legislature of any State may empower the executive thereof to make temporary appointment until the people fill the vacancies by election as the Legislature may direct.

This amendment shall not be so construed as to affect the election or term of any Senator chosen before it becomes valid as part of the Constitution.

AMENDMENT XVIII

(Ratified on January 29, 1919.)

Section 1
(Prohibition of Liquor)

After one year from the ratification of this article the manufacture, sale, or transportation of intoxicating liquors within, the importation thereof into, or the exportation thereof from the United States and all territory subject to the jurisdiction thereof for beverage purposes is hereby prohibited.

Section 2
(Enforcement Power)

The Congress and the several states shall have concurrent power to enforce this article by appropriate legislation.

Section 3
(Provision for Ratification)

This article shall be inoperative unless it shall have been ratified as an amendment to the Constitution by the legislatures of the several states, as provided in the Constitution, within seven years from the date of the submission hereof to the states by the Congress.

AMENDMENT XIX

(Ratified on August 26, 1920.)
(Women's Suffrage)

The right of the citizens of the United States to vote shall not be denied or abridged by the United States or by any state on account of sex.

Congress shall have power, by appropriate legislation, to enforce the provision of this article.

AMENDMENT XX

(Ratified on February 6, 1933.)

Section 1
(Terms of Presidential and Vice-Presidential Office)

The terms of the President and Vice-President shall end at noon on the 20th day of January, and the terms of the Senators and Representatives at noon on the 3rd day of January, of the years in which such terms would have ended if this article had not been ratified; and the terms of their successors shall then begin.

Section 2
(Time of Convening Congress)
The Congress shall assemble at least once in every year, and such meeting shall begin at noon on the 3rd day of January, unless they shall by law appoint a different day.

Section 3
(Death of President-Elect)
If, at the time fixed for the beginning of the term of the President, the President-elect shall have died, the Vice-President elect shall become President. If a President shall not have been chosen before the time fixed for the beginning of his term, or if the President-elect shall have failed to qualify, then the Vice-President elect shall act as President until a President shall have qualified; and the Congress may by law provide for the case wherein neither a President-elect nor a Vice-President elect shall have qualified, declaring who shall then act as President, or the manner in which one who is to act shall be selected, and such person shall act accordingly until a President or Vice-President shall have qualified.

Section 4
(Presidential Succession)
The Congress may by law provide for the case of the death of any of the persons from whom the House of Representatives may choose a President whenever the right of choice shall have developed upon them, and for the case of the death of any of the persons from whom the Senate may choose a Vice-President whenever the right of choice shall have devolved upon them.

Section 5
Sections 1 and 2 shall take effect on the 15th day of October following the ratification of this article.

Section 6
This article shall be inoperative unless it shall have been ratified as an amendment to the Constitution by the legislatures of three-fourths of the several States within seven years from the date of its submission.

AMENDMENT XXI
(Ratified on December 5, 1933.)
Section 1
(Repeal of Liquor Prohibition)
The eighteenth article of amendment to the Constitution of the United States is hereby repealed.

Section 2
("Dry" States)
The transportation or importation into any State, Territory, or Possession of the United States for delivery or use therein of intoxicating liquors, in violation of the laws thereof, is hereby prohibited.

Section 3
This article shall be inoperative unless it shall have been ratified as an amendment to the Constitution by conventions in the several States, as provided in the Constitution, within seven years from the date of the submission hereof to the States by the Congress.

AMENDMENT XXII
(Ratified on February 26, 1951.)
Section 1[48]
(Limitation on Presidential Term in Office)
No person shall be elected to the office of the President more than twice, and no person who has held the office of President, or acted as President, for more than two years of a term to which some other person was elected President shall be elected to the Office of the President more than once. But this Article shall not apply to any person holding the office of President when this article was proposed by the Congress, and shall not pre-

vent any person who may be holding the office of President, or acting as President, during the term within which this Article becomes operative from holding the office of President or acting as President during the remainder of such term.

Section 2
This Article shall be inoperative unless it shall have been ratified as an amendment to the Constitution by the legislatures of three-fourths of the several states within seven years from the date of its submission to the States by the Congress.

AMENDMENT XXIII
(Ratified on March 29, 1961.)

Section 1
(Electoral Votes for the District of Columbia)
The District constituting the seat of Government of the United States shall appoint in such manner as the Congress may direct:

A number of electors of President and Vice-President equal to the whole number of Senators and Representatives in Congress to which the District would be entitled if it were a State, but in no event more than the least populous State; they shall be in addition to those appointed by the States, but they shall be considered, for the purposes of the election of President and Vice-President, to be electors appointed by a State; and they shall meet in the District and perform such duties as provided by the twelfth article of amendment.

Section 2
The Congress shall have power to enforce this article by appropriate legislation.

AMENDMENT XXIV
(Ratified on January 23, 1964.)

Section 1
(Poll Tax Abolished)
The right of citizens of the United States to vote in any primary or other election for President or Vice-President, for electors for President or Vice-President, or for Senator or Representative in Con-

gress, shall not be denied or abridged by the United States or any State by reasons of failure to pay any poll tax or other tax.

Section 2
The Congress shall have power to enforce this article by appropriate legislation.

AMENDMENT XXV
(Ratified on February 10, 1967.)

Section 1
(Presidential Succession)
In case of the removal of the President from office or his death or resignation, the Vice-President shall become President.

Section 2
(Vice-Presidential Succession)
Whenever there is a vacancy in the office of the Vice-President, the President shall nominate a Vice-President who shall take the office upon confirmation by a majority vote of both houses of Congress.

Section 3
(Presidential Disability)
Whenever the President transmits to the President pro tempore of the Senate and the Speaker of the House of Representatives his written declaration that he is unable to discharge the powers and duties of his office, and until he transmits to them a written declaration to the contrary, such powers and duties shall be discharged by the Vice-President as Acting President.

Section 4
(Congressional Power to Declare and to End Presidential Disability)
Whenever the Vice-President and a majority of either the principal officers of the executive departments, or of such other body as Congress may by law provide, transmit to the President pro tem-

pore of the Senate and the Speaker of the House of Representatives their written declaration that the President is unable to discharge the powers and duties of his office, the Vice-President shall immediately assume the powers and duties of the office as Acting President.

Thereafter, when the President transmits to the President pro tempore of the Senate and the Speaker of the House of Representatives his written declaration that no inability exists, he shall resume the powers and duties of his office unless the Vice-President and a majority of either the principal officers of the executive departments, or of such other body as Congress may by law provide, transmit within four days to the President pro tempore of the Senate and the Speaker of the House of Representatives their written declaration that the President is unable to discharge the powers and duties of his office. Thereupon Congress shall decide the issue, assembling within 48 hours for that purpose if not in session. If the Congress, within 21 days after receipt of the latter written declaration, or, if Congress is not in session, within 21 days after Congress is required to assemble, determines by two-thirds vote of both houses that the President is unable to discharge the powers and duties of his office, the Vice-President shall continue to discharge the same as Acting President; otherwise, the President shall resume the powers and duties of his office.

AMENDMENT XXVI

(Ratified on June 30, 1971.)

Section 1

The right of citizens of the United States, who are eighteen years of age, or older, to vote shall not be denied or abridged by the United States or by any state on account of age.

Section 2

The Congress shall have power to enforce this article by appropriate legislation.

Glossary

administrative law The rules and regulations issued by departments and agencies of the executive branch of government.

adversary system A judicial process characterized by the conflict of two or more opposing parties before an impartial third party, the court.

affirmative action Programs created by government and private organizations that are designed to provide greater opportunities for women, African-Americans, and other minority groups who have been victims of past discrimination.

agency An organization within the federal bureaucracy that is headed by a single administrator and performs specialized functions but does not have departmental status.

amendment A formal addition to the Constitution that either changes one of its sections or adds matters that were not included in the original document.

amicus curiae brief ("friend of the court") A written brief in support of one of the parties in a legal dispute that attempts to influence the decision of the court.

Antifederalists Opponents of the Constitution of 1787 who wanted to preserve the authority of state governments.

appellate jurisdiction The authority of a court to review on appeal the decisions of lower courts.

appropriation bill A bill that allocates funds to a program of the executive branch of government.

Articles of Confederation The document that created the United States' first central government. It was ratified in 1781 and remained in effect until 1788. Congress, the only branch of government created by the Articles, did not have the power to tax or to regulate commerce and was unable to address the economic problems of the nation.

authorization bill A bill that permits the executive branch of government to undertake a specific program and limits the amount of money that may be spent on it.

bill of attainder An act of a legislature that singles out specific persons or groups and orders them to be punished without judicial trial. Such acts are prohibited by the Constitution.

bill of information A method of obtaining an indictment in which the public prosecutor presents a written statement of the evidence to a judge or magistrate.

Bill of Rights The first ten amendments to the Constitution, ratified in 1791. These amendments guarantee the basic rights of citizens.

blanket primary A type of primary election in which voters do not have to declare a choice of political party and are free to vote in more than one primary (e.g., voting Republican for one office and Democratic for another).

block grant A sum of money that is given by the national government to a state to be used for a broad, general purpose.

brief A written argument submitted to the court by attorneys for the parties in a case.

bureau The largest working subunit of an executive department that performs specific functions.

bureaucracy A way of organizing people to achieve a specific goal; a means to get work done.

Cabinet A body that advises the President and serves to coordinate and implement governmental policy. It is composed of the heads of the executive departments. Other high officials, including the Vice President, may also attend cabinet meetings.

calendar Bills reported from a standing committee of Congress are assigned to a calendar, which is used to schedule debate on the floor of the House and Senate.

caucus A meeting of party members at the local or precinct level to select delegates to the national convention. Also, a meeting of all the members of one party in the House or the Senate.

checks and balances A system of organizing the power of government in which the executive, legislative, and judicial branches possess some power over each other's activities, thus preventing arbitrary action by any one branch.

civil law Law that defines the legal rights of citizens and thereby provides rules for resolving disputes between individuals and/or corporations or between individuals and/or corporations and the government.

civil liberties The rights of the individual that are guaranteed by the United States Constitution.

civil rights The right of individuals not to be discriminated against on the basis of their race, sex, or nationality.

civil service A system of employing government workers that is based on merit and grants tenure to those employees.

class action suit A legal action brought by one or more individuals as representatives of a group of similarly situated persons.

closed primary A primary election in which participation is limited to voters who have formally registered as members of a particular political party.

cloture vote A procedure to end debate in a legislative body in order to obtain a vote on a bill that is being considered by that body.

coattail effect The ability of a popular presidential candidate to help elect legislative candidates of his party in a presidential election.

commercial speech Advertising used for business purposes. The Supreme Court has granted First Amendment protection to certain forms of truthful commercial advertising when used by lawyers, doctors, and other professional people.

common law Law established by past judicial decisions, often referred to as "judge-made" law.

concurrent powers Powers that are shared by the state and national governments.

concurring opinion A written opinion of a judge who agrees with the decision of the majority but feels that the majority opinion does not adequately express his own reasoning.

confederation A system in which the legal power of government is held by state governments; the central government has only the powers that have been given to it by those governments.

conference committee A joint committee composed of members from each house of Congress, whose purpose is to create a compromise version of a bill that has been passed by both houses in different forms.

confrontation clause Part of the Sixth Amendment to the Constitution requires that in all criminal cases an accused person has the right to confront the witnesses who testify for the government.

Connecticut Compromise A compromise between the New Jersey and Virginia plans worked out at the Constitutional Convention. It was agreed that the national legislature would be bicameral, and representation in the House of Representatives would be based on population, but in the Senate each state would have equal representation.

Constitutional Convention A meeting in 1787 of fifty-five delegates selected by the states to revise the Articles of Confederation. The result of the Convention was, however, an entirely new constitution, which was ratified in 1788.

constitutional court A court authorized and created under the provisions of Article III, Section 1, of the Constitution.

constitutional democracy A form of democratic government that places limits on the power of a majority to act and defines these limits in a written constitution.

constitutional law Law based on the provisions of state and federal constitutions.

convention A meeting of either elected or appointed members of a political party that may nominate candidates for public office, elect party officials and delegates, and write party platforms.

criminal law Law that defines acts that constitute a violation of the public order and provides specific punishments for these acts.

de facto segregation Segregation ("in fact") that is a product of private actions and not of governmental policies.

defamation Spoken or written words that are false and hold an individual up to public ridicule and contempt. (See **libel** and **slander**.)

defendant The party against whom a legal suit is brought.

de jure segregation Segregation ("by law") that has been created by the policies and actions of government.

delegated powers Powers specifically granted by the Constitution to the federal government, especially those given to Congress by Article I, Section 8.

democracy A system of government in which the policy decisions of the government rest on the freely given consent of the people and that guarantees certain basic rights such as freedom of speech and the right to vote.

department The major administrative unit within the federal bureaucracy, headed by a Secretary who is a member of the cabinet.

deregulation A process by which supervisory laws and regulations are removed from various parts of the economy.

direct democracy A form of democracy in which the people themselves meet to discuss and decide issues of public policy.

discharge petition A petition that requires the signatures of a majority (218) of the members of the House of Representatives in order to remove a bill from a standing committee and bring it to the floor of the House for consideration.

dissenting opinion An opinion written by a judge to record his disagreement with the majority decision and to express his reasons for voting against it.

double jeopardy The retrial of an individual for a crime of which he or she has already been acquitted. Double jeopardy is prohibited by the Fifth Amendment in federal courts and by the due process clause of the Fourteenth Amendment in state prosecutions.

due process clause Section 1 of the Fourteenth Amendment, which declares that no state ". . . shall . . . deprive any person of life, liberty, or property without due process of law. . . ." Also found in the Fifth Amendment to the Constitution.

electoral college The name given to the group of electors chosen in each state in the November voting and who actually elect the President and the Vice President.

elitists A school of political thought which believes that political power in the United States is concentrated in the hands of the few.

English Bill of Rights A list of the rights of Englishmen adopted by Parliament in 1689. Included in the list are the right to trial by jury and the right to petition the government for the redress of grievances.

equal protection clause Section 1 of the Fourteenth Amendment, which declares that no state shall "deny to any person within its jurisdiction the equal protection of the laws."

equity A system of law that provides relief in situations in which common law or statutory remedies are inadequate, especially through the issuance of injunctions to prevent injuries.

establishment clause A provision of the First Amendment that limits the power of Congress to create a state religion or provide aid to any religion by legislation. This restriction also applies to state governments through the due process clause of the Fourteenth Amendment.

exclusionary rule of evidence A requirement that any evidence in a criminal case obtained illegally by police cannot be used as evidence in a trial.

executive agreement An international agreement between the United States and a foreign nation made by the President; unlike a treaty, it does not require the advice and consent of two-thirds of the Senate, but it has the same legal status as a treaty.

ex post facto law A law that imposes a penalty for performing an act that was not considered criminal when it was committed, or that increases the punishment for a crime after it has been committed. Such laws are prohibited by the Constitution.

federalism A system in which the legal power of government is divided between a central or national government and smaller units of state government, usually under the authority of a written constitution.

Federalists Supporters of the Constitution of 1787 who favored a stronger national government.

felony The more serious forms of crimes such as robbery or murder.

field service The regional, state, and local subunits of the federal bureaucracy.

filibuster The use of extended speaking by a minority in the Senate to prevent the passage of a bill favored by the majority.

First Continental Congress A meeting of delegates from twelve colonies in 1774 for the purpose of coordinating colonial opposition to the policies of Great Britain.

free exercise clause A provision of the First Amendment that prohibits the national government from restricting an individual's right to the free exercise of his or her religion, as long as the religious practices involved do not violate the law. The free exercise clause is also applicable to the states through the due process clause of the Fourteenth Amendment.

full faith and credit clause A provision of Article IV, Section 1, of the Constitution that requires states to honor the final civil rulings of other states.

gerrymandering The division of a state, county, or city into voting districts in such a way as to give an unfair advantage to one party in elections.

government The institutions and processes by which decisions or rules are made and enforced for all members of a society.

government corporation A governmental body that, under policy regulations established by Congress, provides a public service but is organized like a private business corporation.

grandfather clause A device used by southern states during the late nineteenth century and early twentieth century to disfranchise blacks. The grandfather clause excused most whites from taking literacy tests by allowing all who had voted prior to 1867, or whose ancestors had voted before that date, to vote in future elections without having to pass such a test.

grand jury A jury that decides whether there is enough evidence to indict and bring to trial a person accused of a criminal act. Grand jury indictment is required in federal cases involving capital or otherwise infamous crimes.

grant-in-aid A sum of money that is given by a higher level of government to a lower level to help finance programs.

guarantee clause Article IV, Section 4, of the Constitution, which provides that the United States ". . . shall guarantee to every state in this Union a republican form of government. . . ."

impeachment Indictment of the President, Vice President, federal judges, or other civil officers of the United States by the House of Representatives on charges of treason, brib-

ery, and other high crimes and misdemeanors. Conviction and removal from office requires a two-thirds majority of the senators present to vote.

implied powers Powers given to Congress in the necessary and proper clause of Article I, Section 8, of the Constitution, which enables the federal government to carry out its delegated powers by any constitutional means.

impoundment A President's refusal to spend money that has been appropriated by an act of Congress. A 1974 law sharply limited the President's right to impound money.

independent A voter who does not identify with a political party.

independent regulatory commission A government agency that is responsible for the regulation of a major sphere of the economy. It is headed by a number of commissioners who are appointed by the President, with the advice and consent of the Senate, for overlapping terms. The commissioners exercise executive, legislative, and judicial powers.

indictment A formal accusation of a named person with the commission of specific criminal acts; the indictment is made either by a grand jury or a bill of information.

injunction A court order issued by an equity court forbidding a person or group of persons from committing an act that they are attempting to commit, or restraining them from continuing to commit such an act, or requiring them to perform an act.

interest group An organization of people who share certain attitudes and interests and try to affect the political system by shaping public opinion, opposing or supporting candidates for public office, and influencing the decisions of government officials, especially legislators and administrators.

interstate compact An agreement between two or more states, adopted by the state legislatures and often approved by Congress, in which arrangements are made to deal with interstate problems.

interstate rendition clause Article IV, Section 2, of the Constitution, which provides that an individual who is charged with a crime in one state and is found in another state may be returned to the state with jurisdiction over the crime.

item veto Rejection of specific provisions or items in a bill passed by a legislature. Although the President does not have this power, most state governors do.

Jim Crow laws Laws that enforced the practice of segregation or discrimination against blacks in public places, employment, and so on.

joint committee A committee, composed of members from both the House and the Senate, that has been created to deal with issues that require joint consideration.

judicial activism The belief that the judiciary should be willing to exercise its authority to declare unconstitutional actions of the other branches of government and to establish new rules of public policy.

judicial review The power of a court, and especially the Supreme Court, to review the acts of legislative bodies and executive officials to determine whether these acts are consistent with the Constitution.

judicial self-restraint The belief that judges should exercise self-control in using their judicial power and should generally defer to the policies of the elected branches of the government.

jurisdiction The legal authority of a court to hear a particular kind of case.

law Principles and regulations established by a government that are applicable to the people and enforced by the government.

legislative court A court created by Congress under Article I, Section 8, of the Constitution.

legislative veto A device used by Congress to control executive power. Many laws contain provisions that a presidential policy can be rejected if one or both houses of Congress adopt a concurrent resolution that opposes the decision of the President. The concurrent resolution is not submitted to the President and is, therefore, not subject to his veto. Declared unconstitutional by the Supreme Court in the 1983 case of *INS* v. *Chadha*.

legitimacy The belief that certain principles or rules are right and proper; according to Max Weber it is based on tradition, charisma, and legality.

libel Written material that publicly defames the character of an individual.

line agency An agency that carries out government policies and provides various types of services.

literacy test A written or oral test used to determine eligibility for voting. Used by Southern states from the late nineteenth century until the 1960s to prevent African-Americans from voting.

lobbying Attempting to influence government policy by persuading legislators to vote for or against a particular proposal or by convincing members of the executive branch of government that a particular program is or is not desirable. Lobbying is the primary method used by interest groups to affect public decisions.

Magna Charta An English document of 1215 stating that the king was to be bound by the law and was to respect the rights of his subjects.

majority leader A legislator, chosen by the majority party in each house of Congress, who serves as a chief strategist for the party and as spokesperson for the majority party's position on issues.

majority opinion An opinion of a court that has the support of a majority of the members of the court.

majority rule A basic principle of democracy under which public policy is set by the freely given consent of the majority, either directly by the people or through elected officials, but limited by the recognition of certain basic rights of the minority.

merit system The civil service system established by the Pendleton Act in 1883, in which people compete for jobs in the federal government and are hired on the basis of ability as demonstrated in a standardized test.

minority leader A legislator, chosen by the minority party in each house of Congress, who serves as a chief strategist for the party and as spokesperson for the minority party's position on issues.

minority rights Those rights of the minority recognized in a democracy. These include the rights to vote, to run for political office, and to express dissenting political opinions. In the American system of government, these rights are found in the Constitution and especially in the Bill of Rights and the Fourteenth Amendment.

minor party A political party that lacks the power or resources to get its candidates elected but exists to oppose present policies and to advance its own ideas.

misdemeanor Less serious forms of crimes such as trespassing.

multiparty system A political system in which there are more than two major political parties.

national chair The top official in the national organization of a major political party, who acts as the party's national spokesperson.

national committee The executive committee of the national party. Its members, who serve four-year terms, are formally elected by the national convention but in reality are chosen by the state parties by such methods as direct primary or state convention, depending on state procedures.

national convention A national meeting, held by each major party every four years, at which elected or appointed delegates nominate candidates for President and Vice President.

national supremacy The doctrine, set forth in Article VI of the Constitution, that the Constitution and all national laws and treaties are the supreme law of the land.

necessary and proper clause Article I, Section 8, of the Constitution, which provides that Congress can ". . . make all laws which shall be necessary and proper for carrying into execution . . ." its delegated powers and the powers of any other branch of the United States government.

New Jersey Plan An alternative to the Virginia Plan presented to the Constitutional Convention by William Paterson of New Jersey. It called for a unicameral legislature that would have the authority to tax and to regulate interstate commerce, a national executive office presided over by two people, and a national judiciary.

no prior restraint Censoring or preventing the publication of material before it is actually released.

open primary A direct primary in which a voter may choose the party primary in which he or she wishes to vote without having formally registered as a party member.

original jurisdiction The authority of a trial court to hear a case "in the first instance."

override A situation in which a president vetoes a bill, and it must be returned to the Congress. If both houses of Congress then approve the bill by a two-thirds vote, the bill becomes law.

oversight The power of Congress to supervise the activities of executive departments and agencies.

party identification The loyalty of voters to a particular political party.

party platform A political party's statement of general policy, adopted at the party's national convention.

party vote Legislative votes in which a large percentage of one party votes for a bill while a large percentage of the opposing party votes against it.

plaintiff The party who brings suit or initiates court action.

plea bargaining An agreement between an accused person and an attorney for the government in which the former agrees to enter a plea of guilty to a lesser criminal charge in return for the government's dismissal of more serious charges.

pluralists A school of political thought that believes that political power in the United States is dispersed among many individuals and groups.

popular sovereignty The political and legal idea that the people are the source of all lawful authority in a society.

pocket veto A form of veto power. Bills that are sent to the President during the ten-day period before the adjournment of a session of Congress automatically die unless the President signs the legislation.

policy agenda A list of proposals on problems that government officials are concerned with at a given time.

political action committee (PAC) A group created by labor unions, business corporations, or private individuals and groups to engage in political activities and campaign spending.

political culture The fundamental, widely supported values that hold a society together and give legitimacy to its political institutions.

political executive A government employee who is appointed by the President with the advice and consent of the Senate.

political opinion Attitudes expressed by members of a particular community on political issues.

political party An organization that attempts to influence the political system by gaining the support of voters and especially by getting its members elected or appointed to public office.

political power The influence of an individual or group on the political behavior of others.

political socialization The process by which people form political opinions; it is influenced by group membership, social categories, and historical events and political issues.

political system A set of institutions whose activities result in the authoritative decisions that become public policy.

politics A process by which values are authoritatively allocated for a society; a method of deciding who gets what from government.

poll tax A special tax, formerly used in the South as a requirement for voting, that prevented many blacks and poor whites from voting.

precinct The basic unit of party organization in many states, corresponding to the small local area in which elections are administered.

presidential primary A primary election used by a majority of states to select delegates to the presidential nominating conventions of the major political parties.

President of the Senate The presiding officer of the Senate, who is also the Vice President of the United States.

President pro tempore ("for the time being") A senator who is elected by the majority party to preside in the absence of the President of the Senate.

primary An election in which voters select a political party's candidates for local, state, and national office and in some states select party officials, such as members of party committees, convention delegates, and other leaders.

privileges and immunities clause Article IV, Section 2, of the Constitution, which prohibits a state from discriminating against citizens of another state.

public hearing A meeting of a committee or subcommittee of Congress at which members of the public are permitted to testify about proposed legislation.

public opinion The range of opinions expressed by citizens on any subject.

public policy All the rules of conduct (laws, treaties, regulations, etc.) that are enforced within a political system.

ratification Legalization of a constitution or an amendment to a constitution by formal consent; to become legal by formal procedures defined in the document.

reapportionment The redrawing of legislative district lines on the basis of new population information supplied by the United States Bureau of the Census.

reasonableness test A standard used by the Supreme Court to interpret the equal protection clause of the Fourteenth Amendment. The Court assumes that the law in question is constitutional and will uphold it if the government can advance reasonable argument in its defense.

registration The procedure by which a person proves to an election official that he or she is qualified to vote.

regulation A rule or order issued by an administrative agency of government which has the force of law.

removal power The power of the President to remove from office any appointed official who performs strictly executive functions.

representative democracy A form of democracy in which public officials who represent the people are elected by popular vote in free elections.

reserved powers Powers that are neither delegated to the national government nor denied to the states by the Constitution; they are "reserved" to the states or the people by the Tenth Amendment.

revenue sharing A system under which states and cities were given a certain portion of federal tax revenues to be used in financing their programs, with no strings attached.

rider A provision attached to a proposed piece of legislation that is not related to the main subject of the bill.

rule A special order, issued by the House Rules Committee, that determines when a bill will come up for debate and sets time limits on the debate.

runoff primary A second primary in which the two candidates receiving the highest number of votes for a party's nomination for local or state office compete with each other, both having failed to win a majority of votes in the first primary.

sampling A process used in public opinion polling that involves choosing a relatively small number of cases to be studied for information about the larger population.

scientific polling A means of finding out about public opinion through the use of scientific methodology and mathematical probability.

Second Continental Congress The second meeting of colonial delegates in May 1775. Although it had no specific authority, the Second Continental Congress printed money, raised troops, coordinated colonial efforts in the war against England, and adopted the Declaration of Independence.

sedition Oral or written advocacy of rebellion against the government that is designed to overthrow the government.

select committee A committee created to do a specific job, such as conducting an investigation into a specific problem.

self-incrimination Being compelled to be a witness against oneself. Self-incrimination is prohibited by the Fifth Amendment and is applicable to the states through the due process clause of the Fourteenth Amendment.

senatorial courtesy The informal rule under which the President must clear his nominations for federal positions within a state with the senior senator from that state who is a member of his party, or risk Senate rejection of those nominees.

seniority system The system under which chairs of congressional committees were appointed on the basis of length of service on a committee.

separate-but-equal doctrine The standard used by the Supreme Court to interpret the equal protection clause of the Fourteenth Amendment from 1896 until the mid-1950s. The requirement that a state must provide equal protection was held to be satisfied if the government provided separate facilities for blacks, as long as they were equal to those provided for whites.

separation of powers A system of organizing the legislative, executive, and judicial functions of government, characterized by the creation of independent institutions to perform these functions.

Shays' Rebellion A protest in 1786 against mortgage foreclosures and high taxes in Massachusetts led by Captain Daniel Shays.

single-issue interest group An interest group that is concerned with only one public issue.

slander Spoken statements that publicly defame the character of an individual.

social contract An agreement by the people creating the political community and the government.

Speaker of the House The presiding officer of the House of Representatives, nominated by the majority party and formally elected by all members of the House.

spoils system The system used in the early part of the nation's history to fill government jobs. Jobs were awarded to friends and supporters of the party in power.

staff agency An agency that gathers information and makes it available to the President.

standing committee A permanent congressional committee with authority to consider bills in specific areas.

statutory law Law written and enacted by a legislative body.

substantiality test A standard used by the Supreme Court in determining whether laws based on gender are constitutional. To pass this test, a law must serve "important governmental objectives" and be "substantially related to achievement of those objectives."

survey research A method of data collection in which information is obtained from individuals who have been selected to provide a basis for making inferences about the larger population.

suspect classification A term used to describe the category in which the Supreme Court now places all laws based on race. Such laws are assumed to be unconstitutional forms of discrimination under the equal protection clause of the Fourteenth Amendment.

symbolic speech The communication of ideas by certain acts (such as wearing an armband or flying a flag) to dramatize a person's beliefs.

telephone poll A type of public opinion poll in which information is obtained by telephone interviews based on random selection of phone numbers.

trade associations Business interest groups organized on the basis of a single industry, such as steel or coal.

treaty An international agreement negotiated by the President that requires the advice and consent of two-thirds of the Senate to become effective.

two-party system A political system in which only the candidates of two major political parties have any real chance of being elected to office.

unanimous consent agreement A procedure in the Senate to establish the terms for consideration of a bill and set limits on motions, amendments, and debate.

unitary government A system in which the legal power of government is possessed by the national or central government.

universal suffrage The right of every adult man or woman who is a citizen of a country to vote.

veto The power of a President to reject a bill passed by Congress. A veto can be overridden by a two-thirds vote in both houses of Congress.

Virginia Plan   The fifteen resolutions presented by Governor Edmund Randolph of Virginia to the Constitutional Convention. It influenced the decision to abandon the Articles of Confederation and write a new constitution. The plan called for a national government consisting of executive, legislative, and judicial branches. The legislature was to be bicameral, with representation based on population and taxes paid.

voter turnout   The percentage of eligible voters who actually cast ballots in an election.

whip   An assistant floor leader who is appointed by his or her party and whose task is to keep party members informed on party-sponsored bills, notify the party leader regarding the support that may be expected when the bill comes to a vote, and obtain the voting support of as many party members as possible on key bills.

whistleblowers   Corporate or government employees who make public the mistakes or misdeeds of their superiors.

white primary   A device used prior to 1945 in the one-party southern states to prevent blacks from voting by denying them the right to participate in Democratic party primary elections.

writ of certiorari   ("to be made certain") A discretionary writ granted by the Supreme Court directing a lower court to send up a case for review.

writ of habeas corpus   ("you have the body") An order issued by a court requiring that the government bring an arrested or detained person before the court to determine whether that individual is being legally held. Habeas corpus is guaranteed by the Constitution.

writ of mandamus   ("we command") A court order to a public official to perform an act that is legally required.

Photo Credits

Chapter 1: 1 Art Stein/Photo Researchers. 3 Tom Grill/Comstock. 4 UPI/Bettmann Newsphotos. 6 Farrell Grehan/Photo Researchers. 7 New York Public Library. 9 The White House Collection. 10 The Granger Collection. 12 Bulloz/Art Resource. 15 Lowell Georgia/Photo Researchers.

Chapter 2: 19 Dale E. Boyer/Photo Researchers. 22 New York Public Library. 23 Richard Frear/Photo Researchers. 25 The Granger Collection. 27 The Cleveland Museum of Art, Hinman B. Hurlbut Collection. 29 Colonial Williamsburg Foundation. 32 Courtesy of The New-York Historical Society, New York City. 37 Supreme Court.

Chapter 3: 45 S.M. Wakefield. 46 AP/Wide World Photos. 51 Laima Druskis. 53 Robert Goldstein/Photo Researchers. 57 Jerry Schad/Photo Researchers.

Chapter 4: 67 R. Maiman/Sygma. 69 Charles Gupton/Uniphoto. 73 UPI/Bettmann Newsphotos. 75 Susan Greenwood/Gamma Liaison. 81 Michael Sargent/The White House. 87 Library of Congress. 88 UPI/Bettman Newsphotos.

Chapter 5: 101 S.M. Wakefield. 112 S.M. Wakefield. 115 Bob Daemmrich/Uniphoto. 117 AP/Wide World Photos. 118 Laima Druskis. 122 Howard Sachs/Consolidated News Pictures/Uniphoto. 123 Jose Lopez/The New York Times. 125 Handgun Control, Inc.

Chapter 6: 131 Robert Phillips. 134 Jim Wilson, The New York Times. 136 UPI/Bettmann Newsphotos. 150 AP/Wide World Photos. 153 The New York Times. 158 AP/Wide World Photos.

Chapter 7: 165 S.M. Wakefield. 167 Library of Congress. 172 UPI/Bettmann Newsphotos. 174 AP/Wide World Newsphotos. 185 AP/Wide World Newsphotos. 189 Courtesy Congressman Robert Mrazek. 194 UPI/Bettmann Newsphotos.

Chapter 8: 199 S.M. Wakefield. 203 AP/Wide World Photos. 205 Library of Congress. 206 Eunice Harris/Photo Researchers. 209 Susan Biddle/The White House. 211 Harry S Truman Library. 213 Carol T. Powers/The White House. 217 AP/Wide World Photos. 218 The Bettmann Archive. 223 Reuters/Bettmann Newsphotos. 226 Susan Biddle/The White House. 228 Brown Brothers. 232 UPI/Bettmann Newsphotos.

Chapter 9: 237 Bob Daemmrich/Stock, Boston. 241 Federal Trade Commission, Washington, D.C. 245 AP/Wide World Photos. 249 Bob Daemmrich/Stock, Boston. 253 Charles Feil/Uniphoto. 256 AP/Wide World Photos. 258 U.S. Department of Treasury.

Chapter 10: 265 Supreme Court Historical Society. 267 Irene Springer. 271 Robert J. Bennett. 275 The Supreme Court Historical Society. 279 The Supreme Court Historical Society. 282 Roger Sandler/Black Star. 283 AP/Wide World Photos. 287 AP/Wide World Photos.

Chapter 11: 293 Ed Elberfeld/Uniphoto. 297 John Ficara/Woodfin Camp & Associates. 299 The New York Times. 301 AP/Wide World Photos. 302 UPI/Bettmann Newsphotos. 304 Jan Halaska/Photo Researchers. 308 Randy Taylor/Sygma. 310 Stacy Pick/Stock, Boston. 312 AP/Wide World Photos. 313 Paul Conklin.

Chapter 12: 321 AP/Wide World Photos. 323 Courtesy of the New-York Historical Society, New York City. 324 New York Public Library Picture Collection. 325 Library of Congress. 327 Library of Congress. 328 Puerto Rican Community Development Project. 331 AP/Wide World Photos. 332 AP/Wide World Photos. 334 AP/Wide World Photos. 338 Shirley Zeiberg. 340 Laima Druskis. 343 AP/Wide World Photos. 345 S.M. Wakefield.

Name Index

Subject Index

Dred Scott v. *Sanford*, 286, 323, 324
Dual court system, 269–74
  constitutional, 271–72
  federal courts, 269–70, 271–74
  legislative, 272
  state courts, 270–71
Dual federalism, 56
Dual government, 38
Due process clause
  of Fifth Amendment, 330
  of Fourteenth Amendment, 51, 293–94, 314, 339–41

Economic equality, 13–14
Economic interest groups, 118–19
Economic Report of the President, 213–14, 244
Economy, President as manager of, 219
Education. *See also* Schools
  political socialization and, 70
  public, 50, 51
  universal, 14–15
  voter turnout and, 92
  voting patterns and, 94, 96
Education Amendment (1972), Title IX, 339
Education for All Handicapped Children Act (1975), 344
Election(s), 12–13, 151–54. *See also* Voting
  balloting, 12–13, 152
  congressional, 157–61
    House of Representatives, 12
    off-year, 160–61
    Senate, 12, 31
    voter turnout in, 89–90
  as constitutional issue, 30–32
  constitutional provisions for, 36–37
  date of, 151
  of electors, 154
  free, 12–13
  media coverage of, 79, 82, 114
  national party committees and, 110
  popular, 150, 156, 157
  presidential, 12, 31–32, 82, 133–35. *See also* Electoral college
    by House of Representatives, 154–56
  primaries, 77, 79, 132–33
    national, 141
    polling in, 77
    presidential, 133–35
    runoff, 132–33

television advertising and, 79
  white, 87, 327
  registration, 152
Electoral college, 31–32, 37, 149–50, 152–57
  problems with, 154–56
  reform vs. abolition of, 156–57
  two-party system and, 157
Electoral functions of Congress, 172–73
Electoral support from interest groups, 126
Electors, 153–54
  proposed elimination of, 156
Elitist view of political power, 3–4
Emancipation Proclamation (1863), 323–24
Eminent domain, 49
Employees, public, 119
Employment, equality in, 335–36
Engel v. *Vitale*, 296–97
English democratic institutions, 11
English legal tradition, 20
Entitlement programs, 168
Enumerated powers, 47–48, 166–70
Environment, interest groups representing, 119
Equal Employment Opportunities Act (1972), 339
Equal Employment Opportunity Commission (EEOC), 335
Equality, 13–14
  categories of, 13–14
  in employment, 335–36
  in public facilities, 333–35
Equal protection clause of Fourteenth Amendment, 51, 293–94, 341
Equal Rights Amendment (ERA), 40, 338
Equity, 266
Escobedo v. *Illinois*, 311–12
Establishment clause, 296–97
Ethics, interest groups and, 121–22, 126
Ethnicity. *See also* Minority groups
  congressional membership by, 178
  voting pattern and, 96
Examinations, civil service, 249–50
Exclusionary rule of evidence, 308–9
Executive agreements, 207–8
Executive branch, 31, 253. *See also* President(s)

congressional authority over, 257
  departments, 238–39
  legislation from, 191
  lobbying, 123–24
  organization of, 238–46
    line agencies, 238–42
    staff agencies, 238, 242–46
  removal from, 255
Executive Office of the President, 243–46
Executive power, 36. *See also* President(s)
Executives, political, 250–51
Executive session, 192
Exit polls, 76–78
Expertise, bureaucratic, 251–52
Ex post facto laws, 34, 50, 307
Expressed powers, 47–48, 166–70
Extradition, 52

Fair trial, 305–6
Family, political socialization through, 69
Family court, 270
Farmers, 117
Federal Communications Commission (FCC), 240
Federal courts, 269–70, 271–74
Federal deficit, 168
Federal Election Campaign Acts (FECA), 144–45
  1974 amendments, 120
Federalism, 45–65
  centralized, 58–59
  competitive, 56
  Constitution and, 35, 47–53
    concurrent powers, 49
    interstate relations, 51–53
    limitations on national government, 50
    limitations on state government, 50–51
    powers of national government, 47–49
    states' powers, 50
  cooperative, 56–58
  dual, 56
  grant-in-aid system, 57, 59–60
  growth of interest groups and, 116
  mutual obligations in, 53–55
  national supremacy, 54–55
  nation-centered, 56
  New, 60–63
  state-centered, 56
Federalist Papers, The, 29, 34
Federalists, 32–34, 41

Issue attention cycle of the public, 225–26
Item veto, 216

Jeffersonians (Republicans), 41
Jews, 95
Jim Crow laws, 325
Joint committees, 184–85
Joint undertakings, 57
Judges, federal
  selection of, 278–84
    for lower courts, 278–79
    Reagan appointments, 279–80
    Supreme Court appointments, 280–81
  terms of office, 37
Judicial power, 36
Judicial review, 37–38, 284–86
  criticisms of, 286
  federal bureaucracy and, 259
  Presidency and, 220
Judiciary, 265–91. *See also* Supreme Court
  dual court system, 269–74
    constitutional, 271–72
    federal courts, 269–70, 271–74
    legislative, 272
    state courts, 270–71
  interest groups' influence on, 124
  law and, 265–68
    adversary system in, 268
    civil, 267–68
    criminal, 267
    defined, 265–66
    role of courts, 268
    role of judge, 268–69
    types of, 266–67
  restrictions on, 287–88
  selection of federal judges, 278–84
    for lower courts, 278–79
    Reagan appointments, 279–80
    Supreme Court appointments, 280–81
  self-restraint vs. activism in, 288–89
Judiciary Act (1789), 285
Judiciary Committee, 278–79, 282
Jurisdiction, 269–70
  appellate, 270
  congressional power over, 287
  original, 53, 270
Jury
  grand, 310–11
  petit, 310
  sequestering of, 305

Justice, Department of, 239
Justice of the peace, 270

Katz v. *United States*, 309
"Keating Five" hearing (1990), 174
Korean War, 210, 211

Labor unions, 118–19
Language minorities, 328–29
Law(s), 265–68. *See also* Legislation
  adversary system in, 268
  civil, 267–68
  criminal, 267
  defined, 265–66
  English common law as basis of American, 20
  equality under the, 14
  ex post facto, 34, 50, 307
  Jim Crow, 325
  legitimacy and, 4–5
  natural, 7
  preventive detention, 314
  race-based, 341
  role of courts, 268
  role of judge, 268–69
  sedition, 299–300
  shield, 306
  statutory, 266
  suspect classifications, 341–42
  traffic and safety, 302
  types of, 266–67
Lawsuits, class action, 335
Leadership
  of Congress, 179–82
    majority leaders, 182
    minority leaders and floor whips, 182
    in Senate, 181–82
    Speaker of the House, 179–81
  of President, 255
Legal equality, 13
Legislation, 189–95. *See also* Congress; Law(s)
  calendar, 192
  committee stage of, 191–92
  Constitution and, 166
  to end sex discrimination, 339
  from executive branch, 191
  floor procedures, 192–93
  impoundment, 257
  introduction of a bill, 189–91
  legislative power, 36, 165
  presidential approval or disapproval of, 195
  voting on, 194–95
Legislative bureaucracy, 188–89
Legislative caucus, 132
Legislative courts, 272

Legislative function of Congress, 166–70
Legislative oversight, 171–72, 257–58
Legislative veto, 220–21
Legislature, bicameral vs. unicameral, 28–29
Legitimacy, 4
Lend-Lease Agreement (1940), 208
Lexington, Battle of (1775), 22
Libel, 304–5
Libertarians, 108
Liberty
  defined, 10
  equality and, 14
Liberty Bell, 23
Libya, bombing of (1986), 170
Limited government, 11
Line agencies, 238–42
Listening devices, electronic, 309
Literacy tests, 87–88, 326, 327
Lobbying, 122–24
Lobbyists, legislative efforts at controlling, 127

Machine, political, 111
Magna Charta, 20
Majority, tyranny of, 9–10
Majority leader, congressional, 181, 182
Majority opinion, 275–76
Majority rule, 8–10, 68, 286
Malloy v. *Hogan*, 310
Management jobs, minority-held, 336
Managers, 185
Mandamus, writ of, 285
Mapp v. *Ohio*, 308
Marbury v. *Madison*, 37–38, 285–86
Maryland, 25–26
Massachusetts, 25
Massachusetts (office-block) ballot, 152
Mass media. *See* Media
McCulloch v. *Maryland*, 48, 55
Media, 78–84. *See also* Press; Television
  election coverage of, 82, 114
  free, 79, 80–82
  freedom of the press, 306
  interest groups' use of, 125–26
  as limit on presidential power, 225
  paid, 79–80
  political debate on, 13
  polls by, 74, 75–77
  President as national opinion leader and, 217–19
  prior restraint of the press, 299

Media (continued)
  reform proposals, 82–84
  as restraint on federal bureau-
    cracy, 260
Merit system, 248, 249–50
Military policy, 210
Miller v. *California*, 303
Minorities, language, 328–29
Minority groups
  civil rights of, 322–36
    employment equality,
      335–36
    equality in public facilities,
      333–35
    organizations promoting,
      325–26
    school desegregation,
      329–33
    voting rights, 326–29
  voter turnout and, 92
Minority leaders, congressional,
  182
Minority rights, 10–11, 68
Miranda v. *Arizona*, 312–13
Misdemeanors, 267
Mississippi, 329
Missouri Compromise, 322–23
Mistrial, 311
Mixed caucus, 132
Montgomery, Alabama, 333
Morals, public, 303–4
Mothers Against Drunk Driving
  (MADD), 120
Motivations of President, 227–29
Multiparty system, 103
Muskrat v. *United States*, 268

NAACP v. *Alabama*, 306
National American Suffrage Asso-
  ciation, 336
National Association for the Ad-
  vancement of Colored People
  (NAACP), 124, 326
National banking system, 49
National Budget message, 213
National Center for State Courts,
  271
National chair, 109
National committee, 109–10
National conventions. *See* Con-
  ventions
National government. *See also*
  Federalism
  limitations on, 50
  obligations to states, 53–54
  powers of, 47–49
  states' obligations to, 54
  states' rights vs., 27–28
National Opinion Research Cen-
  ter (NORC), 74

National Organization for Women
  (NOW), 337
National primary, 141
National Rifle Association, 124–25
National Security Adviser, 208–9,
  245
National Security Council (NSC),
  244–46
National supremacy, 35, 38, 54–
  55, 56
National Voter Registration Act
  (1990), 93
Nation-centered federalism, 56
Native Americans, 322
Natural law, 7
Natural rights, 7
Near v. *Minnesota*, 298
Necessary and proper clause,
  48–49
Negative advertising, 80, 83–84
Network, cue, 194
New Deal, 58, 95, 287–88
New England Confederation, 20
New Federalism, 60–63
New Jersey Plan, 28
Newspapers, truth boxes in, 83
New York Times, 260
New York Times Co. v. *Sullivan*,
  304–5
New York v. *Quarles*, 313
Nix v. *Williams*, 308–9
Nominations, 131–41. *See also*
  Election(s)
  of presidential candidate,
    133–41
  delegate selection, 133–36
  national conventions, 109,
    133, 137–41
  preconvention campaign,
    136–37
  procedures, 131–33
  of Vice President, 139–40
Nonwhite Americans, civil rights
  of, 322–36
  employment equality, 335–36
  equality in public facilities,
    333–35
  organizations promoting,
    325–26
  school desegregation, 29–33
  slavery and, 322–24
  voting rights, 326–29
North Dakota, 53

Obscenity, 303–4
Occupation
  political socialization and, 70
  voting pattern and, 96
Office-block (Massachusetts) ballot, 152

Office of Management and Budget
  (OMB), 168, 244
Off-year elections, 160–61
Omnibus Crime Control and Safe
  Streets Act (1968), 309
One-party districts, 157
Open primary, 133
Opinion(s)
  political, 71
  public. *See* Public opinion
  Supreme Court, 275–76
Opposition, organized, 13
Oral arguments, 274–75
Order, public, 302–3
Oregon v. *Mitchell*, 88–89
Original jurisdiction, 53, 270
Oversight, legislative, 171–72,
  257–58

Panama invasion (1989), 170
Parliamentarian, 181
Participation, political, 84. *See
  also* Interest groups; Political
  parties; Voting
Parties, political. *See* Political par-
  ties
Party-column (Indiana) ballot, 152
Party votes, 194–95
Passive-negative presidents, 230
Passive-positive presidents, 230
Patronage, 214, 217, 248
Peer group, political socialization
  from, 70
Pendleton Act (1883), 248
Pentagon Papers (*History of the
  U.S. Decision-Making Process
  on Viet Nam Policy*), 220, 260,
  298–99
Persian Gulf War (1991), 170, 211,
  223
Personal diplomacy, 209
Personality, power and, 4
Petition
  discharge, 191
  freedom of, 298–306
Petit jury, 310
Philadelphia v. *New Jersey*, 55
Plaintiff, 267
Plank, 137
Plea bargaining, 317
Pledge of allegiance, 69
Plessy v. *Ferguson*, 324–25
Pluralist view of political power,
  3–4
Plurality, 150
Pocket veto, 215–16
Police court, 270
Policy agenda, 189
Policy representation, 170–71

registration and, 90–91,
92–93
by women, 336–37
Voting Rights Acts, 88–89, 327–29

War, undeclared, 211, 220
Ward, 111
War declaration powers of Congress, 210, 211
War Powers Resolution (1973),
169–70, 211, 221–24
Washington Post, 260
Watchdog functions of Congress,
171–72
Watergate scandal, 143, 225
Ways and Means Committee, 166,
186, 188

"Weak" Presidents, 227, 229
Webster v. *Reproductive Health
Services*, 341
Whips, congressional, 182
Whistleblowers Protection Act
(1989), 260
Whistleblowing, 259–60
White House Office, 243–44
White House press conference,
218
"White House rose garden" approach, 148
White male suffrage, 86
White primaries, 87, 327
Women
affirmative action for, 347
Bill of Rights for, 337
civil rights of, 336–43

Constitution and, 339–43
Equal Rights Amendment
(ERA), 338
legislation to end sex discrimination, 339
organizations supporting,
337
voting, 336–37
in Congress, 178
interest groups representing,
119
suffrage for, 86
voter turnout among, 92
World leader, President as,
209–10
Writ of certiorari, 277
Writ of habeas corpus, 34, 50, 315
Writ of mandamus, 285